Books by Stanley Noyes

Poetry

Faces and Spirits 1974
Beyond the Mountains beyond the Mountains 1979
The Commander of Dead Leaves 1984

Novels

No Flowers for a Clown 1961
Shadowbox 1970

Editor
(With Gene Frumkin)
The Indian Rio Grande:
Recent poems for 3 Cultures 1977

Los Comanches

LOS COMANCHES

The Horse People, 1751 – 1845

STANLEY NOYES

University of New Mexico Press
Albuquerque

Library of Congress Cataloging-in-Publication Data

Noyes, Stanley.
Los Comanches : the horse people, 1751–1845 /
by Stanley Noyes.—1st ed.
p.   cm.
Includes bibliographical references and index.
ISBN 0-8263-1548-8 (pa)
1. Comanche Indians—History.
I. Title.
E99.C85N69   1993
973'.04974-dc20
93–13951
CIP

Book design by Julie Noyes Long

For Nancy

The Comanche are scattered from the great Missuris [sic]
River to the . . . frontier presidios of New Spain. They are a
people so numerous and so haughty that when asked their number,
they make no difficulty in comparing it to that of the stars.

Athanase de Mézières, 1770

The only real American don't use much stile aney more Unkle
Sam lets him play Injun once a year and he dances under the flag
that made a farmer out of him once nature gave him everything he
wanted. now the agent gives him bib overalls hookes his hands
around plow handles and tells him it's a good thing push it along
maybe it is but thair having a hell of a time proving it.

Charlie Russell, 1925

The future depends on man's transcending the limits of
individual cultures.

Edward T. Hall, 1976

Contents

III   Los Comanches Versus Three Republics

The Comanche people dominated the southern plains from the middle eighteenth century until the end of the Spanish period in 1821. They continued to do so throughout the Mexican period, as well as during the nine-year existence of the Republic of Texas. The United States' annexation of Texas in 1845 precipitated the Mexican War. Also it soon made enemies of Comanches and Americans, who had been on fairly good terms up until that time. But once the U.S. Army began defending the Texas frontier, and its soldiers began killing marauding warriors, Comanche goodwill toward Americans quickly dissipated.

Los Comanches portrays a people—the People—principally through their actions in shaping and responding to events, but also through taking their culture into account. The book's purpose is to address several questions: Who were the Comanches? What course did they follow from the middle of the eighteenth century, when they completed their conquest of the southern plains, until 1845, when we Americans automatically became their enemies?[1] And *why* did they act and react as they did? The last question is, of course, often difficult, if not impossible, to answer.

The narrative concludes at 1845 because the history of the Comanches after this date is well known and has been related in several books. As the historian Grant Foreman has pointed out, the Mexican War represented a fissure in the annals of the southern Plains Indians.[2] With its close in 1848, the whites increased their slaughter of the buffalo, making the hunt, and life, ever more difficult for the Comanches and their Kiowa and Wichitan allies.[3] These peoples, as a result, became increasingly hostile toward the whites, especially toward the Anglo-Texans pushing toward—or into— their hunting grounds. Annexation and the Mexican War announced the final act of the People's tragedy, an act whose details had been foreshadowed by earlier events.

In his preface to *Great River*, the historian Paul Horgan advises the reader that he has taken "every opportunity to stage a scene." The present work also progresses by scenes whenever possible, profiting from each chance to render the Comanches through eyewitness accounts. From such perspectives the reader may, it is hoped, experience historical individuals, including Native Americans, as fellow human beings and not as stereotypes.

There is a trend these days to charge studies of Native American peoples with "ethnocentrism" or "Eurocentrism."[4] Here it must be said, and without apology, that *Los Comanches* is frequently both ethnocentric and Eurocentric. How could it be otherwise when such a work depends upon the first-hand accounts of historic observers? All had European roots, and each viewed the Comanche people through the sometimes myopic lens of his or her particular culture. Yet the observations of Spanish and Mexican officials, of Texas Rangers and American officers, of Missouri traders and French scientists, of Mexican and Anglo captives of both sexes, while reflecting the biases of those cultures, would seem otherwise to be tolerably objective. Many compliment the People. Still the reader is advised to consider each of these accounts critically, always keeping in mind the fact that none was written by a Comanche presenting his own point of view. In addition, the reader should periodically recall the admonition from a modern ethnohistorian to the effect that observations about Comanches from a certain time and place may not apply to tribal members at another place and time.[5] But then, of course, they may.

For the viewpoint of the historic Comanches, or its reasonable semblance, we must turn to the American anthropologists who began their study of the People in the 1930s, as well as to their successors, the contemporary revisionist scholars.[6] They give us a look from within the culture, as it were. Yet while granting the value of ethnology's contributions to an understanding of the Comanche people, the student of the past may also suspect that the sizable part of its data that relies upon memory ethnography is probably no more reliable than carefully considered eyewitness accounts by historic observers.[7]

None of the scenes presenting these accounts is fiction. Some are based upon captivity tales, which can read like fiction. But such tales, when carefully selected, are valid historical documents, nonetheless. This book, while thoroughly researched, is intended for a general audience. Consequently not every quotation has been labeled by page number in the notes. The context will supply the source. All sources appear in the three-part bibliography, and any interested scholar should be able to track down specifics without a great deal of difficulty. Although liberties have been taken with the letter of these sources—such as converting indirect discourse into dialogue and stilted dialogue into colloquial speech—fidelity to their spirit has remained paramount.

The book progresses, it will be observed, by two time systems. The chronological pattern advances in a relatively orderly fashion and is limited at either end. But a second scheme is arranged for significance and effect.

there were, as will be seen, both Spaniards and Frenchmen on the Great Plains, which were by no means "unexplored." As late as 1852, Captain Randolph B. Marcy, U.S. Army, in a report to Congress, stated his belief that he had been the first white man to reach the headwaters of the Red River.[16] Yet Captain Francisco Amangual, a Spanish officer, had led an expedition through that area more than forty years before Marcy. Pierre Vial, a Frenchman in the service of Spain, had been familiar with the region since the late eighteenth century.

We forget that by 1821 the Comanches already had over a hundred years of recorded history behind them. When we think of the tribe, we think of the final third of their historical experience. Yet when the People are permitted the full scope of their history, they reveal themselves to have been far more interesting than the lurid image conjured up by their reputation.

The stereotype of the historic Comanches that seems still to haunt the popular imagination is the nineteenth century one of "ferocious savages." It doubtless came into being during the period from about 1835 to 1875, when the People were fighting for their territory, and for their way of life, against the advancing Texas frontier. As they became increasingly desperate, these Native Americans did indeed at times become "ferocious." Yet that is only a small part of their identity and their story. In 1870 an Austin newspaper compared them to "rattlesnakes" and "Mexican tigers."[17] This sort of image has lingered in the popular mind, but it does the People a grave injustice. The Comanches, to be known more than superficially, must be seen in their entirety within the context of their culture. The portrayal of a people exhibiting as many contradictions as ourselves is the task the present work seeks to accomplish.

Many institutions and individuals have been helpful throughout the years of research and writing that went into this book. I would like to thank, among the institutions, the Santa Fe Public Library and the Panhandle-Plains Historical Society Library. Laura Holt, Librarian at the Santa Fe Laboratory of Anthropology, has been extremely helpful. The librarians of Zimmerman Library at the University of New Mexico—particularly those in the Anderson Room, in Special Collections, and in Government Publications—often aided me, as did Irene Moran, director of public service at the Bancroft Library of the University of California at Berkeley. I am also indebted to the U.S. Cavalry Association and the Comanche Tribe Enrollment Department for useful information. I am grateful to the librarians at the New Mexico State Library, where I did much of my research, especially to Betty Sena and Norma Jean McCallan in the Southwest Room, and to everyone at the reference desk. Finally I wish to thank my friend Orlando Romero, librarian at the History Library, Palace of the Governors, Santa Fe, for frequent assistance reaching back over a decade.

Numerous other individuals provided help of various kinds. My friend Blythe Brennan permitted me to use her idea for a southwestern historical work. Although I was unable to realize the potential of that particular idea, the resulting research, and a great deal more later, ultimately engendered *Los Comanches*. My true subject evolved, I believe, out of the urging of my friend Edward T. Hall that I write a book on the Comanche people. Through Ned Hall's suggestion, E. A. Mares, another friend, and at that time curator of the Albuquerque Museum, invited me to speak to the docents of that institution about the Comanches. This I did in the fall of 1984. That talk, which was well received, marked the true beginning of the present work.

While investigating the original subject, I consulted with Albert H. Schroeder, archeologist, and with Myra Ellen Jenkins, historian. Each responded to numerous questions, a courtesy for which I am grateful. Later two friends, both writers themselves, read the earlier, incomplete manuscript. I am indebted to Gene Frumkin and Mary Cable for this kindness. Al Hart, John Sayler, Abel Davis, and Phil Long rendered other, much appreciated, forms of assistance, as did Margot Schevill, Barbara A. Hail, Carol Canty, Daniel J. Gelo, and Enrique R. Lamadrid. Later still Anne Valley-Fox, poet, and Marc Simmons, historian, earned my heartfelt thanks by reading a near-final draft of the present work—as, even more recently, did Gene Frumkin (once again, beneficently), E. A. Mares, and Natalie Schram. Last of all, I wish to express to my old friends, Ferol Egan and James Schevill, my profound appreciation for their help and support throughout the composition of this and other books over the years.

Stanley Noyes
Santa Fe, 1992

Prologue

The Comanches were Shoshones, who, on obtaining horses, split off from their parent tribe in the seventeenth century, riding from the mountains of present Wyoming southeast into the Great Plains.[1] In 1706 Sergeant Major Juan de Ulibarrí, of the Santa Fe presidio, reported to New Mexico's governor, Cuervo y Valdez, that Taos was preparing for an attack by the Utes and Comanches. That same year the Comanches and their linguistic kinsmen, the Utes, began raiding the Jicarilla Apaches, who lived at the edge of the plains, across the Sangre de Cristo mountains, east of Taos. At this historical moment, when the Comanches began mounted raiding, the mighty Lakotas, or westernmost Sioux, were still pedestrian farmers. The "fighting Cheyennes," and probably the Arapahoes too, were still village horticulturalists. The Cheyennes would remain so until about midcentury, with the Arapahoes, in all likelihood, converting to a nomadic life not long before them.[2]

Earlier, when Comanches were still Shoshone, or Snake, Indians, they were a simpler people who lived an arduous life, stone-age hunters-gatherers constantly struggling to wrest a living from a harsh environment. The western branch, in fact, existed mostly on nuts and wild vegetables. By the last decades of the seventeenth century, the eastern Shoshones and their Comanche offshoots had already moved out onto the northern plains adjacent to the Rockies. The Kiowas, later to become an enemy, then a potent ally, of the Comanches, appear to have lived to the west of the Black Hills in present northeast Wyoming. The Shoshones proper occupied the country between them and the mountains. The Comanches lived just south of the Kiowas. Although the Kiowas must have had to communicate by sign language with their neighbors, the three peoples were on friendly terms at that time.[3]

Around the beginning of the new century, the Comanches began moving southward. Probably the principal reason was a desire to gain greater proximity to the Spanish settlements of New Mexico, with their herds of horses. Up until this time, Apaches had had a virtual monopoly on acquiring the animals, through raiding, from this source. The Comanches wanted access to the supply. But there may have been another reason for the move. The southern plains, stretching below the Arkansas River, were swarming with buffalo and other wild game, such as elk, antelope, and deer. What was to become "Comanchería," as the Spaniards came to call the region, was bounded on the west by the Sangre de Cristo Mountains and the Pecos River. Its eastern limit was marked by the Cross Timbers, twin bands of oak extending down from the Arkansas to the Brazos. In the south the Balcones Escarpment, below the Edwards Plateau, was its approximate boundary. In all the southern plains constituted one of the richest hunting grounds on the continent. The Comanches came ultimately to dominate some 240,000 square miles of them.[4]

There was only one drawback to the nascent migration—the southern plains were already occupied by another, formidable people.

Seven years before Jamestown, in 1601, when the first soldier-colonists of New Mexico rode out on the plains in search of Quivira, fabled land of gold, they encountered men on the ninth day, just as the army reached the Canadian River. Appraising its sheer walls, Don Juan de Oñate and his advance guard were surprised to see some twenty Indians appear. They recognized them as belonging to "the nation called Apache." The warriors were dressed in buckskin jackets reaching to the knees, or were wearing tanned buffalo hides draped over their shoulders. Although armed with bows and arrows, shields, and war clubs, they raised their hands to the sun in a sign of peace.

As the army followed the Canadian eastward, deeper into the Plains of Cibola (named for the shaggy "cows" Coronado had discovered sixty years before), it encountered from time to time encampments of red-and-white tepees. The Vaquero Indians occupied these lodges, which some in the expedition compared to Italian pavilions. The Spaniards called these Apaches "Masters of the Plains." Their portable camps, or *rancherías*, consisted of thirty or forty tents of tanned and waterproof buffalo hide, each capable of holding four or five people. The Apaches, standing by their lodges, would boldly greet the procession of armored horsemen as it passed.

Occasionally the expedition would come upon a ranchería on the move. A woman would stride in the lead, followed by a long packtrain of dogs in single file, as many as five hundred of them, each dragging its travois over the short grass of the high plains. Behind the train trudged the remainder of the women, with the children and the old. The dogs, which padded along at an even pace, frequently snarling, were medium-sized, shaggy, and mostly white, or white with black spots. Anyone close enough could see the flies pestering them in the hot sun, hovering near sores under their harnesses. The band's warriors, their bows and arrows in their hands, traveled at a distance from the side of the packtrain, keeping between it and the army. Always, though, as they approached the Spaniards, they would raise their arms to the sun.[5]

These were the Plains Apaches. The original "Masters of the Plains" were hunters and traders, sometimes raiders, nomads who planted no crops. They relied on the bison for their sustenance and for the hides, jerked meat, and tallow they traded each fall at the pueblos of Taos, Picurís, and Pecos for the produce of the Rio Grande Valley. The early Apaches, whatever the individual bands called themselves, roamed the mountains of New Mexico and the entire southern plains, often exceeding its northern limits, before either Spaniards or Comanches traveled there. They were destined to become the enemies of both and, ironically, to help draw together those two very different peoples. The Comanches—or at least their war parties—rode, by contrast, aggressively into the southern plains, and into history, in the early eighteenth century. To understand them one needs some knowledge of the historical context they entered, and of the Athapascans whom they displaced.

It is possible to generalize about the southern Apaches, since their tribal divisions shared certain traits. Certainly the Spaniards did generalize. As early as 1634, Fray Alonso de Benavides wrote that the Apaches were "very spirited and belligerent." He conceded that they also prided themselves on "never lying but on always telling the truth."[6] Later, in 1668, a Father Bernal wrote authorities in Mexico City that the province was at war with the Apaches, who murdered all the Christian Indians they could lay hands on. Every road was risky, because the heathens watched all of them. The Apaches, he wrote, were a bold people who threw themselves into peril as if there were neither God nor hell.[7] But the best early description of the Apache people was written by Lieutenant Colonel don Antonio Cordero at El Paso in 1796. Cordero was later governor of Texas and was, incidentally, so widely respected at that time that a prominent Comanche chieftain adopted his name. The colonel had fought the southern Apaches, spoke their language, and probably knew them better than any other Spaniard of his time.

Colonel Cordero believed that the adult men of the tribe were more proud of their courage than anything else. But courage alone did not determine their prestige among their people. According to Captain John Cremony, an American who also fought the Apaches, learned their language, and wrote about them seventy-one years after Cordero, a warrior's cunning might give him a standing in the band higher than that of a man braver than he. Since each male was trained from childhood to look upon all humankind as his natural enemy, his principal aim in life became the deception of others. To reach this goal, he had plenty of motivation. Cremony observed that the women bestowed their attentions upon the cleverest thief among the men, possibly because he could best supply their wants. He heard one Apache remark that "Gianata" was a great brave. Why? Because he kept seven women. Cremony knew that, with respect to courage, Gianata was by no means the foremost warrior in his band, but he was the cleverest thief.

A people with these characteristics was certain to have uneasy relations with its neighbors—especially when, as Colonel Cordero pointed out, the different divisions of the tribe sometimes fell into bloody battles among themselves. The Faraon division, for instance, raided the Jicarilla Apaches, who lived north of them, as well as the Spaniards. Yet to his credit, Cordero did not blame the long war between Apaches and Spaniards on the Native Americans. "Perhaps it was originated in former times," he wrote, "by the trespasses, excess and avarice of the colonists themselves . . ."⁸ Since he was writing his report by order of General Field Marshal don Pedro de Nava, Cordero diplomatically refrained from referring to past excesses and avarice among high Spanish officials.

When did the long war begin? Probably immediately. Apache livestock raids commenced with the founding of Oñate's New Mexico colony in 1598. The following year Spaniards and Apaches fought each other for the first time, when the Athapascans assisted warriors of Acoma Pueblo in defending their great rock from a punitive force of *conquistadores*. But the principal causes of the extended conflict seem to have been the slaving practices of early Spanish officials, as well as their interruption of the traditional trade between the Apaches and the Pueblo peoples. The enslavement of peaceful Indians had been forbidden since the time of Queen Isabella, but Spaniards had found ways of circumventing the royal decree. Slaving expeditions were common during the seventeenth century along the northern frontier of New Spain. Several of New Mexico's governors perpetrated outrages against peaceful Apaches, including some of those who traded at Pecos Pueblo. Spanish policy clearly dictated "reducing" *indios bárbaros* and establishing them as Christians in missions, each mission with its presidio in the vicinity. This method worked successfully with many settled tribes, such as the Pueblo Indians, but it proved impossible with fierce nomads like Apaches, who valued their independence far too much to settle down under the discipline of a padre.

In New Mexico by the 1660s, Apaches had become a formidable menace to Pueblo Indians and Spaniards alike. But reprisals against their raids continued a vicious circle. If punitive expeditions captured Apaches, which they made every effort to do, Spanish officials and officers then punished the infidels by selling them as servants to colonists or by marching them south in chains to the mines at Parral. The province of New Mexico was poor, the Spanish administrative system lent itself to corruption, and such expeditions, while decried by the clergy, could be profitable ventures. As a result Apaches grieved for the captives and ground their teeth in hatred against the Spaniards and their Christian Indian allies.

By the early eighteenth century, the more advanced northeastern Apaches (Carlanas, Cuartelejos, Palomas, and Jicarillas, to name a few) had become partly agricultural, probably from Pueblo influence. Semisedentary, they lived on the western High Plains, one band, the Palomas, even dwelling somewhat south and east of present Denver. During the growing season they lived in small houses in the midst of fields where they planted, irrigated, and harvested their crops, consisting of maize, beans, and pumpkins. Significantly they were friendly toward the Spaniards, with whom they had apparently had only limited contact before the early 1700s. In striking contrast to the southeastern and western divisions, some of these people actually allied themselves, in time, with the conquerors. After 1786, for instance, the Jicarillas were virtually an arm of the New Mexico militia.[9]

The southern bands continued to be hostile. But these southern Athapascans were predators, who were especially active when food was scarce. Even if they had lacked grounds for hating the Spaniards, they would probably have found Spanish and Pueblo herds of exotic livestock irresistibly tempting. Once having acquired a taste for beef and mutton, and for the flesh, especially, of horses and mules, they would almost surely have continued raiding the settlements and pueblos where the animals might be seized.

These Apaches soon learned that the horse had uses beyond providing a feast. In 1621 Spanish authorities gave New Mexico settlers permission to mount Pueblo Indians on horses as herders. Throughout that decade, and afterward, some of these converted Christians deserted their masters to take refuge among the Apaches. Some must have driven horses with them to assure a welcome. In any case during the 1630s and 1640s, fugitive Pueblos taught the Apaches to ride. This, of course, greatly increased the speed, range, and destructiveness of Athapascan raids. The southern Apaches responded to the opportunity by attacking not only along New Spain's northern frontier but by striking into Chihuahua and Sonora.

No one can say precisely when the Plains Indians first obtained horses. Apaches surely traded away some. In any case by 1700 horses were widely diffused, many of them bearing Spanish brands. Certainly the 1680 Pueblo

Revolt in New Mexico had something to do with their dispersal. The flee-ing colonists had time to drive with them only a fraction of their livestock. Either Apaches ran off most of the multitude of horses and mules remain-ing in the province, or the victorious Pueblos traded the animals, having no use for large numbers of them. Tribes like the nearby Utes, newly pos-sessing horses, allowed them to breed and eventually had a sufficient num-ber so that they were able, in turn, to barter some to other peoples, such as their Shoshonean relatives, the Comanches.[10]

It is scarcely possible to think of Comanches without thinking of horses. Wresting the initiative from Apaches, the People made themselves the great horsemen, horse breeders, trainers, traders, and distributors of the plains. By 1754, according to the anthropologist Clark Wissler, the Black-foot Indians on the far northern plains already owned great numbers of horses. Where had they obtained them? Almost surely from the nomadic Kiowas, Kiowa-Apaches, or Comanches. John C. Ewers, another anthro-pologist, cites the account of a fur trader who first bartered with the Crows in 1827. Old people among the tribe told him they remembered seeing the first horses introduced into their country—and that Comanches had brought them. This apparently occurred during the early 1760s. In any event beginning in the first quarter of the eighteenth century, the People played a major role in dispersing horses throughout the entire region, trad-ing them to Shoshones and other neighboring tribes who, in turn, passed them on to others. Horses came to represent wealth to all of the Plains Indians, among whom the Comanches were the wealthiest. By the early nineteenth century, each Comanche division had enormous herds attached to it. The Texan captive Clinton Smith claimed that his band had possessed around six thousand head of horses, while his foster father, Chief Tosaco-wadi, had personally owned about a hundred of these. But any accom-plished warrior apparently might acquire fifty to two hundred head, while one chief, A Great Fall by Tripping, was reputed to have possessed some fifteen hundred of the animals.[11]

The horse not only symbolized wealth but also represented mobility and military power. In recognition of these benefits, the Comanches named the animal the "God-dog." To them it meant the difference between a constant threat of hunger and the assurance of plenty, between vulner-ability to their enemies and relative security through strength. As a result the population explosion among horses had, by the late eighteenth century, begot a more modest population increase among the People, from an es-timated seven thousand in 1690 to a possible twenty thousand in 1786.[12]

Perhaps only someone deeply involved with horses can understand the Comanches, with their passion for horses. An American cowboy, for example, might smile at hearing that many Comanche five-year-old boys could saddle their own ponies, then ride off alone with their bows, arrows, and reatas. Older boys acquired other accomplishments. Colonel Richard I. Dodge, who spent many years on the plains, was one day relaxing on a bluff above a valley, when he noticed, about a half-mile up a stream, a herd of about twenty ponies. They attracted his attention because, although gathered together, they seemed constantly to be in a flurry, a motion he could not account for. Studying them through field glasses, he found that their wrangler, an Indian boy of ten to twelve, was roping one after another. This boy, alone with his little herd, would snare one with his lariat, slide off and release the horse he rode, mounting the other bareback. Presumably guiding the new horse with his knees, or perhaps with a hackamore, he would pursue yet another, casting his loop three to a half-dozen times before catching the next pony, and so on. When Dodge left, a half-hour later, the boy was still entertaining himself in this manner.[13] The colonel did not specify his tribe, but it is certain that Comanche boys spent hours in such practice. Before there was an American cowboy, the Comanches had learned the art of *la reata* from captive *vaqueros*. From the People its use had spread to other Plains tribes.[14]

Both Thomas James, an American trader, and George Catlin, the artist, described Comanches capturing mustangs with lariats. In 1823 James watched from beside his Comanche "brother" as a group of well-mounted braves hid in a ravine, while others drove a herd of wild horses into it. At the proper moment, the concealed riders burst forth. Each one succeeded in roping a mustang, throwing him by quickly turning away. Leaping from his horse, he tied the wild pony's hoofs together, "two by two"—all in a few minutes of violent confusion. James alleged that within twenty-four hours of their capture, the mustangs had become tame and ready to ride—possibly because having been nearly choked to death had made a strong impression upon them.

Catlin in 1834 depicted a variation of the method related by James. In Catlin's description, as soon as the Comanche snared the mustang, he slid from his horse, running at full speed while allowing the rawhide lariat to drag slowly through his hands, until the pony choked and fell, strangling, to the ground. The brave advanced slowly toward its head, keeping the rope taut, until he could slip hobbles on its front feet. Slacking the noose to allow the animal to breathe, he formed a loop around its lower jaw, by which he controlled it when it recovered its breath, regained its feet, and began rearing and plunging. He then advanced, hand over hand, toward its head, preventing it from throwing itself over backward. The warrior placed his palm on the pony's nose, next over its eyes, enabling him, at last, to breathe into its nostrils. After this, according to Catlin, it soon became gentle, so that all the Comanche had to do was remove the hobbles and lead or ride it back to his encampment.

For the American cowboy, the intriguing part of James's description would be the ability of the warrior to throw (or "bust") the mustang without "dallying" (from *dar vuelta*), or wrapping, his rope around a saddle horn. (If tied down, a rawhide reata will break.) A man relying upon his own weight and strength alone can easily be jerked from his horse's back by a second, terrified horse at the end of his rope. That terrified horse can also drag a man trying to run behind him, or at least rope-burn his hands. But of course the animals were choking, and the mustang, like the Indian's own mount, was light in weight and, on average, barely fourteen hands high—truly a pony. Still the techniques described by James and Catlin clearly required superior skill both as a roper and as a horseman.

Learning to ride nearly as early as they began to toddle, the Comanches took for granted even the most extreme forms of riding, such as "topping off" broncos. In this respect their sense of humor, like that of the American cowboy, could be harsh. In 1869, for example, when Clinton Smith was around the age of twelve, he and his younger brother, Jeff, were abducted by a mixed party of Lipan Apaches and Comanches. In the midst of their flight, the warriors amused themselves by roping a two-year-old buffalo calf and placing the boys on its back. Clinton bucked off, but Jeff clung to the wool on its hump. When Clinton pursued it, fearing it would disappear with his brother, the calf whirled and charged him, knocking him "about fifteen feet." He regained his breath, rolled over, and got up, with blood dribbling from his nose and mouth, to find his audience highly entertained and laughing at him.

But after Clinton Smith had been adopted by the Comanches, such challenges became part of his daily play, whenever his band was camped for a time. During these periods he and boys his age would swim every day, race horses, and rope and ride buffalo calves. They would also take wild horses out into deep sand, where it required more effort for the broncs to pitch, and ride them. Later Smith recalled that, by then, he had become "pretty well Indianized" and "quite an expert rider."[15] Colonel Richard Dodge considered the Plains Indian boy of from about twelve to fifteen to be "the best rough rider and natural horseman in the world."[16]

The Comanche boy was, of course, all of this time preparing to become a warrior. Starting at an early age, he practiced constantly shooting with his bow and arrows at various targets from horseback, and from every possible position. When George Catlin was visiting the "Great Camanchee Village" with the dragoon expedition of 1834, he was at first astonished and baffled by one feat of horsemanship involving the bow and arrow, and practiced by the young braves who were continually showing off before the soldiers' tents. In this "stratagem of war" the youth would, in passing before an enemy, drop on the far side of his pony, with only his heel and perhaps the top of his head and an eye visible over the horse's back. In this position, at a dead run, encumbered by his bow and quiver and shield and lance, the brave could accurately discharge arrows over the pony's back, or under its neck, could instantly return to his usual seat on the animal, or swing over to its opposite side.

By offering a plug of tobacco, Catlin at last persuaded one youth to approach closely enough so that he could examine his pony and equipment. The artist found the feat was made possible by a hair halter braided into the mane at the withers. The resulting loop formed a sling into which a warrior could drop his elbow. With his body's weight supported by the middle of his upper arm and his heel, a youth, or man, was free to peer at the enemy, shielded by his horse, while loosing arrows at him. Clinton Smith contended that if such a warrior's horse were shot, the man usually landed on his feet, covering himself with his shield. But obviously no mere hair loop "explained" this horsemanship. To attain such expertness, as Catlin realized, required hours, days, months, and years of practice.

James Hobbs, another adopted Comanche, told of having to reach down from the saddle at a gallop and pick objects from the ground. But Hobbs failed to explain the reason for this stunt, one related to what was perhaps the most difficult and important equestrian feat performed by Comanche men. Each warrior had the obligation of rescuing wounded and dead comrades from the field of battle. He rescued the wounded for obvious reasons—it was a dishonor to desert a wounded companion. The dead he recovered whenever he could, because the People believed, in common with other Plains tribes, that a scalped person was denied an afterlife. The Comanche warrior consequently considered it a sacred duty to save either the wounded or the unscalped dead from his enemy's hands.

Plucking objects from the ground at a gallop was part of a military drill, of which the People had a number. Each youth practiced it again and again, and continued practicing it as an adult. At first he would swoop down and retrieve small, light objects. Mastering this, he learned gradually to seize and recover larger and bulkier objects. When he could do this, he began to drill with two comrades, one of whom took a turn at playing the role of a wounded or dead man. The youth and his partner would race side by side toward the fallen and "wounded" friend, who would try to help them by extending his arms and legs. Passing on either side of the prone figure, the two riders would reach down simultaneously, seize the third brave as best they could and, together, swing his body in front of one or the other of them, bearing a pretended victim off to safety.[17]

This became an even more demanding drill when one of the three warriors played dead. In that instance the supposed corpse not only offered no assistance to the other two men but lay, by turns, in every kind of position a dying man might drop into. As with the previous drills, Comanche braves practiced this one repeatedly, until they and their ponies could perform it successfully again and again. Last of all, the most difficult drill consisted of a single rider swooping down from a gallop to seize another man's prostrate body and to swing it up on his horse before him and to ride off with it. This extraordinary maneuver required perfect timing, great agility and strength, and expert riding. If performed today during a rodeo, it would probably leave even our hypothetical American cowboy shaking his head. Yet every Comanche warrior was supposed to be able, if the need arose, to effect such a rescue by himself, and this at the risk of his own life from enemy arrows or gunfire.

For all their superlative horsemanship, the Comanches did not sentimentalize horses and could, in fact, be ruthless toward them. A famous spot on their westernmost war trail to and from Mexico is a former ford on Rio Pecos still called, "Horsehead Crossing." This ford received its name from the number of horse skulls that had once accumulated there. The skulls were partial remains of horses that Comanche war parties had stolen in Mexico. Having first driven the herd rapidly, night and day, to the Rio Grande, they continued to push it through hot, broken country to the Pecos River. There the exhausted animals drank so heavily that many died as a result. On the war trail, or otherwise, when Comanches were short of food and in a hurry, they thought nothing of slaughtering horses for meat. In 1836 when the Englishwoman Sara Ann Horn was first captured in southern Texas, and her Comanche captors brought her into their camp, her first impression was of the stench of spoiling horse meat. A few years later, in the early 1840s, when buffalo were already becoming less abundant, an English visitor to Texas, William Bollaert, reported (it is not clear how accurately) that "the Comanches it is supposed have eaten 20,000 mustangs during the last 5 years. They *barbecue* mustangs sometimes whole . . ."[18] To the general mass of horses the Comanche warrior had only a limited attachment.

Yet his feeling for an exceptional horse, such as his own buffalo or war pony, was generally one of affection. Each man had his favorite pony, which he staked beside his lodge at night instead of allowing it to graze at large with the herd. Some men were said to love such favorite animals more than their wives or children. Captain Randolph Marcy, U.S. Army, once tried to buy the favorite horse of Sanaco, a southern Comanche chief, offering him a large price for it.[19] But Chief Sanaco would not consider the offer. The animal, he said, was one of the swiftest in his band's herd. If he were to sell it, all of his people might suffer, since they all depended on its speed in hunting buffalo. Besides, he said, patting his pony on the neck, "I love him very much."[20]

At the start of the eighteenth century, the Comanches had horses and wanted more. They wanted the great southern-plains hunting grounds, where buffalo blackened the land like cloud shadows. They wanted a chance at the Spaniards' horses. To get both of these they were prepared to fight.

I

Nuevo Mexico

El Apache y el Comanche
Se citaron pa' la guerra,
El Apache gime y llora,
Y el Comanche se le aferra.

[The Apache and the Comanche
Met each other for war,
The Apache moans and cries,
And the Comanche tightens his grip.]

From a New Mexico folksong

The Comanche excel all the other nations
in breeding, strength, valor, and gallantry.

Athanase de Mézières, 1777

Ay, nanita, alli vienen los cumanchis!
[Oh, granma, here come the Comanches!]

From a New Mexico folksong

Comanchería and the Southern Plains, ca. 1786
(Placement of Comanche divisions, after Thomas W. Kavanagh, "Comanche
Politics," Ph.D. diss., 1986)

1706	The Comanches appear in Spanish records for the first time.
1714	The French found Natchitoches Post; the Spanish establish Los Adaes sixteen miles west of the French post.
1718	The Spanish establish San Antonio de Béxar; the French found Nouvelle Orléans.
1719	New Mexico Governor Valverde mounts an unsuccessful punitive expedition into the plains against the Utes and Comanches.
1720	Pawnee allies of the French massacre the Spanish Villasur reconnaissance expedition on the Platte River.
1739	The trading expedition of Pierre and Paul Mallet reaches Santa Fe from Pawnee villages near the Missouri River in present Nebraska.
1743	The Comanches visit San Antonio de Béxar for the first time.
circa 1749	The French broker a peace between the Wichitan confederacy and the Comanches. The Comanches break their alliance with the Utes.
1750	By mid-century, the Comanches have driven most Apache bands such as the Jicarillas, Carlanas, Mescaleros, Faraones, Lipanes, and so forth westward and southward from the southern plains.

1751   New Mexico governor Vélez, responding to aggression, defeats a band of Comanches in what has become *Comanchería*.

1758   The Comanches begin raiding in Texas, starting with the San Sabá presidio and mission.

1762–1763   In the treaty of Paris closing the Seven Years War, France cedes Louisiana west of the Mississippi to Spain.

1766–1768   The Marqués de Rubí inspects the military defenses of the entire northern frontier of New Spain.

1770   The French town of St. Louis is transferred to Spain.

1775–1783   The British colonists win their freedom from England in the American Revolutionary War. Spain declares war on England in 1779.

1777   Teodoro de Croix, commander general of New Spain's Interior Provinces, holds councils of war in Coahuila, San Antonio de Béxar, and Chihuahua. The third council results in a decision to seek an alliance with the "Nations of the North" (the Comanches and Wichitan confederacy, etc.) against the Apaches.

1779   De Anza defeats the notorious Comanche chieftain, Cuerno Verde.

1780–1781   A smallpox epidemic, originating in Texas, spreads to New Mexico and throughout the Plains tribes.

1785   Governor Cabello of Texas concludes a peace treaty with the Comanches.

1786   New Mexico's Governor de Anza achieves a treaty with the Comanches, making them allies of Spain in "continual war" against the Apaches.

ONE

Governor Vélez Battles Comanches, 1751

The province had been quiet for months. In the capital city of Santa Fe, the only sounds were those of church bells or of dogs barking. Already it was early November of the year 1751, and nights were chill, with the scents of piñon and juniper smoke in the blackness under near and brilliant stars. During the warm days *pobladores*, or colonists, were still cutting wood in the high desert or the foothills of the Sangre de Cristo mountains, which had yet to receive their first snow. Each afternoon settlers, men and boys, rode into the city leading horses and mules loaded with firewood. It was a season of peace before the first storm.

But the city's tranquility was broken by news of an Indian attack on Galisteo Pueblo, about twenty miles to the south. As expected, the squad of presidials stationed there had fought well. They had repelled the assault of three hundred *indios bárbaros* by firing their arquebuses from a trench, killing six of the enemy. The horse Indians had drawn back. The sixteen warriors armed with muskets had fired at the mouth of the trench. The others, in black warpaint, had galloped by, speeding arrows from their ponies' backs. In the end the war party had ridden off with their dead lashed to horses, having accomplished nothing but the slaughter of twelve tame cows pastured outside the pueblo.

The young governor was furious. Had not he, Tomás Vélez Cachupín, warned a band of this very people last summer at Taos that he was admitting them to the trade fair on the condition they neither steal horses nor raid the pueblos of Pecos and Galisteo? The chief and his principal braves had acted humble and had promised not to attack the province. Now, this. Well, he resolved to make an impression on the tribe.

Vélez must also have recognized an opportunity. For he was only ad interim governor, and that by chance. Probably a younger son in an aristocratic family, he had previously served for fourteen years as a cadet in Havana. At the end of this stint, his superiors transferred him to New Spain. Viceroy Revilla Gigedo stationed him in Santa Fe, where he served as captain of the cavalry at its presidio. In late 1748 or early 1749, the king appointed Colonel don Francisco de la Rocha Ferrer to be governor of New Spain's northernmost outpost. But the colonel, unable to serve, named the young captain as his "lieutenant general" to rule "the kingdom of New Mexico." Vélez had already governed for two years, and now the ambitious young officer saw a chance further to prove himself and to advance his career.[1]

The governor gathered a force of fifty-four presidials, thirty citizen militiamen, and some forty Pueblo auxiliaries. On the morning of the second day following the attack, he set out with his troops to punish those deceitful and arrogant Comanches. The weather was cold. Brown and yellow leaves rattled on cottonwoods in canyons. Vélez urged his mounted column along rapidly, traveling day and night. He kept scouts moving ahead to seek out any enemy lurking behind. They found no enemy but did discover burnt-out Comanche campfires. As a result the governor felt secure in allowing a few tiny fires at night, where soldiers, settlers, and Pueblos could huddle, warming their hands against freezing temperatures. On the fourth day the force rode out onto the plains, and on that gray expanse the weather grew milder. Soon they encountered a fork in the enemy's trail, where one set of hoofprints headed northeast, the other southwest. Vélez chose to follow the second. The next day the trail of this band became increasingly fresh, as if the raiders were now traveling more slowly. That night the governor pushed his horse through the dark at a faster pace, sensing the Comanches to be not far ahead of him and still unaware of pursuit.

When dawn came the following morning, Vélez found his command moving among a great herd of buffalo. Well, they would provide cover. Now he must reconnoiter. Convinced the enemy was near, he sent a squad of Pueblo Indians about eight miles ahead to learn whether the enemy had spent the night on the side of a mesa, where he knew there were springs. As the day wore on and the sun hung overhead, he continued cautiously to lead the force forward. In another twelve miles he came upon the scouts waiting for four of their party. These Pueblos were spying from behind a mound to the left of the springs. Soon they returned, excited, to report seeing two Comanches walking from the springs along the mesa top.

Fearing he had been discovered, Vélez acted. He placed a presidial sergeant in command of the two squads of soldiers and twenty Indian auxiliaries and dispatched him to capture the two Comanches. He followed with the main force, trotting at double quick time. The two Comanches, seeing the sergeant and his men galloping behind them, sprinted to shout the alarm, arriving first at the brushy water hole where the war party had halted. In response, Comanche braves leapt onto their ponies and loped out to attack in a half-moon formation that bristled with bows and lances.

The sergeant and his *soldados de cuera* drew up close to face the oncoming horseman. The soldiers wore identical black broad-brimmed hats, six-ply deerskin jackets, leather leggings and spurs, with leather shields on their arms, lances in their hands. The Pueblo Indians waited behind them, bows and lances ready. As the enemy charged, the sergeant drew his musket from its scabbard. The whooping braves racing before him in confusing maneuvers were not easy targets, but he aimed, fired, reloaded, fired again. Twice, in the dust and gunsmoke, he saw a Comanche fall from his pony. The enemy with their few guns were firing back. Other warriors, riding at a gallop, were showering him and his men with arrows. Standing firm, the Spaniards and Pueblos defended themselves.

As the sun drooped over the horizon, Vélez took in the situation before him and gave his horse full rein. The main force followed him into battle. Reaching the sergeant, he found him bleeding from an arrow wound in the head. Two soldiers and a Pueblo warrior had been wounded by gunfire. He signaled forward with his sword. Without haste the enemy withdrew to the water hole. Vélez pressed the attack, ordering his men to surround their position. Retiring farther from the Spanish onslaught, the Comanches dismounted and formed a wall with their ponies and their shields.

From the edge of the water hole, Governor Vélez sent his ensign with three squads into the brush where there was a passage. They attacked the enemy's flank, while he led a frontal attack, concentrating fire on the ring of shields and ponies. The Comanche men, forced into disorganized retreat by the fury of the twin assaults, left many of their horses dead or kicking on the ground as they splashed into the concealment of a reed and rock-rose thicket at the center of the water hole.

Sunset had passed. The sky was darkening. Vélez ordered his men closer to the thicket and had them build huge, blazing fires, so he could watch any attempt of the enemy to escape. Other soldiers kept up a steady fire into the reeds where the Comanches were concealing themselves, standing waist-deep in water. During the evening the trapped warriors twice attempted to fight through the circle of soldiers and Pueblos. Each time the presidials and militiamen fired directly at the advancing forms, driving them back into the darkness. At about nine o'clock the governor ordered two squads, with forty Pueblos, to advance into the thicket, sword in hand, and finish off the enemy sheltered there. But his men could move only very slowly through the water and dense brush. In the flickering light Vélez soon divined that the Comanches, lightly clothed, and also armed with lances and swords, had the advantage in that terrain. Calling out the soldiers and their Indian allies, he decided on new tactics. Although the enemy was by now evidently out of both powder and arrows, they refused to surrender.[2]

At the governor's command, the two squads and the Pueblos set fire to the thicket. The hidden braves tried to put out the fires, revealing themselves sufficiently so that the Spanish soldiers were able to fire volleys at their partly illuminated forms. At that some women and children among them began screaming. Relenting at the outcry, Vélez ordered his men to stop firing. Through an interpreter he told the Comanches he was punishing them "because of their arrogance and maliciousness in attacking the pueblo of Galisteo." But he promised to spare their lives if they would surrender and give up their arms. The Comanches yelled from within the thicket that they knew this was a trap to "seize and execute them." They refused to surrender, even though the night had grown painfully cold, and they were standing in water. Losing patience, Vélez told them that if they had not surrendered by sunrise he would finish them off without pardoning anyone.

About midnight the first one surrendered, a youth of sixteen with a badly wounded foot. Shivering from the cold, he limped from the brush carrying a cross fashioned of reeds. The governor dismounted and accepted the cross. Embracing the boy, he led him to the nearest fire and seated him by it. For a while longer the others endured the icy water, undoubtedly watching the boy's shaking body gleam in the firelight. Finally, one at a time, at intervals, others came out of the thicket, suspicious, expecting to be killed. The first to appear were the most seriously wounded warriors, sixteen of whom died the next day. They were weeping, seemingly from pain. Vélez judged this a display calculated to evoke his sympathy. He could not have known that Comanches believed they would lose their chance for life with their people in another world by drowning or dying in the dark. In all, forty-four Comanches, including six women and children, came reeling out of the brush, to be seated around the fire.

After a time, finding no further harm had been done to them, they began calling to the chief and seven of his braves who had stayed in the thicket, urging them to surrender. The chief refused. For the remainder of the night Governor Vélez waited astride his horse, his weapons in his hands, with his men in the same posture, so as not to be cheated out of a complete victory.

By three o'clock in the morning, the moon had risen and was shining on the thicket, reflecting from patches of water within. The captives were seated or lying by the fires, while armed Spaniards and Pueblos waited on their horses in a circle around the silvery thicket. A war whoop sounded. On the side where the ensign and his soldiers stood guard, the defiant chief and his seven warriors hurled themselves at the line with their lances. The Spaniards fired muskets, killing the chief and two braves, wounding the others. Shortly afterward the five wounded men stumbled, splashing, out of the brush to surrender, begging for their lives. Vélez received them as he had the others.

Dawn revealed a dismal sight. The water hole and its vicinity were strewn with the dead bodies of ponies and warriors. The governor ordered his men to search the thicket. The soldiers found nothing alive, only dead Comanches and their guns, shields, lances, swords, and bows. Vélez had these collected. He ordered them distributed, with the saddles and trappings of the ponies, among his Pueblo auxiliaries, while he gave the surviving ponies to his militiamen. The Comanches who watched this grim business were not reassured. Gathering together and shaping another cross, they presented it to Vélez with veneration, pressing it first to their lips, then to his. Governor Vélez later reported to the viceroy that "this pious demonstration among barbarian heathen" had deeply moved him. Again and again he reassured his prisoners that they had indeed earned their lives and freedom by surrendering. But he warned them to keep peace with New Mexico; otherwise he would not allow them to trade at Taos—and, yes, he would persecute them until they were utterly destroyed.

The governor also stipulated that the tribe return two Spanish women carried off from Abiquiù in 1747, during the previous administration. The Comanches agreed to do so, informing him that the two women and a boy were with another chief, who lived beyond the Arkansas River, where they also lived, at a distance of ten days' travel. More important, they assured him they would "inform their whole tribe of the great charity of the Spaniards, who, after having conquered them, had kept their promise to them."

The total number of this Comanche war party had been 145. The survivors numbered 49, including the 6 women and the 3 children. Virtually all of them were wounded. (Of the Spaniards, 8 soldiers had been wounded, 1 of them fatally; Pueblo casualties were not given.) Governor Vélez took 4 hostages with him to insure the return of the Spanish women and boy. Leaving the Comanche leader tobacco and a bow and ten arrows with which to kill buffalo, Vélez and his command rode away across the plains while, dwindling behind them, the surviving Comanches stood forlornly at the scene of their disaster, watching them go.

The following April a small Comanche band appeared at Taos. Vélez found the chief so conciliatory he released the hostages to him before the return of the captive Spaniards. To his surprise he discovered that one of the four young men preferred to remain with him, the youth had been so happy as a guest in the governor's house. Two of the others, who did leave with the chief, spread the news of their hospitable treatment at Vélez's hands. This also impressed the tribe.

But, especially, the Comanches did not forget their defeat. Nearly a year later, a former captive of theirs, a Kiowa woman spoke to a Spaniard of the "horror which the havoc of the pond of San Diego caused among them."[3] They did not forget Governor Vélez, whom they dubbed the "Boy Captain" or the "Captain Who Amazes." But it was not merely Vélez's ability as a soldier that earned their respect; the previous governor, Codallos, had badly defeated them in 1747. No, it was something besides. Vélez had deeply impressed them by his magnanimity in granting life and freedom to Comanches who had surrendered. This was generosity beyond the code of plains warfare, the generosity of a great *capitán*. Most of all, though, under his leadership the Spaniards "had kept their promise to them."

TWO

Expeditions to the Plains, 1706–1749

Vélez Cachupín was the first New Mexico governor to achieve prolonged and satisfactory treaties with the Comanches. Earlier, during the administration of the Marqués de Peñuela, between 1707 and 1712, the Utes and Comanches had ridden into the province requesting peace. But after the marqués had granted them a treaty, their first of innumerable pacts with the Spaniards, they had continued to enter the kingdom and steal under the protection of the agreement.[1]

In 1716 the Comanches and their Shoshonean-speaking Ute allies committed depredations at Taos, at Tewa pueblos, and at Spanish settlements. Using these provocations as a pretext, Don Félix Martínez, the ad interim governor, sent Captain Cristóbal de la Serna against a large Ute camp below the Cerro de San Antonio, a mountain rising from the prairie south of today's Antonito, Colorado. De la Serna augmented his command with fifty Indian auxiliaries, possibly including Jicarilla Apaches. The Utes, having sent peace feelers to the capital, evidently felt secure, believing the Spaniards were coming to discuss terms with them. The captain and his force fell upon the camp. In the ensuing melee the Spaniards and their Indian allies routed the panic-stricken Utes, killing some, while others fled. Cristóbal de la Serna marched a large number of prisoners to Santa Fe. From there Governor Martínez sold the captives south into slavery in Mexico, pocketing the proceeds from the sale. Although Spanish authorities investigated the incident, none of the prisoners returned. Partly as a result of this outrage, both Utes and Comanches grew increasingly hostile toward New Mexico.

Three years later, in 1719, the number and intensity of Ute and Comanche raids against the province had so greatly increased that the new governor, Don Antonio Valverde Cosio, called a council of war to decide on a course of action. Owing to the number of robberies and murders committed by the two tribes, the gathering of New Mexico frontiersmen recommended a campaign against them. Late that September, leading a large and well-equipped expedition, Governor Valverde set out for the plains to chastise the Comanches in what was already becoming their home territory.[2]

Valverde crossed the mountains eastward to what is now Cimarron, marched north to the Purgatoire River, rode north again over foothills to join the Arkansas River east of the present town of Pueblo, and finally traveled along the river eastward again for about ninety miles to a spot somewhat beyond today's Las Animas, Colorado. There Apache scouts informed him that the Comanches moving before his army had changed course. He commanded a halt and called a council of settlers and soldiers.

To the governor the noteworthy events of the journey were probably not incidents such as a bear chasing Pueblo Indians into camp, but rather encounters with various groups of Apaches. The first of these occurred just east of the Sangre de Cristos, when an officer discovered a small adobe house. The Apaches living there cultivated fields of maize, which they had already harvested. They complained to Valverde through interpreters that the Comanches were harassing and killing their relatives and other members of their tribe.

On September 22 the army traveled about eight miles, to the vicinity of Rayado Creek.[3] Again the soldiers found fields of Indian corn, beans, and squash. The governor ordered them to disturb nothing. On the creek "at the distance of an arquebus shot" they came upon some Apache families living in an adobe house whose flat roof supported a cross. As the mounted column proceeded upstream, the soldiers observed eight more houses, occupied by other families.

During a halt, as Valverde was dining with the chaplain and some officers, Chief Carlana, of the Apaches, rode up to them.

"Ave Maria," said the chief.

"Sin pecado concevida," the Castilian replied.

Carlana swung off his horse. The governor welcomed him, handing him his own plate of boiled meat and vegetables. After the chief had eaten, Valverde asked him why he had come. Carlana explained he was fleeing, with half of his people, from his traditional country, a spur of the Rockies crossed today at Raton, New Mexico. He had come to seek assistance from the Jicarillas, while the remainder of his people had sought refuge with other Apaches. Why? He was compelled to do all this because of constant Ute and Comanche raids. Governor Valverde told of his plan to punish their mutual enemies. Delighted, Carlana offered to go with some of his warriors to guide the army, showing them campsites and springs on the way to the region of the Comanches. Valverde accepted the offer, and Chief Carlana quickly departed.

Five days later, on September 27, the army was bivouacked along the

Purgatoire River when Chief Carlana returned with sixty-nine mounted warriors. They loped their horses around the camp, singing and whooping, then danced around the fire for most of the night, some of them painted white, others red. The next afternoon, after the daily march, Carlana presented himself at Valverde's tent with seven of his young men, each armed with bow and arrows, a machete, and an oval leather shield. Through the interpreters he told the governor the time had come to send out scouts to reconnoiter the country lying ahead. Valverde agreed. Giving the braves chocolate and tobacco, he sent them off.

The Spaniards received little news of the enemy until early on October 3, when some of the scouts appeared out of the darkness. They reported discovering three enemy riders driving twenty horses and a colt before them on one of the beaten paths leading from Santa Fe. The trail was plain, and it led toward Comanche country. The next definite sign of the foe came four days later. During a spell of cold, overcast weather, the expedition camped at a spring with a pond. Chief Carlana, on examining tracks there, declared that the Utes and Comanches had "ranched on the spot." He estimated that they had set up more than sixty tepees. The travois poles of these had left dragmarks in the earth that clearly showed the direction in which they had departed. The next day, which was also cold and disagreeable, the army traveled eastward about fourteen miles and pitched their tents in an arroyo among cottonwoods. Here, once more, there was evidence of the enemy, who had decamped only a few days before, leaving piles of firewood. Sleet began falling, and soldiers heaved the wood on their fires.

The turning point came on October 14. On the previous day the army had again encountered a recent enemy campsite. This time scouts found the charred remains of two hundred fires. The Spaniards estimated at least five persons around each, making a total of some one thousand men, women and children. In this area by the Arkansas River, thousands of buffalo wandered, grazing, on the plains. But their myriad tracks could not conceal those of the enemy. Early on the 14th the vanguard again struck the Shoshoneans' trail. The tracks were clear, obviously made by a great number of people and horses, heading northeast.[4]

The governor ordered a halt to confer with Chief Carlana. Through the interpreters he told him of his plan to pursue the two enemies along the now distinct trail until he overtook and chastised them. For a moment Carlana must have gazed sadly at the hoofprints before him, at the interweaving lines of dragging lodgepoles. It would be impossible to follow them farther, he replied. They had craftily changed direction and were now taking a route with sparse waterholes and springs. What water did exist along the way was insufficient to support the caballada and the army, especially after the passage of a thousand Utes, Comanches, and their ponies.

For the Apache chief and his warriors, the campaign ended there, with the sight of trampled grass and innumerable parallel lines pointing northeast. Had the Utes and Comanches become aware of the army on their trail? Undoubtedly. In any event the Carlana Apaches were now without a home or hunting grounds of their own. Their allies, the Jicarillas, were gradually retreating from the same enemy. The Spaniards, even with their elaborate expedition and their generous promises, had proven unable to help them.

That same year, 1719, from the opposite, eastern side of the plains, Bénard de la Harpe left the little wooden fort of St. Jean Baptiste de Natchitoches to lead an expedition up the Red River. Near the present site of Texarkana, he built a stockaded trading house among the Nasonis, a tribe of friendly Caddoan Indians. He bought horses from them, and with a party of only ten, struck out north and west through woods and across plains, despite the danger of attack by Apaches. Soon, though, he joined a group of some fifty Caddoans en route to his own destination, a village of the Tawakonies, a division of the Wichitan peoples. Early that September the party reached the village of conical grass huts on the Canadian River near its confluence with the Arkansas.

Far west of there, across the plains and beyond the mountains, in the colonial kingdom of New Mexico, Governor Valverde was preparing for his expedition. Yet he would not be departing from Santa Fe for over two weeks.

Fortuitously de la Harpe arrived during a great gathering of the Wichitans (Tawakonies, Iscanis, Taovayas, and Wichitas proper). Most of these people had never seen a white man, and it was almost as if he had ridden in on the wind. After a friendly and ceremonial reception, the explorer held council with nine chiefs representing the six thousand people assembled there, many of them encamped in their buffalo-hide tepees. At this council, where Caddoans served as interpreters, the Frenchman managed to conclude a treaty between the Wichitan divisions and his own nation: it would endure as long as a French king ruled Louisiana.

The Wichitans needed a treaty with a strong ally. Although they were an agricultural people living part of the year in villages by rivers and cultivating corn, squash, and melons, during the winter months they were nomadic, warlike hunters who followed the buffalo. At this juncture in their history they were confronted, to the east and north, with hostile neighbors—the feared Osages. To the west they had new enemies in mounted Comanches, while their oldest and most hated enemy remained the Plains Apaches, who had traditionally raided them for slaves, even when they had lived in present Kansas in the villages Coronado and Oñate had known as Quivira. They, in turn, had traditionally captured Apaches, whom they likewise sold into slavery . . . sometimes.

De la Harpe had made a successful visit to the Wichitan peoples. He was leaving the fleur-de-lis flying over the Tawakoni village of grass huts. He had opened negotiations for trade, with his eye on horses, of which the tribe had plenty. Now as he prepared to depart, the chiefs presented him with a gift, a little Apache girl, eight years old. But what was this? They were apologizing. The translator explained that the chiefs regretted making such a modest present, only a single slave. If only he had come a month earlier, they would have given him several; unfortunately, at that time they had offered a great feast and had eaten seventeen other Apache captives. Yes, and they hoped he would return soon and bring the muskets he had promised to trade with them. In the meantime, they wished him a good return journey.

Cannibalism? Yes. And muskets?

Spanish law strictly forbade any trade of firearms to the indios bárbaros. And now Frenchmen were going to trade muskets to the Plains Indians? Yes, the French were going to trade firearms for buffalo hides, slaves, and horses. This barter would make a difference in the balance of power on the southern plains, particularly to the Apaches and the Comanches.

French and Spanish rivalry soon presented the People with opportunities. Seizing upon these, they accomplished their conquest of the southern plains in less than fifty years, and this with the unintentional assistance of the French. France, "the reluctant imperialist," was, in contrast to Spain, far more interested in trade than in conversion of the Indians and colonization.[5] (John Law's Compagnie des Indes, for instance, held a trading monopoly in Louisiana from 1717 to 1731, virtually controlling the colony during that time). The French had long been intrigued by New Mexico, with its supposed rich mines, and by the prospect of trade with Santa Fe. Their strategy in approaching this northern kingdom of New Spain was one that they had used successfully elsewhere. They would progress toward a profitable business arrangement by making treaties with and between hostile tribes. In this instance they must have concluded that they might monopolize the trade of the Plains Indians while, at the same time, establishing a lucrative commerce with the Spaniards of New Mexico. Possibly it never occurred to them that such a scheme would be abhorrent to high Spanish officials, whose attitude toward their provinces, and toward trade with outsiders, particularly the French, can only be described, in today's expression, as "paranoid."

Spanish colonists in New Mexico shared their vice-regal government's apprehension about the intentions of the French. In the 1690s, according to Bancroft, the settlers had feared a French invasion. Certainly they knew that the French were out there, somewhere, far east of the Sangre de Cristo range of mountains. During the same decade a Padre Niel had ransomed two little French girls from a war party of Navajos returning from the plains. Then, in 1698, the French had nearly destroyed a Navajo force of four thousand men. Even if this had been a figure greatly inflated by rumor, the Spaniards isolated in New Spain's northernmost outpost were understandably alarmed.

Probably neither officials nor settlers knew it, but in 1703 twenty *voyageurs* from New France had tried unsuccessfully to explore their way from the Illinois country to New Mexico, hoping to trade with Santa Fe.[6] Nor did Spaniards know that, sixteen years later, during the same fall de la Harpe had visited the Wichitas on the lower Arkansas, Lieutenant Claude-Charles du Tisné had reached and treated with two additional Wichitan villages, apparently on the Verdigris River at the site of the present town of Neodesha, Kansas. But in 1706 a Spanish military expedition out of Santa Fe had, for the first time, encountered direct evidence of French penetration toward New Mexico. This occurred when Apache chieftains at El Cuartelejo, a cluster of rancherías located, in all likelihood, near today's Scott City, Kansas, had shown Sergeant Major Juan de Ulibarrí a captured musket. One of Ulibarri's men, Jean de l'Archevêque, a Frenchman suspected by historians of being one of La Salle's murderers, promptly identified the gun as French. The Cuartelejos explained they had taken it from the body of a white man. This person, who had been bald and accompanied by a pregnant woman, had come with a war party of Pawnees to attack them. The Pawnees, on being discovered, had retreated, but the man and woman, trudging slowly, had lagged behind. Apaches had killed them both and scalped the woman, returning with the musket and powder, a kettle, and a cap with red lining, part of the traditional garb of the voyageur.

The Cuartelejo chiefs pointed out that the "other Spaniards," or French, were trading guns to the Pawnees, enemies who were selling Apache women and children to their new allies—just as they, the Apaches, sold Pawnee and Wichitan captives to the Spaniards. They went on to invite the captain and his command to join them at once in a joint campaign against their mutual enemies. Ulibarrí declined, saying it was his duty to return sixty-two runaway and apostate Picurís Indians to their New Mexico pueblo, that winter was coming on, and that, besides, so as not to alarm them, he had intentionally omitted bringing along a bugle or a drum.

Back in Santa Fe, his task accomplished, Sergeant Major Ulibarrí reported to Governor Francisco Cuervo y Valdez. Of minor importance to the governor, no doubt, was the news that the "infidel enemies of the Ute and Comanche tribes" had attacked two Apache rancherías. No, the big news was the appearance of a Frenchman, with Pawnee allies, so near the province. This was the principal piece of information which Governor Cuervo, in turn, sent on to Mexico City, where the viceroy and other officials received it with interest, if not alarm.

Thirteen years later Governor Valverde, returning from his fruitless expedition against the Comanches, met with a host of Apaches on the Arkansas River among cottonwoods, a little east of modern La Junta. There were more than a thousand of them in some two hundred tepees—Cuartelejos, along with two other bands that the Spaniards called, respectively, Palomas and Calchufines. Among these people was a Paloma chief with a healing gunshot wound. On questioning the man, the governor learned that the French, with Pawnee and Wichitan allies, had attacked the Palomas from ambush while they were planting corn in their own country, which was probably in today's northeastern Colorado, along the South Platte River. The chief, wounded while defending himself, maintained that he and his people would have been massacred if night had not fallen, providing them with an opportunity to escape. As it was the enemy had retained the Palomas' lands, so that they, themselves, had been forced to relocate, for safety, to this present river, the Napestle, or Arkansas.

The viceroy surely found this news of increased French activity on the plains even more disturbing than anything in previous reports. What made it particularly alarming was England's and France's declaration of war upon Spain that same year, 1719. Viceroy Valero must have agreed with Valverde's conclusion that the enemy's purpose appeared to be "to penetrate little by little into the land." As a result he ordered the governor to reconnoiter, so as to determine the location and strength of the French on the plains.

But Valverde was busy with the problems of the province. Instead of leading the expedition himself, he dispatched his lieutenant governor, Pedro de Villasur, with forty-two presidials; several settlers; a priest, Father Juan Mínguez; the frontier scout José Naranjo; an interpreter, Jean de l'Archevêque; and sixty Pueblo auxiliaries.[7] If the lieutenant governor failed to locate the French, he succeeded in finding their allies, the Pawnees, on the Platte River between today's towns of Maxwell and Brady, Nebraska. The Pawnees behaved in a strange and hostile manner, and the expedition withdrew, having discovered no definite evidence of a French presence. But early on the morning of August 14, 1720, a swarm of Pawnee warriors, possibly including some Frenchmen, ambushed the Spanish camp. Villasur, "a man inexpert in military affairs," had selected a campsite bordered by high grass near the confluence of the North and South Platte Rivers. His experienced *maese de campo* (master of the camp), Tomás Olguín, had objected to the spot, because it was not defensible against an enemy.

"That is fear," Villasur had snapped. "We will stop in this place."

"I have never known fear, sir," said Olguín. "I spoke only of what seemed wise to me."

Both men died around dawn the following morning.

The attack by running, whooping warriors, who had crept from the river through grass, took the Spaniards and Pueblos entirely by surprise. Forty-eight of the Indian allies managed to break away and flee in panic. Because the Pawnees attacked on foot, soldiers of the horse guard somehow fought their way into camp from the pasture, rescued a few other men, and escaped with the herd. Thirteen Spaniards escaped. All the others died, although in the struggle they inflicted heavy casualties on the Pawnees. Among the dead were the priest, the frontiersman Naranjo, and, ironically, the renegade Frenchman Jean de l'Archevêque. The survivors fled southwestward. Villasur's reconnaissance left thirty-two widows in the province of New Mexico. The war declared by England and France against Spain in 1719 ended that same month.

The Comanches may have gloated over the defeat of the Spaniards, but there was an aspect of it that no doubt disturbed them. The Pawnees were their enemies, too. The new white men on the plains were giving firearms to the Pawnees. They knew and feared these weapons that spit out noise, smoke, fire, and death. Yet they had no superstitious dread of them. Their Ute allies, and probably they, too, had already fought Spanish soldiers who had used muskets. They had learned that a gun did not make a man invincible, and the shots did not always kill, or even strike. Still every warrior wished he had one. But how to get the weapons? That was a hard question. The fact that the French were friends of their enemies made them enemies of the People also. Another thing—what if the Apaches were to get their hands on a quantity of firearms?

In 1723 a Frenchman, Etienne Véniard de Bourgmont, with a small company of soldiers, constructed a post, which he called Fort Orléans, near the mouth of the Grand River on the Missouri.[8] There he traded with the Kansa Indians, who were enemies of the Padoucas, or Plains Apaches. But the strategy of de Bourgmont's employers, La Compagnie des Indes, compelled him to make peace with the Padoucas, who were known to barter regularly with New Mexico.[9] Peace with the Plains Apaches, they believed, would clear the way for French trade with Santa Fe. After one unsuccessful try, de Bourgmont journeyed in the fall of 1724 southwestward across the plains of today's Kansas. For ten days the party traveled—de Bourgmont, his officers and soldiers, his young son, and delegations of Indians from several tribes. Finally, on October 18th, he was met by two French emissaries he had sent ahead. They came at a gallop (*à grand galop de cheval*), accompanied by Apache chiefs and bearing the French flag, with its royal fleur-de-lis.

The French pitched their tents a pistol shot away from the Padouca encampment. Soon a small crowd of Apache warriors arrived among them. Laying a great buffalo robe on the ground, they placed upon it de Bourgmont, his son, and two officers. Fifteen men hoisted up the robe and carried it to the tepee of the head chief of the Padoucas (probably Cuartelejo Apaches who had harvested their crops and were hunting buffalo out of a temporary camp). There the chief feasted the group until nightfall, when they returned to their own tents.

The following morning de Bourgmont unpacked his goods, separating them into large piles: guns, powder, musket balls, sabers, picks, hatchets, mirrors, red cloth, and blue, along with piles of needles, vermilion, awls, scissors, bells big and little, and so forth. Before the imposing array he spoke to the crowd of Apaches, telling them his master, the King of France, wished them to be at peace with the French, as well as with all the tribes whose representatives were present: the Missouris, the Osages, the Kansas, the Otos, and the Pawnees. Further, he said, when Frenchmen came to them wishing to travel to New Mexico, they, the Padoucas, were to serve as willing guides, a favor for which they would be paid. He then presented the head chief with the French flag, which he demanded he maintain as spotless as it was at that moment. "My friends," he concluded, "the goods which you see before you are for you all. Thanks to the king, our master, you have only to take them. It's he who gives them to you, and who sent me specially to bring his message to you, and to give his flag to the great chief of the Padoucas."

The Apaches were stunned by this generosity, hardly able to believe the French wanted nothing in return for the gifts. Immediately, and during the remainder of de Bourgmont's visit, the *Grand Chef des Padoucas* thanked the party in oration after oration, meanwhile entertaining them with his people's most lavish hospitality, and at once presenting its leader with seven horses. "Is it true," he asked, "that you are really men?"

The Padoucas regaled even the common soldiers, who were permitted to go, a few at a time, into their camp, where the people gave them "mille caresses et ils leur offroient de leurs filles" (that is, stroked them and offered them their young women). Later, in another speech to the Indian delegations accompanying the party, the chief exclaimed at how lucky they, the other tribes, were to live near the French. It was true, he said, that they themselves traveled to barter with the Spaniards, but the Spaniards would only trade horses to them, along with a few knives and bad axes. They refused to trade guns, or lead, or powder, or kettles, or blankets, or any of the goods the great French chief had given them. Therefore the French were their real friends. Picking up a handful of earth, he said loudly, "I consider the Spaniards now as this dirt"; then, speaking directly to de Bourgmont, he added, "And thee I consider to be like the sun."

No wonder officials in the miserably poor colony of Nuevo México felt threatened by the French advance! In Mexico City the viceroy recommended establishing a presidio at El Cuartelejo in order to guard against a possible invasion by French troops. Governor Valverde and his successor, Juan Domingo de Bustamante, requested instead a garrison at La Jicarilla, for protection not only against the French but also against Ute and Comanche incursions. They pointed out that among other disadvantages to the first plan, Cuartelejo was at a distance of over 340 miles from Santa Fe, whereas La Jicarilla was within a distance of about 100, and was situated before a principal trail over the mountains to Taos. This counterproposal was considered with Spanish bureaucratic deliberation, and letters passed back and forth for several years, until it was dropped in 1726, as recommended by *Visitador* (Inspector) Pedro de Rivera, largely because of the anticipated cost to the royal treasury.

Meanwhile as some Apaches were receiving arms from the French, others were defending themselves from Ute and Comanche attack. In 1723 Chief Carlana rode into Santa Fe to complain of the constant raids and to plead for Spanish help, declaring the willingness of his people to become Christians and Spanish subjects. Governor Bustamante visited La Jicarilla, whose rancherías may have stretched along Cimarron Creek. He found that many of the Apaches were apostates. Still he promised them all Spanish protection—promises that, like those of Valverde, would probably have been honored if the viceroy and his advisors had been able to see the Apache crisis from the viewpoint of the colonists, who needed a buffer to protect them from the new plains raiders.

The following year, during which de Bourgmont treated with the Padoucas, Governor Bustamante received another group from La Jicarilla, who again pleaded for help. This time the Governor sallied out with his troops after a war party of Utes and Comanches, pursuing them so hotly that he managed to rescue sixty-four Jicarilla women and children from probable slavery.

Comanche policy during the 1720s and beyond was clear: to seize the lands of all Apaches in their path and either to kill, capture, or drive them from their traditional territory. French policy, on the other hand, was less evident, and sometimes seemed downright contradictory. Plainly the French wished access to New Mexico. In 1724 they made allies of the Padoucas, but only two years later they appear to have been courting the Comanches. In 1726, when *Visitador* Rivera was in Santa Fe, he interviewed some Paloma and Calchufines Apaches who had fled to the capital to escape a force of Comanches with Frenchmen among them. Around the same time, or perhaps the next year, a Taos chief reported the presence of Frenchmen at El Cuartelejo about to assist a war party of Cuartelejo, Paloma, and Sierra Blanca Apaches in a campaign against the Comanches. In any event the Apaches told Governor Bustamante they believed the French had gained the friendship of most of the Indians of the plains.

But the Apaches were only partly right. French strategy, in the end, alienated the Comanches.[10] Undoubtedly the Nuhmuhnuh resented the gift of firearms to the Padoucas—whether Cuartelejos or some other band. Possibly some of their warriors died from that gift, or from others similar to it. Like all tribes, they wanted guns badly. For this reason they were willing to trade with the French. But from the 1720s on, they mistrusted French traders. The head chief of the Padoucas had asked Bourgmont to send Frenchmen to live with them. The Wichitan peoples welcomed French residents in their villages. But the Comanches never permitted either *coureurs de bois* or squaw men to live among them. More important, they evidently proved unwilling, no matter what blandishments were offered, to smoke the calumet with the Apaches.

As the Nuhmuhnuh drove southward, their policy for some fifteen years was to bar the westward progress of French traders across the plains, so as to keep guns out of the hands of Apaches. Ironically, Gallic strategy, so successful at first, finally produced the opposite effect of that intended. The French made the mistake of forming alliances and bartering with the People's enemies. Instead of opening the way to New Mexico, their tactic created, in Comanche alienation and mistrust, an insuperable obstacle to trade with the Spaniards of Santa Fe.

Out on the plains the Comanches were already winning their war. Spanish documents refer, for example, to a rumored nine-day battle between Comanches and Apaches in 1725. This sustained conflict, unusual among Plains Indians, was supposed to have occurred on the Rio de Fierro, apparently the Wichita River. By Spanish accounts the Comanches were victorious, and the Apaches fled.

Most battles, though, resulted from the kind of swift, mounted raid the Comanches and Utes directed so expertly against the Jicarillas. In these the

Apaches fought for their lives. Knowing where to find the northeastern Apaches during the growing season, the raiders were able to plan attacks from as far as two to four hundred miles away. They would suddenly strike, kill and burn, then gallop away with scalps, plunder, and prisoners, escaping into the vastness of the plains. Moreover in the war itself, the Comanches had the unwitting assistance of the Caddoan-speaking tribes on the eastern margin of the prairie (these included the Arikaras, Pawnees, Wichitas, and Caddos proper). After having acquired horses, the Apaches had mercilessly raided the Caddoans for slaves. Now, armed with French trade muskets, these peoples, though still enemies of the Comanches, were helping the Comanches to push the Apaches southward. Finally, another reason for Comanche success may have been the cohesiveness of the People, as opposed to an endemic tendency toward divisiveness among the Apaches.

Some few Apaches, for a time, were able to defend themselves with firearms. But guns require powder, lead, and—often—repairs by an armorer. To Apaches cut off from these necessities, guns became useless, and the French by 1728 could not afford to sustain all of the trading ventures they had initiated. That year they abandoned Fort Orléans. Eventually old enmities among the tribes reasserted themselves, and the alliances carefully fashioned by the French—for example, between Osages and Pawnees—disintegrated. In any event by 1730 the Comanches, Utes, and perhaps other tribes hostile to the Apaches, had swept the Cuartelejos, too, from their traditional homeland. Three years after that the Franciscan clergy in New Mexico established a mission for the Jicarillas in Taos Valley, where these Apaches had fled from the Utes and Comanches. Six years later another expedition by the French demonstrated just how successful the Comanches had been in harrying their enemies westward and southward, out of the path of their migration.

At the end of May 1739, two brothers from New France, Pierre and Paul Mallet, struck out with a party of six to discover on horseback a route from the Missouri River, near what is now Omaha, to Santa Fe. Leaving Pawnee villages, they followed the Platte River westward across the treeless plains of present Nebraska, where they frequently used *bois de vache*, or buffalo chips, for fuel. On the twentieth, now traveling southward, they lost seven heavily laden packhorses in crossing the deep and swift Kansas River. Four days later, at the Arkansas River, they discovered on rocks *marques des Espagnols*—traces of Spanish passage. At that point they estimated that they had traveled approximately four hundred miles since departing from the Pawnee villages.

On July 5, probably in present southeastern Colorado, they encountered an encampment of "une nation Sauvage, nommée Laïtanes," Indians whom Americans would later call "Hietans" or "Ietans."[11] They presented the Comanches with a gift, receiving several deer in return. But the people of the band behaved so suspiciously that they traveled another league (about 2.5 miles) before pitching camp. The next morning they turned south from the Arkansas. As they were riding from the site, an Arikara Indian, a slave among the Comanches, came up and informed them that the People wished to destroy them. The intrepid Frenchmen sent him back with a message, saying, in effect, "come on ahead—we're waiting." They remained at the spot until the Arikara returned, alone. Then, on questioning the man, they learned that he had earlier been a slave of the Spaniards, even having been baptized. Promising to try procuring his freedom, they persuaded him to guide them to New Mexico.

On July 10 they first saw "les Montagnes Espagnoles" (the Sangre de Cristo range), and on the thirteenth they spent the night by three Comanche tepees, to whose occupants they made a small present. Two days later they encountered three Pueblo Indians, to whom they gave a letter for the commandant at Taos. The next day they received, in return, a gift of mutton and wheat bread *fort beau*. When they were about a league from the first Spanish post, after a long climb in the mountains and a descent into green alpine valleys, and were approaching the pueblo and mission of Picurís, the commandant and the padre, at the head of a crowd of people, came out to meet them. They entered Picurís with bells ringing.

The Mallet brothers arrived in Santa Fe on July 22, having traveled, they estimated, around seven hundred miles since leaving the Pawnee villages. For the next nine months they remained in the capital, waiting for the annual caravan from Mexico to bring the governor a response from the viceroy concerning their disposition. In the response, when it finally came, that official directed the governor to try persuading them to remain in New Mexico, or even to try recruiting them to explore farther westward in the service of Spain. But he did not suggest holding them against their wills. So on May 1, 1740, the party rode out of Santa Fe toward Pecos Pueblo—all except for one Moreau, who had meanwhile married a local girl and become a resident. As for the Mallet brothers, their plan was nothing less than to find the Mississippi, somewhere out there east of the mountains, and to glide down that river to New Orleans. This they did. But first they found the Canadian, which may owe its name to them. They followed that river across the plains, like other explorers after them, to its junction with a larger stream. There they were agreeably surprised to find themselves at the Arkansas, where a little downstream, some fellow *canadiens* were hunting game and salting meat.

In the meantime, en route, they had again encountered Comanches, who this time were friendly. On May 13 three of the seven men left the party to return by way of the Pawnee villages to Illinois, a feat they accomplished. On that same day the remaining four came upon eight Ietan warriors, with whom they camped that night. Two days later they reached a Comanche ranchería, with a multitude of horses pastured in the vicinity. They spent the night there, and the band offered them a feast. The next day they traded a few knives and other *bagatelles* for horses and continued to follow the Canadian southeastward on their journey.

On May 30 they met some "Padokas," two men and three women. The four Frenchmen shook hands with these people, but the Apaches were so nervous—perhaps recognizing Comanche horses and tack—that soon afterward they took fright and ran off, throwing away the meat with which they were loaded. By June 19 the brothers were considering a change of plan. With only two knives remaining among them, they somehow succeeded in building two *petits canots*, or dinghys, out of elm bark. On the twentieth day they released their eighteen horses onto the prairie and embarked in their dinghys, to slip downstream with the sluggish current. Four days later they reached the mouth of the Arkansas River. After hunting for a time with the other Canadians, they loaded a pirogue with salted meat, proceeded to Arkansas Post (a French trading community), and from there paddled down the Mississippi to New Orleans.

The Frenchmen's extraordinary expedition demonstrated that important changes had occurred on the southern plains within fifteen years or so. The fact that the first, unfriendly band of Comanches permitted the Canadians to pass beyond them to the Spaniards indicated they no longer feared firearms reaching the Apaches; there were no more Apaches on the plains in that region. The Mallets' return trip demonstrated further change. Their Santa Fe host, Lieutenant Governor Juan Páez Hurtado, had in 1715 led a punitive expedition against the Faraon Apaches down the Canadian River, where the Jicarillas and the Picurís Indians, from whom the Faraons stole horses, had reported their rancherías to be. Hurtado had failed to find the Apaches, who had apparently been warned in advance by their trading partners, the Pecos Indians. But his Picurís guide had led him to a place slightly north of the river where there was water, pasture, and a multitude of hoofprints said to be those of Apache ponies. The Mallet brothers, on the other hand, encountered only Comanches along the stream, except for a single small party of frightened Apaches. Clearly by 1740 the Comanches had driven the Plains Apaches south of the Canadian River. The southern plains, which the Spaniards had long considered a part of Apachería, were on their way to becoming Comanchería.

Tomás Vélez Cachupín began his first term as governor of New Mexico in 1749. But between the time of the Mallet brothers' return trip and the year of his inauguration, there were important developments involving the Comanches. In 1740 the two Frenchmen reported the People to be at peace with the Spaniards. They also reported, significantly, that there were only eighty soldiers in the Santa Fe presidio, "mauvaise troupe et mal armée" ("a sorry troop, badly armed"). The Comanches were doubtless aware of the relatively few presidials garrisoned in the province. Shortly afterward they began the raids of the 1740s, which cleared the eastern frontier from Albuquerque northward, causing *genízaros* (former Indian captives of the Comanches, or these former prisoners' children) and settlers, alike, to desert their farms and villages and flee to safer, more populated regions in or near the Rio Grande Valley.[12] The Comanches were now attacking with French muskets, and some warriors were better armed than either the provincial militia or the soldados de cuera, as the leather-jacketed presidials were called.

Although La Compagnie des Indes had surrendered its trading monopoly in 1731, allowing Louisiana to revert to a royal colony, there were still independent French traders on the southern plains. These entrepreneurs continued to sell guns to the Comanches, resulting in increased raiding for horses in New Mexico, as well as war against all whom the People considered to be their enemies. Between 1744 and 1749, for example, the Nuhmuhnuh reportedly slew 150 Pecos Indians, those friends of the Apaches.[13]

In 1747 Governor Joachín de Codallos y Rabal of New Mexico defeated a Comanche and Ute war party that had penetrated as far west as Abiquiù. In this period the Comanches themselves participated in two important changes. Around 1749 the French arranged a peace between the People and the Wichitan confederacy. From then on the Wichitan tribes were to be, intermittently, both allies and trading partners who supplied the Buffalo Indians with French muskets. Then about the same year, the Nuhmuhnuh broke with the Utes, who became their enemies. Yet even without their old allies, the People prospered and grew continually stronger. Only the year before, for instance, Indians friendly to New Mexico had reported thirty-three French traders at La Jicarilla, that former home of the Apaches, selling guns to the plains warriors. The Comanches had—discovered a wonderful formula, which was to bring them the military power they wanted and help them continue their conquest of the southern plains—the barter of Apache slaves and stolen Spanish horses for French muskets, powder, and lead. This trade made them what Spaniards had once called the eastern Apaches, "Masters of the Plains."

THREE

Who Were the Comanches?

✢

Much, much later, during the final quarter of the next century, a group of Comanche men were talking and laughing around their small fire, somewhere in the southern plains. The figure watching them from the darkness guessed they were recounting events of the day. Ignorant of their language, as he was, he could not be sure. But he did recognize them as Comanches. Longingly he watched them for about a half-hour. For over a year now he had been living alone, roaming from one deserted place to another, fleeing from all men, red or white, hiding, with only his horse for company. He was desperately lonely. At last, drawing a deep breath, he stood and walked out of the dark into the firelight among them.

With whoops and shouts the warriors sprang to their feet, dashing into the dark. For moments he felt their eyes upon him—a sixteen-year-old, with long, unkempt hair, dressed in worn buckskins, clutching a bow and a fistful of arrows. With more whoops, the Comanches charged back into the firelight, surrounding him.

Giving the sign for peace, the boy signaled he was alone and hungry.

The first to approach him was an old woman with the party. Standing close, she peered at him fiercely out of her single eye, all the while chattering excitedly in that language he could not understand. Worse, he was unable to meet her gaze, even though he knew this was making a bad impression. Luckily a young brave stepped up and addressed him in the Athapascan tongue.

The youth told his story.

He had been an Apache, he said, by necessity. He had been driven from the tribe for killing a medicine man who had murdered his master and friend, Carnoviste. Born white, he was now an Indian. He hated the whites. On his shield were the scalps of white men he had killed. He had risen to minor chief under Carnoviste, but their warriors had all been slain in a drunken fight by other Apaches, who would now like to kill him, too. He wanted, he declared, to become a Comanche and help them fight whites and Apaches.

When the youth had finished speaking, a second warrior joined the first. He remembered seeing him, he announced, among the Apaches. Once they had even raced horses, and the youth's horse had beaten his. Also he had known Carnoviste and other Apaches, with whom they had usually fought but had sometimes been at peace, in order better to make war on the whites.

In the end, in spite of the old woman, who advised killing him, the youth was invited to eat and sleep with the party and to accompany them the next day to the main camp. There, the warriors said, their principal chief, Cotopah, would welcome him.

Cotopah did.

The youth who threw himself upon the mercy of the Comanches was Herman Lehmann. A German immigrant boy, he had been captured by Apaches at the age of eleven. Five years later the Comanches welcomed this fugitive from the camp of their enemies. Never did Lehmann regret walking out of the dark into the light of their fire. Years afterward, recalling his decision to reveal himself, he could still picture those Comanche men talking and laughing in the flickering light. The Apaches with whom he had lived never had laughed unless someone injured himself or suffered a disaster.[1]

In spite of their being infamous among some whites, especially the Anglo-Texans, the Comanches were a brave, generous, and hospitable people. In contrast to the Apaches, they were a close-knit tribe.[2] To a certain extent their various divisions and the bands composing them, resembled a single big family. The ethnologist Thomas Gladwin has pointed out that Comanches rarely addressed each other by their proper names. Instead they treated each other as relatives (which they often were), using kinship terms. As Gladwin observes, this must have made it easier for individuals and for groups to change band allegiance, which they were always free to do. Even when speaking to an older stranger, the polite Comanche, desiring to show good will or respect, might address the person as "father" or as "mother's father." But the Comanche male's closest relationships were with his brothers (rather than with his wife), or with an exceptionally close friend whom he would address and in turn be addressed by as "brother." Comanche women may have recognized among themselves a similar, though weaker, kind of institutionalized friendship.[3]

Brave, generous, and hospitable, with numerous warm relationships within the tribe, the Comanches were a generally cheerful people. In 1828, for instance the French botanist Jean Louis Berlandier, accompanied a band of some seventy Comanches on a hunting trip for bear and buffalo. Beginning with the first night, he noted a marked contrast between the manner of the Comanches in camp and their behavior as he had earlier observed it in San Antonio. In town he had found them distrustful, taciturn, and mysterious. But when camped with his fellow hunters and their escort of thirty Mexican dragoons, they revealed, he wrote later, a frank and light-hearted side of their natures that seemed to conform more closely to their true temperaments.[4]

Years later Robert S. Neighbors, Indian agent under the Republic of Texas, corroborated Berlandier's observation, finding the Comanches to possess "a gay cast of mind," along with a passionate spirit. Neighbors also remarked upon the tribe's unusual generosity, writing in 1853: "From the liberality with which they dispose of their effects" on ceremonial occasions, "it would induce the belief that they acquire property merely for the purpose of giving it to others."[5]

As a people the Comanches were also hospitable, a trait shared in varying degrees by all the Plains tribes. Berlandier, for example, wrote of an incident that occurred somewhere on the southern plains prior to 1828. Two Osage warriors, lost, hungry, exhausted, stumbled into a Comanche encampment and appealed for help. Although the Osages were among the Comanches' mortal enemies, and the two tribes were then at war, the Buffalo Indians warmly welcomed the helpless strangers and provided them with food and shelter. The two recovered quickly. Soon one of them began bragging to his host of his exploits, telling of how he had killed a Comanche in battle at a certain well-known spot. The host, recognizing the place and battle, realized his guest had slain one of his relatives, a death he was obligated to avenge. Bound by the rules of hospitality within the ranchería, he invited his guest to hunt with him. Once at a distance from camp, he revealed his relationship to his guest's victim and challenged the enemy warrior. In the following struggle he killed the Osage.[6]

On another occasion a band of Comanches welcomed and fed a fearsome supernatural being—or at least a personage they took to be supernatural. According to the Abbé Domenech, a French Apostolical missionary who visited Texas in 1846 and for several years afterward, an old German priest once decided to walk, alone, from New Braunfels to Fredericksburg. Although nearly blind, the old man was an ardent naturalist, and he hoped to gather scientific curiosities en route. With this purpose in mind, he set out one morning outfitted only with a double pair of glasses on his nose, a tin box hanging from his shoulders, and a few comestibles for the trip. From the first day out, he began filling his box with rare plants and jamming his pockets with mineral specimens. On his hat he pinned a variety of insects, undoubtedly including butterflies, until it was virtually covered with bugs. Having killed several large snakes, he knotted them and let them hang from over his shoulders. On the second day he killed another rattler, this one seven or eight feet long, which he wrapped around his waist, using it as a belt.

By the morning of the third day, the old priest had consumed his supply of food and was beginning to be acutely hungry. As he advanced, continually searching for specimens, he happened to glance up and notice smoke rising from a clearing ahead. Its source, he discovered, was an Indian camp, and he trudged in confidently. But the Comanches—men, women, and children—screamed and ran. The old man, gesturing frantically at the retreating people, succeeded in making them pause long enough to understand that he was extremely hungry. For some moments there must have been, among them, a conflict between the instinct for flight and their code of hospitality. The tradition of hospitality won. With trembling hands, as Domenech described it, the women brought coffee, corn, and mule meat, which the devoted naturalist ate voraciously. Later, leaving as he had come, the nearly blind priest meandered off across the empty country, to arrive safely at Fredricksburg the same day.[7]

It is impossible to know whether the Comanches really considered the German priest to be a supernatural creature. Certainly they lived in a world where they were constantly in contact with the supernatural. Each wild animal had a spirit with supernatural power, while those of the eagle, the elk, the buffalo, the deer, the coyote, and the wolf were especially strong. This power, as will be seen, could be shared with an individual. Mesas and bluffs and hills, rivers and springs, the vast plains themselves could be the homes of spirits, each with its power. It is not surprising, then, that the Comanche band took their bizarre visitor for either a supernatural creature or a mortal possessing great power—potent "medicine." In offering him food they were not only following their code of hospitality but placating a potentially dangerous being.

Living as they did in a world where the supernatural was everywhere, and where visions and dreams had the solid reality of rocks and trees and grass, the Comanches neglected some worldly matters that caused them to be criticized by the descendants of Europeans. One of these was physical cleanliness, which for them had nothing to do with godliness. (Supernatural contamination and hygiene were, of course, entirely different matters). Hubert Howe Bancroft, who classified the Comanches as a division of the Apaches, wrote of these peoples that "in common with all primitive humanity they are filthy." In a footnote he quoted an 1867 U.S. government report stating that "they defecate promiscuously near their huts; they leave offal of every character, dead animals and dead skins, close in the vicinity of their huts." Other Americans, or Anglo-Texans, who, as captives or traders or soldiers, came into contact with the Comanches, confirmed Bancroft's judgement that these Plains Indians, among others, were "filthy beyond all power of descriptions," as Captain Robert G. Carter, U.S. Cavalry, wrote concerning his own observation in the 1870s.[8]

About a decade earlier, when the cattle baron Charles Goodnight was a young man scouting for Ranger Captain Sul Ross, he identified a captured "squaw," survivor of the Pease River massacre of a Comanche supply camp, as a white woman. His captive turned out to be the long-sought Cynthia Ann Parker. Afterward Goodnight recalled that it was "a little difficult to distinguish Cynthia Ann's blond German features, as her face and hands were extremely dirty from handling so much meat." The Comanches, he added, "adhered very little to cleanliness."[9]

Yet for a people constantly interacting with the spirit world, certain practices were simply not important. The habit of physical cleanliness was one of these. The Comanche people, while as human as any of us, lived as an integral part of nature, and nature was not—in any soap-and-water sense—"clean." Tribal members might, for instance, swim in both summer and winter, even breaking ice to do so. To Captain Carter's dismay, though, they only seem to have swum for enjoyment (except in rare instances of ritual purification.) What was important to them were the ceremonies—such as puffing pipe-smoke to the six directions—that placed an individual, or the band, or its representatives, in harmony with the spiritual forces of the earth and sky; also crucial were the observance of taboos and the more mundane avoidance of grease and menstrual blood which, they believed could negate any warrior's "medicine."

As will be seen, the Comanches were a religious people. They believed in an afterlife. They believed in a Great Spirit, whom they identified with the sun. Or rather they thought the Great Spirit lived behind the sun. They believed in an Earth Mother. Still these were abstract entities. Each male Comanche's principal concern, insofar as "religion" went, was with the source of his own supernatural power, or "medicine," the earthly phenomenon or animal spirit that had once revealed itself to him in a vision or a dream. Few of his beliefs, from a European or Anglo-American perspective, had much to do with what are normally considered to be ethics or morality within those cultures.

"No individual action is considered as a crime," wrote Robert S. Neighbors. But Neighbors unknowingly exaggerated. Many of the chiefs, in particular, displayed over and again the virtue that James Mooney, the noted anthropologist, attributed to the entire people, when in 1907 he wrote that the Comanches, besides bearing "a reputation for dash and courage," possessed "a high sense of honor." The Spaniards learned early that many, if not all, chiefs conscientiously tried to enforce among their young men compliance with treaties. Furthermore, a number of chiefs, over the years, scrupulously returned horses stolen by their warriors in violation of treaties to Spaniards, Mexicans, Anglo-Texans, and Americans.

The chiefs' task of restraining their followers could be delicate because, as the ethnologist Ralph Linton has observed, the tribe "attached tremendous importance to individual freedom of action." The Comanches "love their liberty so much," wrote Juan Antonio Padilla, a Spanish official, in 1820, "that they will not bear servitude; and to have peace with them it is necessary to subdue them by arms. It is certain that they are not reducible to the Catholic religion." Yet even by Euro-American standards, many Comanche leaders possessed a distinct ethical awareness, as well as the moral courage to exercise their significant but limited authority.

A Comanche warrior absorbed from childhood the tribal ethic, an informal system of obligations and constraints that influenced his conduct whether he knew it or not. He did know, for example, like all the People, that it was "wrong" to swear an oath falsely, especially if he called upon the sun as his witness. Further, he believed he would die as a result. If he were married, he knew that it was his duty, should the ranchería be attacked, to help his mother-in-law escape. This was not only "right," but should he fail to do so, she could reclaim her daughter from him. This same man, if he possessed exceptional supernatural power and were a medicine man, also knew that it was "right" for him to employ that power to help himself and others in the hunt or in war, but that it would be "wrong" to use it in putting a curse upon another Comanche—and in fact might lead to his death at the hands of his fellows.

So ethics and mores blended imperceptibly into "law." Each male Comanche, who, according to E. Adamson Hoebel, spent much of his energy toward "individual aggrandizement in war . . . and the maintenance of prestige within the tribe," realized that other Comanche men would not abide insults from him and that loss of control toward another could lead to his death. The same could happen if, in anger, he should kill another man's favorite horse. His own death, however, would activate the law of retributive justice, and his relatives and friends would avenge his murder. The matter would end with the slaying of the other man. Yet everyone knew the limits of tolerable conduct, and such instances were rare within such a unified tribe, whose constant warfare created a high degree of male bonding.

Even so, from the perspective of the descendents of Europeans, there is a distinct difference between the historic Comanches' viewpoint concerning the settlement of disputes and the one that Europeans have traditionally taken for granted. The "outstanding factor around which the settlement of a dispute turned was not the question of the right or wrong of the situation," notes Hoebel, "but rather the relative bravery in warfare of the two parties involved. . . . It is very clear . . . that the Comanches tended to attribute moral rightness to the braver man."[10] This judgment may strike those from other cultures as odd, in fact the Comanches' entire way of life appeared to be immoral or amoral to most eighteenth- and nineteenth-century European and Anglo-American observers.

In blunt terms, the People lived, apart from their dependence upon the bison and upon trade, by theft, kidnapping, and murder. One observer, Captain Randolph B. Marcy, wrote that the Comanches looked upon "stealing from strangers as perfectly legitimate and honorable . . ." (Yet they virtually never stole from each other.) With respect to captives, José Francisco Ruíz, Mexican Indian agent and officer, reported of the Comanches in 1828 that they held an estimated nine hundred prisoners, adding that "the lot of the women is most pitiful." As for murder, twenty-one years later an acculturated Choctaw, Peter P. Pitchlynn, arguing against a proposed bill to formally establish an Indian Territory, declaimed as follows: "the first bill introduced [in the territorial legislature] would probably be to suppress and punish piracy—that is, in plain English, to prevent murder and robbery; [but] as soon as this was interpreted to the delegates from the wandering tribes, they would consider it in the same light as your honors would a proposition to punish honesty and truth . . ."[11] Beyond all of this, and most repugnant from the Eurocentric viewpoint, especially to the Anglo-Texans, Comanche warriors regularly raped captive women, whether Indian, Mexican, or white.[12]

During their brief span of history, the Comanches earned a bad reputation among *mexicanos*, Anglo-Texans, and Americans. But they did not consider themselves a bad people. They were true to their concept of the supernatural. They were true to their customs and even to their own notion of honor. In essence they were a tribe of proud predators. From their own cultural perspective, they saw nothing wrong in that. The Comanche warrior, mounted on his pony, swooping upon his prey, could be said to resemble an eagle, the animal the People believed to possess the most powerful medicine—and the one later chosen to symbolize the United States.

The Comanche warriors quickly accepted Herman Lehmann because of his daring act. They belonged to a people who, above all, admired courage.

As the anthropologist Ralph Linton noted, "war was the main activity of Comanche men, also *the mainspring of the culture.*"[13] Most Comanche values derived from personal bravery. Such a value system, which was not so different from that of the Apaches, nor from that of the Cheyennes or Kiowas, served as the basis for a warrior ethos. (Today it would be called, if found in a modern culture, the extreme of *machismo*).[14] Masculine strength and courage embodied in a skilled, lucky, war chief combined to form an ideal inspiring entire peoples. It was the ideal every Comanche boy wished to emulate.[15] Battle provided the ideal death, like that of the defeated chief who defied Vélez by charging, with only his lance, into a line of Spanish muskets. A Comanche motto proclaimed "The brave die young."

Possibly the single remark most revealing of Comanche attitudes was one made by chiefs to Governor de Anza of New Mexico in late 1786 or early 1787, after their treaty and alliance with the Spaniards. Learning that delegations of Lipan Apaches had been visiting New Mexico to sue for peace, they begged de Anza not to grant a treaty to this mutual foe; otherwise, they pleaded, *they would have no enemies to fight and, as a result, would become effeminate.*[16]

In such a culture, women understandably ranked lower than men in tribal esteem. Long before, when the Comanches had been Shoshones in the mountains of Wyoming, the women had foraged for roots and nuts, helping to feed the tribe. They had been somewhat respected in their former roles as providers, but were less so on the plains, where buffalo were abundant and men the mounted hunters. Now they performed the tribal drudgery, from breaking and pitching camp to undertaking all but the heaviest skinning and butchering of the bison their men had killed. Now they were merely the property of their fathers, older brothers, or husbands.

Needless to say there was little tolerance for weak or crippled individuals. Jean Louis Berlandier wrote that men wounded in battle in such a way as to be permanently crippled chose suicide "rather than be hateful in the eyes of their women," who apparently mocked them. At first this is hard to credit, but Thomas C. Battey, a Quaker teacher among Kiowas and Comanches in the 1870s, during the early reservation days, observed that neither tribe knew anything about setting bones. He reported seeing, as a result of their ignorance of this art, instances where "the bones of the fore-arm" were "shoved down into the hand to the knuckle joint" and an "ankle" was "turned over so that the foot was bottom upwards . . ." It is understandable that proud warriors might prefer death to living with such deformities.

The horse culture similarly devalued very old men, except for important chiefs and tribal leaders who retained their vitality and acumen. Formerly, as Shoshones, old people had been respected for their accumulated experience, including their knowledge of the region, and their wisdom. But as Comanches, out on the plains, hunting and fighting on horseback and filled with a new sense of power, the tribe exalted youth, with its energy and strength, while regarding the weakness of the old with condescending pity or scorn. As Linton observed, the young warrior was by nature "vigorous, self-reliant, and pushing." He lost prestige by ignoring slights. "The old man, on the other hand, was expected to be wise and gentle, willing to overlook slights and, if need be, to endure abuse."[17] Thomas Battey even knew of rare instances among the Comanches (though not among the Kiowas) when old or infirm people had been abandoned, or "thrown away."

In their attitude toward the old, Comanches resembled their Athapascan enemies rather than the people who were to become their closest allies, the Kiowas. Colonel Cordero noted that the Apaches despised decrepit or old men, including formerly renowned warriors, who came finally to be, each of them, "a plaything of their *ranchería*." The Kiowas, in contrast, venerated their old men. Lieutenant James W. Abert, U.S. Army, observed in his 1845 journal that while meeting with a band of Kiowas under the celebrated Chief Dohasan ("Little Mountain"), he placed a crude map before an informal gathering of elders and other men. But the old ones, who were treated with great courtesy, disagreed as to whether or not a certain Buffalo Creek drained into the Canadian River. The Kiowas drew a new map in which, in deference to the old men's disagreement, the watercourses on the southern plains were depicted running parallel to each other, indefinitely.

In their treatment of old men, as in most other respects, the Kiowas were a more nearly typical Plains tribe than the Comanches.[18] Because the Comanches were less "typical," it is illuminating to compare these two peoples whose destinies were eventually to merge. Staunch allies after 1806, they remained culturally quite different.[19] Certainly the Kiowas embraced the warrior ethos too (they were supposed to have killed more whites per warrior than any other tribe), but their culture was richer than that of the Comanches.

For one thing the Kiowas' religious practices were relatively formal. The Comanches, while also genuinely religious, took a more relaxed view toward existence, and even toward the supernatural, whose principal function was to help individual warriors safely gain glory and horses. (They also seem to have been adverse to elaborate religious display.)[20] The Comanches were relative parvenus, originally Great Basin bands hailing from the West, while the Kiowas were an ancient tribe whose origin remains a mystery. Like the Indians of Taos Pueblo, the Kiowas spoke a Tanoan language. Ethnologists speculate they may have had a southwestern origin, although the earliest available evidence places them, like the Comanches, first in the Rockies, then on the northern plains. In any event their social organization, their myths, rituals, and ceremonies, indicate a complex cultural tradition strikingly in contrast to that of the Comanches.

Of the Kiowas' ceremonies, the most important was their annual sun dance. The ceremony was characteristic of the Plains tribes, yet the Comanches appear to have held it only sporadically. The Kiowas possessed, like the northern Plains Indians, a tribal medicine, the sacred Tai-me dolls, as well as medicine bundles known as the Ten Grandmothers.[21] The Comanches had no equivalent. The Kiowas, like the Dakotas, kept a pictographic calendar, while the Comanches kept none. The Kiowas pitched their lodges in a carefully planned "camp circle," while the Comanches usually camped more or less at random, their tepees often spread out along a stream. The Kiowas had warrior societies, like other Plains tribes. In contrast to the Kiowas and other tribes, the Comanches lacked hunt police, but Jean Louis Berlandier described a "no-flight" society of elite older warriors who called themselves "wolves," and modern research has disclosed several other military groups, such as the Crow Tassel Wearers, the Fox Society, and the Little Horse people. Still a contemporary ethnologist concludes that "by diffusionist standards, it would be difficult to imagine a High Plains tribe more 'marginal' than the Comanches."[22]

But if the Comanches fail to fit neatly within the definition of "Plains Indians," the definition, itself, must yield. The Comanches' culture remained relatively simple in contrast to the cultures of some other Plains tribes.[23] Yet these upstarts from the Basin and the backwoods had made themselves powerful and rich by the middle of the eighteenth century. Their peers among Plains tribes—Dakotas, Blackfoot, Crows, Cheyennes, Arapahoes, and so on—respected and sometimes envied them. Most smaller tribes feared them.

The Spaniards adapted "Comanche" from "Komantcia," a Ute word meaning "anyone who wants to fight me all the time." Wallace and Hoebel explain that the Utes originally employed this term to describe Comanches, Arapahoes, Cheyennes, and Kiowas, all of whom they warred against. But sometime (probably long) after 1726 the Utes began applying the word specifically to the Comanches. The Spaniards borrowed the term from the Utes, and the Americans received it from the Spaniards.

Lieutenant Colonel Richard I. Dodge, who spent over thirty years among the horse Indians, referred to the Kiowas and Comanches as "these modern Spartans."[24] Around a hundred years later, a contemporary scholar has echoed the comparison. Writing of "the prevailing theme of Comanche culture, the glorification of war," he declares that "the Spartan quality of Comanche culture cannot be overemphasized."[25] Yet this metaphor is only partially valid. Both Spartans and Comanches developed warrior societies. Spartan elders, for example, examined every male baby to determine whether he appeared physically capable of evolving into a soldier. If not the infant was abandoned in the mountains. Similarly with the People. If a child were born deformed or sickly, the medicine woman or midwife would abandon it on the plains. At the age of seven, a Spartan boy left his mother in order to begin his military training. At twenty the youth became a soldier, a role he was expected to fill until the age of sixty. During these years his life was marked by rigorous discipline, frugality, and austerity.

The Comanche male, too, was expected to become a warrior; there were really no other options for him. But the Nuhmuhnuh indulged their children, almost never disciplining them physically. By around the age of five, the boy was riding his own pony and practicing with his toy bow and arrows. As he grew older, the young Comanche ran free with a gang of boys his own age. Theodore Babb, a Texan captive, told of how, during his first winter with the Nakoni Comanches, the women made him help them with their chores, such as hauling wood and water. The other boys finally told him to assert his male rights. After that all he did was help care for the horses and play with his friends. He and the others would catch ponies from the herd, riding them all. On horseback they would chase and hunt deer, antelope, and buffalo. But starting about the age of fourteen, a Comanche youth would accompany older men on war parties. After a few such experiences, if he acquitted himself well, the youth was considered a warrior.

The Comanche warrior experienced the Spartan's discipline, frugality, and austerity on the warpath. He was obliged to obey unquestioningly the orders of the war chief in command of his party (although he could leave it if he became disaffected). Throughout any war party, he was expected to be able to endure severe hardships, often doing without rest, food, or even water, for extended periods. If trapped by an enemy, a Comanche was expected to fight to the death rather than surrender. If somehow captured, he was expected to endure the most excruciating tortures the enemy could devise, without a whimper, until death released him. This was the ideal. Needless to say, not every warrior could live up to it.

But in camp the Comanche brave was no Spartan. Jean Louis Berlandier, writing from his own cultural perspective of course, called the Comanche male both "sensual" and "indolent." Beyond this the typical man was apt to be competitive, aggressive, personally vain, particularly about his hair, and boastful—though only in the socially approved manner about deeds he had really accomplished and which had been confirmed by witnesses or by an oath. He was often a womanizer, even with other men's wives, was usually a passionate gambler, especially with regard to horse racing, but was almost never a drinker, until the final stage of Comanche history.

In Comanche culture, vengeance was a tribal obligation, second in importance, perhaps, only to the demonstration of courage. Taking revenge for the death, say, of a relative killed by the enemy was a near-sacred personal duty. Any offense committed by another tribe against the People called for a group retaliation and was almost certain to initiate warfare. In the ensuing hostilities, each family who lost a man to the enemy had its personal feud with the foe until one of its war parties took an enemy scalp. In this manner intertribal strife might prolong itself indefinitely, like the endless wars between Comanches and Osages.

Occasionally, though, the ideals of courage and vengeance conflicted with each other; that is, the courage of an enemy warrior might so arouse Comanche admiration as to preclude revenge, even if that enemy should fall into the People's power. This paradox could result in interesting situations. Berlandier, for instance, tells of Keiuna, a Comanche chief he knew, who once captured an especially courageous Lipan Apache. Chief Keiuna, by Berlandier's account, did no harm to his prisoner, "simply" dislocating his shoulders so that he could not escape. When Keiuna learned that other Comanches wished to kill his captive, he hid the man in a forest, fed him until he had recovered, then gave him weapons and allowed him to escape. The scientist reported, besides, that the Comanches would sometimes offer an especially brave prisoner hospitality, and—in order to "perpetuate the race of a warrior"—would offer him their women.

On the other hand, the Comanches were unpredictable, and the desire for revenge might override their admiration for an enemy's courage. Pedro Espinosa, a Mexican captive who had escaped from the Comanches after nineteen years, and who then became a tracker and trailer for the U.S. Army, told Colonel Richard Dodge this story:

A war party from his band attacked a rancho in Mexico, quickly killing all the defenders except for one man, a big, powerful *mexicano* who fought them with an axe. In the struggle he managed to kill one or two of his assailants. A warrior finally subdued him by standing on a wall, tossing a lariat over his head, and jerking him off his feet. The raiders returned with the man to Comanchería, Nuhmuhnuh home country. On the way they treated him well, flattering him about his courage and promising to make a chief of him when they reached their camp. Crossing the Llano Estacado, they stopped by a waterhole for several days, where they put the prisoner to work digging a hole, telling him they needed it for a religious ceremony. When the captive, using a knife and his hands, had completed digging a pit about five feet deep, they bound him with rope, placed him in it, filled the hole with dirt, packing it around his body and exposed head. They then scalped him and cut off his ears, nose, lips, and eyelids. Leaving him bleeding, they rode away, counting on the sun and insects to finish their work for them. Later, back at their encampment, they told the story as an excellent joke, one which gained them a certain celebrity throughout the tribe.[26]

Clinton Lafayette Smith, another Texan captive among the People, told years later of how, in contrast, his foster father, Chief Tosacowadi (Spotted Panther) once chose, like Chief Keiuna, to honor courage rather than to exact vengeance.

✠

Smith was accompanying a scouting party during the 1870s when they discovered a camp of eight buffalo hunters with two Tonkawa guides. The Comanches loathed the white hunters, who were wantonly destroying their source of food merely for the hides. They hated the Tonkawas equally, who besides being cannibals, regularly scouted for the Texas Rangers and the U.S. Army. Surrounding the camp, the Comanches opened fire. The hunters fought with grim composure, killing several braves. But the warriors slew seven of them. The eighth hunter, looking around him, dropped his gun and raised his hands.

The party returned with the hunter and the Tonkawas, who had been seized trying to escape from the camp. At the ranchería, where the scouts' return with prisoners caused an uproar, the white man appeared cool, without fear. When warriors rushed at him with tomahawks and lances, he stood unflinchingly, smiling. By signs the braves showed they intended to shoot him. Loading guns with cartridges from which the lead had been removed, they handed the weapons to Smith, a captive youth named Kahn, and a Mexican boy, instructing them to fire point-blank at the man. When this impromptu firing squad moved up and aimed at the white man, he waited, undaunted. When they pulled the triggers, the guns flashed and boomed, and the powder blackened his face. The buffalo hunter merely wiped the black off, continuing to confront the crowd of Comanches.

Chief Tosacowadi whooped, walked up to the man, patted him on the back, and exclaimed, "Bravo!" [27]

✛✛

For the remainder of the time the hunter was with the band, he was well treated. One night he stole a horse and fled. Tosacowadi made no attempt to pursue him. Later he released the Tonkawas. [28] These were perhaps the sorts of acts the Marqués de Rubí had in mind when writing, in the eighteenth century, that the Comanches and other "Indians of the north" were, "because of generosity and gallantry," the "least unworthy" of the native nations to be the enemies of the Spaniards.

Juan Bautista de Anza
(Courtesy, Palace of the Governors, Museum of New Mexico, neg. no. 50828)

Spanish Presidial Soldier
His leather jacket of seven-ply buckskin is an experimental model rather than the thigh-length *cuera* worn by frontier troops in New Spain. (Courtesy, Archivo General de Indias, Sevilla, Spain)

Lipan Apache Warrior
(Courtesy, Museum of New Mexico, neg. no. 6974)

Comanche Village, Women Dressing Robes and Drying Meat
(George Catlin, Courtesy, Smithsonian Institution, Gift of Mrs. Joseph Harrison, Jr.)

Breaking down the Wild Horse
(George Catlin, Courtesy, Smithsonian Institution, Gift of Mrs. Joseph Harrison, Jr.)

White Wolves Attacking a Buffalo Bull
(George Catlin, Courtesy, Smithsonian Institution, Gift of Mrs. Joseph Harrison, Jr.)

Comanche Feats of Horsemanship
(George Catlin, Courtesy, Smithsonian Institution, Gift of Mrs. Joseph Harrison, Jr.)

Comanches Moving Camp, Dog Fight en Route
(George Catlin, Courtesy, Smithsonian Institution, Gift of Mrs. Joseph Harrison, Jr.)

Little Spaniard, a Warrior
Evidently captured as a boy, Jesús Sánchez was a Mexican, or even New Mexican, who had become a leading warrior among the Comanches. (George Catlin, Courtesy, Smithsonian Institution, Gift of Mrs. Joseph Harrison, Jr.)

Kah-kee-tsee, The Thighs
This Taovayas girl was one of two young women returned by the dragoons to their people. (George Catlin, Courtesy, Smithsonian Institution, Gift of Mrs. Joseph Harrison, Jr.)

FOUR

The Peace Policy of Governor Vélez, 1752–1766

O n August 6, 1752, two Frenchmen, guided by a woman of the Aé tribe (probably Skidi Pawnees) entered the gates of the mission and pueblo of Pecos. A group of Jicarilla and Carlana Apaches, who had found them on the Gallinas River, were conducting them on this, the next-to-last leg of their journey. The woman, Manuela, was a runaway "servant" (meaning, slave), whom the travelers had encountered and persuaded to guide them back to New Mexico from the northern side of the Arkansas River.[1] The party's leader bore a white flag formed from a length of linen on a stick with a cross. Behind the two men and the woman straggled nine pack horses loaded with goods intended for sale in Santa Fe. The mission priest, Fray Juan José Toledo, installed his guests in the cloister and immediately penned a note to Governor Vélez, telling him of the foreigners' arrival, and sent it by a Pecos Indian to the capital.

Although Father Toledo ended his letter with conventional compliments, signing as, "your most grateful chaplain, who kisses the hand of your lordship," this elegant closure probably did not reflect his true attitude toward the governor. A constant characteristic of life in the province of New Mexico, as in Texas and elsewhere, had been since the beginning the incessant quarrels between the clergy and governors, along with members of the governors' secular administrations. The favorite charge of each faction seemed to be that the other abused, exploited, or seduced the Pueblo Indians. In the seventeenth century this bitter hostility had led even to excommunication and murder. While the climate was no longer so extreme, the Franciscans bore a special animosity toward Vélez, in spite of his being energetic, intelligent, and conscientious, and did so with some reason, as will soon be evident.[2]

In any event Father Toledo knew better than to welcome these new Frenchmen with mission bells. In the thirteen years since the Mallet brothers had arrived, there had been several more French interlopers. The priest may not have known that the king had forbidden the return of any of them to Louisiana or Canada, but he did know that the present governor lamented the return of the first party, whose trip had served, he believed, as a reconnaissance of routes to and from the province, and whose trading success was an enticement to others. Only two years previously, one member of that original party, Pierre Mallet, had reappeared with three other Frenchmen, after having been robbed of most of their goods en route by Comanches. Receiving them sternly, Governor Vélez had auctioned their remaining articles and sent the men as prisoners to Mexico City.

This time Vélez's welcome was no less severe. On August 9th he interrogated the traders from New France, using as interpreter Louis Fèbre, a tailor who had deserted, with two others, from Arkansas Post in 1749, had arrived in Taos, and had been permitted to remain in the province. In his three years of residence, Fèbre had learned to understand and speak a little Spanish. Under questioning, both French subjects claimed neither to have heard of the second Mallet expedition nor of the Spanish prohibition of trade to foreign nations with "the kingdom of his Majesty in America." But they were able to provide the governor with current information about the Comanches, who at first had not wished them to proceed to New Mexico. The band had relented after the traders gave them presents, finally even furnishing directions for reaching the province.

Vélez asked one of the two, Jean Chapuis, how he and his partner would have managed to pass regularly through the tribes all the way from the Missouri River to New Mexico, if trade had been permitted. Chapuis said they would have navigated the Platte with large canoes to "the boundaries of the kingdom," where they would have bought caravans of horses from the Pawnees and Comanches and have proceeded to Santa Fe. They had entire faith in the Kansas, Osages, Wichitas, and Pawnees; but because of the Comanches, in whom they lacked confidence, they would have required escorts of fifty or sixty armed men for each caravan. The other Frenchman, Louis Feuilli, told the governor that not only were the Comanches and Wichitas firm friends—so much so that they now campaigned together against the Kansas and Osages—but that the Wichitas had recently brought about a new, friendly relationship between the Comanches and the Pawnees, which would have made the trade route possible.

Governor Vélez was particularly concerned that French authorities had formally licensed the two Canadians to trade with New Mexico. Perhaps, like the *fiscal*, or attorney general, at New Spain's capital, he suspected the two of reconnoitering for France. At any rate after having questioned them he ordered their goods sold at auction and sent them off to Mexico City. The viceroy, in turn, shipped them on *La Nueva España* in 1754 to Spain, probably to be imprisoned as the Council of the Indies recommended, instead of being executed, as Spanish law required. If the young governor thought at all about the traders' harsh fate, it was probably without much pity. He recalled all too well that French traders had been arming the Comanches since at least 1740 and were partly responsible, therefore, for the repeated invasions of the province before his peace with the tribe the previous year.

Besides, Vélez had other matters on his mind. On first assuming office, he had realized that the split between the Comanches and Utes presented an opportunity that he might exploit to New Mexico's advantage. Unfortunately his predecessor, Governor Codallos, sometime before April 1849, had misconstrued the intentions of Utes on their way to make peace with the Spaniards after their breach with the Nuhmuhnuh, and had surprised, captured, and "put to the sword a ranchería of more than one hundred tipis." Responding to that appalling error, the enraged Utes had revenged themselves on the Cañada district (near present Española) with "fuego y sangre" (fire and blood), to use a favorite phrase of the conquistadores. But in 1752 Vélez took advantage of a ruse employed by some battling and outnumbered Navajos, who sent a cross and Franciscan calendar to their Ute adversaries, explaining that the calendar was a letter from the Spanish chief commanding the two tribes to be friends, or he would declare war on both. The Utes, deceived by the ploy, reported to Taos to treat with the Spaniards. Vélez rode there immediately, acknowledged the calendar as his letter, and concluded a peace with these former allies of the Comanches.

The youthful governor also took care to maintain good relations with the remnants of the northeastern Apaches. During the same year, he reported to Viceroy Revilla Gigedo that he continued to have confidence in the Carlanas, Palomas, and Cuartelejos. Throughout the previous winter, three hundred men of these tribes had been living peacefully, along with their families, in the vicinity of Pecos Pueblo. When they ventured eastward onto the plains to hunt buffalo, they left their wives and children safely within the pueblo walls. He explained to the viceroy that he did his best to keep these friendly Apaches settled in that area, in case of a Comanche attack, in order to augment his own forces—including 150 colonists he had recently trained and drilled in cavalry tactics. Also he employed the Apaches as scouts. They knew the plains so well, he added, that they were able confidently to reconnoiter out upon them for some 260 miles. Even the hated Faraon Apaches, farther south, were "peaceful in a rare manner," and presently causing "little injury in the villa and jurisdiction of Albuquerque."

Two years later, at the end of his first term (1749–54), Governor Vélez wrote a detailed *Ynstrucción* for his successor, Francisco Marín del Valle.

This document, written at the order of the viceroy, demonstrates Tomás Vélez Cachupín's mastery of diplomacy. In his long letter of advice, he addressed such matters as his own opinion of the ability of individual officers of the presidio and militia and the settlers as a whole ("perverse, poor, and lazy," yet deserving sympathy because of their extreme poverty and their vulnerability to Indian attack), as well as measures for the defense of the province.[3] Vélez recommended a policy of firmness with the colonists. But he reserved most of his advice for dealing with the Apaches, the Utes, and the Comanches, and for successfully administering the annual Taos trade fairs, when bands of all three tribes might be present at once.

Again as in his report to the viceroy, he stressed the importance of "keeping the Carlanas and the rest of the Plains Indians at peace, always sympathetic," and identified with Spanish interests. It was especially important to prevent them from being influenced by the southern Apaches, such as the Faraones, in case "a change should come over the Comanches."

The new governor must also take care to preserve friendly relations with the Utes, who had the power to devastate the north of the province, and whose trade was particularly important to the northernmost settlers. Vélez urged his successor to be humane, generous, simple, and kind with them, "without revealing fastidiousness or repugnance at their rude clownishness and manners." He cautioned Marín del Valle to protect them from being cheated in trade with the settlers. "To their captain, named Tomás," he wrote, "show all courteousness, great friendship, and love." Further, he warned, when an individual Ute stole horses, the new governor should resist threatening the entire tribe or even complaining harshly to the chiefs. Instead he should do as Vélez had done: notify the chiefs so that they, themselves, might punish the guilty man and return the horses. In his experience they had been "exact in giving satisfaction in such thefts."

In his advice concerning the Comanches, Governor Vélez raised the subject of the Taos trade fairs, which the People loved to attend. First of all the new governor must not permit the settlers or the Pueblo Indians to rob them, as they had done in the past, of hides or horses or any "other priceless possession." To prevent such thefts, the governor must take certain measures. Most important, he, himself, must be present at every fair and immediately available to resolve disputes. He should, of course, be "surrounded with a suitable guard" and have his "person adorned with all splendor possible." The new governor would need to station in the Comanche ranchería soldiers in charge of an officer, with special responsibility for guarding the horse herd. No one should be permitted to enter the camp unless the fair was open and the governor present. "The Comanches have such confidence in this action that, with their horse herd under the vigilance of the soldiers," he wrote, "they feel themselves completely relieved from responsibility, a condition they appreciate in the highest degree."[4]

On arriving at the fair, the governor should receive the chiefs cordially, seating himself and smoking with them, making them feel welcome while appearing to enjoy their company. "You should introduce yourself with skill and with expressive words, maintain in your looks a mien, grave and serene, which they may observe and thus continue the faithful friendship they have at present." Vélez advised his successor to unbend with the chiefs. "Permit their familiarities," he wrote, "and take part in their fun at suitable times. . . . I have done so and have been able to win the love they profess for me."

The greatest challenge to Vélez's diplomatic talent occurred when the three tribes—Apaches, Utes, and Comanches—attended a trade fair simultaneously. When that happened, he warned, the new governor must make every effort to prevent the Apaches and Utes from doing any mischief to their mortal enemies, the Comanches. Vélez related proudly that he had succeeded in maintaining between the two sides "as much harmony as if they [had been] friends." Remaining ever present among them, ready to adjudicate concerning prices, he had overseen their peaceful barter of horses and weapons and had even assisted the Apaches in ransoming family members from the Comanches. "Show yourself indifferent in general," he urged. "But, in particular cases, persuade each one for his best interest."

In spite of the benefits Governor Vélez had provided New Mexico, he was by no means universally admired there. In 1761, for instance, the father provincial, Fray Pedro Serrano, complained bitterly to the viceroy of a custom at the trade fairs during Vélez's first term. Father Varo, the priest at Taos, had reported it to him. He would happily remain silent on the practice, if he did not wish a change so badly, since this infamy was "so obscene and unfit for chaste ears."

The friar, in his gray habit, moved among the jostling summer crowd. Within sight some two hundred tepees were pitched, with a horse herd pastured nearby. Here, at the fair, many other horses, except for prohibited stallions and mares, had been tied by settlers who wished to sell them. The grounds smelled of manure and the greasy smoke of countless cooking fires. Moving between Pueblo Indians, colonists, an occasional soldier, the friar passed by collections of ironware displayed for trade—a multitude of hoes, wedges, axes, picks, trade knives, machetes, and bridles.

At a crowd a little apart from the rest, he elbowed his way forward, but no one turned. Everyone watched, the Indians impassively, the Spaniards as if each had withdrawn into himself, all in a silence contrasting with the hubbub of the rest of the fair. He craned to see. Before the crowd stood a barbarous heathen Indian with an Indian girl, a captive he had apparently just sold to a settler, who stood by, ready to claim his purchase. The girl was naked, a child. Behind the pair the priest saw other barbarian men and other captives, also female and young. When the man turned sideways, the Franciscan saw more clearly than ever his extended penis. Placing his hands on the girl's shoulders, the warrior pushed her down into a bending position, with her legs apart. For a time he struggled to force himself into her. At last entering her, the man gave a series of brutal thrusts, then pulled away. Roughly he drew the girl straight and turned her toward her purchaser. The child stood, hanging her head, so that her face was invisible. The Franciscan saw blood on her leg.

"Now you can take her," the Indian declared in Spanish. "Now she is good."

Pivoting, white-faced, the friar left the crowd of men, already preparing in his mind the report he would write the father provincial.

"It is the truth that when these barbarians bring a certain number of Indian women to sell, among them many young maidens and girls, before delivering them to the Christians who buy them, if they are ten years old or over, they deflower and corrupt them in the sight of innumerable assemblies of barbarians and Catholics . . ." Father Serrano had written.

Possibly the "barbarous heathen Indians" Father Varo referred to were Apaches or Utes, but probably not. Since the two tribes were mostly restricted to the western margin of the plains, and at risk even there, they lacked opportunities to take captives, while the Comanches (whom Father Serrano had mentioned in his previous paragraph) continued to seize many, especially Apaches. Furthermore the boast of that particular "barbarian" was, in all its arrogance, pure Comanche.[5]

Vélez Cachupín seems to have been a devoted Catholic; that, at least, is the image conveyed by his letters and reports to the viceroy. But like most eighteenth-century governors in New Spain, he was a professional soldier and predictably impatient with the clergy. In response to the clergy's complaints, he was said around this time to have threatened "to make the religious leave the kingdom for Mexico thrown across a mule in two pairs of irons."

Governor Marín del Valle probably considered his predecessor's advice impertinent and offensive, even though the viceroy had commanded it. In any event, apparently of a proud and vengeful nature (like the Comanches themselves), he seems to have determined to pursue his own policy toward the Plains Indians. As a result during his term (1754–60), the Nuhmuhnuh began once more attacking New Mexico. The worst of these attacks occurred in 1760, evidently in revenge for those Spanish allies, the Taos Indians, dancing before the People while flourishing fifteen Comanche scalps, perhaps at a trade fair. It was the sort of incident that Vélez would not have permitted to occur. That August a band of Comanches raiding throughout the Taos Valley attacked the Villalpando ranch house, where numerous Spanish families had gathered for defense. Assaulting the building with more than usual ferocity, the warriors battered their way in, massacred the men, with a loss to themselves of forty-nine warriors, and abducted fifty-six women and children. With the help of Apache auxiliaries, Governor Marín del Valle pursued them out onto the plains for over two hundred miles before turning back, unsuccessful.

Two interim governors followed Marín del Valle; Mateo Antonio de Mendoza and Manuel de Portillo y Urrisola, whose successive administrations ruled until 1762, the year of Vélez's return to office. The second of these men, Governor Portillo, was a throw-back to the seventeenth century. At Taos in 1761 the band appeared that had been responsible for the previous year's massacre. Meeting with the chiefs, he ordered them immediately to return all of their Spanish prisoners. When they refused, he seized them as hostages, an act of treachery by both European and Indian standards. In response the band's warriors charged—into a trap, a field-piece loaded with grapeshot, and reinforced with soldiers firing shotguns at close range. Portillo boasted, after the slaughter was finished, that he had killed more than four hundred Comanche men and captured some three hundred of their women. It was not surprising that Vélez, on his return, found the entire Comanche tribe about to declare war on New Mexico.

One of the governor's first acts was to dispatch six Comanche women captives as ambassadors of peace to their people. A month later nine warriors and four women appeared at Taos. On learning this, Vélez ordered the delegation escorted to Santa Fe by fourteen Pueblo Indians. When they arrived he received them warmly, especially so as they were "individuals of the highest position and distinction in their tribe," and as he had known them during his previous administration. Significantly the men were armed with French muskets and were bearing full powder flasks (with two pounds of powder each), shot, tomahawks, and lances.

The following day Governor Vélez smoked and conferred with the delegates, two of whom were chiefs. Through an interpreter they told him they had come to confirm that he was truly the same governor they had known in the past. They were happy to find this so. Since his departure eight years before, they had had bad relations and war with his successors. In fact when the women messengers had arrived, the chiefs had been gathered in council discussing how best to prosecute a general war against the province. After recent events they had no longer desired peace or trade with the Spaniards. They were particularly incensed, they complained, at former Governor Portillo, who had denied them permission to trade, anyway, and who had murdered their warriors in Taos and captured their women, when these people had gone there "with their hearts full of kindness to establish peace . . ." As for Portillo himself, they remarked bitterly, he had never wished "to hear them speak directly to him."

Vélez expressed sympathy with the Comanches' resentment, although he did reproach them for their violence against the province during the term of Marín del Valle. Still it was insane, he said, for Spaniards and Comanches to fight each other when they should be good friends, united "under obedience and vassalage to the great and powerful captain of the world, the king and lord of the Spaniards, who so ordered it." The governor suggested that the two sides make another sincere effort at friendship. They should begin, he said, by exchanging prisoners. They should, of course, also engage in trade, as before; and the Comanches should feel free to visit the kingdom confidently whenever they wished. For his part he promised to punish any subject of his who did them any injury during the trade fairs. But he asked that they behave reciprocally, having their chiefs punish warriors who visited New Mexico only to steal horses or to raid the settlements.

The delegates bound themselves to repeat the governor's words faithfully to the chiefs of the tribe, who had sent them for just that purpose. Concerning the prisoners they had held for two years now, they promised to make a special effort to gather them together and return them "within the time of three moons." They did, though, ask to be excused if they could not recover some of them, who might have died or been sold to the Wichitas and French. Still they would endeavor to buy back any such Spaniard they might find.

On June 10, while Vélez was waiting for the designated July moon, four more chiefs, accompanied by seven warriors, five women, and three children, all in three tepees, arrived at Taos. The corporal of the squad manning that post sent the party to Santa Fe, where the governor received them "with pleasure and attention," fed them, and gave them tobacco. On the following day he held council with the four, who informed him they had been empowered by the head chiefs to tell him the earlier emissaries had returned and that they, the leading men, had ordered the various rancherías of the tribe to hold councils in order to expedite the return of their Spanish captives, "large and small." The present delegates had also come for further reassurance that Vélez really was pursuing his former, friendly policy, since Governor Portillo's massacre was still fresh in many Comanche minds.

Understanding their point of view, Vélez invited the four chiefs to put him to the test by asking for a sign that might convince them of his sincerity. His guests were clearly pleased at the offer. The oldest among them, a chief and medicine man ("whom they honor in their false religious and diabolical misconceptions"), told him they would like to see some of the Comanche prisoners. Not only that—each one of the four would like to take back with him a relative, or even his own woman, providing she were with the group. If the governor were willing to do this, said the medicine man, the act would reassure even the most resentful and suspicious of their people.

Governor Vélez sent at once for all of the captives dispersed among the settlers in the capital. His subordinates gathered and brought them to the palace. Vélez soon placed before the chiefs thirty-one women and children, among whom, luckily, there was a relative of each. Every man chose the prisoner most closely related to him. Thanking him repeatedly, each of the chiefs embraced Vélez around the neck, telling him they now knew he had no sinister intentions and that he retained the attitude he had shown during his previous administration. The governor, taking leave of his guests, sent them back to Taos with tobacco for themselves and for the head chiefs and other important men of the tribe. To guard against an accidental meeting with Utes, he provided them with an escort of thirty Pueblo Indians.

In spite of this auspicious renewal of friendly relations, Governor Vélez was careful to protect the frontier settlements. From his Santa Fe presidio he sent detachments to guard the most vulnerable of them (presumably including Pecos and Galisteo), as well as dispatching scouts to watch the routes by which Comanche war parties usually entered the province. In concluding his letter to the viceroy, the Marqués de Cruillas, Vélez wrote, "If the Comanches refuse the proposals which I have made for their satisfaction and wish to follow the road of vengeance, I have sufficient justification to make war upon them. However, I shall always . . . do what is best, that is, keep the peace."

For once the Comanches rejected "the road of vengeance." Vélez Cachupín concluded another peace, which seems to have lasted five years, throughout the extent of his second term. Earlier, in his *Ynstrucción*, he had written: "There is not a nation among the numerous ones which live around this government in which a kind word does not have more effect than the execution of the sword." During both terms he verified this statement through his policies. Yet he never sentimentalized the Comanches. His diplomacy was a mixture of military preparedness and firmness, tempered by just dealing and personal presence. Although he used the kind word whenever possible, the sword also had its place. "As the Comanche nation is so astute," he wrote, "and, like all, revengeful and bloodthirsty, it is a prudent measure to deal with them with the left hand and keep the sword unsheathed in the right, ready to ward off any treacherous blow."

The Franciscans had protested Vélez's return to govern the province a second time. In spite of the clergy's opposition, the king had commanded the viceroy to reinstate him promptly, "*con pretexto ni motivo alguno.*"[6] Yet the Franciscans, especially those at exposed posts such as Taos, Picurís, Pecos, and Galisteo, were certainly in a position to appreciate the peace on the eastern frontier, even if it meant only that fewer Pueblo Indians were murdered or abducted. Upon a Spanish map of about 1760, the cartographer wrote across the plains a little northeast of the Pecos River: "All these lands on this side of the mountains and their rivers are dominated by Comanches, who invade said kingdom plundering and murdering. They are extremely skillful in horsemanship and the use of firearms, which they get from the French nation." During both of Vélez's terms, the Comanches, once they were defeated in 1751, refrained from plundering and murdering in New Mexico.[7]

The Nuhmuhnuh now possessed the power to punish the kingdom whenever they cared to. By midcentury the Great Plains to the north and east of New Mexico were occupied by three major bands, or divisions, of Comanches. (Robert H. Lowie, the noted anthropologist, defined a "band" as "a local group of people jointly wandering in search of sustenance"; this book, however, uses "division" to describe combined bands under the leadership of a principal chief. A division could fragment and recombine, according to the availability of game, water, firewood, and grass for the horse herds). The northernmost division during the time of Vélez was the Yupe (or Jupe), "People of the Timber," who roamed from the southern part of Wyoming south to the Arkansas River. The Yamparica ("Eaters of the Yap Root"), shared part of their range, hunting and roving from today's northern Colorado to the Arkansas.[8] The third division was the Cuchantica, or Cuchanec ("Buffalo Eaters"), who followed the herds south from the Arkansas River to the Red, ranging as far eastward as the Wichitan trading villages. Their easternmost bands were known by the Spaniards as the *orientales.* Later, in the nineteenth century, the tribe's major divisions were to multiply, changing some names and territories. But the new era, that of the People's greatest power, still lay before them.

If American colonists and European nations failed, understandably, to notice the Comanches' conquest of the southern plains, they were entirely attentive to another event occurring during Vélez's second term. This was the signing of the Treaty of Paris, which, in 1763, concluded the Seven Years War (known in North America as the last of the French and Indian Wars). Great Britain, France, and Spain were the signatories. But the part that affected Spain, New Mexico, Texas, and the Comanches was France's cession in 1762 of Louisiana west of the Mississippi to its ally, Spain, in order to compensate for Spain's loss of Florida. The territorial transfer ended fear by Spanish authorities that the French were encroaching westward. Yet a greatly enlarged frontier in Louisiana and Texas created new problems for them, with concern about English colonists and traders on the east bank of the Mississippi, as well as about the additional host of Indian tribes now settled or roving within their borders. The matter of highest priority became the reorganization of military defense along the entire northern boundary of New Spain, especially in such a way as to minimize the increased strain upon the royal treasury. For this purpose Spanish officials began employing established French traders to persuade France's former Plains Indian allies to switch their allegiance to Spain. From Spain itself, the Bourbon king, Carlos III, dispatched a personal emissary to review for him the situation along a frontier stretching from present Arizona to Louisiana at the Mississippi.

So it happened that the principal event during Vélez's second term was the 1766 visit to New Mexico of the Marqués de Rubí. Rubí's stop there was part of his seventy-five-hundred-mile trip to inspect even the most remote outposts of northern New Spain. The governor no doubt received the king's representative with as much ceremony as was possible in Santa Fe. The two men must have conferred in the adobe Palace of the Governors. The marqués had decided to recommend moving the El Paso garrison to some more northern point on the road to Santa Fe, in order to protect caravans from the kind of Apache harassment his own party had experienced. Did the governor know of an appropriate location along the way? Vélez respectfully suggested that Robledo, a Río Grande settlement near the present Radium Springs, would be a suitable spot. Rubí included this proposal among his own to the king. But the inspection's most significant moment occurred when Rubí realized the implications of Vélez's peace with the Comanches, and when he had satisfied himself that the Plains tribe was actually honoring the treaty. The marqués was favorably impressed by the People. This fact was to have important consequences for the settlers of New Mexico and for the Comanches.

FIVE

Governor Mendinueta and War, 1767–1778

Colonel don Pedro Fermín de Mendinueta replaced Vélez as governor in 1767. Conceivably he was the equal of the "Captain Who Amazes" as a soldier; he was certainly his inferior as a diplomat. During his tenure he did manage once, in February 1771, to effect a treaty with the Comanches, which the People broke, at the latest, in July of the following year, when they also elected to attend the Taos trade fair. But Mendinueta's policy was primarily one of war. Throughout his consecutive administrations, a total of eleven years, he mostly struck an inflexible stance toward the Nuhmuhnuh. In the end his uncompromising war policy nearly destroyed the province.

During his first year he wrote the viceroy that he still hoped to achieve a peace with the Comanches. But he distrusted them. As a precaution against attack, he ordered a detachment of fifty men, (presidial soldiers, militia, and Indians) to establish an outpost on San Antonio Mountain, west of the Río Grande and a little south of the present Colorado line. They were to protect Ojo Caliente, a Spanish settlement at a hot springs some twenty-five miles west and south of Taos. He also ordered scouts to be stationed east of the mountain, in a position enabling them continually to observe the river.

What happened next was typical of events during Mendinueta's years in office. On June 1, six Comanche chiefs rode into Taos with a white flag. They told the *alcalde mayor* (mayor) they were coming to ask for peace and that their people would arrive the following day. They were in a hurry, they added, and could remain only long enough to trade the few things they had brought. A messenger rode hard to bring the governor the news. Mendinueta gathered his troops and horses and struck out at once for Taos, traveling some twenty-seven miles that day. At midnight another messenger told him the Comanches had declared war. He ordered the horses resaddled and resumed the march in the dark. At four in the morning he received word that the Comanches had fled after killing five colonists and a Taos Indian. Against the alcalde's orders these men had visited the Comanche camp in order to trade. They had died for their disobedience, but had killed four Comanches in the struggle.

Reaching Taos Mendinueta learned just how cunning the raiders could be.[1] The chiefs had reasoned that settlers, hearing of peace and trade, would descend on Taos, leaving Ojo Caliente undefended. Accordingly they had sent a hundred warriors to attack that settlement, while the main party proceeded to Taos to engage in a hurried trade. But the governor's scouts had been alert. The troops, militia, and friendly Indians posted at Cerro de San Antonio had intercepted the hundred Plains Indians. Taken by surprise the Comanche war party had fled, eluding their pursuers, although several had drowned in recrossing the Río Grande. The others rejoined the main encampment at Taos. The chiefs vented their anger on the five Spanish settlers and the Taos Indian, then departed with "such speed that they left dead horses along the trail, together with supplies, saddles, buffalo skins, and bits of clothing."

The episode was characteristic of Comanche forays into New Mexico during the second half of the eighteenth century. The Nuhmuhnuh were continually probing, sometimes with large war parties, scheming, looking for weak spots, trying to catch their intended victims off guard. When possible they avoided confrontation with an armed and prepared enemy. Strangely it was also common for only a few settlers and Christian Indians to be killed, and for the raiders to lose an equal or greater number of warriors. Formidable as they were, the Comanches were not invincible. The worst part of their intermittent raids must have been the atmosphere of anxiety they created among both Spaniards and Pueblos.

During Mendinueta's two administrations, there were relatively quiet years and active years. The next year, 1768, was a "quiet" one. That summer the governor set out from Santa Fe with 546 presidial soldiers, militia troops, and Indian allies (Pueblos, Utes, and Jicarilla Apaches) "in search of the Comanche enemy to punish their unfaithfulness and hostilities." Eventually his scouts sighted two Comanches with seven horses at a distance. They were beside a creek flowing into the Arkansas River. The colonel ordered a detail of soldiers to construct a barge. On this, a few at a time, the army crossed the river. Although the governor had directed that the two braves be captured, alive or dead, his Ute and Jicarilla allies proved to be too eager. Rushing ahead, they revealed themselves to the two Comanches, who fled and gave the alarm. Their band scattered. Like Valverde before him, Mendinueta was obliged to give up his punitive expedition.

In September a war party of twenty-four Comanches killed an unarmed settler at Ojo Caliente. Next they rode by the settlement, firing at it but hitting no one. The garrison, along with sixteen colonists and some Ute

Indians, gave pursuit and caught up with the group. The Comanches entrenched themselves, a defense that had worked badly for them in the past. In this instance the expedient worked no better; the Spaniards and Utes killed twenty-one Comanches and captured two others, while one managed to escape. Two days later one of the prisoners died, after, curiously enough, "entreating for holy baptism, which was given him."

Even the loss of nearly an entire war party was no deterrent to the plains raiders. At the end of the following month, five hundred Comanches surrounded the plaza at Ojo Caliente before dawn. For a time they tried to enter, but all the gates were locked. They then rode to a knoll within musket range and began firing at the settlement. The Spanish soldiers and settlers returned the fire. Soon part of the enemy force advanced, led by a chief wearing "as a device a green horn on his forehead." The defenders were not impressed. The Spaniards leveled some accurate fire at the oncoming warriors, hitting several. As other braves tried to recover the bodies of the fallen, the marksmen within the settlement shot down four of their horses.

Evidently to the Comanches this was an ominous development. Three hundred of them departed southward and burned two empty houses. A dozen Comanches later encountered another house, whose occupants were armed and on guard. They contented themselves with killing a feeble-minded deaf man who came to greet them, taking them for Utes. Soon, reassembling, the raiders began their withdrawal. They burned fields as they went, but once again they fled so swiftly that "they left in a camp a quantity of bows and arrows, bits of clothing, some dead horses, and five live ones." The Spaniards interpreted this as evidence they had suffered severe casualties.

The foray was unexceptional in all respects but one. This was the presence of the chief wearing a green horn on his forehead. Later the Spanish viceroy, the Marqués de Croix, noted that "a barbarian has raised himself up among that nation," posing as a "little king." The viceroy apparently did not ask himself where the Comanche chieftain got the idea of "a king"—surely the chief was powerfully influenced by those same Spaniards he affected to despise. Cuerno Verde (Green Horn), as he began to be called, constantly surrounded himself with a bodyguard of warriors and had "pages" who served him when he mounted or dismounted from his pony and who held a canopy of buffalo hides over him, in whose shade he seated himself. From Mendinueta's report de Croix inferred that the little king had died in the raid on Ojo Caliente.[2]

So much for a quiet year. More relatively quiet years followed until 1774, an active twelve months. That fall Governor Mendinueta wrote the

viceroy (now Bucareli) that his province had up to then endured five Comanche invasions, which he had twice countered with punitive expeditions.
The first two incursions were typical nuisance raids. The remaining three
were, as the governor remarked, of greater consequence. On July 27 more
than a thousand Comanches rode through the district of Chama, north
and west of Santa Fe, and penetrated to the Río Grande pueblos of Santa
Clara and San Juan. Mendinueta pointed out that in spite of their great
number, the enemy killed only seven New Mexicans, wounding six others
and carrying off three boys. They succeeded, though, in destroying
twenty-five head of settlers' horses. The settlers themselves put up a vigorous resistance. At the settlement of La Cañada, for example, the alcalde,
his lieutenant, and some settlers held out in a fenced field behind a house
against a large enemy force.

The Pueblo Indians also proved once again that they were not, never
had been, the tame folk they are sometimes reputed to be. At Santa Clara
nine men fought so furiously they put to flight fifty Comanches who attacked them outside their pueblo. The men of San Juan also defended their
horse herd from a large force of Comanches. In the struggle the marauders
killed three of the San Juan warriors, but then the Plains Indians "fled
precipitately to recross the river, where they were pursued with lance in
hand." As a result of these skirmishes the raiders lost twenty-three men.
What had they gained? Horses. A sizable herd.

In August of that year the people of Pecos were working in their fields
when some 100 Comanches galloped down upon them. In this attack the
plains warriors shot or lanced or smashed to the ground seven men and
two women, before riding off with another seven struggling captives. The
following day Governor Mendinueta sent 114 men to pursue the war party.
Most of the men were presidials, supported by militiamen and Indian
auxiliaries. Riding hard the troop came upon the Comanche camp four
days later on the plains, about 180 miles from Santa Fe. This band of
Nuhmuhnuh was spread out by a stream. Their tepees stretched along it
for such a distance the Spaniards could not see the end of them.

Swinging into formation, the leather-jackets attacked, riding among the
lodges, killing Comanches before them and on either side as they advanced. Ironically the first they encountered were the raiders themselves,
dressed in their best regalia to celebrate their success, probably with a scalp
dance. The Spaniards succeeded in wresting from them their single surviving Pecos captive, a woman. Killing on both sides, the Spaniards and their
Indian auxiliaries continued to advance beside the stream ever deeper into
the camp.

As the Comanches realized how few the attackers were, they began to organize a defense, falling upon the Spaniards with constantly increasing strength. Soon the outnumbered soldados de cuera had to abandon their horse herd and form a square, so as to be able to fire on all four fronts. In this formation they kept up a constant fire until four o'clock in the afternoon. Again they attacked, driving the Comanches from the stream, where they remained until "the evening prayer, when they retired in such good order that the enemy did not dare to molest them."

The Spaniards rode back with twenty-two wounded and one soldier killed, whose body they brought with them. Among themselves they agreed that in the first assault alone they had slain some forty of the enemy, including seven whom they took to be chiefs. They could not estimate the number of others killed during the remainder of the day. But they reasoned that there had been many, judging from the wails and lamentations of the Comanches, who, within sight of them, had been throwing away the belongings of the dead.

The Plains Indians had also abandoned the Spaniards' horse herd shortly after adding it to their own, since most of the horses were exhausted and wounded. One soldier, formerly a captive among the Plains tribe, smiled in explaining how he had shouted to the enemy the news that the troop consisted of scouts for a larger force soon to arrive. Later they learned that the band had believed him and had fled that night, abandoning their lodges along with many horses and dead bodies.

The morale of the entire colony was lifted by the news of this victory on the plains. To Governor Mendinueta the mood of the kingdom seemed right for a punitive expedition against the enemy, in order to pursue the advantage already gained. That September, about six months later, he sent out an army of six hundred men, consisting of soldiers, militia, and Indians, under the command of an old frontiersman, don Carlos Fernández, who "in spite of his advanced years," was "well known for his valor and capacity."

By taking an unpredictable route and by marching at night, Fernández managed on the fifth day to surprise a Comanche band in its camp. Eighteen warriors, by leaping on their ponies and riding for their lives, were able to escape the attack. The others, men and their families, tried to take refuge behind a barrier of trees in a wood protected on one side by a small, deep pond. For two hours the Spanish army fired into the wooded enclosure. "As shot and shell has no respect for sex or age," wrote Mendinueta later, "when the battle was over only one hundred fifteen individuals, women and children, were alive," most of them wounded. The governor estimated from the number of tepees that more than four hundred of the enemy had been killed or captured. The Spanish force, in contrast, lost only one Indian auxiliary, with twenty-eight other men wounded. The surviving women and children were placed under the charge of the Franciscans for religious training.

It is instructive to compare the results of Mendinueta's victory with that of Vélez. The Spaniards since 1598 had followed a policy of punitive expeditions as a response to raids by hostile Indians. While these expeditions sometimes obtained revenge, without diplomacy in addition, they never achieved their objective; that is, if their objective was to stop the raiding. In keeping with his intransigent attitude, Mendinueta offered the Comanches nothing, not even the possibility of surrender, until all the men had been killed. Fernández carried out a massacre for the governor. But to what effect? The guerrilla war went on.

The following year, in May of 1775, the Comanches opened hostilities by again attacking the Pecos Indians in their fields. Three people were killed on either side. A week later the same war party murdered a youth in the evening, while he was herding oxen "near one of the first houses" of Santa Fe. The situation was becoming grave when Spaniards were not safe at the edge of their capital city.

Even the viceroy, after reading Mendinueta's reports, began to recognize the seriousness of the province's plight. In February 1775, he wrote the governor that, "if your lordship considers it suitable to arm the settlers," he would arrange to sell them arms from the royal warehouse at cost. The colonel's reply, at once tactfully reminding his superior of the true state of affairs and appealing for aid, gives a picture of the damage done to the province by raids from the Navajos to the west, Apaches to the south, and Comanches to the north and east.

Most Excellent Sir: I am giving your Excellency the most fervent thanks for the expressions which you deigned to extend to me in your esteemed letter of February 8 last. I assure your excellency that, as a result of the satisfaction, I shall attempt as always to fulfill most exactly the functions of my duties.

Your Excellency is aware of the conditions of this province. You look upon it with pity, and it is worthy of that as its valorous settlers are extremely poor, without horses, and are raided by the Comanches, Navajos, and Gilas [i.e., Gila Apaches]. Although your Excellency, overflowing with kindness, may wish to provide them with arms at cost, it is impossible for them ever to be able to pay, both because of the miserable condition of their existence and the fact that money does not circulate in this province.

Because of the new [regulation?] introduced for the company, the individuals of it will dispose of their old arms in favor of the settlers by bartering them for produce of the land. In this respect we are not badly off, as I count some six hundred guns and one hundred and fifty pairs of pistols in fair condition in all the realm. It is not the same in regard to the horse herd, as the rearing of the animals has been destroyed by the enemy. We do not have the tame horses with which to defend ourselves from the three enemies who surround us. Thus, Most Excellent Sir, if the kindness of your Excellency and your strong desire to develop this province do not provide this unfortunate and valiant community with a horse herd on the account of the king, perhaps to the number of fifteen hundred horses, I fear its desolation will follow . . .[3]

On October 18, 1775, Viceroy Bucareli sent Governor Mendinueta's letter to the *fiscal*, or attorney general. Three days later the fiscal replied, supporting the governor's plea for fifteen hundred horses, to be supplied at the king's expense. But he recommended that the proposal next be cleared by the Royal Tribunal of Accounts. On October 24, the Royal Tribunal of Accounts agreed with the fiscal and urged "the most prompt and efficient measures . . ." Two days later the governor's request was considered by the Council of the Royal Treasury, which also approved of the purchase. The official decree was then sent to don Hugo O'Conor, the inspector of the interior provinces, "so that he may provide for their purchase in a suitable manner and . . . dispatch them with all possible haste to the above-mentioned governor for the rehabilitation of the province."

All of this took place in the fall of 1775. The fifteen hundred horses, upon which the defense of the province depended, actually arrived nearly three years later, in the spring or summer of 1778. That same summer, after Colonel Mendinueta's departure in March, the Comanches again invaded New Mexico and, in a single raid, killed or captured 127 settlers.[4] Even if the "tame horses" had arrived prior to this calamity, the beleaguered *pobladores* must have felt, in its wake, demoralized, abandoned, and perhaps doomed. In their isolation, who might they call upon to save them from death or capture and the horror of possible death by torture, in the face of such determined enemies and such odds?

By 1776 the situation along the entire northern frontier of New Spain had become so critical that the Council of the Indies created the Commandancy General of the Interior Provinces of New Spain. By this act the northern provinces were split off and removed from the control of the viceroy. Charles III appointed as commander general Teodoro de Croix, who had most recently served as *castellan* (governor) of the port of Acapulco. De Croix, though born in Lille, France, had joined the Spanish army at the age of seventeen. Rising gradually as an officer, he had served under his uncle, the Marqués de Croix, during the latter's term as viceroy of New Spain, 1766–71.[5]

Although the new commander general returned to Mexico at the end of 1776, he required some months to familiarize himself with conditions in the northern provinces. When de Croix grasped the true situation prevailing in the vast territory under his command, he could scarcely conceal his dismay from José de Gálvez, minister of the Indies. In a letter written in April of 1777, he expressed not only his concern for the province of New Mexico but his awareness of its strategic value, writing that "if we lost the important barrier of New Mexico, which I pray God may not happen, the Indians would be masters of that immense country, and accustomed to living by robbery would indubitably approach us. If today an army is needed only to make war on the numerous and vagrant Apache, what force would be necessary to curb the other nations?"

By the following year, de Croix was beginning to come to terms with the dreadful condition of his provinces. He marked the year with three councils of war, the first in Coahuila, the second at the capital of Texas, San Antonio de Béxar, and the third in Chihuahua. For the country lying on either side of the Pecos River, the third and final council was to prove the most significant. Present besides Don Teodoro de Croix, were Mendinueta, who had been promoted to brigadier; Colonel don Jacobo Ugarte y Loyola, new governor of Sonora and later (1786–91) to be himself *commandante general*; and Lieutenant Colonel don Juan Bautista de Anza, the new governor of Nuevo México. After the preliminaries the secretary briefed the council by reading reports of absent officials, including those of Lieutenant Colonel Atanasio de Mézières, lieutenant governor of the fort and district of Natchitoches, and of the Baron de Ripperdá, governor of Texas. The members then addressed sixteen points already discussed by the two previous councils, all of them concerned in one way or another with the defense of the northern frontier.

Much attention was given to warfare with the Apaches, the major problem of the northern provinces except for New Mexico and Texas, where it was only one of many. The sixth point, for example, asked about the advantages or disadvantages of the temporary peace then existing with the principal Texas band, the Lipan Apaches. In response the Chihuahua Council concurred with the two before it, agreeing that "in none of the provinces should peace be extended to the Apaches because their friendship will always produce very funereal effects." In contrast the council answered the tenth point in favor of peace with the Comanches and other "nations of the north." ("Nations of the north" referred to the Wichitan tribes—Taovayases, Iscanis, Wichitas proper, Tawakonies, and, later, Kichais. The phrase also included other peoples of slightly lesser importance to the Spaniards: the Tejas, or Hasinais; the Panismahas, or Skidi Pawnees; the Tonkawas; and others).

In 1768, two years after his visit to New Mexico, the Marqués de Rubí had recommended to the king a "war of extermination" against the Apaches, who kept only a "perfidious peace." By contrast the Comanches, as he himself had noted, were capable of honoring the terms of treaties. Their friendship should be cultivated. As Spanish allies they might be employed in joint campaigns against the Apaches, whose enemies they already were. The marqués made his recommendations to the king in the form of *dictámenes*, or opinions. These in turn were incorporated into a royal edict, the new "Regulation of the Presidios," promulgated in 1772.

Now, six years later and a decade after Rubí's New Mexico visit, the council noted that the "Regulations" actually forbade all but the most enforceable treaties with the Apaches. On the other hand, the council reasoned that the Plains Indians lived in open country rich in wild game and with access to great herds of buffalo; certainly they would prefer to remain where they were. Only if the Comanches should become hard pressed by their enemies, the Osages for example, would they be likely to encroach upon Spanish frontiers. If a treaty were made with the nations of the north, or *norteños*, those frontiers would be secure for a long time to come.

For these reasons the council of Chihuahua confirmed what was probably the most important decision of the previous two meetings: "the alliance with the Indians of the north was agreed upon," an alliance to be directed against the Apaches. Ultimately the council's decision rested upon Vélez's peace. Thanks indirectly to "The Boy Captain," Lieutenant Colonel Juan Bautista de Anza had set an alliance with the Comanches as a principal objective for himself when he started out that summer or early fall for Santa Fe.

SIX

The Meaning of Captivity

The anthropologist E. Adamson Hoebel, who in conjunction with the historian Ernest Wallace has written the most complete ethnographic account of the Comanches, makes an important point in discussing the Nuhmuhnuh's treatment of captives. In that account he points out that the People did not invariably, or even customarily, torture their prisoners. But if they were angry, they could be extremely cruel in gaining revenge. "For the most part," he writes, "the treatment an individual captive received depended on the personal character of his captor." Hoebel cites a Comanche informant, Nayia, who remembered a man known to castrate the boys he captured, and who had once crucified a prisoner. In contrast he mentions a medicine man who freed the first Mexican boy he seized to herd his horses, because he could not be bothered with teaching him Comanche. After that he released or gave away the subsequent prisoners he took.

The war party that captured Theodore Babb in 1865 was of the first variety. After a raid in which one of the warriors murdered the boy's mother, the party fled the Texas frontier, riding day and night until reaching the Red River. Two days later they camped on the banks of the Canadian. That night Mrs. Luster, a young widow captured with Babb, escaped with his help on one of their captors' best horses. (The boy, nearly discovered, had to return to his sleeping place). The young woman gained an hour on her pursuers, whose search for her proved fruitless. Holding Babb responsible for the escape, the warriors stood the thirteen-year-old against a cottonwood, informing him by signs they were going to kill him with arrows and bullets, scalp him, and hold a scalp dance. The boy's nine-year-old sister began wailing and sobbing as she watched the line of braves with guns and bows aimed at her brother. Babb tried to comfort her, but the child threw herself on the ground and hid her face. Unable to bear the suspense, Babb signaled for the men to shoot.

A few warriors impulsively came forward, placing themselves before the line of executioners. But the others pushed them aside. Tying the boy to a tree with a rawhide reata, they piled dry grass and dead branches around and over him. They placed a flint and steel by the brush pile and gathered for what appeared to be a final council, while all this time, the nine-year-old girl continued to wail and sob. Once again Babb signaled the group to proceed. At this the men crowded around him, saying, "Heap wanna you," and untied him. Later Babb learned that his fearlessness and defiance had saved his life; the warriors saw in him a future Comanche brave. His sister, watching them free him, ran to him and embraced him, weeping this time with joy.[1]

Probably each war party and each band took its tone from its leader. In New Mexico in the 1770s the most dreaded Comanche chieftain was known as Cuerno Verde. The "little king" who wore a green horn on his forehead had died in the 1768 attack on Ojo Caliente.[2] But his son had claimed the "ridiculous device" he had worn. Because his father had been killed by Spaniards, Cuerno Verde *fils* carried on a murderous vendetta against New Mexicans, raiding with exceptional ferocity. In doing so he became notorious throughout the province. By 1779 the new governor, Juan Bautista de Anza, considered him "the cruel scourge" of the kingdom.

Every Spanish settler feared capture by the People. During the eighteenth century, these plains raiders made prisoners of many individuals of both sexes, probably because they had value as slaves or because they might be traded for captured Comanches. Later, after the first of several devastating epidemics, starting with smallpox in 1780, the tribe may have viewed captives not only as investments for future ransom but also as a means of replacing heavy tribal losses through disease and war. The Nuhmuhnuh usually adopted and raised children as full members of the tribe, although they might sometimes enslave or kill them.[3] Warriors frequently took captive women for their wives or for slaves of their wives. The People took few adult men as prisoners. Even so there were exceptions to the norm in both directions. As Hoebel has indicated, while there were notoriously cruel chiefs, like the second Cuerno Verde, others existed who were exceptionally forbearing. In attempting to get a sense of a diverse people, a student of the past often finds the exceptions to the rule more instructive than the rule itself.

It was probably around 1846, just after the United States had annexed Texas. By then the Comanches had long since known the meaning of surveying. Some had probably known it since 1833, when a mysterious Alexander Le Grand, rumored to have been half French and half Comanche, had been out surveying on what is now the Texas panhandle. Most Comanche divisions surely knew by 1837 or 1838 that surveyors "stole the land." The People hated them. In any case it happened that a survey group was working on the San Sabá River, far from the settlements. During this period a half-dozen men left the main party, after establishing a time and place to reassemble. One late afternoon these men—Wylie Hill, Richard Cheek, James L. Jobe, and George Hancock—were riding along when they suddenly became puzzled by a distant brightness reflecting the sunlight. Soon, though, they realized that the shining emanated from the shields and, probably, lance points of some fifty Comanche warriors who were standing and evidently watching them.[4]

By the time the Comanches were within rifle range, the Anglo-Texans had taken cover in chaparral under a cliff. To their surprise the leading men of what appeared to be a war party, instead of opening fire, drew up and signaled that they wished to talk, expressing a desire to meet with the white men's captain. The surveyors hurriedly chose George Hancock to act in that capacity, although several of the group, fearing treachery, strongly opposed his going. But as Hancock walked resolutely out of the thicket, the old chief dismounted from his pony and advanced toward him while making friendly signs. He gave the *tejano* "an earnest hugging," calling him "Big Chief."

The remaining Anglos had moved forward, standing in view of the chief and his followers, fingers on rifle triggers, ready to defend Hancock if necessary. But at a sound in their rear they turned to see the crest of the hill behind them nearly covered with Comanches. John Holland Jenkins, the Texas pioneer who wrote of this incident in his memoirs, observed that the surveyors realized at this juncture they were at the mercy of a "savage and hitherto merciless foe." Meanwhile the chief continued to question Hancock in detail, presumably through signs, concerning the location and number of the main survey party. When satisfied, the old man informed the "captain" and his men that he and his warriors would accompany them to their rendezvous with the others.

Having no choice the Texans rode along "all mixed up with a large band of Comanches." By now the sky was darkening, and there was still no sign of the main body of surveyors. One of the men, Wylie Hill, had a shout uniquely his own which carried a great distance. In hope of receiving a response, he took a deep breath and uttered his cry. There was only silence from the country through which the mixed group rode, but the warriors, no mean whoopers themselves, were delighted and amused by the sound and insisted on Hill's repeating it at intervals, all the while trying to imitate it. Yet by the time darkness had enveloped the crowd of riders, the Texans, in contrast, were finding their fix anything but amusing.

"Boys," said Hill at last. "They're going to kill us for sure. We'd better take the main bulge on them."

"No," replied one of the braves riding near them. "These Indians aren't going to kill you."

"What? Who are you? How do you know English?"

Warren Lyons, for that was the warrior's name, told of how, when he had been seven or eight, he had gone with his father to the fields. A party of Comanches, surprising the older Lyons plowing, had killed him, seizing Warren. Since that time Warren had grown up as a Comanche and was content with his present life among the People, a fact his Anglo interlocutors had difficulty in understanding.

Ultimately Wylie Hill's whoop was answered, and the half-dozen Texans led their Comanche escort into the survey camp, perhaps not receiving as warm a welcome as they might have under other circumstances. Later, at the Texans' campfire, the chief, feigning ignorance of the surveyors' task, innocently asked them what all the blazes on the trees meant.

"Why do you cut them like that?"

"Oh, we're out here bee hunting."

Still in a kindly tone, but in one containing a threat, the old chief recommended they leave the woods alone and return to the settlements:

"This is our hunting ground, and you'd better plan to leave in the morning."

That night, according to Jenkins, "the lion and the lamb" lay down peacefully together and slept, except for one Ben Heines, who "refused to trust either Providence or Comanches and sat up the whole night long." But before stretching out by the embers, the Texans spoke for some time with Warren Lyons, especially those who knew his mother and relatives, trying to persuade him to return to his own people. But Lyons appeared saddened by the thought of leaving the Nuhmuhnuh and, in the morning, rode off with the old chief and his followers, "turning his back upon those of his own race without sign of hesitation or regret."

Warren Lyons finally visited his mother and rejoined the Texans, eventually becoming a ranger and fighting the people who had murdered his father but who had also raised him, happily it seems, from childhood.

Lyons's mild and genial old chief was probably a southern Comanche, or Penateka, and his division had, around this time, signed treaties with the Texans. What is more, many of the old chiefs genuinely wanted peace with the tejanos, provided that their own territory remain inviolate. But surveyors? Working within Comanchería? Most chiefs would have, at the least, attempted to kill Hancock, Hill, and their companions. The Texas pioneer J. W. Wilbarger related, for example, an anecdote of nine surveyors working above New Braunfels in 1838. Apparently unknown Indians, probably Comanches, surprised and slew them all. Much later searchers found their bones, but could identify only one skeleton, "that of a young man by the name of Beatty, which was found lying at the root of a tree, on which, with his pocket knife he had rudely carved his name." In another instance Captain Randolph B. Marcy wrote in 1852 of how Comanches had once "massacred a party of twenty men who attempted to survey a tract of land in Western Texas." (Unfortunately the U.S. Army officer provided no date or other details.) Comanche leaders to the opposite extreme of the old chief might even have attempted to take one or more of the surveyors alive.

There are, understandably, no eyewitness accounts from former captives of the cruelest chiefs. Apparently none of these victims survived. Yet there are descriptions of the kinds of torments to which the Cuerno Verdes subjected at least some of their adult male prisoners. In 1828, for instance, Lieutenant José María Sánchez y Tapia, artist-cartographer of the Mexican *Comisión de Límites*, which visited Texas at that time, wrote that the Comanches "do all the evil they can to their enemies, and if one of them falls . . . in their power they bind him, and all try to devise the slowest and most cruel way of putting him to death. Some prisoners they burn by slow fire for several days; others they cut piece by piece, applying burning coals to the wounds; and others they scalp and then put fire on their heads. They also use other horrible methods." Sánchez goes on quickly to point out, however, that the use of torture was restricted to the Comanches' Indian foes and not applied to Mexican prisoners, who were killed but spared the ordeal of torture.[5]

Whether or not most chiefs exercised the same restraint toward earlier Spanish captives is unknown. Again it probably depended to a large extent upon "the personal character" of the Spaniard's captor. Certainly Comanche chiefs in 1786 returned at least one or two healthy men to Governor de Anza. But Cuerno Verde? It would appear he was as extreme an exception in one direction as Warren Lyons's amiable old chief was in the other. By 1779 the new governor of Nuevo México found that this "cruel scourge" had "exterminated many pueblos," or villages. De Anza accused him of "killing hundreds and taking as many prisoners whom he afterward sacrificed in cold blood." Even if Cuerno Verde II refrained from torturing his Spanish captives, their deaths surely could not have been pleasant. It was for this reason, in part, that Lieutenant Colonel Juan Bautista de Anza, that very year, "determined to have his life."

SEVEN

Governor de Anza's Victory and Treaty, 1778–1789

Don Juan Bautista de Anza, soldier, explorer, and founder of San Francisco, had lately suppressed an uprising of Pima and Seri Indians in Sonora. He was already a veteran of that frontier, where his grandfather and father had served, and where his father had died in a battle with Apaches. De Anza himself had already won recognition for his California expeditions. More recently he had killed a renowned insurgent chieftain in hand-to-hand combat. At age forty-three, New Mexico's new governor brought with him experience unusual for an appointee to that post. But the lieutenant colonel was an unusual man, especially so in that, like Vélez before him, he combined the talents of soldier and diplomat.

Colonel de Anza arrived in Santa Fe during the summer or early autumn of 1778 and governed for two terms, departing after the middle of 1789, when he was replaced by another able official, don Fernando de la Concha. Commander General de Croix had instructed the new governor, as his first duty, to open a route between Santa Fe and Sonora. But de Anza, seeing for himself the desperate condition of the province, obtained de Croix's permission first to inflict a defeat on the Comanches. Wisely he perceived that if he were ever going to achieve an alliance with this particular Indian nation, he would first have to compel its respect through a military victory.

On August 15, 1779, he set out from Santa Fe, striking northward, proceeding by a fresh route in order to surprise the enemy within Comanchería.[1] On the second day he reviewed his expedition, which consisted of 103 presidial soldiers along with some 225 militiamen and 259 Pueblo auxiliaries. The regulars he found well equipped. Each man had three horses, was well armed, had plenty of ammunition, and enough food to last for over a month. But the settlers and Indians were badly outfitted. He noted that "because of their well-known poverty and wretchedness," the best-equipped among them possessed only two horses, most of them nearly worthless. Their guns were of equally doubtful value, and they lacked powder and lead. De Anza supplied the most destitute with a good horse. He equipped each man bearing a firearm with a ten-ball cartridge belt.

Marching northward on the west side of the Río Grande, the army camped on the third night at the deserted settlement of Ojo Caliente, bleak evidence of Cuerno Verde's vengeance. On Friday, the sixth day, in the region of the Conejos River in southern Colorado, two hundred Ute and Jicarilla warriors joined the expedition. By that Sunday the force, now nearly eight hundred strong, marched by necessity at night, so that the enemy would not see their dust from the mountains to the east. From the beginning the weather had been chilly. At night, especially, the men suffered from the cold. Crossing the Río Grande near the present site of Alamosa, the army proceeded northward, keeping the Sangre de Cristo range on their right, and as they advanced, the Rockies of the Continental Divide on their left. On Tuesday the twenty-fourth, they camped at a pond where the Utes proudly displayed the decaying bodies of twelve Comanches they had killed there the previous month, when a war party had tried to steal their horses one night.

The army continued to march northward through a ravine with much water. They struggled over Poncha Pass to reach the Arkansas River on Saturday, August 28, after nearly two weeks of travel. In the vicinity of today's Salida, Colorado, de Anza turned his expedition eastward. That Sunday they came upon a herd of buffalo, and hunters killed fifty of the shaggy beasts. The army rested the horses while dressing the meat. The following day the expedition began to force a passage over the Front Range, through ravines and thick forests, still pushing eastward.

When he camped that night by a river, de Anza posted sentinels at lookout points to watch the plains. The next morning one of them reported approaching clouds of dust that appeared to be two horsemen looking for the expedition. The riders turned out to be members of a scouting party sent back by their corporal, camped about four miles away. The corporal had seen "a considerable number of enemies . . . raising the dust." Leaving the baggage train and horse herd guarded by two hundred men, whom he ordered to follow him slowly, de Anza led the greater part of his army to the place where the scouts waited in concealment.

On reaching the outpost, de Anza dismounted and conferred with the corporal of the scouts.

"Sir, in my opinion, they've discovered us."

"What makes you think so?"

"They found my tracks. A little while after they halted—they'd only set up six tents. . . . Four Indians followed my trail nearly to where I was hiding. As soon as they turned back, I reconnoitered their trail. They've already collected their tents and caught all their horses, the mounts as well as the spare ones. It looks to me, sir, as if they're about to run."

The governor reflected. "We'll attack immediately."

At noon the Spanish army moved out, three sections abreast, with de

Anza leading the vanguard at the center. For a moment the Comanches sat their ponies and observed them. Dressed in buckskins, all were mounted, even women and children. Clustered together, they watched the three-pronged formation advance, banners fluttering, the thin sound of bugle and drum in the breeze that stirred the grass. Foremost jogged the presidials in leather jackets, wearing dark, flat-brimmed hats, followed by militiamen, both carrying shields and lances at the ready. Behind them rode Pueblo auxiliaries, with lances and bows. Last came the great war party of Ute and Jicarilla Apache warriors, each mounted on his freshest pony. The Comanches whirled and fled at a run, driving the horse herd, with women and children in front, braves behind them.

Soldiers made prisoners of thirty women and thirty-four children. In addition the Spaniards and their allies captured the entire enemy horse herd, more than five hundred head. They seized all of the enemy's baggage and supplies. There was so much spoil it later took more than a hundred horses to carry it away. But the Spaniards and Indian allies divided it without friction.

The poles of more than 120 lodges had been erected. The Spaniards calculated from 3 to 4 men to a tepee, as well as 7 to 8 women and children. A modest estimate would be about 400 men and some 850 women and children in the band. De Anza neglected to record enemy casualties, which seem to have been light, owing to the speed of the ponies. But the survivors lost everything except for the horses they rode, the weapons they carried, and the clothing they wore.

At 4:30 in the afternoon Governor de Anza began interrogating prisoners, but it was not until 9:00 that evening that he learned the name of the chief whose band he had routed. The last two prisoners told him their chieftain was Cuerno Verde. De Anza also learned that the second "little king" was presently on a campaign in New Mexico. Before leaving, Cuerno Verde had ordered his people to meet him at this well-watered grassland in order to "celebrate the triumph that he flattered himself he would secure." He had been absent now about sixteen days, which was why his band had come to the rendezvous, and why other bands were bound for the same spot; although, of course, they had already been warned by those who had escaped from the Spanish army. Immediately de Anza decided to follow the Comanches' trail, "to see," as he put it, "if fortune would grant" him an encounter, not only hoping to defeat the notorious raider but also wishing to rescue any captives he might have seized.

On the first of September the army broke camp early. At seven o'clock Governor de Anza set out with the vanguard, seeking the chief's trail. By ten o'clock he had found it. He assembled his scouts.

"Always travel to the right and left of it," he ordered them. "By day as well as by night."

Still that particular night he was compelled to stop and camp by a stream. The settlers' horses were exhausted after two grueling days. Again before seven the next morning de Anza was leading his army on the trail of the little king, heading south. After traveling eight miles, he came once more to the Arkansas River, which he crossed. Shortly the scouts announced finding horses belonging to Cuerno Verde. Around the time soldiers were catching the Comanche ponies, most of the Utes, without a word, rode away for home with their plunder.

De Anza proceeded on the trail for another thirteen miles, then halted in a rocky arroyo to rest the horses. At four o'clock he moved out again. About three miles farther along, one of the advance scouts galloped up to inform him that the enemy was approaching, apparently unaware of the Spanish force. At once de Anza gave orders to hide the horse herd, the baggage train, and the troops themselves, whom he placed in preparation for an ambush. Soon he could discern the returning raiders riding spread out at intervals along the edge of the wooded mountains. Between his own troops and the enemy was a narrow valley he lacked time to reconnoiter.

The army was now near what is today called Greenhorn Mountain, in southern Colorado.

At sunset the war party reached the valley. The governor galloped out to attack them with the column under his command. The two forces feinted from a distance. At first the Comanches seemed prepared to defend themselves, but when they noticed two more columns riding to surround them, they fled at a dead run. De Anza was not able to pursue rapidly because down in the valley he discovered a boggy gully, which he and his troops were obliged to cross one at a time. He and his men raced after the Comanches for over a mile on the far side, until most of the party had escaped. Still the Spaniards managed to kill eight warriors and to wound others. Recrossing the gully in the dark, the governor reflected on the quagmire. He concluded that the enemy was probably not aware of it.

At camp officers familiar with the country and the kind of warfare practiced in it urged de Anza not to remain at that place.

"These barbarians can retaliate in the dark."

The governor reflected. From his knowledge of other tribes, he judged this unlikely. Also the suggestion had, to him, a hint of cowardice to it.

"No, the very thing you fear, I desire. Let them come. Even if we hadn't won today, we should for the honor of our arms wait here till dawn. Until then, though, we will remain under arms."

The army spent a chilly, rainy night waiting for an attack. At daylight de

Anza dispatched scouts to reconnoiter the vicinity. Returning they reported no sign of the enemy. By seven o'clock the governor was once more leading his force onward. Soon a few enemy horsemen appeared in the distance. Evidently they intended to cross the valley toward the expedition. Before long these few were joined by others. Beginning his battle strategy, de Anza retained the first and second columns with him in the rear and sent the third, or reserve corps, ahead as vanguard, all the while advancing. The Spanish command was now drawing near a patch of forest. He planned that the first two columns would hold it on both sides.

By the time the Comanches were approaching the far side of the wood, they formed a party of more than forty warriors—some forty braves flaunting before a sizable Spanish army. Riding nearly to within gunshot, they defiantly fired off their muskets. De Anza recognized Cuerno Verde by his green-horned headdress and his act of riding out in advance of his warriors on a curvetting horse. At that moment the governor "determined to have his life."

Continuing to develop his plan, de Anza ordered the vanguard, on issuing from the woods, to attack with two hundred lightly encumbered horsemen. The baggage train and horse herd, with their guards, along with the cavalry, were to form a barricade against which the vanguard would drive the enemy, aided by de Anza leading the rear guard in an encircling maneuver. In this fashion, aware that the Plains Indians were depending on the swiftness of their ponies to strike and escape, he intended partly to surround them, pushing them into the gully.

To carry out his scheme, Colonel de Anza feinted a retreat, riding rapidly away from the Indian auxiliaries, hoping not only to draw the enemy deeply into his trap but to tire their horses as well. Just when de Anza's tactic was succeeding, Cuerno Verde realized what was happening and signaled his warriors to turn back. But the chief had committed himself and his immediate followers too completely to the pursuit. Whirling his horse, de Anza raced with his troop toward the valley, cutting off the Comanche chief from the main body of his war party. Cuerno Verde and his entourage turned and rode down to cross the valley, plunging into the unsuspected bog, where they were trapped.

They leapt from their ponies, took cover behind them, and fought the presidials. Cuerno Verde disdained even to load his own musket, a task a bodyguard did for him. Yet despite a defense that de Anza called "as brave as it was glorious," the Comanche chieftain died there in the gully, along with "his first born son," who was the heir to his command, "four of his most famous captains, a medicine man who preached that he was immortal, and ten more . . ."

After the battle the Spaniards found a musket that an Indian auxiliary had lost in the earlier battle at the Comanche rendezvous. Cuerno Verde had known of the disaster that had overtaken his band. With a mere fifty warriors of his personal guard, he had been both fearless and rash enough to seek out and attack an army of six hundred men. The remainder of his war party escaped, the dust of their flight visible for thirty miles, while among the Spanish force the single casualty was a light-horse soldier who received a minor bullet wound. By 10:20 that morning it was apparent that no more Comanches were going to challenge the army. After the troops had cheered the king and Commander General de Croix, de Anza turned his horse and led his army southward toward home.

De Anza's victory marked the beginning of ineluctable movement toward a treaty between the Comanches and the Spaniards of New Mexico. News of the death of the supposedly invincible Cuerno Verde, he of the powerful medicine, must have reverberated in shock waves throughout Comanchería, causing other chiefs to speculate about the desirability of a peace with the Spaniards. But the time was not yet propitious. That same year, 1779, Spain declared war on England. In Louisiana, Governor Bernardo de Gálvez actively helped the American colonists in their revolution by capturing Baton Rouge and Natchez, Mobile and Pensacola. The Spanish crown made the war against England its first priority, giving little financial support to distant Indian campaigns. The Comanches took advantage of this lull in military activity to continue sporadic raiding. But at the war's end in 1783, Spain and the commandancy general once more turned their attention to the chronic problem of Apache and Comanche attack.

A French trader, Athanase de Mézières, had earlier been enlisted to help execute Spanish policy. De Mézières, who had great influence with the Wichitan tribes, conceived the idea of arming these other "nations of the north" with guns from Louisiana and setting them upon the Nuhmuhnuh. Simultaneously the Spaniards themselves retaliated aggressively against attacks within their borders. Before long the Comanches were suing for peace both in Texas and in New Mexico. Meanwhile in New Mexico, de Anza had been pursuing an amicable but firm policy with the chiefs of the principal divisions of the tribe. The first part of his policy, like that of Vélez, stipulated no trade with the kingdom without a peace treaty. The second part showed his understanding of the plains people: there would be no treaty until all divisions of the Comanche nation entered into the agreement. In this way de Anza worked toward fulfilling the charge he had accepted from de Croix at Chihuahua.

By 1784 the majority of the leading Comanches wanted peace. But one chief of the Cuchantica, Toroblanco (Whitebull), opposed a treaty. That year other powerful chiefs of the tribe conspired against Toroblanco and assassinated him.[2] Except for a part of his band, outlawed by the

Nuhmuhnuh, his followers accepted the will of the People. At de Anza's request, the Comanche bands selected a capitán to represent them all, one Ecueracapa (Leathercloak), the chief "distinguished as much by his skill and valor in war as by his adroitness and intelligence."

To demonstrate his goodwill and largess, Ecueracapa entertained men from Pecos Pueblo, the Comanches' old enemy, out on the plains. The Pecos returned delighted with the treatment they had received and with much praise for the chief. Meanwhile news of the impending treaty had reached the Utes, long-time loyal allies of the Spaniards. In January of 1786 two of their most important chiefs, Moara and Pinto, arrived in Santa Fe, where they harangued Governor de Anza with "insulting and barbarous arguments" against the treaty, "so inflamed that for more than four hours . . . they did not wish to smoke or accept any other present." De Anza patiently heard them out, then soothed them with many reasonable arguments, finally explaining that because of the king's piety, he had to extend the grace of peace to any people who begged for it. Placated, the Ute chiefs asked to be included within the treaty. De Anza promised to do his best with the Comanches.

As gifted in diplomacy as in war, de Anza persuaded the Comanches to make peace with the Utes. On February 28 de Anza accompanied Ecueracapa from Santa Fe to Pecos Pueblo, where numerous leading Comanches were camped. Dismounting among their tepees, the governor greeted more than two hundred warriors, all of them regarding him with pleasure and respect.[3]

Sixty-odd years later, Captain Randolph Marcy, U.S. Army, described the ritual with which Comanche chiefs might greet a leader of another, friendly nation. As Marcy rode toward a Comanche camp, an old, fat chief, "in exceedingly scanty attire," rode out, with his followers, to welcome him. Declaring his friendship for Americans and for Marcy as their representative, the chief grabbed the captain in his muscular arms, while both men were still on horseback. Laying his head upon Marcy's shoulder, he squeezed the American in a bear hug, then placed his head on Marcy's other shoulder and, as the captain later reported, "he rubbed his greasy face against [mine] in the most affectionate manner . . ."[4]

So in 1786, one by one, Comanche tribal leaders came up to embrace de Anza and to rub their painted faces against his; chiefs such as He Who Saw Fire, Bear Bird, The Crafty One, He Gnaws his Master, Seated on the

Mountain Range, Ugly Game, Hoarse Bark, The Feeble Effeminate One, and The Decayed Shoe, of whom we shall heard more later. Some months afterward the new commandant general, Jacobo Ugarte y Loyola described a similar group who visited him in Chihuahua:

> All of these Indians are robust, good looking, and extremely happy. Their faces show forth the martial, frank, and generous character that distinguishes this nation from the others of this frontier. Their dress is decent, fashioned from buffalo skins they provide themselves. They paint their faces with red ochre and other earths, highlighting their eyelids with vermilion. They love adornments and sport them especially in their hair which they wear braided and intertwined with imitation gold buttons, colored glass beads, ribbons and whatever other thing that glitters.[5]

That afternoon, after eating a meal together, the Spanish and Comanche leaders concluded their treaty. One of their prominent capitánes returned to the Spaniards a native of Santa Fe, Alexandro Martín, who had been a prisoner for eleven years. Speeches were delivered on both sides, and the governor promised, among other benefits, safe passage through Pecos to the capital city. He also promised trade fairs at that pueblo, with its ancient tradition of friendship for the Apaches. The Comanches, as part of their commitment, agreed "to employ their arms in incessant, open war against the Apache enemies."

De Anza, as a token that war had ended, presented Chief Ecueracapa with a saber and a banner. The Comanches responded by digging a hole in the earth in which they symbolically buried the war. On the following day, under de Anza's personal supervision, the Spaniards held a trade fair in which the visiting Comanches bartered hides, meat, tallow, a few horses, and three guns. Afterward they expressed their gratification and spoke of transferring most of their trade to Pecos Pueblo.

Never again would the Plains Apaches, with their long dog trains, appear out of the east to erect their lodges before Pecos Pueblo. But neither would feathered or buffalo-horned nomads swoop down on their ponies to murder and abduct men and women working in the fields. From this time on the province would be, with minor interruptions, at peace with the Comanches.

II

Nuevo México and Tejas

*"None of the other tribes dare to fight the Comanches. . . .
The Apache, roaming around in every direction, has no
other check to his depredations than that of his fear
of the brave and honest Comanche, a tribe which
instills fear into all other tribes, which fact
serves to good advantage . . ."*

Pedro Bautista Pino, Santa Fe, 1812

*The Comanches are "treacherous, revengeful, sly,
untrustworthy, ferocious, and cruel, when victorious;
and cowardly and low, when conquered."*

Juan Antonio Padilla, San Antonio, 1820

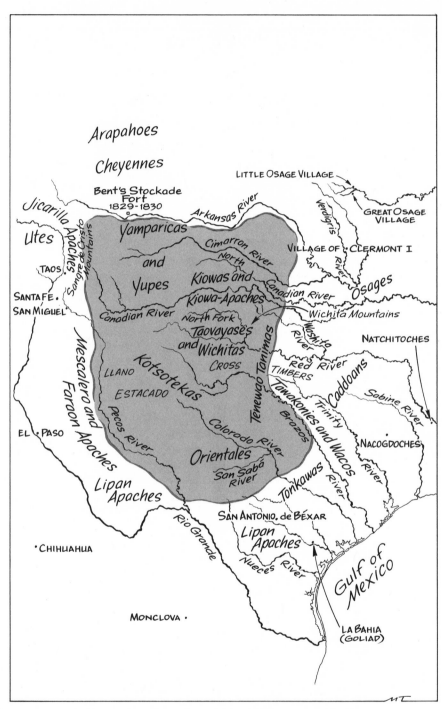

Comanchería and the Southern Plains in the Early Nineteenth Century

1787   Pierre Vial reaches Santa Fe from San Antonio de Béxar.

1800   Napoleon Bonaparte coerces Spain into retroceding Louisiana to France. Nouvelle Orléans and St. Louis again become French towns.

1803   The United States, under President Thomas Jefferson, transacts the "Louisiana Purchase" with France, causing profound anxiety in New Spain.

1804–1806   Lewis and Clark explore the Louisiana Purchase.

1806   Spanish Captain Francisco Viana turns back Jefferson's Freeman-Custis expedition up the Red River. Lieutenant Facundo Melgares visits the Pawnees. Zebulon Montgomery Pike explores to the headwaters of the Arkansas River, and is captured by Spaniards.

1808   Captain Francisco Amangual meets with bands of Comanche allies, while he open a trail between San Antonio de Béxar and Santa Fe.

1812–1813   The Magee-Gutiérrez expedition of American adventurers and republican Mexicans attempts to wrest Texas from New Spain and is defeated by royalist troops in the battle of the Medina River in August of 1813.

1816   Smallpox spreads throughout Comanchería.

1819   The Adams-Onís Treaty settles the boundary dispute between Spain and the United States. Lieutenant Stephen Long leads a scientific expedition (1819–1820) from Council Bluffs (Iowa) to the Rockies and back.

1821   The Mexicans win their independence from Spain. Two American trading parties, that of Colonel Hugh Glen with Jacob Fowler, and that of Thomas James, encounter the Comanches. William Becknell, a Missouri trader, opens commerce on the Santa Fe Trail.

EIGHT

Women: Captives and "Abject Slaves"

De Anza's treaty opened the southern plains to New Mexican traders. Although bands of Comanches continued for a time to attend trade fairs in the province, enterprising traders found it profitable to travel out to seek them, a change that contributed to the decline of at least one trading pueblo; Pecos was abandoned by its last inhabitants in 1838. These traders were first known as *viajeros* (travelers), later as *comancheros*.[1] Their relationship with the Comanches continued for as long as the People roamed the buffalo plains. It was surely an important reason that the Nuhmuhnuh remained generally friendly toward New Mexico from 1786 to 1875. The *comancheros* furnished the various divisions with supplies as well as little luxuries and provided a market for stolen horses and other plunder. Since the traders, whether *nuevomexicanos* or Pueblo Indians, were illiterate, there are no first-hand records of their experiences—or almost none.[2] There is one exception, the account that Vicente Romero, former comanchero, and then an old man, gave to a Works Project Administration writer in the 1930s. Even though the details of the account are recalled from the 1870s, it gives an idea of what such undertakings must have been like, starting from their inception in the late eighteenth century.[3]

Guadalupe Márquez pointed to a multitude of horse tracks crossing the arroyo—surely Indian ponies. Better yet, there were lines traced by dragging lodge poles in the pink sand. One of the older men nodded. This meant women and children; it was not a war party. Márquez urged his horse up the bank of the wash. The others followed, leading the pack animals. Vicente Romero, his nephew, was last in line. Only eighteen, he had already been to the plains with his uncle once before. Silently he laughed. He loved the freedom and adventure of the plains, so different from life in his mountain village. He hoped to bring back bales of dried meat and buffalo hides, horses and mules worth American dollars. His uncle, *comandante* of the party, had said the trail was fresh. With luck they might start trading tomorrow.

Late that afternoon Márquez led his group to a grove of cottonwoods, where he found a spring. As the others began unpacking, he rode to the summit of a nearby hill. With dry wood he built a fire and made smoke signals, using a saddle blanket. On his return he found the men sitting around their own fire. Dismounting, he told them the band of Indians they had been following should show up in the morning. He looked around the group, his eyes resting, especially, on several new faces. His expression was grave.

"Be very careful how you act with the Indians."

Next morning the New Mexico traders were surrounded by people. Occasionally they dealt with Kiowas, but Márquez identified these as Comanches. The women of the band set up the lodges, while children and dogs ran around creating an uproar. The men loafed or occupied themselves with their horses, a large herd grazing at a distance. Vicente, working near a companion, Anaclete Mascareñas, thought the Comanches a fine-looking people, strongly built, with fairly light skins. But he was soon too busy laying out trade goods to pay attention to the Indian camp. With care he displayed blankets, salt, and strips of iron for arrowheads. He opened packs of the hard bread the women of Córdova baked especially for trading. Nearby he displayed a delicacy—dried apples and prunes.

After feasting with the important men of the band, the *comancheros* opened trade. This required patience because each transaction took a lot of talk and gesture on either side. Whether it was for a rabbit pelt or a good horse, it could not be hurried. The whole process went on for weeks. When the band moved, seeking fresh pasturage for the horses, Márquez and his *escuadra* packed up and accompanied them to their next campsite, where the traders once more set up their wares, over and over again.

Always they were careful of their behavior and on guard against treachery by their customers. But they also knew the Comanches needed them. All would probably go well. In the end they would get safely back to their village with their goods, and rejoin their families, if they were careful. But that was chiefly the responsibility of the comandante. In the meantime the younger men, particularly, amused themselves as they could. The children, who had at first been aloof and fearful, now hung around begging for treats and trifles. Vicente enjoyed communicating with them by signs and by a few words. Young braves would arrange foot races or wrestling matches with the traders. Sometimes they held contests of marksmanship with bows and arrows. But what most interested Vicente was racing horses, which the Comanche men did constantly, frequently betting on them. His own favorite hunting horse, a *grullo*, or dun, with a black stripe down its back, was fast. About nine times he raced it against the favorite pony of some

Comanche, betting blankets. Six of these times he won, increasing the quantity of goods he was to take home.

But looking back at the trip years later, he realized they might easily not have returned at all. He thanked God and his uncle. It was all because of a woman, poor thing. He had noticed her the first week, working before a big, handsome tepee. She was pretty and surely a *mexicana*, not a Comanche. Whenever he passed her at her work, carrying wood or scraping a hide, she would look at him hard. But he asked about her and found out she was married to one of the warriors, and so he tried not to think about her. Then one afternoon Anaclete approached with another young man and asked him in a confidential tone to come with them. Surprised, he followed. In some bushes by a stream they came upon the pretty woman, who appeared to have been waiting for them. At first glance she looked like the Indian women in her buckskin dress, but her face was unpainted with the orange rouge so many of them wore, and her eyes, all the time she talked to them, looking from one to another, held theirs with an expression of entreaty.

Her story was simple and sad. She had grown up in Texas at a place called San Antonio del Arbol. When she had been taking clothes to servant women washing at a stream near her father's house, three Comanches had jumped from behind wild plum bushes, seizing her. One had pressed his hand on her mouth. They had dragged her to their concealed ponies. One of them had taken her on his horse and galloped off, with the others behind. They joined more warriors with cattle belonging to her father. Her captors paused to show her the naked, mutilated bodies of two of her father's *vaqueros*. By signs they threatened her with a similar death if she failed to come with them willingly. Since then one of the braves had taken her as his wife. Her eyes glittered with tears as she begged them to rescue her, promising that her father would pay gold and cattle for her return.

Knowing in advance what the answer would be, Vicente went with the others to his uncle, whose word, as comandante, was law, since the very survival of the party depended upon his decisions.

"No, it can't be done," Márquez said. "Any effort to free her might destroy our whole party, far away as we are from home, and few as we are for the number of Indians against us."

Anaclete began to protest.

Márquez cut him off with a wave of his hand. "Look, even if we were lucky enough to get her away with little or no loss, none of us could ever come back and trade with these Indians."

Reluctantly Vicente accepted his uncle's decision. In his heart he knew it was right. He had not cared about the cattle or gold. No, she was pretty.

He had imagined the surprise of the people of the village if he had brought her home as his bride-to-be. Anaclete, he suspected, held that idea even more strongly than he. Mascareñas was two years older, twenty, and it seemed he was in love. He had defied the comandante and had threatened to run off with her anyway. Vicente had given up the thought of a rescue, but he didn't know about Anaclete, who was acting strangely. He sensed his uncle was watching the older youth, and even had some of the other men watching him, too.

One evening just after they all had eaten, Márquez told the party of discovering that Mascareñas had been preparing to carry off the girl. Before Anaclete could even stammer out a defense, the comandante ordered him seized and bound. The others instantly obeyed, grabbing and tying the struggling youth. Márquez told him he would remain bound until he renounced his plan to rescue the girl, and until he swore to obey his leader in every detail. The boy lay by the fire looking pale and defiant. But so it was. Anaclete eventually gave in. The girl stayed with the Comanches, maybe for the rest of her life, poor thing. Such was her lot.

The trading ended and, with pack horses loaded, the little group of comancheros began their journey home. For the first three days, the Comanche band escorted them on their way, as was the custom. Again Márquez led them past Fort Union in the dark, so the American soldiers would not know of their trip. Even after passing the fort, they kept a sharp lookout, since there was still danger from Apaches or from Navajos on a horse-stealing expedition into Comanchería. But finally they passed Mora, then climbed slowly to Peñasco, and finally reached Truchas, urging their heavily loaded horses faster and faster. Soon they halted on the piñon ridge over Córdova. There they fired their guns in a salvo to San Antonio, patron saint of the village. As they rode down toward the church, they could see people standing on rooftops counting to see if any were missing. After all, they had been gone for three months. They rode down the dirt street, and people came out of their houses to greet them. As Vicente's mother hurried toward his grullo, he saw tears of joy in her eyes.

Many observers of the Nuhmuhnuh, such as Berlandier, remarked upon the deplorable situation of women captives, who were subject to sexual abuse by Comanche men as well as to physical abuse by their women. But this was not always so. If a Comanche man took a captive as his wife, she immediately had a protector and became one of the People. The pretty mexicana whom Vicente and Anaclete had wished to rescue was probably homesick, overworked, and unhappily mated, but she was sheltered from the kind of treatment casually dealt out to girls and women who retained the status of prisoners and slaves. In fact many women who had originally been captives preferred, if offered their freedom, to remain with their Comanche mates, especially if they had children by them.

Josiah Gregg, physician and Missouri trader, wrote of encountering one such individual while crossing the plains westward by way of the Canadian River in 1839. After his party had smoked with several Comanche chiefs, a group of Ietan women entered the American camp to barter. Gregg noticed one whose features were Mexican and addressed her in Spanish. Yes, she told him, she was originally from the vicinity of Matamoros, where she had been captured. But now she was married to a Comanche and had no desire whatever to return to her former home.

The incident prompted Gregg to relate another, and more dramatic, story of "voluntary captivity." Dr. John Sibley, surgeon and acting Indian agent for the U.S. Army post at Natchitoches in 1805, had reported the occurrence to Washington. Some twenty years previously, it appeared, the Comanches had kidnaped the daughter of Chihuahua's governor general. This distraught official somehow managed to send a thousand dollars to a *comanchero* to obtain her release. After a short time, the trader succeeded, no doubt paying the captors in goods. But to everyone's amazement, the girl chose to remain with the People. She sent her father a message saying she was married, possibly pregnant, and that her captors had tattooed her. She would be more miserable if she returned, she said, than if she remained with the tribe.

Gregg commented that the anecdote illustrated how "a sensitive female" would sometimes prefer captivity to "the horrible ordeal of ill-natured remarks to which she would inevitably be exposed on being returned to civilized life."

The pioneer Texan Noah Smithwick, who lived for three months in 1837 with Chief Muguara's band, found this segment of the People to be, in his words, "all around . . . the most peaceable community I ever lived in." During the time he dwelt with the band (part of the great southern division of Comanches), he later declared that he had not heard a single quarrel among the adults. Further, he continued, "I never saw a woman or child abused." Of course the women were "abject slaves," but the ranger stated his chivalrous conviction that "an Indian brave would have felt it a burning disgrace to strike a woman." Old Muguara (Spirit Talker) was a prestigious medicine man and probably civil chief of the Penateka division, and his personal band may have been exceptionally harmonious, or else Smithwick may not have been aware of all that took place in camp.

In contrast is the reminiscence of Francesca, a captive seized from New Mexico in 1833. Her mistresses gave her tasks beyond her strength when she was a child, frequently beating her. Later her Comanche husband also beat her regularly. This was probably not typical, but not altogether unusual either. A modern scholar has observed that divorces were common among the Comanches and that "excessive physical abuse" was a ground for separation.[4] Normally the woman's male relatives would buy her back from her husband, especially during the early years of marriage. Women like Francesca with no male kin might flee to another band or even appeal for protection from some warrior more powerful than her husband.[5] Apparently Francesca had no such recourse. Eventually she escaped to Fort Sill, years later telling her story to the Reverend A. E. Butterfield, a Methodist Missionary.

As early as 1787, Commander Jacobo Ugarte y Loyola pointed out in a letter to Governor de Anza the degraded state of the Comanche women accompanying a party of chiefs who had visited him in Chihuahua. In contrast to the men, he observed, "the women were unkempt, had their hair cut short—a sign among them of slavery and abjection—and enjoyed no more esteem than what their masters dispensed in proportion to their services."[6] Yet Comanche women were far from being as powerless as they may have appeared to be.

For example on the return of an important and victorious war party, especially if the men brought back scalps, old men sometimes ran through the village urging the unmarried women to give themselves, as a reward, to these latest heroes. If, on the other hand, the war party had failed, but without losing warriors, the prestige of the leader and his companions would fall among the women, a fact these men could surely read in their faces. If one or more warriors were lost, the women's reaction would be more dramatic. The wives and relatives of the dead would, of course, immediately begin mourning, loudly wailing and sobbing and slashing their arms and legs with knives. But the unsuccessful war chief himself might be the object of their ill-concealed or open anger. Jean Louis Berlandier told of how a Comanche head chief, Paruaquibitse, had once roused the "women of his tribe to a fury against the leader of a minor foray against the Spanish in which one of the chief's nephews had been lost."[7]

Captain John Salmon "Rip" Ford, of the Texas Rangers, observed another instance of feminine irrepressibility.[8] During a truce in 1849, Ford was traveling with a party of Comanches led by Chief Tall Tree. This war chief, serving as a guide for the Texans, was accompanied by among others his sister, over whom, as a Comanche male, he had life-or-death power. But when he began grumbling repeatedly about the short rations (the expedition was running out of provisions), his sister and her female friend finally gave him a scolding that Jim Shaw, a Delaware, interpreted approximately for Ford:

"You ought to be ashamed of yourself to complain. You seem to forget you're a Comanche war captain. Look at the other Indians—look at the white men! They're not saying a word!"

But perhaps the women's greatest power with respect to men was their potential for derision. Wallace and Hoebel report that women from time to time secretly fashioned a warbonnet for a man who exaggerated his deeds. They would present it to him in public (in itself a form of mockery), and the new owner would from then on be obliged to live up to the responsibilities of wearing it. In battle he would be marked out as a leader, having, for instance, the duty of assisting fallen comrades and of covering the retreat of other men. At the worst, if he should at any time give way to panic, tear off his warbonnet, and flee, he would be forever disgraced, and the other men would have the right to address him as "elder sister." But even in less extreme circumstances, no man could feel like a great warrior if he suspected the women of the People were snickering at him behind his back.

In Nuhmuhnuh culture little girls early learned "their place" in the tribe.[9] In contrast to the affection parents lavished on boys, neither mothers nor fathers ordinarily paid much attention to girls. Fathers, especially, took pride in fashioning their sons miniature bows, arrows, and lances, and encouraging their war games. When a boy reached the age of five, his father would usually give him a pony and begin mounting him upon it and allowing him to ride off by himself. The little girls also played at their future adult roles, dressing hides, setting up make-believe lodges, and carrying around dolls on their backs. Still as they grew older, many of them, their warrior fathers' daughters, became as proficient as the boys with bows and arrows and with la reata, while most of them became good horsewomen, some of them expert. Ferdinand von Roemer, a German scientist, noted that all women sat astride their horses like the men and rode "almost equally as gracefully." Captain Randolph Marcy once saw two older Comanche girls, each mounted on a swift pony, start into a dead run after a bunch of antelope; each snared one of the animals at the first toss of her lariat, dragging it, struggling, back with her.

As girls grew toward puberty and started thinking of themselves as women, they began painting themselves, like their mothers and aunts. Although Comanche women paid little attention to their hair, they reddened its part line with vermilion. Their eyes they accented with red or yellow lines, while they painted the insides of their ears red. On each cheek they colored a solid reddish-orange circle or triangle. In addition they sometimes tattooed their faces and breasts. Among the People no special rites (such as the Buffalo God Ceremony among the Teton Sioux) marked the puberty of girls. But afterwards, and presumably after gaining sexual experience, some might sneak into the tepees of boys slightly younger than themselves in order to initiate them sexually. These encounters took place in the dark. Though the Comanches placed no value on virginity, no girl wished to be the object of amused gossip throughout the camp.[10]

Generally girls married young, sometimes even before puberty. Colonel Richard I. Dodge wrote of attending a Plains Indian dance where the "belles of the evening" were "two little girls of about ten years old," who, he believed, were already beginning "to feel matrimonial hankerings." One Comanche chief, Sanaco, he declared, had as a wife "a pretty little maid of about ten years, of whom he was very fond." Chief Sanaco may, or may not, have had sexual relations with his ten-year-old bride. To have done so would not have been unheard-of, as will be apparent later. In any event, the chief doubtless had several other wives of older ages. Some chiefs had as many as eleven, several of whom were, in Hoebel's phrase, merely "chore wives." But the average warrior could support only two or three women, some only one wife.

Evidently there was little jealousy in these polygynous families, especially since the accepted tribal view was that sisters made the best wives. Usually the first wife possessed the most power and prestige. On the other hand, the chief might prefer the youngest and prettiest, whom he would make his favorite, or "sits-beside-him," wife. But the earlier wives welcomed newcomers, since each additional female meant an increased division in the amount of work they needed to accomplish daily. Nor was there ever a problem of too many children. The women of this nomadic people were continually on horseback. Many pregnancies aborted. The rigor of the women's lives meant that none was likely to bear many children. There was even some demand for captive children to adopt.

Although Comanche bands were relatively harmonious communities, one disruptive force was always at work within them. This was the competitive and aggressive nature of the men. It was a tension that frequently expressed itself through adultery. For an ambitious warrior to seduce or steal a rival's wife was a means of increasing his own prestige at the other man's expense. Yet such escapades were risky. If the lovers were surprised in the act, the consequences could be sudden and drastic. Anthony Glass, an American trader, was accompanying a group of Comanches in 1808 when, one morning, a warrior "caught his wife in bed with a man of his party." Immediately the injured husband shot the other man dead, and "then deliberately loaded his gun and shott [*sic*] his Wife also."[11] Usually a couple would run off together, remaining absent from their band for as long as a year. Ultimately, though, they would return, each to pay a price for disturbing social stability. By custom the offending warrior had to make reparations in the form of horses or other valuable property. Or he might choose to endure a public whipping by the aggrieved husband. Many men chose the latter form of repayment. If they endured the beating stoically, it further enhanced their prestige.

As for the woman, the husband had the right to kill her, not only for adultery but for any reason he chose. This form of homicide was not considered to be murder. "Not only was the position of woman largely that of chattel," the ethnologist E. Adamson Hoebel has observed, "but the chattel passed from the original family to the husband." [12] Yet in instances of adultery the injured husband was more likely to inflict the standard Plains (and Apache) punishment upon his wife by cutting off the tip of her nose, disfiguring her for life. Still sometimes he refrained, either because he cared for her, or, especially if she were pretty, because it decreased her value in horses and other goods. Robert S. Neighbors, Indian agent for both Texas and, later, the U.S. Government, contended around 1850 that more frequently than not the woman escaped suffering such penalties altogether. [13]

Ferdinand von Roemer, the German geologist, witnessed such an occasion. One morning an old man appeared before the council of chiefs with a sad expression. The previous night, he complained, some young men leaving on a war party had departed with his two best horses and his wife. Von Roemer recorded that the chiefs, clearly finding the old man's predicament comical, merely suggested that he pursue the war party and recover his property. That evening, doubtless to the scientist's surprise, the old Comanche returned, followed by his good-looking young wife riding on one of two mules. He explained that he had caught the young men, not far from camp, in the act of jerking the flesh of his slaughtered horses. Apparently acting firmly, he had retrieved his wife and appropriated two of his young rivals' mules. He was obviously pleased with this outcome of events. Jim Shaw, the Delaware interpreter, asked the old man why he had not cut off his wife's nose. The old man replied that he was happy to have her back and would not consider doing such a thing. [14]

Strangely, in a culture where females were, in effect, a form of property, any woman had the right to leave her husband—if she could find another man to take her in and pay for her. Using an old woman as a confidante, the discontented wife would ask her to approach several warriors or perhaps an individual warrior. If the go-between were able to find a man willing to reimburse the husband, the wife would simply depart and move into the new man's lodge. On discovering this the deserted husband would complain to the chiefs, who would discuss the matter and fix a price, in horses or other property, for the new husband to pay to the old. This amount was usually proportionate to the new man's wealth. When it had been paid, the matter was closed. The woman, though, had to leave her children with the former husband. Probably for this reason, few women took advantage of the custom, saving it for a last resort. An easier, though less certain, escape was for the wife to be extremely lax in performing her tasks. While this approach may have led to beatings, the exasperated husband often ended by tossing the woman out, severing all ties. Again, though, the wife had to abandon any children she had by the man.

On the other hand, some few Comanche girls were fortunate enough to become a "favorite child." Among Plains tribes there was an institutionalized practice of selecting an occasional child as a "favorite." (Each Comanche boy was apparently a "favorite child.") Wealthy families sometimes bestowed this distinction upon a girl, who, of course, became badly spoiled. Such a child wore good clothes, avoided most work, could order her siblings around, and was never forced into marriage. When she did marry, it was usually to a wealthy and important man, a union that could carry with it a peril for her, as will be seen. Such a woman was almost certain to escape the drudgery that fell to the lot of most Comanche women, and equally likely to escape any mistreatment by her husband.

Besides, if Richard I. Dodge is to be believed, the domestic life of the Plains Indians, in general, would have borne comparison with that in average white communities of the time. The husband was usually kind, he wrote; the warrior governed, but without harshness. The wives rarely quarreled with each other and, as a rule, were "faithful, obedient, and industrious," while the children were spoiled and, though afraid of white men, "a nuisance to all red visitors."

In spite of seeming to be "abject slaves" to Ugarte, Smithwick, Dodge, and other outsiders, Comanche women had a limited amount of power over their own destinies as well as over the direction of the tribe. This is to say that their lives were not devoid of all dignity and joy. Ordinarily girls experienced a period of courtship, when each was free to discourage or encourage one or more suitors. In fact since Comanche youths were shy, girls were expected to make the advances. Later, when a man made an offer for a girl—say, through his uncle—her father or brother made the final decision, with her wishes usually being considered, though not always respected. If the girl were chosen as a favorite wife, she supervised the other women and escaped the hardest chores. As the favorite, she shared in her husband's prestige and carried his shield when the band moved camp (except when she was menstruating). Yet the position of favorite wife could also hold serious risks, for until about the middle of the nineteenth century, the Comanches practiced a form of suttee. If the husband were a renowned warrior, a man of importance in his division, his family would, in the words of Jean Louis Berlandier, "break his weapons, kill his best horses, cut the throat of his favorite wife, and throw them all, together with food and clothing, into a deep trench . . . ," which they then filled with dirt.[15]

But even the ordinary wives, including those who were essentially servants, exercised, along with the other women in the band, some small authority. As Colonel Richard Dodge observed of Plains Indian women in general: they possessed a certain "weight and influence, not only in their own household, but in all the affairs of the tribe." The good and competent woman who had proved herself over the years held the respect of all.[16]

It would have been surprising if at least some of the Comanche women had not been redoubtable beings. Daring young women—and sometimes older ones, too—frequently accompanied war parties, where they not only guarded the extra ponies and plunder during battles, but formed a line of defense, backing the men with bows and arrows. The Texas Rangers found them as dangerous as the warriors and killed them without compunction during combat. Later the U.S. Cavalry did the same, largely perhaps because during the smoke and dust of battle it was difficult to distinguish mounted male warriors from their female counterparts. Captain Robert Carter later defended the practice, generalizing about the women of the Comanches and their southern plains allies: this Plains Indian woman

> when cornered . . . fought with all the strength of her savage nature and desperation of a tigress, using her bow and arrows and six-shooter with both of which she was an excellent shot. There were few or none, of the "peace and order" loving members of the pussy-footed pacifists of that period, or members of the press, who often times referred to her as the "poor *defenseless* (?) *squaw*," who would have cared to put themselves in her way under any conditions of battle, especially when she screamed in a perfect fury of rage.[17]

If Comanche men were known for fighting to the death (Noah Smithwick twice saw wounded warriors lie on their backs and fight until they died) certain of the Ietan women were their equals. During the Mexican period in Texas, for instance, presidials once captured a Comanche woman who, when they were leading her back to the garrison, asked for a knife to remove a thorn from her foot. Immediately upon grasping it, she plunged the blade into her heart.

But the most intriguing hints as to feminine prowess appear in two accounts separated by almost a decade. In the winter of 1835–36, James Hobbs, a captive among northern Comanches, rode south with a war party of some four hundred men to raid deep into Mexico. Hobbs, who had already proved himself and been accepted into the tribe, later described this extended foray, along with a curious detail. The great raiding party, he reported, penetrated as far south as Monclova. Surrounding that town of about two thousand residents, the marauders killed forty or fifty mexicanos, taking twenty scalps. There was nothing unusual in this, of course. But Hobbs went on casually to describe the individual who rode before this army—a young Comanche girl, looked on by the warriors as a kind of "angel of good or ill luck." Riding a fast horse, the girl preceded the line of battle, leading charges, as expert a horsewoman as she was an archer. Evidently the war chiefs of the party later believed their success in this campaign to be owing, in part, to the girl's "boldness and cool daring."

At first the reader of Hobb's memoires is inclined to ascribe this particular to the frontiersman's imagination and his desire to thrill an audience. But eight or nine years later, a corroborating account appeared in *El Registro Oficial*, the department of Durango's newspaper. Among reports of devastating Comanche raids during that November of 1844, a witness mentioned one party of five hundred warriors accompanied by an elaborately dressed Comanche girl riding a big horse with many trappings. Ralph A. Smith, the American historian who unearthed this detail, compared her to a "sort of Indian Joan of Arc," whose role was to inspire the men in battle.

Plainly not all Comanche women were "abject slaves." In fact the most seemingly abject among them possessed, as will be seen, a darker side, which could be as grim and implacable as that of the men on their raids against the settlements.

NINE

Pierre Vial, Explorer on the Plains, 1786–1793

The 1786 treaty made the southern plains relatively safe, though not without risk, for comancheros, as well as for those Hispanic and Pueblo buffalo hunters, the *ciboleros*. It also began an era of exploration of plains country east of New Mexico and north of San Antonio de Béxar. Foremost among the explorers of the 1780s and 1790s was a Frenchman called don Pedro by his Spanish employers. Of course his real name was Pierre, Pierre Vial. Born in Lyon, probably between 1746 and 1755, he shipped to Canada, where he lived for some time. Eventually he roamed down into the upper Missouri country. Next he lived in St. Louis, when it formed part of Spanish Illinois. He may have acquired his speaking knowledge of Spanish there. Apparently a restless man, and possibly a *contrebandier*, he again traveled southward, where at some point the Comanches captured him. He remained with them for several years. Ultimately free again, he resided in one of the Taovayas villages along the Red River. There he practiced the craft of gunsmithing, undoubtedly a reason for his survival.[1]

In 1779 Vial stopped by Natchitoches to release and receive compensation for a Spanish captive he had ransomed. Spanish officials repaid him the value of the ransom and made their report to higher authorities. When the governor of Louisiana, Bernardo de Gálvez, learned of the gunsmith who had been living illegally among the Nations of the North, he ordered that the man be prohibited from returning. In spite of the governor's order, Pierre Vial managed to slip by Spanish outposts and make his way back to the plains, where he remained, again with Wichitan people, for almost another six years.

Another Frenchman, Jean Baptiste Bousquet, on a mission for the governor of Texas, found him in 1785 living in a Taovayas village and persuaded Vial to return with him to San Antonio. Vial accompanied Bousquet, bringing two more captives with him, a little Apache girl and a young Spanish woman, for whose ransom he was again reimbursed. Governor Cabello of Texas willingly pardoned him, pleased to have another interpreter who spoke both the language of Wichitans and that of the Comanches. Pierre Vial joined the little community as smith and armorer. As such he was a valuable asset, especially to the presidio. His presence, in fact, was Spain's great good fortune. From then on Spanish authorities made extensive use of this adventurous blacksmith who was also an extraordinary frontiersman.

In 1786 Vial offered to establish a trail, traveling alone, that would link San Antonio (often "Béxar" to the Spaniards) and Santa Fe. Spain had long wished to connect the capitals of her two northern provinces. This was an opportunity. Jacobo Ugarte y Loyola, commander general of the interior provinces, accepted Vial's proposal, ordering Governor Cabello to outfit and dispatch the Frenchman on the mission. No matter what happened, it would not be any great expense to the crown.

Early in October Pierre Vial left Béxar with a single companion, Cristóbal de los Santos, and a packhorse. On the second day out the packhorse drowned crossing the Río de Guadalupe, and all the supplies for the trip were lost in the stream. Apparently Vial refused to consider turning back. By the middle of the month, though, he had become ill, so ill that on the fourteenth he fell unconscious from his horse in an arroyo, lying senseless for two hours. When he revived, his companion begged him for a letter explaining that, if he should die, Cristóbal was innocent of his death. Vial sat up and said he trusted God he would not die. But they must now change course and head north for the Tawakoni villages, where some Indian might be able to cure him.

The two men rode northwestward, day after day, for about two weeks. By the twenty-ninth, at two in the afternoon, they rode into Chief Quiscat's village on the Brazos River near the present town of Waco. The people came out of their grass huts, astonished to see him, and asked where he was going.

"To the Comanches." He explained that from the Comanches he intended to find a trail to Santa Fe. Now, though, he was sick. Could anyone cure him?

"Yes," said Chief Quiscat. "I'll get someone to heal you."

So he did, keeping Vial in his own lodge. His people took care of the explorer until mid-December, when he was well enough to depart.

From the Tawakonies, Vial seems to have traveled northwestward along the Brazos, then due north to the Taovayas and Wichita villages on the Red River, near what is now Ringgold, Texas. In all there were three villages, two on the opposite side of the river from the other. Each was made up of about seventeen grass lodges. (Captain Randolph Marcy, in 1852, thought they resembled haystacks). The villages were surrounded by fields of beans, maize, pumpkins, and watermelons. Tribal horses grazed at a distance.

Vial remained with the Taovayases and Wichitas until January 6, 1787. On the ninth, in company with many Taovayases, he rode to a Comanche camp. He went directly to the lodge of the band's head chief, Zoquiné, and found him absent; the chief had gone to recover horses Comanches had stolen from the Taovayases, in order to redistribute them to their owners.[2] When Chief Zoquiné returned, he welcomed Vial, calling a council in his tepee. Many chiefs entered to smoke and pass the pipe. They asked first where he was going:

"Santa Fe."

"Why Santa Fe?"

"Your father, the captain at San Antonio," he said, "is sending me to open a road from there to Santa Fe. I'm taking a letter to the captain at Santa Fe, so the Spaniards and Comanches can ride freely from one place to another. You know, the Spaniards look on the Comanches as brothers. The captain sees them as his sons."

The chiefs said they were pleased. Right now, though, it was not possible to travel, because of the great cold and deep snows at Santa Fe. They invited him to spend the winter with them. In spring they would go with him to Santa Fe. In the meantime, had he heard that the Comanche chief he had known at San Antonio had been killed?

No, he had not.

"Yes, that chief had been killed by the Spaniards."

By the Spaniards . . . ? But, why?

Then they told him this story:

Many Comanches left on a campaign against the Apaches. They were riding across a plain when they came upon the tracks of horsemen. They followed the tracks and reached a camp of men they believed to be Spaniards, because they made so much noise. The war party rode off to continue looking for Apaches. But they sent two young men back to spy on the camp. That night the young men came back and reported hearing the people talk, but they could not be sure what nation they were from.

Then the Comanches prepared to attack, believing the strangers to be Apaches. At daybreak, about four in the morning, the war party started off at a gallop. But the two young men, who had faster ponies, or whipped them harder, got there first. This time they saw the people really were Spaniards. By then the soldiers had seen them and had begun shouting to the Comanches, behaving as friends, as they had often done in the past. Still, the young men proposed stealing the Spaniards' horses. A chief named Patuarus, who had just ridden up, objected. The Spaniards were friends, he said. Why harm them? The young fools then accused the older warriors of being afraid. They even told Patuarus that if he insisted on being friends with the Spaniards, they would not recognize him as chief any more. Patuarus became furious.

"Not all you Comanches are fit to face danger before the Spaniards!"

At this taunt the Comanches immediately fired into the camp. The soldiers returned fire, killing Patuarus and another chief. The Spaniards laid down such heavy fire that the Comanches spun their ponies and galloped away. At a little distance, they stopped. The chiefs rebuked the youths for having started the fight. They raised a Spanish flag. A chief named Tanicón, who was Zoquiné's brother, and Chief Guaquangas, rode back and surrendered to the Spaniards. The Spanish captain, don José Menchaca, came up to the two chiefs and embraced them. Other Spaniards and other Comanches rode up. They buried the two dead chiefs and set the flag at the head of the most important one.

After that the Comanches traded with the Spaniards and came home.

Don't worry, though, the chiefs reassured Vial. We won't harm you, even though the relatives of the dead men are here around you. Because the dead men were guilty.

Silence in the lodge.

"But you aren't guilty," Vial said, at last. "The Spaniards look on all of you as brothers—even though you're not like them. When the Spaniards believe a nation is friendly, they don't act treacherously toward them, as those chiefs did."

The council agreed that was true.

Nearly a week later, on January 17, the chiefs again gathered in Zoquiné's lodge to smoke with Vial. At their request he scribbled a note to Governor Cabello, asking him to send some tobacco, which they were nearly out of. They dispatched the note by a minor chief, with a strong young warrior for company. Even though they had sent only two men, the chiefs now complained about the risky distance of San Antonio from their usual range. En route there was danger from both Tonkawas and Apaches. The chiefs were even audacious enough to suggest that the Spaniards reestablish their abandoned presidio on the San Sabá River (avoiding the awkward subject of the massacre they and their Wichitan allies had perpetrated at the San Sabá mission twenty-nine years earlier). That site would be much more convenient for them. Or the Spaniards could found a settlement on the Pedernales River. In that case they could trade there. The young men could hunt in their home range, without being tempted to make trouble near Béxar.

Vial no doubt assured the Comanches he would convey their suggestions to the captains in San Antonio and Santa Fe. The council ended with a sense of accord and good feeling. The Frenchman should have congratulated himself on his sure handling of meetings that could have been dangerous. Possibly he even imagined he had put the most precarious moments of the trip behind him. But as experienced as he was, he must have known that on the plains, and with the Comanches, a man could never predict what crisis might arise next.

On January 18 the Comanches broke camp and traveled west until they stopped for the night in a gully with a stream. The following day the women again dismantled the tepees and loaded all their baggage on travoises. Once more the band set off westward, riding under the winter sun, until they halted, later that day, by the same stream. There this band of the Nuhmuhnuh established their winter camp, with their lodges erected at intervals along the creek, in the general vicinity of today's Burkburnett, Texas. They remained at that site nearly until spring.

In early March the band broke camp and traveled uneventfully until the night of April 7. That evening two Comanches from another band arrived. At once they put the Frenchman in a precarious position. Before Chief Zoquiné and others, they told Vial that three Comanches had come to their camp from San Antonio. These three had warned them that the explorer intended to trick the People: the captains at Béxar and Santa Fe had exchanged letters agreeing that any large groups of Comanches coming to trade in either city were to be massacred. They accused him of leading Zoquiné and his people to Santa Fe so that they might be murdered there.

"You Comanches shouldn't believe Spaniards would act so treacherously," said Vial calmly, turning to the messengers. "Because these two have bad hearts, they think the Spaniards are like themselves."

Zoquiné stood by Vial. He would not leave him, the chief asserted, until he saw him in Santa Fe. By his presence of mind the explorer had overcome what was probably the most dangerous challenge of his journey. On May 2 Vial and de los Santos left the band of Comanches with whom they had wintered. Accompanied by four chiefs (surely including Zoquiné) and two braves, along with their wives, the explorer and his companion struck out westward, following the Canadian River. Somewhere near the site of present Logan, New Mexico, the party encountered a camp of Yamparica Comanches. The chief, Paranuarimuco, produced a Spanish flag and escorted the group to his lodge. There he hosted and entertained them, talking to them especially about the captain in Santa Fe (de Anza), with whom he was pleased.

Now within some ten days travel of his destination, Vial did not linger.

The next day the party set out again, northwestward. By May 25 they had reached Pecos Pueblo. The following day don Pedro, with de los Santos and the dozen Comanches, who were no doubt painted and in their dress regalia, rode into Santa Fe bearing the Spanish flag. Presidial troops trotted out to greet them. Vial jogged with the soldiers to the governor's palace. Presumably before the palace, he formally delivered the banner to Captain don Manuel Delgado, with this ritual marking the end of his journey.

Vial's trip, the first by a Spanish emissary into the plains since the peace of 1786, illustrates how vast a change had occurred there. Although the southern plains were still dangerous, and the tribes living on them could be alarmingly unpredictable, the Frenchman and his companion had traveled some 1,157 miles, coping with the loss of their supplies, serious illness, parleys with proud and sometimes self-righteous chiefs, even with accusations of treachery, and had survived it all to enter Santa Fe with an illustrious escort of the very Indians who until recently had been the Spaniards' most deadly enemies. It was a remarkable achievement.

But during this period of exploration, several other journeys, equally extraordinary, followed Vial's. The same month that don Pedro arrived in Santa Fe, July 1787, Governor de Anza dispatched a retired presidial corporal, José Mares, on a return trip to San Antonio. Mares was accompanied by Cristóbal de los Santos and Alexandro Martín, the former captive, who served as interpreter. On the outward trip they fell in with a Comanche band who led them out of their way to the Taovayas villages, where the People were going to trade, so that Mares retraced Vial's route. But on the return trip, the corporal traveled more directly, once again guided by Comanches. For the final leg, in fact, a friendly chief lent him two of his sons to show the Spaniard the way to the capital city. Mares arrived there in June of 1788, shortening Vial's distance by some 125 miles.

Pierre Vial led the following two trips. The first reached from Santa Fe to Natchitoches, Louisiana, in itself a stretch of over 900 miles, then to San Antonio, then back to Santa Fe. This time the explorer had more company. Three cavalrymen escorted him to the Taovayases on the way out, before turning back. Four New Mexicans, volunteers for the adventure, accompanied him throughout the entire trip, which began in 1788 and ended the next year. But the second of the two explorations was the fateful one.

In 1792 Vial left Santa Fe with two young New Mexicans, Vicente Villanueva and Vicente Espinosa, with a letter from de Anza's successor, Governor don Fernando de la Concha, to the governor of Spanish Illinois, Zénon Trudeau. En route, by the Arkansas River, he and his companions encountered hostile Kansa Indians, who slashed their clothes from their bodies and were about to kill them. A Kansa whom Vial had known in Louisiana saved their lives, but the three men were held naked as prisoners for three months, first in the Kansas' hunting camp, later in their village on the banks of the Kansas River, which empties into the Missouri. Finally they were freed by a French trader who had ventured upstream. The trader took them in his pirogue down the Missouri River to St. Louis, where they arrived a dozen years before Lewis and Clark pushed off on their epic journey up the same waterway. There Vial reported to the commandant and received instructions for his return trip.

The Frenchman and the two Vicentes left St. Louis the following June, arriving in Santa Fe late that fall. Meanwhile Vial had parleyed with Pawnee chiefs, following his orders to try arranging a treaty between the Pawnees and Comanches. Nearly successful, he was frustrated by encountering a Pawnee war party bent on revenge against the Comanches. Beside what was probably the North Canadian River, the warriors attacked his little camp at midnight. Luckily they recognized Pawnee horses before injuring any of his group, although they did send back the Pawnee peace envoys who were accompanying him. Some two weeks later, in the region near Tucumcari Peak, New Mexico, the explorer rescued a lone Comanche who stumbled into camp naked, without weapons or even moccasins, dying from exposure, hunger, and thirst. Clothing and feeding the man, he brought him with him. Finally on November 15, 1793, after an absence of a year and a half and a round trip of nearly twenty-three hundred miles, Vial and his companions rode into Santa Fe at nightfall. The explorer immediately went to the palace and sought out Governor de la Concha, handing him a letter from Trudeau in St. Louis.

The explorer's third journey was fateful for two reasons. For one thing it alerted Spanish officials to the relative proximity of Santa Fe and St. Louis. It made them aware of New Mexico's vulnerability to aggressive American frontiersmen. Commandant Trudeau wrote the governor of Louisiana that Vial had claimed he could have made the trip out in twenty-five days, if he had not been captured by the Kansas. Equally important from a historical perspective, when Vial and his two companions pioneered a route between Santa Fe and St. Louis, they inaugurated the Santa Fe Trail. William Becknell of Missouri is usually credited with initiating the trail in 1821, and he did, in terms of trade. But the honor of the first round trip by men of European descent probably belongs to Pierre Vial and the two young New Mexicans in 1792 and 1793.

Some thirteen years later, in 1806, the Comanches participated in an event of great consequence to them. The event is recorded in a story passed down from one generation to the next among the Kiowas; their tradition has it that two separate parties of Comanches and Kiowas, enemies at that time, arrived at the house of a New Mexican, possibly a comanchero, who was on good terms with both peoples. This nuevomexicano was able to arrange a parley between the hostile groups of warriors. During the talk a Comanche chief, Pareiya (Afraid-of-Water), invited a Kiowa chief, Gui-k'ati (Wolf-Lying-Down), to return with him to his camp and spend the summer there. During that time they could talk about peace between the two peoples. Wolf-Lying-Down, the second most important Kiowa in the tribe, accepted the invitation. But he told his braves to return to the trader's house when the leaves turned yellow. If he were not there, the Kiowas were to avenge his murder.

The party of Kiowas left. Wolf-Lying-Down rode off with Afraid-of-Water and his warriors. They traveled south of Pareiya's camp on the Brazos River, where the Kiowa spent the summer among the Comanches. The People entertained him as a guest. That fall Wolf-Lying-Down met his warriors, as agreed upon, at the trader's house, and there was peace between the tribes.

The historian Elizabeth John has found evidence in the Santa Fe archives that bears out at least part of the Kiowa account and places that treaty definitely in 1806. Possibly the Spanish go-between, if there was one, was *Carabinero* Juan Lucero, an interpreter friendly with both Comanches and Kiowas. In any event the Gui-k'ate of the story appears almost surely to have been a Kiowa chief the Spaniards knew as "El Ronco" ("the hoarse one"). That same year he married a daughter of Pareiya and moved in with the Yamparicas. This was the beginning of lasting peace between the two peoples.[3]

TEN

American Advances, 1800–1807

Napoleon Bonaparte in 1803 sold Louisiana to the United States, contrary to his agreement with Spain. The limits of this vast region were so vague that Thomas Jefferson, despite the doubts of knowledgeable advisers, became convinced that the new American territory extended westward to the Río Grande—an interpretation that would have made El Paso, Santa Fe, and Taos American settlements. For sixteen years Spain and the United States disagreed over the boundary of the Louisiana Purchase, with many Americans persuaded that Spanish Texas rightfully belonged to their own nation. Finally in 1819 the Adams-Onís Treaty settled the dispute.

By the terms of that agreement, Spain reluctantly ceded Florida to the United States. In return Washington assumed a five-million-dollar Spanish debt to American citizens, dropped its claim to Texas, and agreed with Spain upon a boundary line separating U.S. and Spanish North American possessions. This line ascended the Sabine River to the Red, running northwest along it until the hundredth meridian. There it rose directly north to the Arkansas, following that river west to the Rockies, and stretching from those snowy peaks to the Pacific. Meanwhile, early in 1804, Spain claimed the Missouri River as the international boundary. In the interim, until 1821, when the Adams-Onís Treaty was ratified, some Americans trespassed into northern New Spain, while the Spaniards held their ground and continued to cultivate their Plains Indian friends, including the Pawnees, who lived on the Platte River, far north of the Arkansas, in present Nebraska.

Even before the Louisiana Purchase, one American adventurer, Philip Nolan, was entering Texas to seize wild horses for sale in the United States. On good terms with the Comanches, he lived with them intermittently for two years during his first trip, probably made shortly after 1790. As a result of this first effort, he drove back 50 horses. On his second trip he was more successful, returning to U.S. territory with 250 head. These he sold in what would become the states of Mississippi (a territory as of 1798) and Kentucky (admitted into the Union in 1792). In all Nolan made four expeditions before 1800, bringing back some 1,00 head on one occasion. But Spanish officials became increasingly suspicious of him, and in 1801, when he entered Texas without a passport, he paid with his life for the illegal entry.

With the help of Tawakoni scouts, Lieutenant Francisco Músquiz, commander at Nacogdoches, found him on a tributary of the Brazos, now called Nolan's Creek, in today's Hill County. Músquiz, leading 120 men, called on Nolan and his party of 24 to surrender. But the mustanger and his mixed group of Spaniards and Americans chose to resist from within their fortified camp, whose corrals already contained 200–300 head of horses. After exchanges of fire, the Spaniards killed Nolan. His companions surrendered. From that time on, Spanish authorities, who suspected Nolan of having been a spy for the United States, if not a filibuster, remained constantly on guard against American interlopers.

The Lewis and Clark Military Expedition up the Missouri River (1804–6) increased apprehension among Spanish officials from Havana to Santa Fe. As one result the governor of New Mexico, Don Joaquín del Real Alencaster, again dispatched Pierre Vial in 1805 on a mission to the Pawnees. In particular Alencaster instructed him to "acquire news and knowledge of the state of Captain Merri's expedition of the Missouri River and the trade and commerce of the nations located on it with the Anglo-Americans." If the opportunity should arise, Vial was to influence all tribes he encountered against the expedition. He was to persuade the Indians that the Spaniards alone deserved their friendship. There could be no risk, he declared, in trading with Spaniards. But the only motive of the Americans in trying to win their friendship was the desire to destroy them in a few years, so as to possess the Missouri River and the land on either side of it.

Don Pedro left Taos October of 1805, commanding a force of fifty men. It was the first sizable military expedition to strike out for the Pawnees since the Villasur disaster in 1720. If Vial had not been in command, it might have ended as badly. The expedition followed the Purgatoire River northeastward to its junction with the Arkansas. Somewhere in the vicinity of today's Las Animas, Colorado, on November 5, three bands of whooping horsemen attacked their camp at midnight. The enemy numbered more than a hundred. The main objective of the raiders, who uttered no word except for their cries, seemed to be to capture the horse herd. Vial and most of his troops galloped to help the horse guard. After some three hours of fighting, in which the herd changed hands several times, the explorer and his soldiers drove the enemy into the Arkansas River. But on returning to camp, he found that the strangers had looted it, stealing virtually everything. Without utensils, supplies, or presents for the Pawnees, Vial was obliged to turn back. That morning as he was leaving, the hostile

Indians attacked again, harassing the expedition for eight miles before disappearing. The crippled expedition returned to Santa Fe.

But who were the attackers? Vial, that expert on the Plains Indians, was baffled in his attempt to identify them. They did not fight half-naked, so they were not Kiowas. They were not Pawnees, who did not employ horses in warfare. Might they have been Comanches? New Mexico's governor thought perhaps they were, but probably none of the Nuhmuhnuh could have deceived Vial. Who, then, were these unknown Indians who concealed their language, each with a cloth tied around his head, carrying a gun, not bow and arrows, and fully dressed in colors of *red, white, and blue?* Governor Alencaster was convinced that Americans were behind the attack. He wrote the commandant general of the interior provinces, Don Nemesio Salcedo y Salcedo, that the Indians, whatever their nation, had been "incited by the Americans" in order to discourage Spanish friendship for and trade with the Pawnees. As for Vial, the Frenchman made two important recommendations to his superiors. First, he suggested that future expeditions be larger, with greater firepower, writing that "one cannot travel on these roads with so few men nor with so few munitions. All these nations are very avaricious when they go out on a war raid or campaign; if they meet anyone, whoever it may be, if they have some goods, they take these away from them; and he runs the risk of being killed . . ." [1] This was advice that later American travelers on the southern plains might have done well to memorize. Second, he wrote that "for the security of our province, it is advisable to construct a fort on the Arkansas River in order to subdue all the tribes, as well as to avoid the entrance of the Americans . . ."

The higher Spanish authorities rejected Vial's second recommendation, although it was endorsed by Alencaster. Some twenty-eight years later, Charles Bent, holding a United States' permit, began trading with the Cheyennes and other Plains Indians from his fort on the Arkansas River. That fort, flying the American flag, was located on the north bank opposite the region where the mysterious Indians wearing red, white and blue had attacked Vial and his Spanish troops.

Spanish officials proved more receptive to the explorer's first recommendation. In 1806 Commandant General Salcedo dispatched Lieutenant Facundo Melgares to Santa Fe with 105 men.[2] In the provincial capital, the lieutenant added 400 militiamen and 100 Indian auxiliaries, leading them down the Red River on two missions. First he was to halt the advance of Thomas Freeman's reconnaissance party of 50 men, 45 of whom were an American military escort, up that stream. Second he was to achieve a treaty with the Pawnees.

Two years before, Thomas Jefferson had written Freeman, a civilian explorer, with instructions for his expedition up the Red into the heart of Comanchería. Among these directions the American president had emphasized the importance of winning over the Texas Indians, ordering the civil engineer to "court an intercourse with the natives as intensively as you can" and to "inform them that their late fathers the Spaniards have agreed to withdraw all their troops from the Mississippi and Missouri *and from all the countries watered by any rivers running into them . . .* "[3] Of course the "late fathers" of the Texas tribes had done nothing of the kind and had absolutely no intention of doing so. On July 28, 1806, another Spanish officer, Captain Francisco Viana, leading 212 men, turned back the Freeman probe a little east of today's Oklahoma border, abruptly terminating what has been called the "Lewis and Clark expedition of the Southwest."[4]

Learning this, Lieutenant Melgares marched his troops northward toward the Arkansas River. En route he encountered a band of Skidi Pawnees, with whom he held what seemed to be a successful parley. But that night the Panismahas disillusioned him by running off a large number of horses from his caballada of some two thousand head. Undiscouraged the lieutenant posted half of his command on the Arkansas and rode northward to meet with the main body of the Pawnee nation. He found them on the Republican River. (Pawnee territory seems to have extended at that time from the Niobrara River in present northern Nebraska southward through the valley of the Platte to the Republican River in present northern Kansas). There he successfully concluded a treaty with the tribe. Satisfied he had fulfilled his mission, Lieutenant Melgares rode back to the Arkansas River, retrieved his waiting troops, and returned to Santa Fe.

Melgares missed an American expedition by a month.[5] He had hardly returned when First Lieutenant Zebulon M. Pike left St. Louis (in July 1806) for the purpose of reconnoitering the region between that city and the Rocky Mountains; as well as, it seems, of scouting the Santa Fe area. Pike acted only by authorization of the treacherous James Wilkinson, governor general of Louisiana Territory, and the man, incidentally, who had raised Philip Nolan. (Wilkinson, also a secret agent for Spain, was a party to the Burr conspiracy to separate the Louisiana Territory from the United States and, with British help, to establish it as an independent nation; later he betrayed Burr.) By the use of diplomacy and daring, Pike passed through the Pawnees and made his way to the Rockies.

That February Spanish soldiers captured Zebulon Montgomery and a small party of his men west of the Río Grande near today's Sanford, Colorado, where they had built a log fort. Governor Alencaster sent Pike and the fifteen men to Chihuahua. Commandant General Salcedo returned the lieutenant to Natchitoches in July 1807, after directing a letter of protest to General Wilkinson. Eight of the American soldiers remained as prisoners for the next two and a half years (with a Sergeant Meek held until 1820), arousing indignation among the American public. The Spaniards had reason to be alarmed over the affair. Pike was obviously scouting and spying, and it was apparent to them that this had been the intent of his expedition from the beginning.

If the presence of Americans on the eastern frontier of northern New Spain made Spanish officials increasingly uneasy, the evidence suggests that the Comanches, on the other hand, held a largely favorable attitude toward the newcomers. In 1822, for example, Stephen Austin, "the father of Texas," was traveling between San Antonio and Mexico City. In Mexican Texas, near the Nueces River, a war party of fifty Comanches captured him and a companion. But when the Comanches learned the two men were Americans, they returned nearly all of their belongings and released them. That same month, in a letter, Austin interpreted the incident by noting that the Comanches' "partiality for Americans [was] explained by their illicit trading relations with certain Americans . . . ," who were probably operating mainly in the vicinity of Natchitoches.[6] Also indicative of the People's attitude toward *americanos* was the fact that three years later, when Comanches were raiding San Antonio, they left Austin's little colony alone.

Most of the Comanches raiding sporadically around San Antonio throughout the 1820s and 1830s probably belonged to that branch of the Cuchanticas, or Cuchanecs (later, Kotsotekas), whom the Spaniards called the *orientales*. In the first half of the nineteenth century, these eastern Comanches evolved into, or produced an offshoot known as, the Penatekas (Honey-Eaters), destined to become famous and infamous in Texas history. Precisely when this change occurred is uncertain. A modern scholar, Thomas W. Kavanagh, believes the new division emerged in the middle to late 1840s, noting that the appellation first appeared in 1846. Until 1845 it is probably fair to continue referring to these bands as orientales, but since most Texas historians use "Penateka" consistently to designate the southern Comanches, the present work will employ the terms interchangeably through 1846. Whatever their name, these Comanches ranged principally within the boundaries of what is now the state of Texas, pitching their tepees and hunting especially upon the Edwards Plateau, north and west of the Balcones Escarpment and the town of Béxar.

The increasingly frequent appearance of the orientales in the vicinity of San Antonio was only one of several developments among the Nuhmuhnuh around the turn of the century. These developments included a substantial population increase along with a continued tribal drift southward. Clearly the People were prospering on the plains, each division subsisting upon the enormous herds of buffalo, no matter what its name implied. The Yupes disappeared around this time or earlier, probably becoming absorbed as bands of the Yamparicas. The Yamparicas, still the northernmost division, dragged their travoises from the vague boundary of the Arkansas River southward to the indefinite range of the Kotsotekas (Buffalo-Eaters), who roamed throughout what is presently western Oklahoma, frequently setting up their lodges along the Canadian River and farther southward to the lower Río Pecos. East of the Buffalo-Eaters, and probably somewhat later, ranged the Nokonis (Wanderers), a smaller division that had emerged by 1846. Also in existence by the time of Texas annexation was the Tenewa division (Downstream People), a cluster of bands occupying the region yet farther eastward, within and around the Cross Timbers, from the Arkansas River to the headwaters to the Trinity. According to Kavanagh, this cluster probably included the Tanimas (Liver-Eaters). Finally the Quahadas, thought to be another offshoot of the Kotsotekas, appeared in the 1860s and prowled across the Llano Estacado, becoming known as the most remote of all these unions of bands.[7] Yet whatever the names and ranges of their divisions, the Comanches were culturally a single people and shared both enemies and friends. For nearly half a century a significant number of them placed Americans in the latter category.

Fifteen years before Stephen Austin's capture and release, an incident occurred in American Natchitoches that had an interesting, if largely symbolic, import—that perhaps of a straw in the wind. In 1807 it happened that a party of Yamparica, or possibly eastern Kotsoteka, Comanches visited John Sibley, M.D., the acting Indian agent there.[8] Sibley treated his visitors courteously and distributed presents to them. He then convened a great council of almost three hundred Indians belonging to tribes in the region. Before this assemblage, with the comanches about to depart, the doctor later reported to the Secretary of War that, in his words, "the Principal Chief produced a Spanish flag and Layed it down at my feet, and desired the Interpreter to tell me, that he received that Flag from Governor Cordero of St. Antonio and wished now to exchange it for a flag of the United States, that it might be better known in their Nation." At first Dr. Sibley coyly demurred, explaining that his country was at peace with Spain, and that he had no wish to offend the Spanish government. But the chief insisted, saying it was all the same to him whether Spain was offended or not. He went on to promise that if Sibley would give him a flag, "it Should wave through all the Hietan Nation, and they would all die in defence of it before they would part with it." At that John Sibley, no doubt jubilantly, gave in and presented the chief with an American flag.[9]

One of the chiefs with that Ietan party may have been Pisinape, or the "Decayed Shoe" of de Anza's 1786 treaty.[10] (By 1810, three years later, he was to become increasingly involved with American traders.) In any event, at some time before their departure, Sibley invited the four chiefs to his home, "Entertain'd them, Gave them Tobacco, Smok'd with them etc. Offered them Spirits, which they refus'd . . . Sent for a Taylor & had them Measured each of them for a Scarlet Coat faced with Black Velvet & trim'd with white Buttons . . ."[11]

Ironically Zebulon Montgomery Pike, now Captain Pike, had left Natchitoches only a few days before this. The captain, during his expedition to the Rockies the previous year, had vainly sought the Comanches in order to "establish a good understanding" with the people whom General Wilkinson had called "that distant powerful nation." Pike told Sibley the American government wanted friendship with the tribe, and that this was the first opportunity available to any American official of implementing the policy. So it appears that not only were the Nuhmuhnuh intrigued with the Americans, but that the United States government long before the Dragoon Expedition of 1834 was determined to court the Comanches.

ELEVEN

Encounters in Comanchería, *1808–1845*

B ecause there are only so many eyewitness perspectives on the Comanches, the person wishing to tell their story, or any significant part of it, must also rely on actions of their adversaries and allies to advance the narrative. This in no way violates the limits of the subject. It is in fact an occasional enlargement of scope justified by the importance the Nuhmuhnuh gave to the distinction between enemy and friend. An early Texan, Victor M. Ross (a source for James T. DeShields' *Border Wars of Texas*), erroneously called the Comanches "veritable Ishmaelites," with "their hands . . . raised against all men, and every man's hand against them." To the contrary, the People were keenly aware of the responsibilities owed to allies. In 1812, for example, a prominent New Mexican, Pedro Bautista Pino, praised them for honoring "with the greatest care all the conditions of treaties," going on to write that the Spaniards made a mighty effort to do likewise.

In the early nineteenth century, relations between the Comanches and their Kiowa allies gradually grew closer even than those existing between the Nuhmuhnuh and the Spaniards of New Mexico during the period of their greatest cordiality. As the nineteenth century progressed, the Comanches and Kiowas, while remaining culturally distinct, became at times virtually a single people. Frequently they camped together, hunted together, traveled on raids together, even deep into Mexico. They fought, side by side or separately, against the same enemies and traded, both of them, with the comancheros and the Wichitas.

In contrast the Comanches' relationship with the Wichitan peoples, their other traditional allies, fluctuated over the decades, ranging from friendship to outright hostility and war. For instance as early as the spring of 1778, the Taovayases complained to Athanase de Mézières that the Comanches visited them as friends but stole from them, a breach of amity they were then overlooking. They did so because they and the Comanches needed each other. The Nuhmuhnuh needed the outlet for trade that they found, especially, at the Taovayas and Wichita villages on the Red River.

All of the Wichitans, including the Tawakonies and the Iscanis (later known as "Wacos"), badly needed the Comanches as allies against their enemies, the Lipans and the powerful Osages, who were armed with English guns. The Lipans and Osages were also among the People's principal enemies before white settlers approached the southern plains. As a result the Comanches and the Wichitan peoples rarely remained at war for long and were far more often friends and allies than they were enemies. Peace between Comanches and Wichitans, of course, included the Kiowas. This alliance, in turn, tended to look upon Americans with a generally favorable attitude, at least until around 1846.[1]

In response to American activity, Governor Manuel Antonio Cordero y Bustamante of Texas wrote Commandant General Salcedo early in 1808, proposing a military expedition to Santa Fe. It would make sense to find a route, with adequate water, suitable for wheeled vehicles, just in case. At the same time its leader might reaffirm and strengthen ties with the Comanches. Evidently Salcedo concurred with Cordero's reasoning. That March the governor began organizing the expedition. It would consist of two hundred mounted regulars and militia, along with carts and about six hundred head of horses and mules, and would start from San Antonio with a Comanche guide. In command he placed Captain Francisco Amangual, a veteran frontier officer who, at the age of sixty-nine, was waiting for promotion to the rank of lieutenant colonel. At the end of March, Captain Amangual rode out of San Antonio de Béxar before the billowing dust of his mounted troops. It was the beginning of his journey across the plains to Santa Fe. Each day from then on he dutifully scribbled in his diary.[2]

1808—11 April

At dawn this morning two Comanche Indians appeared. They said they were on their way from Chief Cordero's ranchería to Béxar. We remained camped here in order to rest the horse and mule herds, which are thin and lame owing to all our travel over rocky country with sparse grass. The San Sabá River has plenty of water, with a big grove of walnut and other trees. There are fish in the river and the country abounds in wild turkey, bear, and other animals. From our camp to the abandoned presidio is about twelve miles.

Later I set out with ten men to have a look at the presidio. There is still a small plaza surrounded by a rock wall, which is in bad repair. I noted signs of bastions in each corner, and the ruins of a two-story house on the north side. There are also remains of a covered road leading to the river . . .

Gazing at the country from the ruins, Captain Amangual could not have helped imagining a March morning in 1758—and three miles away across the river a mission of palisaded logs, where a few brown-robed priests and some soldiers stared from the parapet at an army of Comanches and other northern Indians in war paint, many of them firing French muskets in the air as they circled the mission on decorated war ponies. One of them trotted to the stockade gate, slipped from his horse, and in an unhurried manner, swung it open. A mass of warriors jostled each other riding in. Then, after a time, screams and whoops, shots, smoke, and flames, while the remainder of the two thousand horsemen continued to circle. The captain scratched his head. While from here Colonel Parilla, the post commander, with about sixty men (whose horses had already been stolen) must have watched in helpless anguish, as the mission that was to have housed the Apache enemies of these barbarians dissolved in roiling smoke and orange flames.[3] Amangual looked hard at his vision, then blinked. That was why he and other Spaniards must work to continue the alliance with the Comanche nation.

"The presidio is north of the river and close to it," he wrote that evening. "The river is deep here. From it, one sees a fine view . . ."[4]

In May of 1821, Thomas James, an experienced frontiersman, set out for Santa Fe at the age of thirty-nine from Harisonville, Illinois. With him he bore ten thousand dollars worth of goods. His companions consisted of eleven others, "young and daring men, eager for excitement and adventure," including his brother as well as his friend John McKnight. Early on their way up the Arkansas River, the party bought twenty-three pack horses from the Osages. This unwise purchase, on their way into Comanchería, was destined to guarantee them an ample amount of excitement and, in fact, was nearly to lead to their deaths.[5]

James's expedition does not seem to have been typical. Of course entering Comanche country or trading with the People always entailed risks. In 1838, for example, fifteen traders left from San Antonio for Comanchería, never to be heard from again. Their friends later learned that the Comanches had accused them of deliberately introducing smallpox into the tribe and had put them all to death. But such an occurrence was exceptional, and scores, if not hundreds, of traders from New Mexico and from the Louisiana and Arkansas frontiers had already bartered in Comanche territory and had returned safely.

A more or less representative encounter with the tribe was probably that experienced by a trader named Anthony Glass in 1808, the year, of course, that Captain Amangual was leading Spanish troops across the plains from Béxar to Santa Fe. The Glass expedition was authorized by Dr. John Sibley of Natchitoches. When Comanches had visited him in 1807, they had evinced a desire for American traders among them. A year later Glass, a pioneer hardware merchant from Natchez, had offered to accept a Wichitan invitation to traders and to seek out Comanche camps as well. Sibley, eager to win over Spain's Indian allies, had licensed him.[6]

Glass set out that July with ten men. By October he had left the Wichitan villages on the Red and was roaming, with a mass of Wichitans and Comanches, the country between the upper Brazos and Colorado rivers. In his diary entry for October 9th to 14th, Glass complains that eight of his companions have temporarily abandoned him to search for a "larger horde of Hietans" (Comanches) with whom to trade. The American grumbles that he is hundreds of miles from the nearest settlements, surrounded by thousands of Indians, responsible for valuable merchandise and a great herd of horses, and has only two of his men available to help him. Yet, he continues, "all the Indians appear very friendly and say they will not leave me as long as they can be of any service to me, and some say they will go with me to Nackitosh and not only assist me in driving my horses, but assist me also in Purchasing more."[7]

Glass did have a problem with other Comanches stealing his horses. Frequently, though, diligent chiefs managed to deliver some back to him, and he believed that they "did all in their power to prevent their people from stealing." On February 6, 1809, for instance, he noted that Comanches had taken more horses. Following the thieves to their camp, he found that they had fled farther into the plains with the animals. The principal chief was apologetic. There were bad people in all nations, he told the trader, informing him that his tribe had no laws to punish theft. He asked Glass not to "condemn a whole nation for the conduct of a few individuals . . ." Why, when he, the chief, had been in Natchitoches, he went on to explain, thieves had stolen a number of ponies from him. Yet he did not think less of the Americans as a nation. He hoped Glass would have the same consideration toward his people.

Two days later this same chief sent the trader some of the stolen horses he had managed to recover.

Thomas James and his men experienced far more serious problems. Many days after buying pack horses from the Osages, they were camped on the Cimarron River in what is now the Oklahoma Panhandle. Before dawn their dogs began barking. The men seized their guns, half-asleep, sitting up quickly. Out of the darkness they heard a clapping noise, then sounds like footsteps. They rose, gathered together, listened, waited. Just after daylight they saw more than a hundred Plains Indians galloping toward their small herd of horses, which had wandered a little distance from camp. A warrior in the lead shoved his lance, underhand, into a horse.

James, a tall, muscular man "of the coon-hunter type," seized an American flag, which he began waving.

The Indians whirled their ponies and rode at the traders, loping into camp with fierce expressions, snatching up everything that lay loose. The party's Spanish interpreter conferred briefly with the chiefs. This was a Comanche war party, he told James, advising him to make peace by giving presents. The tall trader opened packs of goods and distributed gifts. One of the two chiefs was soon appeased. The other regarded the Americans with hatred from a single eye. He and his followers clearly wished to kill them. Inspecting the traders' gear, they seemed to become increasingly angry. Through the interpreter they told James he was using Osage horses. They were at war with the Osages.

"You're spying for them."

Luckily the friendly chief's followers outnumbered those of the One-Eyed Chief. Soon One-Eye and his warriors, after final, baleful glances, rode away. The friendly chief demanded more presents for having intervened in behalf of the Americans. With little choice, Thomas James obliged and passed out more trade goods.

"Whatever you do, don't go up the Arkansas River," this chief warned.

Three weeks later James and his companions reached the Canadian River. They had just made camp, when he was startled to see Comanche horsemen bob over a rise and make for them. He recognized the rider in the forefront. The friendly chief galloped toward him with outstretched arms, crying, "*Towaue, towaue!*" He knew this meant "Good, good!" The chief pulled up his pony, leaned over and embraced him. The interpreter, after a brief exchange with the leader, told James the Comanches wished him to accompany them to their ranchería. At the same moment a warrior reached down, snatched up a brass kettle, and rode off with it.

"Can you protect my things, if I go with you?"

The chief replied that he could not.

James, who spoke some Spanish, told the friendly Comanche he would be able to go in the morning. In the meantime he wanted some dependable braves to watch over his camp that night. The chief left some of his men, and the Americans passed a peaceful night.

The Comanche encampment, consisting of a thousand lodges, was near the Canadian River, in bottomland by the base of a great mound. A civil chief came out to meet the traders. He was an old, small man with a malignant stare. When the party of Americans had been conducted to a spot near the base of the mound, near the old chief's tepee, they pitched camp, piled up the trade goods, and covered them with hides.

A crowd of men had been gathering. Now a great number of chiefs and warriors surrounded the party, demanding presents. James and his companions laid out piles of tobacco, vermilion, lead, powder, calico, and other items. But after the crowd of men had collected their gifts, they were still not satisfied. Some of the braves began breaking open bales of cloth and dividing among themselves the best woolens, intended for sale in Santa Fe.

James had finally persuaded the warriors to stop pillaging just as the head chief, Big Star, arrived and told the throng they had taken enough. By this time the plunderers were sharing their loot. They tore the woolen cloth into breechclouts and blankets. The silk handkerchiefs they tied in their hair, letting them flutter. Later, after the camp had quieted, James informed the chiefs he was about to depart. They forbade him to do so. At that moment Thomas James must have cursed the plan that had led him to trade for Osage horses before striking westward into Comanchería.

1808—12 April

Today we continued our march through country with good views, good grass, and thinly scattered trees. After traveling about nine miles, we came to some low, rocky hills. The Indian guide told me we were now approaching Chief Cordero's ranchería. I sent two soldiers and an Indian to inform him of our arrival. Soon a Comanche raced up on his horse to tell me Cordero had moved to a spot with plenty of grass and water for everybody, and was expecting us there. We at once changed our course and rode across some low, grassy hills.

From the crest of one of these, I saw the village, which resembled a city, occupying a beautiful plain. A great number of mounted Indians rode toward us, led by Cordero and his chiefs. They had painted themselves with red ochre and had dressed in a variety of trappings. I received them with the troops drawn up in columns, and with drums beating a march. After all of the friendly formalities, the companies filed by and proceeded toward the ranchería. Chief Cordero and his head men escorted me, with the remaining braves riding along on one side, until we drew near the village. When we halted, we formed a square, then set up camp. Our guide went off with the other Indians.

This afternoon I accompanied two chiefs to visit Cordero in his lodge. He had made seats for us by covering the earth with buffalo robes, and he welcomed us jubilantly. Later, I returned to our camp with no unusual incident.

In the spring of 1839, a party of Americans led by Josiah Gregg was traveling westward, with wagons, along the Canadian River.[8] Gregg, a physician and experienced Santa Fe trader, was attempting to open a route far south of the Arkansas and the Santa Fe Trail, reasoning that the grass would green earlier and would better sustain his draft animals. The frontiersmen accompanying the fourteen wagons, with their mule and ox teams, were well armed. Better yet, for the time being a Lieutenant Bowman and his forty dragoons were escorting them, at least to the approximate Mexican boundary.

The previous month, around mid-May, the caravan had encountered their first Comanches. This meeting had occurred at Chouteau's Fort, a trading post some five miles east of modern Purcell, Oklahoma. In charge of the party of about sixty was a Chief Tabbaquena (Sun Eagle), a fat, squint-eyed old man with no special token of rank about him (the same, incidentally, that George Catlin had encountered and portrayed five years before.)[9] As the chief admitted understanding a little Spanish (*un poquito*), Gregg queried him concerning the expedition's proposed route to Santa Fe. The merchant soon learned that the old Comanche not only possessed an intimate knowledge of southern plains' geography but was equally familiar with the Mexican frontier from Santa Fe to Chihuahua and from there east to the gulf. Gregg handed him pencil and paper and asked him to sketch a map of the plains. Rapidly the old chief executed a crude map. To the astonishment of the doctor and other Anglos crowding around, this map provided, as Gregg observed, a more accurate representation of the major rivers, the Santa Fe Trail, and the Mexican communities, than did many of the engraved maps of the same areas.

Later, on May 19, Tabbaquena, leading a much smaller party, rejoined Gregg and his caravan on their way westward. As the trader jogged along with "old Tab" by his side, he conversed with the Comanche, though principally by signs. The chief bragged of his friendship for Americans and warned the merchant to beware of Pawnee and Osage raiders who might run off his oxen and mules at night; not, of course, mentioning the likelihood of Comanches doing the same, if given a chance. The chief and his retinue spent the night in the American camp, departing the next day for their own. Before leaving, the squint-eyed old warrior informed Gregg he had some mules "*para swap*." The doctor immediately traded five mules, to his own advantage, he believed. Afterward "old Tab" and his party rode off to rejoin their people on the Washita.

On the afternoon of June 6, the traders reached a tributary of the North Canadian and pitched camp in a valley surrounded by hills and crags and lying between the Canadian and its northern fork. They had encountered Comanche hunters the day before, and three of the group had departed earlier in order to bring back the capitanes of their band. When the party of some sixty horsemen finally appeared, they approached cautiously. As they drew close, Gregg saw at their head a small man with a pleasant expression, apparently a little under fifty years old. He was wearing the usual plains buckskins but rather than moccasins, he sported a pair of high white cotton stockings, and on his head he bore a single long red plume which nodded with the steps of his pony.

Gregg addressed the party in Spanish, asking if they had brought an interpreter. A warrior with a lean jaw and a grim, gloomy expression kicked his horse forward.

"Sabes hablar en Español, amigo?"

"Sí," coldly replied the Comanche.

Gregg went on to ask where the remainder of the band was and how many of them there were. The interpreter told him his people were camping higher up on the stream, and that there was a huge number of them—nearly the entire nation—since they were preparing to go fight the Pawnees. Well, demanded Gregg, how far was it to Santa Fe?

"Ahí platicaremos después, "the brave said curtly ("We'll talk about that later"), abruptly terminating the conversation.

Gregg and his companions conducted the head chief and his delegation to a place a little distance from the wagons, where they could spend the night without mixing their ponies with the livestock of the Americans. Later he invited all of the capitanes to his camp. Soon he had ten Comanche chiefs seated in a circle inside his tent. But when he brought out a calumet, his guests, to his surprise, refused to smoke with him. The interpreter explained that they customarily did not smoke until after receiving presents. Gregg then offered some Mexican *cigarritos*. Most of the chiefs took a puff, as if they believed that smoking little cigars committed them to no promise of friendship or peace. When Lieutenant Bowman asked Gregg to raise the subject of amity between Comanches and Americans and to invite them to go call upon the *capitan grande* in Washington, the assembled leaders refused to talk upon that subject.

"But aren't we at war?" demanded the interpreter finally. "How can we go see the *capitan grande?*"

Gregg realized at last that the chiefs were taking him and his party for Texans. Carefully he explained that the United States was a separate government, and that the Americans were at peace with the Comanche people and wished them well. As evidence of American friendship, he distributed around the circle some scarlet cloth, along with a little vermilion, tobacco, beads, and other trifles. These gifts, in addition to his explanation, entirely changed the Comanches' mood; they relaxed, now seeming pleased and in good humor.

After a time the head chief began to speak, rather formally, while the interpreter translated his words into Spanish:

"We rejoice," he said. "Our hearts are happy you have come among us.

Our eyes laugh to see Americans walk in our country. We will tell our old and young men, our boys and our girls, our women and children, so they may come trade with you. We hope you will speak well of us to your people, so more of them will seek the roads to our country, because we like trading with the white man."

The following morning when the delegation of chiefs departed, they once more assured Gregg and his companions of their friendship.

"Tell the *capitan grande*," said the red-plumed chief in leaving, "that when he cares to call us, we will be ready to go see him."

From the diary of Francisco Amangual.

1808—25 April

Today I gave Cordero some small gifts to distribute in this encampment. The officers held drill for the companies. In the afternoon I went to the village and met with all the chiefs and the rest of these dummies. Through the interpreter I made a long, clear speech: I told them we came to invite them to visit us. I stressed the love of our king and father for them and our own fidelity toward him. They should act as we do, I said. For example, they should not trade with any other nation, even if others made overtures to them. Because the motive of any other nation could only be to divert them from their loyalty to us. I asked them whether any Americans had come into their country, and, if so, whether they had established a trading post.

The chiefs replied that they considered themselves well informed of events in their region. Also, they thought of themselves as Spaniards and believed the information we passed on to them. They accepted nothing from other nations. As for Americans and such, they knew nothing about them. (This topic caused much discussion in their own language among the chiefs). They enumerated the obligations we imposed on them and declared that they were faithful to all of them, and to us, and were prepared to join us in defense against any enemies. Afterward, the talk turned to the subject of appropriate guides for our trip. I left this matter for them to decide, as long as the guides selected were of good conduct and loyal.

For the past couple of days, the American officers and men had been noticing distant signal smokes, with answering puffs. Knowing themselves to be observed, they took care each night to form the wagons and tents into a semicircle, often closing it with a cliff or the river; or, when possible, completing a circle by felling and dragging trees. As the 1845 survey expedition advanced downstream along the Canadian River, Lieutenant James W. Abert, U.S. Topographical Engineers, continued to see increasing signs of Indians, even recently occupied campsites and a fresh trail.[10] On September 8, a mounted Comanche appeared at a distance. He refused to approach when signaled to. But the next day, after Abert had raised a white flag, a small party of Kotsoteka Comanches rode into camp. The lieutenant feasted them and passed out tobacco, noticing that one brave crossed himself before eating. To his eyes the warriors looked "dirty and mean," with poor clothing, but they were mounted on fine horses with Spanish bridles and saddles. These Comanches departed, evidently pleased with their reception. But on the tenth their band followed the expedition all day, observing the soldiers with curiosity. Abert attributed this to his having told them his party's purpose was neither to make war nor to trade, puzzling them greatly.[11]

On September 11, as the Americans were considering how they might scale a bluff, a group of Comanches signaled them by firing their guns in the air from a cliff across the river. Abert motioned to them to come over, meanwhile placing the wagons in a defensive position by the Canadian. On meeting the small group, he learned they belonged to the same band of Kotsotekas as the others had. They told him they had been watching his party, and had come to have a talk and get some tobacco. They said they had heard of his approach and were not alarmed. Most of their braves, they informed him, had gone south, along with many Kiowas, to fight the Mexicans. These war parties would raid as far south as Chihuahua. Abert passed out tobacco. In return the Comanches showed him a winding trail to the top of the bluff. Unfortunately, when they had gone, he found the path impassable for his wagons.

Following a ravine, Abert and his companions were able to reach the plain above by forcing their wagons up "a frightful steep." For a time they proceeded over level terrain strewn with rose-and-blue-striped agates, until they had to halt at a cliff dropping 250 feet down to the river.[12] They turned back and ended the day camping near their place of ascent, on a point of land between two valleys and at the head of a steep ravine. That evening their guide, Thomas Fitzpatrick, called by the Indians "Broken Hand," warned the guard to watch the ravines on three sides of them, since hostile Indians might attempt to attack the camp by climbing these. Later, in the moonlight, the mules became restless, so much so that several broke their picket ropes. But after the moon set at midnight, all quieted and, except for the guards, the weary men slept.

From the diary of Francisco Amangual.

1808—8 May

After mass we rode out over a high plain. The soil here is composed of red sand. There are many mesquite trees in a kind of valley between the heights.

The ranchería of the big chief Isapampa, whom I have already alluded to, is situated high over the bank of a stream which flows north northwest and spills into the one from which we just came.[13] The site of the encampment is level and grassy, with many mesquite trees. As we arrived, the big chief and other head men of the tribe rode out to greet us. They were well-dressed, but wearing unusual clothing—for instance, long-tailed red coats with blue cuffs and collars, and imitation gold galloons. One chief was dressed in the style of ancient Spain: a red jacket, blue trousers, with white stockings, English spurs, a cornered hat worn cocked. In one hand he clutched a cane with a silver handle in the shape of a hyssop. Other chiefs wore red neckties and otter-skin sashes, decorated with beads and shells. The hair of these Indians was neatly braided and, in some cases, long enough to trail on the ground. Their faces were all painted with red ocher and chalk.

We received Isapampa and the other chiefs cordially, then proceeded to the north side of the creek. There we invited them to dismount and sit down in shade which had been prepared for them. Refreshments were served. Afterward, we talked for around an hour, asking them to continue visiting us at Béxar, so that we would be able to demonstrate our friendship, as well as our loyalty, to them. They returned to their lodges showing every sign of being pleased with our meeting together.

Night came with no unusual incident to report.

As the moon was setting, Hatcher, hunter for the U.S. Army survey expedition, awoke at the noise of the restless mules.[14] He had known earlier that Indians were watching their camp on its perch above the ravines. He and other men had seen several dark shapes whisk across a nearby hill and disappear into the chasm below. Now he rose on an elbow, rolled up his sleeves, scratched his arm. Taking up his rifle, he left his blankets, and went and seated himself in the doorway of his and the officers' tent.

Ten feet from him, in the shadow of the ravine, a man notched an arrow to his bowstring and drew it back, aiming steadily at the silhouetted figure for some seconds. But finally he eased the bowstring back and returned the arrow to its quiver. Silently he piled stones upon one another, leaving a little cairn on the rocky ledge. Then, again in complete silence, he carefully climbed back down the wall of the ravine to join the rest of his party in the black canyon below.

Lieutenant Abert and his men were up by dawn. Soon they discovered prints of moccasins nearby. Next they saw a party of Indians riding toward them. Abert waved. When the riders were near enough, he invited them to join him and his men for breakfast. The Kiowas dismounted in camp, along with several Crows, who were traveling with them. Together, in the friend-liest fashion, all ate a hearty breakfast.

The warrior who had nearly killed Hatcher, taking him for a Texan, showed them his pile of rocks. Ironically Hatcher traded with the Kiowas and was popular with them; later that day, at the Kiowa camp, an old woman wept with joy at seeing the man whom, years before, she had adopted as her son. Now recognizing each other, Hatcher and his near-murderer shook hands warmly. Other warriors told how they had climbed up on the opposite side of the camp. They had crawled to where they could have fatally stabbed the men sleeping under the wagons, then soundlessly escaped. Abert distributed tobacco, and Hatcher made "segaritos." The Kiowas smoked as they rode with the expedition to their camp, which was on the survey route. Laughing, they told the Americans of recently encountering a band of Comanches who had been so alarmed at the sight of the expedition that they had fled, leaving some of their mules and their belongings scattered behind them. They had told the Kiowas that the intruders were as many as "blades of grass on the prairie." But these particular braves had chosen to go see for themselves.

Lieutenant Abert later learned the probable reason for the Comanches' panic from a Kiowa he had encountered earlier at Bent's Fort. He had asked the man to tell his people and the Comanches that he would soon be traveling peacefully among them. Instead the warrior, a practical joker, had told both peoples that a large force of Texans was on its way down the river. At least one band had fled, probably because most of their men were absent, raiding in Mexico. The brave was greatly amused: "I told them a big lie," he said, "but now I've told them the truth."

From the diary of Francisco Amangual.

1808—1 June

We crossed a high, grassy plain near the river. Shortly afterward six men rode up. One was a Frenchman who said his name was don Pedro. They identified themselves as settlers from the city of Santa Fe, and told me they were here with the governor's permission to hunt buffalo for meat. That afternoon five of the men returned to their camp, which is not far from ours. But the Frenchman spent the night with us. In response to my inquiry, he told me that this territory is very peaceful. He also informed me that this river is the Canadian, sometimes called the Colorado, but that it does not pass by Natchitoches. He said that a long way from here it joins the Arkansas, and that later both of them join the Mississippi. He also said that the stream we passed on May 22nd was the Natchitoches—or Red—River, and that we had come to its source.

Pierre Vial in 1808 told Captain Amangual, who had been traveling with Comanche guides, that New Mexico was peaceful. In the same year and part of the following, Anthony Glass traded and roamed with a "horde" of friendly Wichitans and Comanches. In one instance, "ten chiefs and near six hundred men with a large proportion of women and children" of the People joined him. At night he watched them gamble for mules and horses in a game he called "hiding the Bullitt" (or, "button, button—who's got the button?"). By day he met with the leading men, with whom he conversed at length through his interpreter, observing that they professed "great friendship for the Americans or Anglos (as they call us)." Some thirty years later, Josiah Gregg found the Comanches cool, if not downright hostile, toward him and his party, so long as they believed him and his companions to be Texans. Yet once undeceived, the chiefs became as cordial toward Gregg's group as Glass's Comanches had been toward that trader.

Meanwhile in 1821 one of the first American trading parties out of St. Louis, bound for Santa Fe, discovered that even waving the Stars and Stripes did not guarantee your safety if Comanches suspected you of spying for their enemies; and also, possibly, if you possessed goods they wanted. Yet in spite of Thomas James's nearly fatal error, he and his party found defenders in "the friendly chief" and in the chief of the entire Yamparika camp, Big Star. In the end they were to be rescued by a third, "pro-American," chief, one earlier encountered by Francisco Amangual; but that story comes in due course.

Still later, in 1845, one of the People's Kiowa allies was aiming an arrow at a white man when it occurred to him that Hatcher might be an American, and he lowered his weapon. Why did the Comanches, with their Wichitan and Kiowa friends, at peace with the Spaniards and with New Mexico, look favorably upon Americans, while hating Texans? In Comanchería the distinction between the two nationalities was literally a matter of life and death. The Kiowa brave reported to Abert: "Here my heart whispered to me that he might be an American, and I did not shoot."

Bow and Quiver, First Chief of the Tribe
This chief's Comanche name, Isacony, actually translates approximately as
"Returning Wolf." (George Catlin, Courtesy, Smithsonian Institution, Gift of
Mrs. Joseph Harrison, Jr.)

Above: *Mountain of Rocks, Second Chief of the Tribe*
The chief's name, Tabbaquena, actually translates as "Sun Eagle." (George Catlin,
Courtesy, Smithsonian Institution, Gift of Mrs. Joseph Harrison, Jr.)

Below: *Wolf Tied with Hair, a Comanche Chief*
(George Catlin, Courtesy, Smithsonian Institution, Gift of Mrs. Joseph Harrison, Jr.)

Clermont, First Chief of the Tribe
Clermont III was an important leader of the Osages, bitter enemies of the Comanches and Kiowas. (George Catlin, Courtesy, Smithsonian Institution, Gift of Mrs. Joseph Harrison, Jr.)

Teh-toot-sah, Better Known as Tohausen, Little Bluff
The name of this major Kiowa chieftain is now usually written as Dohasan. (George Catlin, Courtesy, Smithsonian Institution, Gift of Mrs. Joseph Harrison, Jr.)

Wee-ta-ra-sha-ro, Head Chief of the Tribe
This leader, whose name is now spelled Wetarasharo, was a principal Taovayas chief.
(George Catlin, Courtesy, Smithsonian Institution, Gift of Mrs. Joseph Harrison, Jr.)

Two Comanche Girls
(George Catlin, Courtesy, Smithsonian Institution, Gift of Mrs. Joseph Harrison, Jr.)

Thunderer, a Boy, and White Weasel, a Girl
At Fort Gibson a charging ram killed the boy; the 1834 dragoon expedition returned his sister to her Kiowa relatives. (George Catlin, Courtesy, Smithsonian Institution, Gift of Mrs. Joseph Harrison, Jr.)

Thomas James
James was a trader with New Mexico and the Comanches and later served as an Illinois legislator as well as a general in that state's militia. (Courtesy, Missouri Historical Society)

TWELVE

The Origins of War and Peace, 1830–1835

When the Comanches began to hate the Anglo-Texans is easier to discover than why. The "why" of that record of progressive animosity and augmenting warfare is a little more complicated. But up until the middle 1830s, the Comanches were still friendly toward the *anglosajones* in Texas. They had done business with illicit American traders since the time of Philip Nolan. The Comanches desired American goods, especially fire-arms, and those who offered the illegal items generally gained the status of friends. It was symptomatic of the tribe's dissatisfaction with Spain's attempt to control their barter when, in 1810, two Comanche chiefs, Chihuahua and El Sordo, rode to Béxar and complained acrimoniously to Texas Governor Manuel de Salcedo about Spanish policy forbidding trade with Americans.[1]

The early Anglo-American colonies were mostly inaccessible to Comanche raiding and, in the beginning, held few temptations, although in 1826 a party of Comanches and Wichitans did raid the de Witt colony on the Guadalupe River. When those colonists moved farther downstream toward the coast, the raiders left them alone to concentrate on the Mexicans. During this early period the Anglo settlers also bartered guns and other contraband to the tribe, in exchange for horses and mules stolen from Mexicans living above and below the Río Grande. American Louisiana was, of course, providing another market for the People's animals and, after about 1816, American settlements, such as Pecan Point on the upper Red River, also offered opportunities for a similar trade.

The Anglo-American colonists first clashed with those occasional allies of the Comanches, the Wichitan peoples, rather than with the Ietans themselves. In 1826, for example, the militia of the Austin colony, using Tonkawa and Lipan scouts, pursued, overtook, and defeated a party of Tawakonies, presumably in retaliation for their raiding. Three years later, in 1829, acting upon a request from the Mexican government, the Austin settlers, with their Indian allies, campaigned against the Wacos and Taovayases. But these initial engagements against the Wichitan confederacy seemed to have little effect upon the Comanches' friendly feelings toward the early colonists.

In 1830 for instance, Caiaphas K. Ham, a settler, resolved to join the Penatekas, wishing to lay the foundation for a business exporting horses to Louisiana. When a chief named Incorry appeared in town (probably San Antonio), Ham hired an interpreter and approached him. In the end Chief Incorry adopted the settler into his family. Ham remained with the Comanches five months, in what was apparently a successful sojourn. "During his stay with the Indians," wrote pioneer Texan historian James T. De-Shields, Ham "gained their friendship completely," and became himself "attached to his red friends."[2]

The following year, in November of 1831, a party of eleven Anglo-Texans under the leadership of James Bowie set out from San Antonio de Béxar to attempt exploiting an old silver mine located near the former San Sabá presidio and mission. They had been traveling for nearly three weeks, when two Comanche braves and a Mexican captive hailed them. The three identified themselves as belonging to Chief Isaonie's band.[3] At present, they said, the chief's party consisted of about sixteen warriors, who were traveling with him to Béxar with a herd of horses they had reclaimed from the Tawakonies and Wacos, in order to return them to their proper owners, citizens of San Antonio. (Rezin P. Bowie, cited by Henderson K. Yoakum, another pioneer historian, failed to say whether this remark by Comanches raised any tejano eyebrows.) The Anglo-Texans smoked and chatted with their visitors, making them a few little presents of tobacco, powder, and shot. The two Comanches and their Mexican companion then departed to rejoin Isaonie's party, which awaited them at the Llano River.

Early the next morning, the Mexican reappeared on his weary horse. His chief had sent him, he explained, to warn them they were being followed by a war party of 124 Tawakoni and Waco Indians, along with 40 Caddoes, who were determined to kill them. Chief Isaonie had parleyed with the chiefs of the party the previous evening, trying to dissuade them from their plan, but to no avail. His chief, declared the Mexican, had told him to say that he, Isaonie, had only 16 badly armed men, but if the *americanos* would come back and join him, he would help them all he could.

Bowie and his companions rejected the idea of turning back, since they would have had to pass by the war party in order to reach the Comanches. Iasonie, on arriving at San Antonio, reported them almost surely dead. But the Anglo-Texans took refuge in a thicket and ultimately outfought and outlasted the larger force, with 1 man killed and 3 wounded to 82 casualties among their assailants. Their survival was an extraordinary feat, but it was perhaps no more remarkable than the Comanche chieftain's offer to risk his life, along with the lives of his warriors, by linking his fate with that of the Anglo-Texan strangers. Comanches could make loyal friends as well as relentless enemies.[4]

Then, in 1832, the commandant of the Río Grande garrison led a force specifically against the Comanches. His command consisted of his own presidials, Mexican militia, and a body of Austin's settlers, along with the usual Tonkawa and Lipan allies. This mixed force discovered and destroyed two small Comanche rancherías on the Llano River. Yet if the Comanches were even aware of the presence of Anglo-Americans on that campaign, they probably blamed the Mexican government, since most of them continued to remain friendly toward the early colonists. Nevertheless the Comanche and Anglo-Texan friendship must have begun cooling around this time. For one thing the Penatekas could not have failed to see what was happening to their sometime allies, the Tawakonies and Wacos, whose traditional lands lay in the path of settlement. Surely this caused the People uneasiness in thinking of their own plains hunting grounds. Then there were the temptations the Anglo-Texan settlers offered, with their often isolated cabins, their big American horses, their women and children, their exotic possessions.

It is also important not to overlook the economic realities of the Comanche-tejano relationship. As already noted, the early Anglo colonists bought stolen Mexican livestock from the Comanches. They must have also bought items that, in 1828, Berlandier found to be the staples of trading Comanches: "Bear grease, buffalo meat, and various furs." This primitive commerce diminished in importance to the settlers with the increased import of American and European goods and as the colonists gradually became increasingly self-sufficient. The settlers therefore were less dependent upon the Comanche trade, and their increased wealth, slight as it was, doubtless aroused the covetous impulses of Indian raiding parties.

Although the Comanches were not a materialistic people, a diminished barter no doubt contributed, among other irritants, to their assuming an increasingly hostile attitude toward their former tejano trading partners. After all, their military power depended to a certain extent upon firearms and ammunition.[5] In 1807, for instance, a group had ridden a great distance to Natchitoches, mainly to obtain firearms with which to defend themselves against, in Dr. Sibley's words, "A Nation of Bad Indians (Ozages) who gave them much trouble and vexation" and who "were more formidable to them On Account of their having arms and they (the Hietans) having none . . ." But an economic explanation alone is insufficient to explain what eventually became a dramatically changed relationship between Comanches and Anglo-Texans. The actions of any people who held celebratory "Give-Away Dances," in which families sometimes reduced themselves to poverty, cannot be explained simply by recourse to economic determinism.[6]

Certainly encroachment on the Comanche raiding range and hunting grounds were also reasons for increasing suspicion and anger on the part of the People. In addition the Anglo-American settlers, becoming more numerous and secure, were freer to display the contempt that most of them felt for Native Americans. As the Texas historian Rupert Norval Richardson observes, the Anglo-Americans, being "bold, aggressive, intolerant, and with little understanding of the Indians or sympathy for them," often behaved toward them "with no more consideration" than they "gave to the dog that trotted at their heels." Richardson concludes that because of these racial attitudes, "war would become almost the normal state of relationship between the two races . . ."[7]

In 1889, over a half-century after the start of the conflict, the Texas pioneer J. W. Wilbarger, looking back, expressed an attitude no doubt characteristic of the more literate settlers of an already vanished frontier, writing: "In our opinion, the aborigines of the American continent, pure and simple, were all naturally incapable of progress, and that their existence was only intended to be a temporary one, and that it should cease as soon as their places could be filled by a progressive people, such as the Anglo-Saxon race." Wilbarger based his argument on "that inexorable law, 'the survival of the fittest' " But essentially what he was saying was: "We are glad . . . that there are no Indians now in Texas except 'good ones' "[8]

With a rationale like this held by even educated frontiersmen, what chance could there have been for peace between Anglo pioneers and Native Americans? Furthermore, as events will demonstrate, there were to be even more compelling reasons after the 1830s for the People to hate the Anglo-Texans. Still according to DeShields, the Comanches remained friendly until 1834 or 1835. While the Nuhmuhnuh, as usual, raided the Mexican settlements along the Río Grande, stealing and killing, they continued to be friendly toward the Anglo settlers until, in DeShield's words, "provoked to hostility."

Although there were many contributing causes, a renegade Anglo settler seems to have triggered hostilities. About sixty miles below La Grange lived a man named Ross. Known as a "desperate character," he traded with the Tonkawas, those enemies of the Comanches, for ponies they stole from the People. Apparently conscious of increasing Comanche anger, a crowd of settlers tried to drive away the Tonkawas camped near Ross's cabin, but he fired on them, and they killed him. In spite of the rigor of this action, the Comanches were not mollified and, in 1834 or 1835, began raiding the Anglo settlements, stealing horses and murdering whites.[9]

During the years 1834 and 1835, when the Comanches began hostilities against the Anglo-Texans, the American government was taking measures to establish cordial relations with the tribe. Already, five years earlier, there had been a battle on the Santa Fe Trail between U.S. troops and the Comanches, in conjunction with their Kiowa allies. In 1832 and 1833, American military expeditions had set forth from Fort Gibson (near present Muskogee, Oklahoma), in attempts to find and treat with the Comanches, whom they rightly understood to control access to the southern plains.[10] The United States wished to protect both the Missouri merchants using the Santa Fe Trail and displaced southern Indians, such as the Choctaws, Cherokees, and Creeks, who had settled or were settling, by the terms of various treaties, in present Oklahoma. Both expeditions failed to achieve their purposes. But the 1834 expedition of the First Regiment of Mounted Dragoons, in contrast, did accomplish its mission.

This was the summer campaign that George Catlin accompanied, by permission of the U.S. secretary of war. Trained as a lawyer, Catlin had renounced that profession to become an artist. Next he had abandoned a lucrative career as a portrait painter in order to join the frontier expeditions that gave him an opportunity to portray American Indians. Particularly fascinated by the "wild" western Indians, he was by now committed to preserving, through his sketches and paintings, as much of their vital cultures as he could. He was especially excited, at the age of thirty-eight, by his "first grand *civilized foray* into the country of the wild and warlike Camanchees," about whom he and his fellow Americans knew virtually nothing, except for some extravagant rumors.

After four days of travel northwestward from a temporary camp at the mouth of the Washita River, Catlin was seeing enormous herds of buffalo speckling the rolling plains far ahead. But columns of smoke rising here and there were of more serious import. That noon he and the officers in the vanguard distinguished a large war party before them, at a distance of several miles. Some at first mistook the force for Mexican cavalry. But on studying the horsemen through binoculars, the officers identified them as Comanche braves watching the regiment from a rise, their lanceblades glinting in the sun as they turned the shafts in their hands.

Colonel Henry Dodge, the officer in command, called a halt so that his dragoons might prepare for possible combat. Next he led his regiment directly toward the war party. But each time the dragoon companies came to within two or three miles of them, the Comanches would disappear over a hill, only to reappear farther away, in a different direction. Colonel Dodge again ordered a halt. With officers of his staff and an ensign bearing a white flag, he rode forward, leaving the regiment behind. Catlin loped his horse to join the advance party. Dodge proceeded until he and his little group were within a half-mile of the Comanches and could make out individual warriors and their ponies. Halting, the colonel sent the ensign a little ahead, ordering him to wave the flag.

There followed what was, for Catlin, "one of the most thrilling and beautiful scenes" he had ever witnessed. A Comanche on a white horse, bearing on his lance a piece of white buffalo hide, galloped out before the massed warriors. Approaching in a zig-zag fashion, he rode his pony back and forth for fifteen minutes across the prairie, simultaneously spurring and reining in, as the pony leapt and plunged. When he reached the white flag, he leaned his lance for an instant against its staff, looking straight at the officer. He spun his horse and galloped to Colonel Dodge with outstretched hand. At once the colonel gripped it. Soon every man in the advance party had seized him by the hand. Upon seeing this, the mass of warriors whipped their ponies and came at a run across the grass to surround Catlin and the vanguard.

The regiment moved up. Every brave rode by the troops, shaking each man's hand as he passed down the line. During this time Catlin could not keep his eyes off the warrior with the white flag, viewing him as a "dashing cavalier." This "little fellow," a harsh horseman by most standards, tightly held in the reins to a heavy Spanish bit, while at every leap of his half-wild horse, he roweled the animal with a huge pair of spurs, until its sides were bloody. The eyes of the brave's "noble little steed" were bulging, and it was in a lather. From the rider's bare back hung his quiver. His left arm bore his shield. He clenched his bow in that hand. He had slung his gun, "in a beautiful cover of buckskin," across his thigh, while in his right hand he carried his fourteen foot lance, with the white leather attached.[11]

In the forefront, officers and Comanche leaders dismounted, including the individual whom Catlin had been observing, and whom he soon began referring to as "the Spaniard." As it turned out, the man's name was Jesús—Jesús Sánchez. A mexicano, or perhaps even a nuevomexicano, he had been seized as a boy and still recalled some of his mother tongue. Culturally, though, he was pure Comanche. Catlin later painted a full-length portrait of this person, who had risen from captive to become one of the prominent warriors of the division and who was, in the artist's opinion, "one of the most extraordinary men . . . living in these regions." Catlin went on to write of the warrior's remarkable strength and agility, as well as his "gentlemanly politeness and friendship . . ."

Sánchez was now consulting with the regiment's interpreter of Spanish. According to Lieutenant T. B. Wheelock, who kept the expedition's official journal, this man, a Cherokee, was lamentably imperfect at his task. Still from the interpreters the colonel learned that this was indeed a war party looking for enemies. Through the Cherokee, Colonel Dodge explained that he and his men had been sent by the president of the United States to make the acquaintance of the Comanche and Wichita chiefs and to smoke the pipe of peace with them. Peace and trade, he declared, were the objects of the Americans in making contact. After conferring the head men offered to lead the regiment to where their people were camped, several days' journey away.

The Comanche encampment lay in a green valley several miles wide, with the Wichita Mountains of present Oklahoma in the distance behind it. Catlin made out, in open timber by streams, the tips of tepees, smoke suspended above them. Some three thousand horses and mules dotted the fields around the camp.

Colonel Dodge drew up the regiment in three columns behind him, placing the white flag before the entire formation. At length, when the warriors of the village below had caught their ponies and raced to the meeting place, a Comanche brave rode out and planted another white flag beside it. Then the two bodies of men sat their horses and faced each other for a half-hour, while waiting for the head chief to appear. During this interval Catlin had time to reflect upon the solid line of warriors facing the dragoons, a line, he noted, that "dressed" like crack cavalry.

At a distance of twenty or thirty yards, the two forces confronted each other, he wrote later, "as inveterate foes that never had met. To the everlasting credit of the Camanchees," he declared, "whom the world had always looked upon as murderous and hostile, they had all come out in this manner, with their heads uncovered, and without a weapon of any kind, to meet a war-party bristling with arms, and trespassing to the middle of their country. They had every reason to look upon us as their natural enemy . . . and yet, instead of arms or defenses, or even frowns, they galloped out and looked us in our faces, without an expression of fear or dismay, and evidently with expressions of joy and impatient pleasure, to shake us by the hand, on the bare assertion of Colonel Dodge, which had been made to the chiefs, that 'we came to see them on a friendly visit.'"

When the head chief arrived, he galloped to the colonel and shook his hand. He rode to one after another of the officers to do the same. Passing to the columns of troops, he rode beside each in turn, gripping the hand of every dragoon in the regiment. All the chiefs and important warriors followed his example, prolonging the ceremony for nearly another hour. Finally the Comanches led the regiment toward their village, leaving the Americans on the bank of a clear stream near a good spring, only a half-mile from their own camp.[12]

This plains encounter, sought by Americans, marked the beginning of friendly relations between the United States government and the Nuh-muhnuh. In the following year, 1835, the ties established were formally recognized by treaty. The American relationship with the Comanches contrasted sharply with the People's relations farther south with Anglo-Texan pioneers, themselves products of an Indian-fighting tradition, who were aggressively pushing their settlements northwestward toward the buffalo plains of Comanchería. But later Comanche attitudes toward tejanos, and toward Texas as distinct from New Mexico, had their source, as well, in events taking place during the eighteenth and early nineteenth centuries.

THIRTEEN

Tejas and the Comanches, 1743–1786

E arly in the eighteenth century, about a decade after Comanches began appearing in New Mexico, the northeastern frontier of New Spain vaulted from the Río Grande to Los Adaes, a mission built for the Tejas Indians across the Red River from the French Natchitoches Post. (The Tejas, or Hasinai, were a confederation of southern Caddoan tribes.) France had established that garrison in 1714. The Spanish mission (1717) and presidio (1721) were partly the result of vigorous efforts by Franciscan friars, partly a response to fears of French influence among the Texas tribes, partly a measure to check French expansion. In 1718, the year the French established New Orleans, other Franciscans founded Mission San Antonio de Valero on the San Antonio River, while several days later Martín de Alarcón, governor of Texas, broke ground for the presidio and village of San Antonio de Béxar. These were to serve as a way station between the Río Grande communities and the eastern boundary to the province, with the capital remaining at Los Adaes (presently Robeline, Louisiana).[1]

During this period and until midcentury, the Comanches were driving Apaches westward and southward from the buffalo plains.[2] The Nuhmuhnuh first entered Béxar in 1743, inquiring after their enemies, the Lipan Apaches.[3] They were to return many times, and by no means always as friends of the officials and settlers there. But they made no major attack on Texas until their assault, with their Wichitan allies, on the San Sabá mission in 1758. That assault was mostly the result of Spanish favors to Apaches, coupled with fears by the "Indians of the North" that Spaniards and Apaches were forming an alliance to be directed against them.

The following year Colonel Diego Ortiz Parrilla led a punitive expedition northward across the plains in order to avenge Spanish honor. His army, drawn from Coahuila as well as from Texas, was composed of 139 presidials and their officers, 241 untried militiamen, 120 Tlaxcaltecan and mission Indians, along with 134 of the Apaches so hated by the Comanches and other norteños. Pursuing a war party of Comanches into a wood, Parrilla rode suddenly onto a plain before the Red River, where he was shocked to confront a palisaded and moated Taovayas village flying the French flag. From within the fort came the sound of drum and fife. In the ensuing battle Comanche and Wichitan warriors fought with French muskets, firing from within the village and from horseback on the plain before it. Each brave riding before the palisade had two dismounted attendants continually ready to hand him a loaded musket in exchange for his empty one. The defenders seemed also to possess an unlimited supply of ammunition. In the face of four hours of sustained and concentrated fire, Parrilla was unable to approach the village. Even the two field cannons on which he had counted aroused only hoots of laughter from the enemy with each shot.

After sundown Colonel Parrilla took stock. Finally he decided to withdraw, after considering the unreliability of his green militia, many of whom had already fled under fire. The Comanche and Wichitan braves had behaved with better discipline during battle than the greater part of his heterogeneous command. Furthermore they greatly outnumbered it, with reinforcements arriving continually. In addition Apache scouts reported sighting fourteen whites inside the fort. Probably, he reasoned, Frenchmen were directing the defense. In any case Parrilla decided to pull out, satisfied that he had killed more than a hundred of the enemy, including the principal Taovayas war chief. He had lost, besides the deserters, nineteen men killed, with fourteen wounded. He considered the punishment sufficient to redeem the honor of Spanish arms, while attempting to take the village would result in heavy casualties, possibly a disastrous defeat. So Colonel Parrilla turned his expedition southward, leaving behind some of his baggage and his two cannons in order to hasten his retreat. As soon as the Spanish army disappeared, triumphant Taovayases dragged the field guns into their village, where they proudly displayed them for some twenty years.

Eleven years later Athanase de Mézières, writing to the governor of "la Luisiana," mentioned in passing the "disgraceful campaign" led by Parrilla in 1759. Not only a trader and planter, de Mézières had served for twenty years as a French officer before joining the army of Spain in 1769. Doubtless his pride as a soldier and as a capitán were reflected in the remark. No, Spanish officials were not proud of the expedition's outcome. But from that time on they knew campaigns against the Comanches and their Wichitan allies were not to be undertaken lightly. Officers on the northern frontier, especially, realized they lacked both sufficient numbers of seasoned troops and sufficient logistical support to confront these tribes in unlimited warfare. As a result they now tended to be more cautious in their relations with the Comanches and other "Nations of the North."

Spaniards in Texas also had their difficulties with the Lipan Apaches. By the middle of the century these nomadic raiders roamed mostly south of San Antonio. But frequently they also hovered around Spanish settlements, partly for protection against their plains enemies, partly in order to prey on settlers, whose horses, mules, and cattle often replaced the buffalo they had been accustomed to hunt. At the same time they usually played a deceptive role with Spanish authorities; for example, in requesting missions that they later found excuses not to occupy.

Up until 1777, at least, Spanish secular officials, as well as those of the church, dreamed of converting Apaches and "reducing" them to mission Indians. For generations the southern and western Apaches capitalized on this Spanish desire, flirting with Christianity but rarely becoming permanent converts. To encourage the Lipans toward baptism, the Spaniards granted them numerous favors, which in turn infuriated the Comanches and their norteño allies. For example Captain Felipe de Rábago y Téran, commander at San Sabá, acceded to Apache pleas for escorts of soldiers to protect them when they ventured onto the plains to hunt buffalo. Comanches and Wichitas soon learned of this practice and began regularly raiding the presidial horse herd.

In their anger the Comanches and their allies did more than raid for horses. Sometimes on encountering a hunting party, they would attack the Apaches and their protectors as well. On one occasion, in 1764, a soldier named Antonio Treviño was a member of a squad escorting Apaches to their winter hunt. Suddenly they were attacked by a large Taovayas war party. Apparently the Apaches and most of the presidials managed to flee, but warriors surrounded Treviño. Standing in the midst of the enemy, bleeding from four bullet wounds and two lance thrusts, the Spaniard fought back so valiantly against the nearly fifty braves surrounding him that their chief, Eyasiquiche, stopped the battle. Like the Comanches, the Wichitan men admired courage above all else. Eyasiquiche needed a warrior such as this soldier to assist in his war against the Osages. Through signs or perhaps a few words of Spanish, he assured Treviño he would not be further harmed if he surrendered. Treviño handed over his arms. The chief ordered his wounds cared for, then mounted the Spaniard on a pony and conducted him, along with his braves, back to their fort on the Red River, not as a captive to be tortured and eaten, but as an honored warrior.[4]

During his six-month stay with the Taovayases, Treviño learned something of their language. Over a period of time he and his captors came to understand and respect each other. As much as Chief Eyasiquiche wished to use the soldier in his forthcoming campaign against the Osages, he decided finally to return Treviño to his own people. This he did as an act of goodwill and a sign of his desire for peace between Taovayases and Spaniards; provided that the Spaniards stop favoring his enemies, the Apaches.

Antonio Treviño furnished his superiors with an oral *testimonio* in 1765. In it he stressed the value of a friendly relationship with Taovayases, along with their neighbors and allies, the Iscanis and Wichitas. Together these norteños could mount and send forth more than five hundred warriors, entirely apart from their Comanche trading partners. The Taovayases' fortified village was as secure as ever. Probably it was more so, since a Frenchman had taught the villagers how to use the two fieldpieces left behind by Colonel Parrilla. The French, in fact, constantly traded at the village, receiving hides, horses and mules, and Apache women and children for muskets and ammunition.

The Taovayases, he pointed out, needed guns and powder and shot, and not only for trade with the Comanches. The Wichitan confederacy, too, had formidable enemies to the north, enemies well armed with guns and expert in their use. These were the Osages, who some eight years previously had driven them down from the Arkansas River, much in the same way in which they and the Comanches had displaced the Plains Apaches. As for the Comanches, they by now had sufficient guns, he reported, so that most warriors possessed one. It would be important, Treviño warned, to come to terms with them before they realized what overwhelming firepower their combined forces represented. But the best way to approach the Comanches, both geographically and diplomatically, would be through his former captors in their Red River villages, a location that Athanase de Mézières was later to call the "Master-key of the North."

Unluckily the governor of Texas at the time, Ángel Martos y Navarrete, had no opportunity to act on Treviño's report. He was replaced that same year by Don Hugo O'Conor, a red-headed, quick-tempered professional soldier determined to brook no nonsense from either settlers or Indians, and with prejudices against the norteños. He ignored Chief Eyasiquiche's act of goodwill, as well as the substance of Treviño's testimonio. In less than a year, the Taovayases were raiding the San Sabá presidio again, as well as the area around Béxar. Yet by good fortune, it happened that the Spanish soldier's direct knowledge of these "Nations of the North," was not to be wasted.

In 1767 the Marqués de Rubí reached Texas, completing the final stage of his inspection tour of New Spain's entire northern frontier. One of the soldados de cuera assigned to escort him was Antonio Treviño. The marqués immediately took an interest in the illiterate common soldier. Throughout his long journey Rubí had frequently been surrounded by officials and officers who had strong opinions about the various Indian tribes encountered on the frontier. He had met no one who had had quite the kind of direct personal experience this soldier had survived. Rubí ordered that Treviño be transferred from San Sabá to the presidio at Los Adaes, where he questioned him extensively. Treviño's high regard for his former captors and his distrust of the Apaches impressed the marqués, even though his view differed from that of Governor O'Conor. As for the soldier's opinion of the Apaches, it confirmed what he had been hearing and observing during the two years of his tour. In Sonora, at the Tubac presidio, the officer who had seemed to him the most exemplary, Captain Juan Bautista de Anza, had given him substantially the same account of the western Apaches as Treviño had given of the Lipans. At the same time the presidial doubtless described for the marqués Comanche trading parties that had visited the Taovayas village and, in response to questions, expressed a favorable opinion of the Nuhmuhnuh as well as of their hosts. When Rubí left Texas, it was with a prejudice in favor of the norteños and Comanches as opposed to any of the Apache bands.

The opinions of the marqués bore fruit, of course, in his *dictámenes* of 1768. These, in turn, were transformed by royal edict into the *Reglamento . . . para los Presidios* in 1772. The "New Regulation of Presidios," as it is commonly called, was instrumental in determining the results of Commandant General Teodoro de Croix's 1777 councils of war in Coahuila and San Antonio de Béxar, as well as that of Chihuahua in 1778; members agreed upon seeking an alliance with the "Indians of the North," an alliance to be directed against the Apaches along the entire frontier.

Meanwhile up until the general treaty of 1786 and 1787, New Mexico and Texas had to fend for themselves. In Texas this meant occasional gifts to important chiefs among the Comanche and Wichitan tribes, as well as several short-term treaties. In 1772 for instance, Captain Athanase de Mézières, lieutenant governor of the now Spanish Natchitoches Post and jurisdiction, conducted a party of norteño chiefs, along with Chief Povea of the Comanches, to Béxar to meet with the new governor of Texas, Juan María, Baron de Ripperdá. Ripperdá had replaced O'Conor. After long days of council, which the Apaches disrupted by killing several of the visiting chiefs, Ripperdá was able to conclude a treaty with all of those attending, although Chief Povea made it clear he spoke only for his own band and for no other Comanches.

Two years later, while de Mézières was on leave, his temporary replacement, Balthazar de Villiers, dispatched a French trader, Gaignard, to the Taovayas villages to attempt arranging a peace with a different division of Comanches, who had been marauding in Texas.[5] The trader was obliged to wait about six months among the Taovayases before managing to communicate with a major Comanche chieftain. In the meantime Gaignard's situation had become unpleasant. His hosts had grown surly owing to losses of their warriors to Apaches—Apaches armed, they believed, by Spaniards. To the Frenchman's relief, the chief finally appeared, with a multitude of his people. During the month this division of the Nuhmuh-nuh, who were probably Yamparicas, camped near the villages, the trader succeeded in arranging a peace between them and the Spaniards. In his report he wrote that "the Naytane are a good nation, and are not cruel. They are numerous, and comprise fully four thousand warriors. They are divided into four bands which are never together. This is the only time that I have seen them all assembled in one place. They are fine men and great fighters. In case the slaves which they capture are grown up, they kill them immediately. They have no fixed village, but are wanderers, following wild animals for a living."[6]

Gaignard returned, satisfied, to Natchitoches that fall and reported to de Mézières, who was back from France. Louisiana was peaceful, the lieu-tenant governor informed him. But, and here de Mézières must have thrown up his hands, Governor Ripperdá was once again complaining of Coman-che raids in Texas, presumably by bands other than those with whom they had taken so much trouble to arrange treaties.

In June when friendly norteño chiefs visited Natchitoches, de Mézières exhorted them to punish the Comanches who were breaking the peace, continuing to raid around San Antonio. The chiefs promised to help him, informing him they had already taken stern measures against the raiders. The previous fall, they related, the Tawakonies had encountered fourteen Comanches returning from Béxar with a scalp. The Wichitan group had attacked and killed the dozen men and the two women of the party. "Those pueblos," reported de Mézières, had then prepared to go to war, treating "as their enemies" all those who were enemies of the Spaniards.

Six years later, in 1780, the Spaniards at San Antonio instigated their own vendetta with the People, although they were far less prepared than the Wichitan tribes to wage it successfully. Hostilities began on New Year's day, when a large force of settlers, soldiers, and mission Indians encoun-tered a group of Comanches along the Guadalupe River. Possibly the party was reconnoitering for a raid on Béxar, or perhaps they were merely hunt-ing buffalo. The Spaniards were probably startled at finding Comanches so close to the capital and assumed the worst. In any case they attacked. A bloody engagement occurred, in which the Spanish command killed some ten Comanches, with the loss to itself of only one soldier. But that summer great war parties of Yamparica Comanches retaliated, striking at ranches around Béxar, murdering vaqueros and lancing their cattle. Governor Cabello, Ripperdá's successor, was virtually helpless confronting such a horde of raiders. The biggest army he could muster amounted to fewer than two hundred men, including settlers and mission Indians. Compared to the hundreds and hundreds of elusive Yamparicas, the number was hardly significant. Gone were the days when Spaniards believed a dozen presidials were a match for a hundred indios bárbaros.

The Comanches camped on a ridge between the Colorado and Guadalupe rivers. All summer they tormented the province. By the middle of September, the situation had worsened. Patrols daily sighted tracks of the raiders' ponies. On September 18th a war party of some eighty Comanches attacked the military outpost at Arroyo del Cibolo, southeast of Béxar. They killed three soldiers and drove off part of the horse herd. Francisco Amangual, then *alférez*, or second lieutenant, was left with twenty-three men to resist further assaults. Governor Cabello could not spare him reinforcements: he had so few troops in the presidio he feared that eighty Comanche warriors could seize the capital itself.

Cabello realized raids would continue as long as the Comanches believed they could prey on the province with impunity. That December, in desperation, he pulled together a force of 172 men and sent them, under Alférez Marcelo Valdés, to locate and fight a party of Comanches reported by his Indian scouts. For a day and a night, he anxiously waited for word of their success or failure. Meanwhile Béxar remained virtually unguarded. On the second day the command returned, elated, victorious, with only a single casualty, a wounded soldier. By the Medina River the scouts had tracked down a warparty of Comanches, some 60 men with about half that number of women and children, as well as a herd of eighty-four horses. A number of the warriors, not liking the odds, escaped before the Spanish onslaught, but the chief and the others sat their horses and waited defiantly. In the ensuing battle, the Spaniards killed 18 braves, including the chief. His horned headdress and his pony's buffalo-horned mask they gave as trophies to the scouts.

Sporadic minor raiding continued over the next three years, but the vengeance attacks that the governor feared did not occur. Then in July 1784, some Taovayas and Wichita youths managed to sneak into Béxar at night and steal two of the governor's best horses. Outraged Cabello sent Amangual and Valdés, with seventy-nine men, to pursue and punish the thieves. On their way the Spanish force surprised a Comanche war party en route to San Antonio. Dropping the pursuit of the Wichitans, the Spaniards immediately attacked the approximately forty Comanches. In woods by the Guadalupe River, the soldiers and warriors fought an eight-hour battle in which the Spaniards killed ten braves and captured others, along with their horses. With three soldiers and a scout badly wounded, Amangual and Valdés turned back to Béxar with their prisoners and captured horses. This fresh defeat at the hands of the Spaniards may have set some of the chiefs to speculating upon the advantage of peace with that particular enemy.

The thefts of horses by young Taovayases and Wichitas also had consequences. As it happened the Spanish officers' abandonment of their pursuit was fortunate. When retired French trader Jean Bousquet, acting as Cabello's emissary, reached the Taovayas and Wichita villages, the chiefs welcomed him in a contrite mood: they did not want war with the Spaniards. Their young men had behaved foolishly. They wished to regain good relations with the governor at San Antonio. In the end Bousquet took with him four representatives of the chiefs on his return trip to Béxar. He also brought back two Frenchmen and a Spaniard who had been living illegally in the Red River villages. One of the Frenchmen was, of course, Pierre Vial.

The governor invited Vial and his polyglot companions to attend the councils that followed. Through the governor's interpreter, the emissaries replied to his complaints with apologies for their irresponsible young men, who had already been censured for their thefts. What their people really wanted was to repair and strengthen their ties with the Spaniards. As a part of that process they had come to ask him to confirm their new head chief, Guersec, as leader of their entire nation. Guersec had already received the cane and medal of office from the former chief, recently deceased, but they wished the governor to make the position official. Cabello, so long in the dark as to the situation north of the capital, was stunned and delighted. Furthermore, they informed him, their people were at war with the Comanches, the same nation that had been pestering San Antonio. Why, the Comanches had even stolen their horses during this trip to visit him, and they had been forced to walk much of the way! Now they wanted an alliance with the Spaniards, so that they might engage the common enemy together. What did the governor think of such a plan?

The governor thought his luck might be changing. Vial and the other former residents of the Red River villages assured him that Chief Guersec was indeed the proper choice for leader of the Taovayases and Wichitas. Cabello gladly agreed to accept the wishes of the two peoples. Still he remembered, without mentioning it, that Spanish policy called not only for peace with these norteños, but for an eventual alliance with the Comanches as well. Governor Cabello invited the Wichitans to gather at Nacogdoches in June in order to receive gifts from the crown. Meanwhile he sent off the four envoys mounted on Spanish horses and bearing a commission for Guersec, along with the flag of Spain and the coat and hat of a captain. In return the chief would now be obligated to rule his people as a faithful vassal of the Spanish king.

In May of 1785 a dispatch from the new viceroy, Bernardo de Gálvez, reminded Governor Cabello of the need to achieve peace with the Comanches. But how would he reach them? Who would venture among them? He called in Pierre Vial, asking his advice. The Frenchman surprised and pleased him by offering to accept the role of peace envoy. Vial would work through his Taovayas friends. They would be in Nacogdoches for their gifts in June. He would meet them there. If they were willing to help him, he would return with them to their Red River villages. From the Wichitan villages he would ride out and seek the Comanches. Cabello agreed, sent off Vial, along with Francisco Chaves, another former resident among the Taovayases, and waited.

As the affair turned out, the time was auspicious for the Texas governor's peace overtures. The Yupes and Yamparicas, denied trade with the Wichitan peoples, were suing for peace in New Mexico, where Governor de Anza was pursuing his own negotiations, using trade as a bait. But the eastern branch of the Kotsoteka Comanches, the *orientales*, were remote from New Mexico. Vial and Chaves, no doubt following directions from the Taovayases, rode out to their plains encampment. The Comanches received them cordially. With just too many enemies and no barter, the whole tribe was in a mood for peace. The Kotsotekas welcomed the opportunity to make peace with Texas, and with the Wichitans as well. Three Comanche chiefs and their wives accompanied the Frenchman and the Spaniard, first to the Red River villages, where they renewed old ties, then southward to Béxar.

Governor Cabello knew that Vial and Chaves had left Nacogdoches near the end of July, but he received no further news of them until, at the end of September, they rode into San Antonio with six Comanches. To say he was pleased to see his emissaries return with the three chiefs is surely an understatement. It must have been the most gratifying sight he had witnessed since his arrival in Texas seven years before. During the councils that followed, Vial and Chaves served as interpreters. Essentially the governor and the Kotsoteka chiefs agreed upon peace and a military alliance between the two peoples. One clause in the compact, though, contained a potential for future trouble: in return for the Comanches' allegiance to the king, the Spaniards promised to distribute annual gifts to their principal chiefs. With the uncertain support that New Spain gave to its northern frontier, this was a risky commitment to make, and it contained within it latent disappointments for Spain's Indian allies. Accumulated disappointments eventually led to bitterness and disaffection. But for now Spaniards and Comanches embraced each other, both sides delighted with the new accord between them and with all their hostility and aggression directed toward the Apaches.

For three weeks Cabello entertained his Comanche guests with the modest best his provincial capital could offer. Frequently the chiefs joined him for talks. He found the men agreeable and their disclosures about the People interesting. But even as he gained knowledge about the tribe that had once been his most formidable foe, he began worrying about the Lipan Apaches, who came and went in Béxar, and who were certain to be informing their people of unwelcome developments in the capital. When he learned of a large force of Lipan warriors hovering around the area, he realized he would have to provide the chiefs and their wives with a sizable escort for a long first leg of their return trip, or his new friendship with the Comanches was likely to be doomed.

Cabello sent off the three chiefs and their wives around the middle of October. In command of the escort was Francisco Amangual, who led forty-two presidials, with ten militiamen to keep watch over the horse herd. Each chief sat his pony dressed in the uniform of a Spanish captain, while every wife carried in her baggage such small but valued gifts as needles, ribbons, and mirrors. Amangual took his orders seriously and accompanied his charges far northward, beyond the Colorado River, three hundred miles from Béxar. After leaving the party well within Comanchería, and secure from Apache attack, he turned his weary troops back toward San Antonio.

Governor Cabello, having few gifts on hand, had invited the Kotsotekas orientales to return in April, in order properly to ratify the treaty with ceremony and presents. In the meantime he was expecting no further visits from them. But beginning the month after the chiefs' departure, he found himself (to his mildly pleased astonishment) entertaining one group of Comanche guests after another. His first visitors were two young warriors who sought out the governor in his home, where they embraced him warmly. The object of their trip was to inform him that news of the treaty had aroused happy excitement throughout their camp, with the people universally pleased. The young men made a favorable impression on Cabello. When they departed after a week, they, in turn, were impressed with his hospitality. The next two guests were a couple who had not been able to wait until April to come and make friends with the Spaniards—and to enjoy the largesse their chiefs had praised. Before the two had left, a war party seeking horses and Apaches fired their guns in the air at the edge of town, then loped down the dusty street to the governor's residence. Riding in advance, dressed in his Spanish captain's uniform, was one of the chiefs who had attended the initial council. And so it went. Finally Cabello ordered a kind of barracks built, with four large rooms, for the purpose of entertaining the many Comanches and Wichitans who continued to drop by.

By the spring of 1786, the governor of Texas was once again pacing with anxiety. June, even, came and went, with no bands of Comanches appearing to ratify and celebrate the peace treaty. Yet he was equally worried that they *would* appear before the caravan with their presents had reached him. Luckily that July a small party of Comanches came to tell him that one of the tribe's two greatest chiefs, Cabeza Rapada (Shaved Head), had died in combat against the Apaches. The other, Ecueracapa, was in the midst of a campaign of vengeance against the Mescaleros and Lipans. The delegation apologized for the delay. Relieved Cabello explained his own predicament and invited them to be his guests in the new building for as long as they chose to remain in San Antonio.

Nine days later a party of Comanches, bearing the Spanish flag, galloped up before the governor's modest *palacio*. At the head of the group rode a tall, muscular young man flanked by two of the Kotsoteka chiefs who had attended the first meeting. Cabello was pleased to learn from the two that the young warrior was Ecueracapa's brother. Welcoming them all, the governor dared hope that this party, at last, was the advance guard of a great Comanche convocation on its way to his capital to ratify the treaty.

But Cabello's hopes were destined to be dashed. Fate and policy changes by his superiors removed the treaty from his hands, denying him a satisfaction that would have made a fitting conclusion to his years of service in Texas. In the council that followed, one of the chiefs spoke of Ecueracapa. The head chief was sorry the need to avenge the dead had kept him from visiting the governor, as he had planned. Now his duty was done, but the year was drawing on, and he had sent his brother to speak for him. Between smokes the brother then warned of some wayward young men coming to harass the Spaniards. Why? They had taken offence because the captain general had not returned their visits to him. Even Ecueracapa believed the Spanish might have come: after all, they would have been perfectly safe in Comanche country.

Cabello was nonplused. Suddenly he must have realized he had violated Comanche rules of courtesy by denying the Kotsotekas an opportunity to repay his hospitality. He knew the fact that he was old and in poor health would not be a sufficient excuse. Recovering quickly, he explained that a shortage of horses had made it nearly impossible to travel. During the years of war, his brothers the Comanches had stolen great numbers of the animals. The supply was now so short that his troops scarcely had enough mounts on which to ride out after the Apache enemy. His response created momentary consternation among the chiefs, so that Cabello immediately changed the subject, inviting the party to be his guests as long as they pleased.

Later he took them to the warehouse and showed them some of the bales of presents reserved for their people after ratification. He also ordered repairs made on their guns and lances at the presidio—possibly by Pierre Vial, who must have been experienced in working on Comanche weapons. Cabello tried to provide Ecueracapa's brother with a uniform, but the young man was so tall and powerfully built that only portions of the clothing would fit him. The Kotsotekas finally rode away, appreciative, proudly bearing the Spanish flag, after reassuring the governor that Chief Ecueracapa would surely come himself, one day, to ratify the treaty.[7]

FOURTEEN

Comanches between Two Flags—Again, 1786–1806

+

Nearly eighty years later, an Anglo boy was standing among sand hills by the Arkansas River. Dressed in breechclout and buckskin leggings, he held an old cap-and-ball revolver. Twenty yards from him, a Comanche chief sat his skittering pony, facing him. The chief was painted and wore a buffalo-horned headdress trimmed with feathers. Restraining the prancing horse, the Comanche raised his shield and leveled his lance at the boy. The boy lifted the heavy revolver, pointing it at the chief's bare chest. Abruptly the warrior charged, covering his upper body with his shield. Squinting as he aimed, the boy fired, suddenly recalling, in the time it took the gun to flash and boom and jolt, the start of all this.

Theodore Adolphus had seen them first, some forty warriors, with bows and lances and shields, riding toward the cabin. At the first whoop, as the raiders' horses broke into a run, he and his nine-year-old sister raced for the house, slamming the door as they entered. His mother and Mrs. Luster, a twenty-two-year-old Civil War widow, had already spotted the Indians, whose ponies the boy could hear stamping outside. Mrs. Luster scrambled to hide in the loft, while Theodore jumped for several old guns in racks on the wall. But the door exploded open, and bare-chested, painted men rushed in. Each time the boy grabbed a gun, a brave would yank it from him, while another whacked him with a quirt. Simultaneously he was aware of his mother offering her hand to other braves, trying, while holding the baby, to make friends with them. The raiders, now looting the cabin, ignored her.

On discovering the young widow, the Comanches trussed her arms and pushed her outside. When others seized the boy's sister, Mrs. Babb leapt to the child and clutched her. In response a warrior stabbed her four times with his butcher knife. The group hustled the little girl from the house. Theodore helped his mother to the bed. He was easing her down upon it when two braves returned. Not finding her dead, one of them, Omercawbey, or Walking Face, shot an arrow into her side. Theodore, as gently as possible, pulled out the arrow and sat down beside the dying woman, trying to comfort her. Omercawbey drew back his bowstring, threatening the boy, commanding him by a gesture to come.

"Go with him and be a good boy," murmured Mrs. Babb.

The other brave seized the arm of the thirteen-year-old and jerked him from the bed. While this warrior dragged him from the cabin, the man's companion, Omercawbey, hammered him with the butt of a quirt. Staggering out the door, Theodore Adolphus turned his head for a last glimpse of his mother, lying in her bloody dress, his baby sister screaming clenched in her arms.

Before the lancepoint touched the boy, the chief spun his pony and galloped off, as he did so swinging his shield to cover his back. Again the boy aimed and fired. Again lead whomped against the shield and was deflected. Three more times the warrior charged the boy, each time shifting his shield to protect his chest or his back. The boy continued to aim at the chief's body, but four more times his lead struck bullhide and glanced off. Now the six-shooter was empty. The boy let it hang from his hand. The chief trotted up to him, telling him in Comanche:

"Good shooting. You'll make a warrior."

The chief was Pernerney, brother of the Nokoni Comanches' headman, Chief Horseback. The boy was Theodore Adolphus Babb, the captive son of a widowed Texas settler.[1]

In 1782 Teodoro de Croix left his position as commandant general of the internal provinces to become viceroy of Peru. Commandant Inspector Felipe de Neve briefly replaced him. Because some settlers and clerics fled New Mexico in 1793 to protest de Anza's reduction of the number of missions (approved by de Croix) and the reorganization of scattered poblador dwellings into defensible communities, de Neve, who may have been jealous of the colonel's successes, took harsh punitive measures against the governor. Among these actions the new commandant general tried in advance to deny de Anza credit for the forthcoming peace with the Comanches. He ordered that Governor Cabello y Robles of Texas take charge of negotiations with the tribe and that the entire treaty process be directed from Béxar. This was, of course, during a time when Texas was still at war with the Comanches. Fortunately for the fulfillment of Spanish policy, de Neve died in 1784. Jacobo Ugarte y Loyola, his replacement (after an interim commandant general), was sympathetic toward de Anza and did all he could to counteract his predecessor's effort to damage him.

One of Ugarte's orders was especially significant for New Mexico and Texas, as well as for de Anza. In 1786 Ugarte commanded that the alliance with the Comanche nation be directed entirely from Santa Fe. Whether this was done primarily to render justice to de Anza scarcely matters. The governor was already conducting negotiations with important chiefs and was respected by the tribe. He was the logical man to complete the agreement. Also Comanche visitors to Santa Fe, who came traditionally to request peace and trade, would impose less strain on the royal treasury than such visitors to Béxar, who came usually for hospitality and gifts. In any event the order favored de Anza and peace.[2]

The Baron de Ripperdá, who governed Texas from 1770 to 1778, and Cabello y Robles (1778–86) were capable and conscientious men. If they sometimes made mistakes, they conducted provincial business remarkably well, considering they were almost always in short supply of everything from soldiers and horses to gifts for the friendly tribes and that they were also at the mercy of decisions made by distant officials who often had little insight into local problems. (For example, trade in firearms with the norteños would have been enormously helpful to Texas in maintaining peace. But the fiscal disapproved, and the viceroy forbade it. Unfortunately for the frontier Spaniards, Louisiana was part of the captaincy general of Havana, while the province of Texas took orders from the capital of New Spain. Many problems developed because the two jurisdictions favored different Indian policies.)

Above all both Ripperdá and Cabello were men whom Indian leaders could respect. This was not true of the pair who followed them and who controlled the destiny of the province until two years before the turn of the century. The first of these was Captain Martínez Pacheco, who governed from 1786 to 1790. Pacheco was an impulsive and erratic individual, whose past behavior suggested mental problems. Characteristically one of his first acts in office was to distribute to the Lipan Apaches some of the gifts Cabello had reserved for the Wichitan confederacy and the Comanches. His successor, Don Manuel Muñoz, who governed from 1790 to 1798, was an even worse choice for *gobernador*. Old, ill, and almost criminally ineffectual, he was hardly the man to win the admiration of aggressive warrior chiefs.

As promised gifts failed to arrive in Béxar during the last decade of the eighteenth century, Comanches more and more often troubled San Antonio and its environs with minor raids. The Kotsoteka chiefs were surprisingly conscientious about trying to restrain their young men, at least until the end of the century, but some old and destructive patterns were reestablished.[3]

Conversely in New Mexico two excellent governors in a row, as well as a series of important events, combined to create a cordial relationship between Spaniards and Comanches. De Anza's administration lasted from 1777 to 1788, over a decade. His replacement, Fernando de la Concha (1788–93), also behaved in a firm but humane manner toward the Indians.

With diplomatic talents equal to those of de Anza, he was able to gain the respect and trust of the Comanche chiefs.

De la Concha succeeded de Anza in the fall of 1787. But before Colonel de Anza returned to Sonora, he held a final triumphant council with the principal chiefs of the Yupes, Yamparicas, and Kotsotekas, traveling that April into Comanchería to do so. At the council's invitation, he officially designated Ecueracapa as captain general over the entire Comanche people. He appointed Chief Tosacondata (White Crane) as lieutenant general of the Kotsotekas and the Yupe leader, Paruanarimuca, as another lieutenant general in command of the Yupes and Yamparicas.[4] The council represented the ratification of the treaty initiated at Pecos Pueblo the previous year. It was surely a summit of the governor's career.

During this period several developments continued to draw the Comanches and Spaniards together. Their new relationship is suggested by the fact that Chief Ecueracapa in 1786 sent one of his sons to de Anza to be educated as a Spaniard. That November a dozen Comanches traveled with the caravan from Santa Fe to Chihuahua. The party included three of Ecueracapa's sons, as well as Chief Tosacondata. The delegation met with Commandant General Ugarte, who entertained them generously. The following year Spaniards and Comanches joined together in fighting Apaches in western New Mexico.

The next events drawing together the two peoples, Spanish and Comanche, were the outcome of natural cycles, repeated over the centuries throughout the Southwest. During the summers of 1787, 1788, and 1789, drought parched large areas of the southern plains. The scarcity of grass meant that the greater herds of buffalo migrated far north. Hunting was difficult and food scarce for many Comanche bands. Aware of the emergency, Governor de la Concha shipped pack trains of corn to Comanche rancherías in 1787 and 1788. Early the following summer, Chief Ecueracapa rode into Santa Fe with 180 of his people to ask for additional help. The governor provided him with 200 bushels of corn on the account of the king, while the people of Santa Fe contributed another 160 bushels from their own stores.[5]

This interaction between Comanches and Santa Fe created reciprocal respect and understanding between the Plains tribe and New Mexicans. It established a bond unlike any existing between Comanches and the Hispanic people of Texas.[6] For example when, during the fall of 1789, Chief Ecueracapa led his warriors against Apaches in the region between San Antonio and El Paso, he reported the results of his campaigns not to Béxar but to Santa Fe. There Governor de la Concha rewarded him with firearms and grateful recognition. Sometimes, though, Comanches operated out of

San Antonio on joint campaigns with their Wichitan friends or other Spanish troops. In 1790 for instance, a large force of norteños found and attacked a combined group of Mescaleros, Lipans, and other Apaches. The Spanish commandant Ugalde, following up, contrived to trap the Athapascans in the Arroyo de la Soledad, west of Béxar. Assisted by 7 Comanche chiefs leading 140 warriors, he attacked with his troops, killing 2 of the Apache chiefs, 28 of their braves, as well as 28 women and a child. In this battle Spaniards and their allies captured an additional 30 women and children, along with eight hundred head of horses and a substantial amount of spoils.

Yet the Comanches never trusted either Ugalde, whom they knew to deal treacherously with the Apaches, or Governor Muñoz, who took office that same year. The following year, 1791, Comanches for some reason murdered five men at San Antonio. Throughout the remainder of the decade, Comanches and other norteños, reverting to a habit that augured ill for the future, regularly committed minor depredations against that capital city while traveling to and from campaigns against the Apaches.

Meanwhile relations with Santa Fe remained good. The northern Comanches, however, had become increasingly involved in warfare with the Pawnees. In 1790 Chief Paruanarimuca asked Governor de la Concha for an escort of New Mexico soldiers to accompany his Yupe and Yamparica followers on their summer buffalo hunt. There was, of course, precedent for this, dating from the years when Spanish presidials from San Sabá escorted Apache hunters to protect them from Comanche and Wichitan war parties. The governor not only complied but lent the Comanche hunters guns, which they afterwards returned.

By 1793 warfare between Comanches and Pawnees had become so intense that Chief Ecueracapa led a force of his Kotsotekas against the enemy. During a battle the Pawnees mortally wounded the great chief. The news caused consternation in Santa Fe. The governor sent the single medical resource of the community, the city apothecary, out to the plains in an effort to save him. But in vain. Ecueracapa died, causing further dismay in Santa Fe. Spaniards now wondered whether the Comanches would choose another head chief over the entire nation, or whether the valuable alliance would simply fragment and dissolve.

That fall when Comanche chiefs called a huge council on the Canadian River, they invited Governor de la Concha to attend. He accepted, joining some forty-five hundred Comanches in an enormous encampment of eight hundred tepees. To his satisfaction the council selected Chief Encanaguane as the new leader of the entire tribe.[7] Unfortunately the governor's health began to fail after his return to the capital, and that winter he left Santa Fe permanently. His replacement, Lieutenant Colonel Fernando Chacón, arrived the next year, 1794, and served for the remainder of the century. Although Chacón lacked the qualities of his two immediate predecessors, he was at least more effective than his counterpart in Texas.

During the new governor's first year, Chief Encanaguane called upon him and requested that he send Pierre Vial again as an envoy to attempt arranging a peace with the Pawnees. Chacón had the good sense to comply. As a result Vial set out upon another important mission. This time the phenomenal frontiersman reached a principal Pawnee village on the Kansas River in only eight days. And in contrast to his return trip from St. Louis the previous year (or his abortive attempt to reach the Pawnees eleven years later, in 1805), this time he succeeded in establishing a peace treaty between the Pawnees and Comanches (both of whom were, incidentally, enemies of the Osages). Even if the peace proved short-lived, his feat must be seen as a triumph for the accord that had developed between the New Mexican Spaniards and the Comanches.

In Texas, on the other hand, Governor Muñoz the following year bungled an opportunity to provide Spain with new allies against the multitude of Americans approaching her eastern frontier. In February a dozen delegates from the Panismahas (Skidi Pawnees, who were closely associated with the Wichitan peoples) appeared in San Antonio accompanied by Taovayases and Wichitas. Through translators the Panismahas informed him that because of problems with Americans, they had left their own region (on the Loup River in present Nebraska) and come to live with their friends, the Wichitans. Their chief had sent them to the governor in order to form a friendship with the Spaniards. They had not undertaken this mission, they explained, for themselves alone. They claimed also to represent thirty-three other nations that desired to be included in an alliance with the Spaniards. Governor Muñoz, without providing details, reported the proposal to Don Pedro de Nava, commandant general of the interior provinces. He then failed to respond to de Nava's excited inquiries in a timely manner. When Muñoz finally turned his attention to informing his superior thoroughly, the Panismahas had apparently become discouraged, given up, and vanished.

The same contrasting trends continued in New Mexico and Texas into the nineteenth century. But in Texas there were some interesting anomalies, as well as one remarkable governor able to elicit the loyalty of major chiefs. Before 1805 there had been minor incidents there, isolated killings of Comanches and a Spaniard. The leading chiefs had tried to smooth these over. In 1802 for instance, an important chief with the unlikely name of "Chihuahua" had offered to form a tribal police force to oversee the

People's compliance with the terms of Comanche-Spanish treaties. Chief Chihuahua, the following year, led thirty warriors to San Antonio, where he asked Governor Juan Bautista Elguezábal to outfit them with appropriate uniforms. He and Chief Isazat also requested that Spanish soldiers be posted in the eastern part of Comanchería to assist in maintaining the peace. Elguezábal, with an empty storehouse, had to temporize with respect to the uniforms. Furthermore Spanish policy prohibited the posting of troop detachments with any tribe. Still relations between Comanches and Spanish Texans, helped by a lively trade and even a joint hunting trip, continued to be good. The following year Elguezábal not only distributed a generous amount of presents but succeeded in outfitting Chihuahua's thirty warriors with uniforms as well.

That same year, 1804, the United States assumed command of the old French (and Spanish) post at what was now American Natchitoches in the District of Louisiana. The Indian agent there, Dr. John Sibley, was, as has been noted, a physician with a penchant for intrigue. Sharing the national ambition to possess Texas, Sibley was the willing instrument of a tacit U.S. policy whose goal was to undermine Spain's Indian alliances, particularly that with the Comanches.

Yet ironically the Comanche-Spanish relationship in Texas grew closer in 1805. To a large extent this was owing to the reassignment of Coahuila's governor, Antonio Cordero, to Texas. Two years before, three Comanche chiefs had met the governor when they had ridden to Monclova to request a licensed trader in their country. Now the same three—Chihuahua, Isazat, and Sargento—traveled to Béxar, with over three hundred followers, to greet Cordero, remaining for three days of talks during which they vowed to bar all foreigners from their country and to raise only the flag of Spain over their rancherías.[8]

Colonel Manuel Antonio Cordero y Bustamante was the same who had written the incisive report on the Apaches from El Paso in 1796. Known as an experienced Indian fighter and an able administrator, Cordero ruled simultaneously as governor of Texas and Coahuila from 1805 through 1808, with the armies of both provinces at his command. In 1807 when Spanish authorities returned Zebulon Montgomery Pike—explorer, U.S. Army lieutenant, and spy—to American territory, Pike traveled through Béxar. There he met the governor and recorded his impressions of the Spanish aristocrat. Physically Cordero was rather tall and fair, with blue eyes and black hair. At that time he was fifty years old and possessed the carriage and demeanor of a professional soldier. The court at Madrid had sent him to America some thirty-five years before, "to discipline and organize the Spanish provincials," at which task he had served in "all the various kingdoms and provinces of New Spain." Pike found him to be the most popular man in the *provincias internas*, respected and loved by all. More than that, Cordero was, in Pike's words, "generous, gallant, brave, and sincerely attached to his king and country."⁹

Obviously Cordero was a man with whom Comanche warriors could identify. In February of 1806, six months before Spaniards halted the American "Freeman probe," when the Louisiana Purchase boundary dispute flared between the United States and Spain, word quickly reached the Comanches. In San Antonio Governor Cordero, on receiving news that American troops had pushed his outposts back, west of the Sabine River, prepared to repulse, in the worst case, an American military drive to the Río Grande. Busy as he was readying defenses, the governor must have been gratified that March to see thirty-three Comanche chiefs, leading two hundred warriors, ride into Béxar to offer him their support. This was the high point, perhaps, of Comanche-Spanish relations in Texas.¹⁰

In the end the crisis on the Texas-Louisiana frontier defused itself. Wisely the American and Spanish commanding officers finally agreed to readjust their positions and respect a neutral area lying between the Sabine and the Arroyo Hondo, a stream somewhat west of Natchitoches. But the Texas governor must have long remembered the Comanche gesture. In fact the offer of assistance may have tempered his reaction the following month, when unidentified Comanche highwaymen robbed a group of travelers of their horses and mules, killing a Spaniard.

The governor's response was to send Captain Francisco Amangual to a large encampment of orientales on the San Sabá River. Amangual conveyed his commander's message to the chiefs, saying in effect that the Comanche police were not fulfilling their duties. It was essential, furthermore, that someone, a single individual, be accountable to Spanish authorities. Consequently the governor demanded that the eastern Comanches elect a principal chief, as western Kotsotekas and Yamparicas had done for years.

The assembled chiefs and influential warriors of the orientales quickly agreed to comply. With Amangual as witness, they elected Chief Sargento to be their top leader. Sargento (tall, straight, with piercing eyes and a Roman nose) in turn promoted himself by changing his name to that of the governor, presumably out of admiration for the colonel. From then on he was known as Chief Cordero, the same who was to host Amangual on his expedition to Santa Fe two years later. Cordero at once set about working to keep the other chiefs of his division faithful to the provisions of their treaty with Spain; until, it would seem, some time later he abruptly became disillusioned with the Texas Spaniards and left the region.

FIFTEEN

Tejas, 1806–1821

In the early 1870s, when Clinton Smith was about thirteen, he was allowed to ride out for the first time with a group of buffalo hunters from his foster father's camp. For the chase he was mounted upon a handsome pinto, but one untrained for buffalo hunting. The party of Comanches approached the herd. When the animals raised their heads, snorted, and began trotting away, the Indians gave pursuit on their fastest ponies. Clinton selected a young cow, leveling his old pistol as he gradually drew within range. After some five hundred yards at a dead run, he fixed her in his sights and fired. Wounded badly, the cow whirled and charged. Clinton drew up, fired again, missing, then tried swinging his horse around to evade her, too late. The buffalo struck the pinto full tilt, hooking him in the flank, lifting and hurling him to the ground. The horse slammed down partly upon the boy, pinning him. It died with its head across his body. Clinton watched, lying stunned, as the maddened buffalo continued hooking the pony, almost above him. Then the cow spun away, running off.

With difficulty Clinton wriggled from under the dead horse. Slowly he walked back to the distant tepees, where he sought out his foster father.

"You're too little to kill buffalo," was all Chief Tosacowadi said, when the boy had told him what had happened. "Don't try that anymore."[1]

From then on Clinton knew, if he had not known already, why the Comanche warrior's well-trained buffalo horse, usually the same as his war pony, was probably his most prized possession.

+ +

Despite Chief Cordero's good intentions, the task of restraining his fellow tribesmen proved impossible. Four years later, in 1810, on the initiative of New Mexico's Governor Manrrique, Spaniards and Comanches launched a joint campaign against the Faraon and Mescalero Apaches. Cordero as well as other chiefs participated in this effort, which achieved some slight success. But in the midst of the campaign, a messenger brought disquieting news from Béxar to Chief Cordero: during his absence other Comanches, especially Yamparikas, had been raiding in Texas, marauding as far south as Monclova. Cordero at once sent his son and 40 warriors to San Antonio as evidence of his desire to cooperate with Spanish authorities. That August the governor of Texas, now Manuel de Salcedo, dispatched 150 soldiers, along with the 40 warriors, to inquire into the raiders' transfer of stolen horses to the Yamparika chief, Pisinape (a name combining "odor" and "shoes"—probably the "Decayed Shoe" of de Anza's treaty). From Pisinape's camp the horses were reportedly delivered to American traders.

On his return to Texas, Chief Cordero charged Yamparika chiefs Decayed Shoe, Chihuahua, and others with complicity in the raids. As a partial confirmation of Cordero's suspicions, Texas officials discovered from a Comanche prisoner that some of the raids, at least, had in fact originated from Chief Pisinape's ranchería. The purpose of the raiding, admitted the prisoner, had been to secure horses for barter with Americans who had set up a camp by a "Colorado" river, possibly the Red. That fall these same Yamparikas abandoned any pretense of honoring the treaty and declared war against the Texas Spaniards.

At this juncture the situation became more complicated. That October a Chief Paruaquita (Bear-scat), alias Oso Ballo (Tawny Bear), who was apparently the Yamparika divisional chief, journeyed south to confer with Chief Cordero. After consulting together the two leaders announced their support for continued observance of the treaty with Spain. To emphasize the seriousness with which they viewed the issue, they proclaimed that any Comanche found guilty of stealing from, or of murdering, a Spaniard would himself be killed. Cordero, to strengthen the ties between himself and his Yamparika counterpart, gave Paruaquita his daughter.

There was now among the Comanche people a peace faction and a war faction, if "war" is understood to mean principally raiding for horses. Since the peace faction was led by two of the most prestigious and powerful men in the tribe, the odds would seem to have favored its success. Yet in this instance the seemingly inevitable failed to occur. During the summer of 1811, Paruaquita reappeared in Texas, evidently with the intention of helping work out, with Chief Cordero and others, a genuine peace similar to that which had existed in New Mexico for twenty-five years. But the efforts of these well-meaning leaders were thwarted by the behavior of a young chieftain named El Sordo (The Deaf One), as well as by a blunder by Spanish officials.

As early as 1803, Spanish soldiers had arrested El Sordo and a party of his followers for the theft of horses and for murder. The group had confessed to the thefts but had declared themselves innocent of the murder.

Fortunately the more serious charge rested upon an instance of mistaken identity, and the truth was discovered. Even at that, Chief Chihuahua, in Béxar at the time, upbraided the youth and his men, threatening to punish any of them who continued to transgress. El Sordo, doubtless reassuring the headman concerning his future behavior, obtained his release through Chihuahua's request. But 1810, seven years later, found him separated from the tribe, living on the Brazos River in the vicinity of the Tawakonies. Meanwhile his camp had become the base for a band of horse thieves—Comanches, Taovayases, Tawakonies, and Skidi Pawnees. Not that there was a stigma attached to stealing horses. Quite to the contrary. But El Sordo was defying his people's principal chiefs and making trouble for all Comanches observing the treaty with Spain.

In 1811 Chief Paruaquita took the initiative toward reestablishing cordial relations with the Spaniards by restoring some horses stolen by Taovayases and by El Sordo's followers. It is likely he also gave the younger chief another stern lecture on the value of the Comanche-Spanish treaty. Although there is no evidence for this, Paruaquita may well have persuaded the deaf chief to travel to Béxar and, as a goodwill gesture, to warn officials there of Taovayas and Tawakoni plans for a series of raids directed against the ranchos of Texas.

If there was at that time a "Most Wanted" list in the minds of Spanish authorities, El Sordo's name must have topped it. But Acting Governor Simón de Herrera, in spite of his suspicions, greeted the Comanche *capitancillo* with a genial hug and made him welcome in the building provided for Indian visitors. After all the man had arrived unarmed, with only one other warrior, two women, and a child. But on the following day, a Spaniard recognized one of the Comanche horses as his own. The governor had no recourse but to investigate. Unfortunately when El Sordo saw the interpreter and five soldiers sent to escort him before the governor, he panicked and resisted, believing they intended to murder him. At this the governor jailed the entire party and immediately assembled a group of leading Spaniards for consultation. Probably because of the deaf warrior's heinous reputation, the group decided that Texas would be improved by his absence, along with that of his companions. Governor Herrera at once shipped off all five to jail in La Bahía, from where they were later transferred to prison in Coahuila.

But—really—two blameless women and a small child to prison? Governor Herrera's and his junta's hasty decision was a grave blunder, destined to sap the loyalty even of Spain's most staunch Comanche allies. Before El Sordo's imprisonment, the deaf chief was something of a renegade, whose death certain Comanche elders would not have lamented. But his arrest and imprisonment, when he had gone innocently to San Antonio unarmed and with the best of intentions, immediately became a cause célèbre throughout Comanchería, winning for El Sordo the sympathy of the most influential chiefs. Moreover the Comanche leadership could only view the young chief's seizure and incarceration as a betrayal of the diplomatic code long established between the two peoples. Like a similar blunder perpetrated twenty-nine years later by Anglo-Texans in the same city, it was viewed by Comanches as an act of treachery.

Early in 1811 Manuel de Salcedo returned to his post in Béxar. Immediately he was compelled to deal with the irate Comanches. With the exception of several Kotsoteka chiefs, who rallied to the Spaniards, the most powerful men among the People were discussing vengeance against Spain. Salcedo discovered that Paruaquita, on the Colorado River, was assembling a formidable force, with the object of demanding El Sordo's release at Béxar. The governor began preparing for any contingency. Meanwhile Chief Cordero sent Pisinape to Béxar to ask for an explanation of the deaf chief's arrest.

Evidently the governor's reply failed to satisfy him. Along with the chiefs Paruaquita, Pisinape, and Izazat, Cordero appeared before San Antonio on April 8, 1812, leading an impressive body of warriors. Governor de Salcedo rode out of the city to confront him, backed by a Spanish army of nearly seven hundred men. For a tense interval, Comanche and Spanish leaders conferred on the potential battlefield, while their respective fighting men waited, arrayed behind them. Finally they agreed to peace; and peace did prevail for a time. Yet an element of trust had been destroyed. For years Comanches were bitterly to remember the deaf chief and his party languishing in Coahuila.² As for Chief Cordero, once so loyal to Spain, and who had "disapproved of the Americans," he virtually vanished from the records of Béxar.³ When he next appears, nine years later, on the plains east of Santa Fe, he has become an even greater supporter of the new Anglo frontiersmen.

After the El Sordo incident and until Mexican independence, the trends of Comanche-Spanish relations in New Mexico and Texas continued to diverge. When the filibusters of the Magee-Gutiérrez expedition invaded Texas from American Louisiana in 1812, the Comanches provided little support for their former allies, the Spanish Royalists. Yet Comanches and New Mexicans continued to enjoy amicable relations. In 1814, for instance, a group of the People visited Santa Fe to propose a plan whereby the Texas Spaniards might make peace with the eastern Kotsotekas, or *orientales*, who were again raiding them. Despite efforts by New Mexico's Governor Ysidro Rey and others, the attempt proved fruitless.

By 1817 the governor of Texas, Antonio Martínez, was calling for help to Coahuila. Sounding like Governor Mendinueta in eighteenth-century New Mexico, he complained that Comanche war parties periodically made off with all the horses and mules at Béxar, leaving him virtually helpless.[4] Two years later, in 1819, Spanish officials in New Mexico warned their western Comanche friends in advance of an impending attack by the Texas Spaniards upon the eastern Kotsotekas. While the New Mexicans maintained good relations with the Comanches up until Mexican Independence and beyond, the Spanish Texans endured increasingly undependable relations with the Plains warriors from 1811 to 1821, a trend that was to continue throughout the Mexican period and into that of the Texas Republic.

In the early period customs and traditions were established that would affect later residents and settlers of Texas, first Hispanic, then Anglo. In New Mexico a long-standing tradition of friendly trade had been reinforced not only by several enlightened governors but by aid to the Nuhmuhnuh in time of famine. New Mexico Pueblo Indians and Hispanic settlers, as well as Hispanic and Indian comancheros, were to continue this tradition of trade for as long as Comanches remained upon the southern plains. Not only friendship counted, of course; New Mexicans provided a convenient source of supply and a market for stolen goods. While the People also came to barter in Béxar, and individual Comanches formed friendships with San Antonians, they often visited the town as a way station to the Río Grande and points south.

At first Comanche war parties rode below Béxar to seek out and fight Lipan Apaches. But as war chiefs became more and more familiar with the country and noted the many ranchos along the Río Grande, they became equally interested in and tempted by Spanish livestock—horses, that is. Farther south, below the river, the wealth of horses was even greater. As early as 1810, a party of Yamparicas raided Monclova. After the Battle of the Medina River in 1813, when royalist troops defeated the filibusters and revolutionaries of the Magee-Gutiérrez expedition, certain rebellious Spanish Texans took refuge with Comanche bands opposed to the government of Spain.

During the chaotic period of the invasion, the anti-Spanish bands had already grasped an opportunity to "make war against the unarmed herdsmen and the peaceable settler, robbing, killing and seizing prisoners," wrote Juan Antonio Padilla, a royalist official, in an 1820 report.

> In these raids, they collected a great number of animals, both horses and mules, leaving horror and devastation in this industry in the Province of Texas and on the frontiers of the other Provinces. At the same time that the

Indians laid waste the haciendas and ranches, the foreigners and various rebel Spaniards, who escaped from the victorious army of our sovereign at Medina, introduced munitions and other things to exchange for animals, making a well worn road through the unsettled region towards Natchitoches. There were not lacking some Spaniards, still worse, who led them and incited them to kill and burn whatever came in their way. With such guides they penetrated to the Villa del Norte del Colonia where these Indians never had set foot before. There is no doubt that they laid waste the country and terrorized the inhabitants . . .[5]

There is little doubt either that these far-ranging war parties drove back sizable herds of horses, whetting the appetites of all the warriors who watched their triumphant return.

Of course the increasing American presence around Natchitoches and in the upper Red River communities, such as Pecan Point, only exacerbated the problem for the Spaniards and, after 1821, for the Mexicans. Americans on their advancing frontier early developed an insatiable hankering for Spanish, and later, Mexican horses and mules. Traders without scruples encouraged the Comanches to raid in Texas and Mexico, so as ensure a plentiful supply of horses and to keep business flourishing.[6] In 1826 the Mexican government appealed to the United States to stop these "traders of blood," but nothing was done about the request.[7] While such commerce was not officially sanctioned, the U. S. government hardly needed a Dr. John Sibley to subvert Spain's and Mexico's Indian allies.

How did this pattern affect the Anglo-Texans? Historical precedents had been set, a Comanche (and Kiowa) habit entrenched. Mexico became the source of the People's wealth and, more important, of their pride and prestige as a warrior nation. Horses, great herds of horses, made them the envy of other Plains tribes. (No wonder they would never make a permanent peace with Mexico, no matter how desperately induced!) The two Comanche war trails to the haciendas south of the Río Grande ran through Texas. Traditionally war parties en route raided through the region, often picking up horses as they came or went. So the Anglo-Texans, once good relations with the People had broken down, inherited thirty years and more, off and on, of bad precedents that had finally hardened into a tradition and a habit nearly impossible to break. The tejanos fell heir to the same troubles that had plagued Spanish and Mexican Texans before them.

In Texas at the end of the eighteenth century, the erratic behavior of old Governor Muñoz was symptomatic of a deteriorating Spain resisting republican ideas engendered by the American and French revolutions. On the continent Carlos III, an enlightened monarch, died in 1788. He was followed by Carlos IV, an incompetent king unable to cope with the momentous events of his time. Under his rule Spain involved herself in both the French revolutionary wars and the wars of Napoleon Bonaparte. In time Napoleon forced both Carlos IV and his son, Ferdinand VII, to abdicate in favor of the emperor's brother, Joseph Bonaparte. French troops marched into Spain in 1808, and the people rose against them. This chaos on the Iberian Peninsula created an equivalent disorder throughout Spanish America. Finally, with the help of the Portuguese and the Spanish popular resistance, a British army under Wellington drove out the French in 1814. Ferdinand VII was reinstated on the throne, quickly proving to be an even more reactionary ruler than his father.

Meanwhile in Mexico in 1810, a priest named Hidalgo led a revolution of the poor and powerless against the viceregal government. This revolution failed, but it was a seismic warning of events to come. In San Antonio the populace responded by first supporting the crown, then revolting and deposing the governor, only to reestablish him later. But Spanish authorities responsible for the north of New Spain had more than domestic revolution to worry about during this period. Since 1803 most Americans had truly believed that the Louisiana Purchase included Texas. Over the two decades following the Hidalgo revolt, there were attempts by Americans, without official sanction, to wrest the province from Spain.

In 1812 an army of American filibusters and Mexican rebels, the Magee-Gutiérrez expedition, invaded Texas from Louisiana and invited the population to join them in a republican revolution. Successful at first, the force of idealists and adventurers was defeated in 1813 by a royalist army led by General Joaquín de Arredondo. Most of the Americans died in a battle by the Medina River. In reprisal for the earlier execution of royalist officers by Mexican republicans among the filibusters, Arredondo ordered that no prisoners be taken. Survivors were executed, along with all men throughout the province suspected of having republican sympathies. Hundreds of refugees fled across the Sabine River to American soil. In San Antonio de Béxar, the general ruthlessly executed some three hundred of the townspeople who had joined the republicans. By the time Arredondo had completed his purge, Texas retained few citizens outside of Béxar, and the capital city's population was drastically reduced.

Another force of three hundred men, mostly from Natchez, under a Dr. James Long, marched into Texas from Louisiana in 1819. The purpose again was that of forming a republic separate from Mexico, presumably with the intention of someday joining it with the United States. A Spanish army under a General Pérez quickly defeated these volunteers. Dr. Long escaped and, in New Orleans, joined a Mexican republican, don Felix Trespalacios, the following year, in leading another expedition to liberate Mexico from Spain. This time the republicans invaded from the gulf. But Long's army, again outnumbered, was compelled to surrender. In 1821, just as Mexico became independent from Spain, Long was shot in Mexico City, possibly by the order of Trespalacios. By 1825, only four years later, Spain had lost most of her American colonies. There was no more Spanish empire.[8]

Back in Spain, the Peninsular War, 1808–14, was partly a guerrilla campaign fought by the Spanish people against the troops of Napoleon. It is called the "War of Independence" there. Although a British and Portuguese army finally drove the French from Spain, the Spanish people in the interim fought courageously—and suffered. Francisco José de Goya y Lucientes created a vivid record of their suffering in his series of etchings, *Los Desastres de la Guerra*. Of these, number 39 offers the naked, mutilated bodies of three men bound to a tree. Their genitals have been cut off. The severed head of one is impaled on a branch, while his arms hang on another. This kind of sight would not have been unfamiliar to the Comanches. Clinton Smith told of seeing the Ietan women of his band occupied on a battlefield by cutting off the arms and legs of the naked enemy dead and hanging them from trees.

Another Goya etching, number 37, is entitled *Esto es Peor*, or "This is Worse." It depicts another corpse of a naked man, his arm lopped off by the shoulder, seated on a dead tree. On close observation, the viewer sees a sharpened branch entering between his buttocks and protruding from his back, a little below the neck. French soldiers in the background busy themselves with the dead or with killing others. If this image of war as practiced by nineteenth-century Europeans had circulated during a council of Comanche chiefs and warriors around 1820, they would have recognized it as an instance of the kind of war they themselves could bring to their worst enemies. It was the kind of war they would bring, in a couple of decades, to the Anglo-Texans, after they had come to hate them as much as they presently did the Apaches and the Osages.

✛

It was still the year 1865.

A war party of fifteen Comanches was riding in rolling plains country, six days southeast of the Arkansas River Nokoni encampment of Chief Horseback. A sixteenth figure, slighter than the others, a boy, rode behind the leader. As the party came over a rise, the leader abruptly drew in his pony. Those following him halted. With his lance, he pointed. At a distance of two or three hundred yards, a small group of riders was pursuing buffalo. Behind them, on the grass, lay the bodies of several of the animals. In all there were seven figures on horses. They were Indians.

"Caddoes," murmured the warrior beside the leader.

Now the Comanches had evidently been seen. With shouts the hunters left the running herd, fleeing at a gallop toward the east. "Kill all of them," ordered Chief Pernerney. "They're Caddoes."

The boy kept behind Pernerney. The Comanche ponies were swifter than those of the hunters, which were already tired from the chase. As the war party drew within range of the Caddoes, then closer and closer, the pursuing warriors began to fire. One by one, the hunters dropped from their horses. Rushing past one of the prone figures, the boy looked down and saw a woman.

The last Caddo rode a fast horse. Still behind Chief Pernerney, the boy continued at a run for another ten miles. Gradually the hunter's exhausted pony slackened its pace. Gradually Pernerney, who had pulled away from the boy, gained and gained. At last within range, the chief leveled his pistol and fired. The Caddo seemed to have been hit, but he continued riding, bent forward over his horse. Pernerney took aim, fired again. The hunter fell from his horse, rolled, drew himself up to a sitting position, facing his pursuers. As the boy approached, he saw that only Pernerney, Tuchispooder (the chief's brother), and he himself had followed this far. Pernerney drew up his lathered, blowing pony before the seated figure. He held out his old pistol to the boy.

"Shoot him in the head."

The boy gripped the pistol, moved his horse to the Caddo, leaned down and fired. The man dropped on his back. Tuchispooder dismounted. With his knife, while Chief Pernerney and the boy watched, he removed the dead Caddo's scalp. Leaving the body as it lay, the two men and the boy rode away over the rolling prairie, with the extra pony trailing behind.[9]

✛✛

Theodore Adolphus, the Texas captive, was becoming a Comanche warrior.

SIXTEEN

La Independencia . . . *and Change, 1821*

In 1821, when Thomas James and his party were detained in the Yamparica camp by the Canadian River, their situation had become rapidly more perilous. Two days after the chiefs forbade the traders to depart, the One-Eyed Chief (called by Spaniards El Tuerto) rode into the village, followed by a hundred men, all of them painted black and armed with guns, or bows and arrows, and lances. Chief Big Star came up to James at once and conducted him into the little old chief's tepee, informing him (presumably in Spanish) that if he remained outside he would be shot. The headman next sent a messenger to ask One-Eye what he would take as a substitute for the lives of the Americans. El Tuerto would accept cloth for his men, but for himself he demanded a "splendid sword" he had glimpsed among the trade goods at their encounter on the Cimarron River. Unfortunately James had already presented this sword to Big Star. Now he was stymied, his life depending upon recovery of the weapon. But while the trader was agonizing over various dismal alternatives, Big Star sent to his lodge for the sword that the other chief coveted. On its arrival, the head chief grasped it, gravely pressed it to his chest, and extended it to the American:

"Take it, and send it to the One-Eyed Chief. You have no other way of saving your life and the lives of your people."

For the second time Thomas James's life had been saved by a Comanche chief.

James accepted the sword and sent it as suggested. El Tuerto was faithful to his part of the bargain. Once again the American spoke to the chiefs of his desire to depart. This time the Comanches delayed him with a promise. The village, they said, was moving downriver the next day. At that time the traders would be permitted to continue their journey toward Santa Fe. James and his companions prepared for an early start the next morning. During the night half of them stood guard while the others tried, without success, to sleep. Years later James remembered this as their third sleepless night. All of the party were by now exhausted from loss of sleep and from anxiety.

Before daylight a gang of boys climbed the mound behind the traders and began hurling stones at them. The friendly chief appeared out of the dark and drove them away. But at sunrise James discovered that, despite the guard, the Comanches had stolen six of his horses. He was about to order his men out to find and retrieve them, when the friendly chief reappeared. The Comanche looked concerned and discouraged in the early, pale sunlight.

"Don't leave this spot," he warned. "Keep together, or you'll be killed. Any men that go out will be murdered. Don't try to get back your horses."

Studying the situation, James saw that the entire village was preparing to decamp, disassembling tepees, hitching horses to travoises. Soon he noticed some fifty chiefs and elders climbing the mound above them. A pack of boys and young braves followed, until an old man turned and waved them away. The two friendly chiefs were not among the group. When the fifty men reached the top of the mound, they seated themselves in a circle and smoked. James watched as one of them began addressing the council, using violent gestures.

"This council will decide our fate," he told the others.

"How do you know?"

He shook his head. "If they come down friendly, we'll have nothing to fear. If they're sulky, we have no hope." He advised his group to look over their guns.

While the council deliberated, the women and children were departing on horseback, dragging behind them the lodge poles that served as part of the travoises. As the women disappeared downstream, warriors gathered in increasing numbers before the traders, some mounted, some on foot, but all of them armed with lances, bows, and guns. Finally the chiefs and elders descended from the mound. James immediately noticed that even the Comanches who had previously been sociable now were sullen and distant. A little later the friendly chief and Big Star came up to the traders, shook their hands, and said farewell to them. James tried to persuade the two leaders to remain with his party. But they sadly shook their heads and walked away.

The crowd of warriors had increased. James and the others stood in a semicircle, their backs to the trade goods and saddles piled above their heads. Facing the chiefs and warriors, they held their rifles at chest height, their fingers resting on the triggers. They knew they would have time for only one shot apiece. In their belts they had shoved knives and tomahawks. One man, without a gun, held an axe poised, while time slowly passed. James stood between his friend, John McKnight, and his brother. Mc-

Knight's face was pale, his jaw and lips trembling. James's brother, standing on his other side, looked desperate but determined.

A half-hour went by in silence. Abruptly a chief dressed in an entire bearskin, with the claws over his hands, rode out rapidly with leveled lance. He drew up his pony about fifteen feet before the traders and sat glaring at James. At too great a distance to use his lance, the White Bear Warrior drew his pistol. He inspected the priming, tossed the powder from the pan, reprimed, and again glared at James. But he carefully kept the muzzle lowered.

"For God's sake, let's start," McKnight exclaimed at last. "James, you'll be the first one killed—but this suspense is worse than death. The black chief is my mark."

"No, McKnight, we've got to hold off as long as they do. For us to begin is folly. At the first shot, we fire, rush in, and sell our lives as dearly as possible."

A trader named Kirker evidently could bear the suspense no longer. Holding his rifle over his head, he walked forward, surrendered his weapon and disappeared into the crowd of warriors without being bothered.

All at once James heard a distant cry, which drew nearer, "Tabbaho, tabbaho"—the word for white man. What did it mean? Some reference to Kirker? But the word was murmured throughout the crowd, and heads of warriors began turning. James glanced to the southwest, in the direction from which the cry was coming. Dust—six horsemen were approaching at a run. As they drew nearer, he heard them shout the words "Sálvenlos, sálvenlos!" Spaniards? Yelling, "Save them?" What could that mean? A sudden hope, almost impossible to credit, made his heart thump.

Minutes later six Spanish officers rode through the crowd of warriors. The man in advance trotted up on his frothing horse to embrace James, exclaiming in his own tongue, "Thank God, we're in time! You're all safe and unhurt."

The officer explained that he had heard of their plight only that morning and had ridden twenty miles to save them. When the commotion had subsided, the Spaniards asked the chiefs why they had intended to kill the traders. Leading Comanches replied that the governor in Santa Fe had told them not to allow any Americans to pass westward. These americanos had insisted on proceeding to Santa Fe. To keep their word to the governor, the Ietans had felt compelled to destroy the party. While James listened in surprise, the officers explained that, yes, that had been the policy under the government of Spain. Now they were free and brothers to the Americans!

In this manner James and his companions learned of the Mexican Revolution.

A historical event, working through the agency of the Spanish officers, saved Thomas James and his men. But an individual was also responsible for their rescue. They met him early the next morning as they drew near the Spanish camp.

A tall peace chief walked out on the plains to greet them. About seventy years old, he was dressed in the regimentals of an American colonel—blue coat with epaulets, red sash, white pants, sword. The straight figure approached the horsemen and saluted. James was impressed by eyes that were still piercing and by the high forehead and Roman nose. Understandably grateful to the man who had saved his life, James thought the chief looked like a "real commander and a hero." The Comanche handed him a note written by the U.S. Indian agent at Natchitoches. It identified him as a chief and requested that any Americans who should encounter him or his people "should treat him and them with great respect and kindness, as they are true friends of the United States."

Although James misspelled the old warrior's name, it was Chief Cordero, the same with whom Francisco Amangual had smoked and consulted thirteen years before, the chief to whom he had given an honor guard, and one of those the captain had warned against American encroachment into Comanchería. Cordero was camped with fifty of the Spanish military and three hundred of his warriors. They were relaxing by hunting buffalo together after returning from a joint campaign against the Navajos. Some of Cordero's men had met a group from Big Star's ranchería and learned of the traders' predicament. The signal for the massacre of the Americans was to have been the dismantling of the last lodge, as the village abandoned the site. Word spread quickly. Many of the young braves rode off for the village, hoping to share in the plunder. But Chief Cordero went immediately to the Spanish officers and explained the situation. He was too old for such a hard ride, he told them, or he would go himself. But he begged them to "mount and ride without sparing the horses."[1]

For a third time Thomas James's life had been saved by a Comanche chief.

It was a moment of harmony between Spaniards (now Mexicans) and Americans and Comanches. The future, shaped by human passions, was to prove treacherous. But for an extended moment, James and McKnight, Chief Cordero in his American uniform, and the six Spanish officers could dine on buffalo meat around a fire, could share fellowship, could rejoice together.

Blessed with ignorance of the future, like all men, none knew of the Council House Fight, lying less than twenty years ahead, and the Comanche war with Texans, which led to war between Comanches and Americans. None knew of the coming war, over Texas, between Mexicans and Americans; and later, to close the century, the war between Americans and Spaniards. None yet knew that American cavalry would drive the lofty People from the plains, as they, themselves, had once driven the Apaches, and that the Comanches would vanish from Comanchería as surely as the countless herds of buffalo that had sustained them throughout their 169 years of recorded history. But for that moment of concord, the men seated around the fire were friends, and trusted the future together.

III

Los Comanches versus Three Republics

*The most common vices of the Comanches are vengeance,
pride, and excessive laziness; but at the same time
they are frank and loyal friends even to the Mexicans.
When at war with us if Mexicans are in their camps,
the Comanches will not harm them, showing that he who
lives with them is their friend, regardless of his nationality.*

José María Sánchez, San Antonio, 1828

*The Camanche is a fine looking Indian. . . . The squaws are dressed in deer
skins, and are good looking women . . . appearance of a
Camanche fully equipped on horseback, with his lance and
shield by his side, is beautifully classic.*

T. B. Wheelock, first lieutenant dragoons, Fort Gibson, 1834

We found the village of the Principal Chief *to be filled
with naked, half-starved savages; and of the very lowest
order of the human species. . . . They were badly armed—not
having more than six or eight guns in the village, and
were but indifferent marksmen. It was a general impression
that our company of thirteen might have whipped the
whole village.*

"X.Y.," correspondent of the *Telegraph and Texas Register*,
Houston, 1838

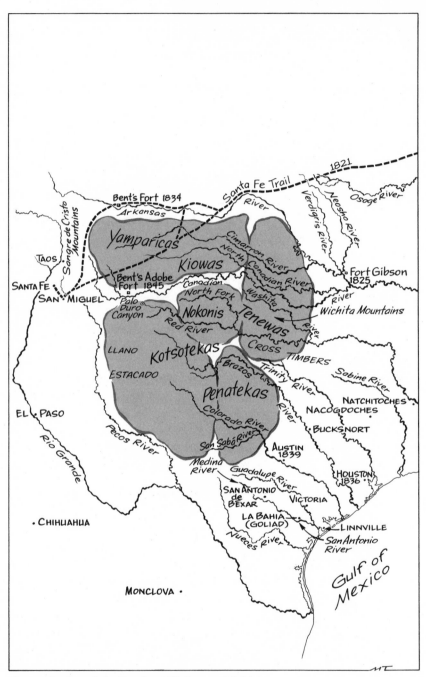

Comanchería and the Southern Plains, ca. 1845
(Placement of Comanche divisions, after Thomas W. Kavanagh, "Comanche Politics," Ph.D. diss., 1986)

1823   The Mexican government's Imperial Colonization Law confirms the Texas land grant to the deceased Moses Austin and transfers it to his son, Stephen.

1825   The United States begins construction of Fort Gibson near present Muskogee, Oklahoma.

1829   Comanches and Kiowas battle U.S. infantry on the Santa Fe Trail.

1830   The U.S. Congress passes the Indian Removal Bill, exiling the Cherokees, Creeks, Choctaws, Chickasaws and, ultimately, Seminoles to Indian Territory in present Oklahoma, land the Comanches, Kiowas, and Wichitan peoples have traditionally considered theirs.

1832   Construction of "Bent's Old Fort" begins on the Arkansas River near present-day La Junta, Colorado.

1833   Sam Houston, as the envoy of U.S. President Andrew Jackson, meets with Comanches in San Antonio.

1834   Artist George Catlin accompanies the First Dragoons from Fort Gibson and sketches Comanches, Kiowas, Taovayases, Wichitas, and Wacos near the Wichita Mountains of present Oklahoma.

1835   At Camp Holmes on the Canadian River, U. S. commissioners conclude a treaty with the Comanches, Taovayases, Wichitas, and Wacos. In Texas, at about this time, the southern Comanches begin their raids against the Anglo-Texans, who simultaneously revolt against the Mexican government of President Antonio López de Santa Anna.

1836   The Anglo-Texans, led by Sam Houston, defeat Santa Anna's army at the battle of San Jacinto, winning their independence from Mexico. Comanche raiders capture Rachel Plummer, Cynthia Ann Parker and Sara Ann Horn.

1839   The Comanches suffer another outbreak of smallpox.

1840   Anglo-Texans kill a delegation of southern Comanche leaders at the "Council House Fight" in San Antonio and defeat a retaliatory raid led by Buffalo Hump at the battle of Plum Creek.

1841   Sam Houston begins his second term and reintroduces his peace policy toward the Comanches and other tribes.

1843   Colonel J. C. Eldredge, commissioner of Indian affairs for the Republic of Texas, and Tom Torrey, trader and Indian Agent, and young Hamilton Bee, meet with Comanche chief Pahayuko at his camp on Pecan Creek, near the Red River.

1844   At Brazos Falls Sam Houston meets in council with the southern Comanche chief, Potsanaquahip (Buffalo Hump), along with other Indian leaders.

1845   The United States annexes Texas.

1846   The Butler-Lewis commission concludes a treaty with the Comanches for the United States.

1846–1848   Mexico and the United States wage a war over the annexation of Texas. Mexico loses Texas, New Mexico, California, and a vast region of the West to its enemy.

1849   Some three thousand forty-niners follow the Canadian River route to the goldfields of California, bringing smallpox and cholera to the Comanches.

1850, 1853   The United States government concludes treaties in each of these years with the Comanches and their Kiowa and Kiowa-Apache allies.

1855   The state of Texas institutes a small reservation for the southern Comanches. Two years later a little more than half of the Penatekas are occupying it.

1858   Both U.S. Army troops and Texas Rangers, acting separately, punish the Comanches north of the Red River.

1860   In the Pease River "Fight" (more accurately, massacre), Ranger Captain Sul Ross recovers Cynthia Ann Parker.

1861–1865   During the Civil War years, the Comanches, essentially neutral, intensify their raids against the Texas frontier in late 1862 and depopulate some sections by 1864 and 1865.

1864   At Adobe Walls, the former Bent post, United States troops under Kit Carson engage a multitude of Kiowas, who are supported by some Comanches, Kiowa-Apaches, and Arapahoes.

1867   At the Medicine Lodge Treaty council, the Comanches (except for the Kotsotekas and Quahadas) agree to renounce their claim to greater Comanchería and to live upon a reservation of some fifty-five hundred square miles in Indian Territory.

1869   The federal government establishes Fort Sill near present-day Lawton, Oklahoma) in order to control the reservation Comanches and Kiowas.

1874   Under the influence of their young prophet, Isatai (Wolf- or Coyote-Droppings), the Comanches hold a Sun Dance this spring. Two days later a great war party of Comanches, Kiowas, and Cheyennes attacks Adobe Walls, a buffalo hunters' station near the old Bent trading post. This battle begins the Red River War. That fall the U.S. Fourth Cavalry surprises and routs a vast encampment of Comanches and their allies at Palo Duro Canyon, striking them a decisive blow.

1875   In June, Quanah Parker leads a band of Quahadas into Fort Sill. His surrender signals, in effect, the end of the Comanches's free life upon the southern plains.

SEVENTEEN

Power and Puha

During his 1834 visit to the "great Camanchee village," George Catlin employed his pen as well as his brush to describe his impressions. [1] The Comanches he saw as quintessential horsemen. On foot they were, in his view, "unattractive and slovenly-looking." Short and often plump, they moved heavily and awkwardly. Another observer later compared them to sailors on shore leave, walking as if the earth were billowing beneath them. Some were as bowlegged as the proverbial old cowhand. But once these horsemen leapt upon their ponies, they were transformed into graceful beings. Catlin wrote that the moment a Comanche laid his hand upon his horse, his face became handsome. But another, and prejudiced, observer found the People handsome all of the time. Writing in 1812 from Cádiz, the New Mexico Spaniard Don Pedro Bautista Pino declared that "the Comanche is known . . . for his magnificent size and graceful appearance, his frank martial air, and his modest dress . . ."

Catlin's view of the Comanches is the prevailing one. Yet there is such a variety of differing and contradictory contemporary descriptions of the Comanches that some should be balanced against the predominant view. In 1786 for example, Governor Domingo Cabello y Robles of Texas was struck by the height and muscular development of Comanches visiting the capital at Béxar. But when he complimented these chiefs on their fine physiques, they told him there were many more powerful men than they among their people. When he tried to outfit them with Spanish officers' uniforms as gifts, he found his visitors so tall that nothing in his warehouse would fit them. Forty-two years later, Jean Louis Berlandier, also at San Antonio, wrote that "the Comanche people are all tall, well-proportioned, and not at all disagreeable as to physiognomy." (He was especially struck by the men's absence of beards and by "the way they completely pluck out their eyebrows and lashes."). Around 1849 Captain John Salmon "Rip" Ford, of the Texas Rangers, observed that the Comanches were "generally tall and well formed." Later yet, Captain Randolph Marcy, U.S. Army, in an 1853 report to the Senate, depicted Ietan warriors in these terms: "The

Comanche men are about the medium stature, with bright, copper-colored complexions and intelligent countenances, in many instances with aquiline noses, thin lips, black eyes and hair . . ."

Of course Spanish soldiers of that period may have been short. But average Frenchmen? And Texas Rangers? Not to be overlooked was the intermarriage with captives among all Comanche divisions. These unions probably produced individuals who were taller than average for the tribe, and this may account for some of the discrepancies in contemporary descriptions of the men. In any event the Comanches were a robust people. Although shorter on the average than other Plains Indians, and inclined toward corpulence, the men were proud of their muscular development and vigor, those basic manifestations of male physical power.

But, like later Americans, the Comanches desired other forms of power. The kinds concerning the Nuhmuhnuh were of two sorts. The first, and most important, was "medicine," or supernatural power, usually obtained through a vision. No chief could be without it. Warriors would not follow a man on a war party unless they had confidence in his medicine. Any individual who lost faith in that power was justified in dropping from the group. The other type of power is more familiar to contemporary Americans. Although personal prestige rather than wealth was primary among the Comanches, this concept of power includes wealth, which even today may be measured symbolically in terms of "horse power." Most of all, though, it includes the right legally to influence or command the actions of others. Comanche culture rested upon the use of all forms of power, even those of reason and persuasion when these were wielded in council by a respected peace chief. But it rested especially upon those of medicine and the socially recognized right to influence or command. These two principal kinds of power were frequently combined to be employed outside the tribe against the People's enemies.

Of the Comanche warrior's "arms," those extensions of his will and personal strength, the lance, bow, and arrows had no supernatural associations.[2] The lance, ordinarily ranging from six to eight feet in length, was traditionally tipped with a Spanish sword blade and was thrust underhand, while the short bow, a horseman's weapon, was made of Osage orange and was gripped horizontally while shot. (According to Mildred Mott Wedel, Claude du Tisné, the French explorer, as early as 1719 mentioned Indian lances fitted with Spanish swords). But the object joining both kinds of power was the warrior's *chimal*, or shield. From a practical standpoint, it was a defensive weapon of tough bullhide stuffed with horsehair or, later, paper—even the pages of an entire book. From another point of view, it was an object partaking of the sacred. Rimmed with feathers, it was painted with symbolic designs and often had fixed at its center an amulet to which the warrior offered reverence.

Puha (or *pouha*) was the Comanche word for "power" or medicine, and the amulet at the shield's center was called a *pouhahante*. Its main purpose was the supernatural protection of its bearer from injury in battle. Jean Louis Berlandier noted that the pouhahante might consist of bones or entire dried animals, such as rats, birds, lizards, or snakes. The shield represented a kind of shrine and, except in battle, was protected from contaminating moisture or grease by a cover of tanned and painted leather. The chimal hung on a lance, or on a tripod of three lances, outside the warrior's tepee and was never allowed to touch the ground. But the idea of the amulet's power was taken even further: Berlandier also observed that the pouhahante on the shield was sometimes consulted like a small oracle, who might then reply in a dream.[3]

All dreams among the Nuhmuhnuh were not of equal importance. Ordinary dreams had little significance. Others, whose transcendence the dreamer could recognize, were portentous and revelatory. Comanches paid great attention to these. But equally important were visions, which had to be sought in a prescribed manner. The belief among Comanches that comes closest to Western ideas of religion was their faith in the effectiveness of efforts by an individual to gain supernatural power, or puha. This was expressed, in action, by that person's quest for a vision.

The Comanches believed, of course, in a Supreme Being, who lived behind the sun. This Universal Father was complemented by the earth, Mother of all living things. But the Comanches regarded the sun and earth with some detachment. These deities lacked the immediate, vital connection associated with a personal vision. David Burnet, first interim president of the Texas Republic, spent much of 1818 and 1819 near or among the Nuhmuhnuh. Describing them later, and clearly from a Eurocentric viewpoint, he managed to make them sound like eighteenth-century deists, writing that "indeed they consider the Supreme Being, to be so far removed from them as not to wish to interfere directly, in their temporal concerns, and as equally unwilling to be interfered with. They therefore leave him to enjoy his repose without molestation, and expect the same indulgence for themselves."[4]

With a man's personal medicine, it was a different matter. The warrior probably remembered his quest for puha and its acquisition as belonging among the most important moments of his life. The vision through which he first received communication from the supernatural may have seemed to him the summit of his spiritual experience.

At the time of puberty, before venturing upon the warpath, a youth would take the steps necessary for initiating a vision quest. There was a socially recognized pattern for this; the anthropologist Ruth Benedict actually believed the social recognition of the vision to be the "fundamental and typical religious fact" among North American Indians.[5] Probably a medicine man would instruct the novice, requiring him first to bathe, in a preparatory rite of purification. When the time was appropriate, the youth would set out alone, on foot, from the camp, wearing only his breechclout and moccasins. With him he would carry a buffalo robe, tobacco, a pipe, and the means to light it. Four times he would halt on the way to his destination. At each spot he would smoke and pray to the spirits. On reaching the chosen place, often near a hilltop, facing south, he would again smoke and pray. With nightfall he would cover himself entirely, keeping his head under the robe until dawn, an act that, in itself must have taken courage. At the first rays of the rising sun, he would stand and face the light, in order to absorb the sun's power.

For at least four days and nights the youth would remain, without water and fasting, on his lonely hilltop, waiting and praying. Unlike the young men of many other Plains tribes, he would practice neither self-abasement nor self-torture. It was not for him to beseech the supernatural like an Arapaho—or like a Crow or a Cheyenne, to cut off a finger as an offering to the sun or to the spirits he sensed to be watching him.[6] Smoking and praying in humility, the Comanche would address himself to the spirits with confidence. Compared to them, he was weak, while they were strong. But a mark of the great and powerful was generosity. So he waited, trusting that some spirit would, out of sheer beneficence, share its power with him.

Sometimes the quest failed. No vision came. The youth would have to return another time. But often it did come—in a waking dream, a voice heard in a trance, a hallucination. In this manner the successful aspirant encountered the spirit that was to become his supernatural guardian. It might manifest itself visibly to him in the form of an eagle, a buffalo, a bear, or as almost any wild animal. Spirits were also associated with natural forces, and the vision seeker might succeed in summoning one on his hilltop, or in a canyon, or at a spring. Whatever its source or manifestation, the spirit would instruct the young man, using the Comanche tongue, emphasizing the prescripts and taboos he must observe if he were to use his new puha effectively and with good, not evil, results. The spirit would give the youth one or more songs to be chanted when he wished to "make medicine," or consult with his guardian. On the basis of this experience, a young Comanche would later select the contents of his medicine pouch, which would also aid him in contacting the spirit. The pouch might contain almost any natural objects—feathers, herbs, fur, or fangs. But the instruction received in the vision remained among the most valuable and sacred of a male Comanche's psychic possessions, especially when he was preparing for, or actually upon, the warpath.

And if the youth were unable to induce a vision? A young man among the Comanches could always ask a medicine man to share some of his power with him. The other would not ordinarily refuse.[7] But all the shaman could do was to prepare the novice for contact with a certain guardian spirit—say, a wolf. The youth was still obliged to go out again and seek an encounter with that wolf-spirit through a vision. The boy's family would reward the medicine man for such sharing, probably with a horse and other gifts, agreed upon in advance. But among the Nuhmuhnuh there was no regular commerce in supernatural power, such as the buying and selling of medicine bundles (really visions) by the Blackfoot, or the trade in guardian spirits among the Crows and Arapahoes; although a Comanche medicine man might capitalize upon a reputation for successful cures and other rituals.

In common with other Plains tribes, with their individualistic attitudes, the Comanches had no class of priests among them.[8] All men had direct, personal relations with the supernatural, principally through the medium of the vision. Visions might be sought repeatedly, as for example during mourning, for curative power, or for success in the hunt or on the warpath. Individuals who demonstrated what appeared to be a favored relationship with the supernatural, who possessed exceptional "power," came to be considered medicine men, but they formed no class and were deemed to be no more exalted than wealthy men or outstanding warriors.[9] There were even, among the Comanches, postmenopausal medicine women.

As a young man grew older and acquired experience as a member of successive raiding, vengeance, or war parties, he would begin to think of leading such a foray himself. (The Comanches distinguished between the three types of groups; this book generally employs "war party" to include all of them.) Perhaps around this time he would have an important dream or evoke a vision and would interpret either one as a summons to lead such an expedition. He would probably sing and make medicine, consulting with his guardian spirit by means of the medicine pouch he carried within his breechclout. Should he believe his guardian spirit favored the foray, he would invite comrades into his lodge to discuss the project. If the other men believed in the young warrior's medicine, and if he were a brave man with qualities of leadership, his comrades would smoke the pipe with him, indicating their willingness to join the party. Any among them who doubted would allow the pipe to pass.

After leading a series of successful raids, the warrior would, over a few years, acquire a reputation for his valor, good sense, and the potency of his medicine; which, in a superficial way, might be equated with "luck." Because he was a Plains Indian, he would also have gained prestige by such war honors as stealing horses from an enemy camp, taking scalps, and counting coups. The coup (French for "blow," which can also carry a suggestion of "deed") was a far greater honor than collecting a scalp.

Specifically it signified the touching of an enemy with the hand or, among the Cheyennes, a specially striped "coup-stick." The Comanches, though, might apply the word to other daring deeds. The People gave credit for a blow by two separate warriors on the same individual. The Cheyennes allowed three touches, each by a different man, while the Arapahoes permitted four. Touching a dead foe during battle gained one the honor, but the greatest deed was to touch a living enemy, an act that could be extremely dangerous, even if the man were fallen and dying.[10]

If the Comanche warrior were also generous in his distribution of horses and other booty to members of his parties, he would have no trouble in finding followers to accompany him on raids, unless his puha was perceived on any occasion to fail him. Then he, and his wives and children as well, would suffer a loss of prestige, since status was based to such an extent upon apparent supernatural power and upon the war honors presumed to be associated with it. But if he continued to be successful in raiding and in war, he would probably become a war chief, a social advancement that more or less just "happened." Later if he lived long enough (there was a high mortality rate among war chiefs), he might even become the head war chief of a band or a division. Then he would wield a certain amount of power over his people.

Yet like that of even the greatest of Comanche chieftains, an Ecueracapa, for example, this ambitious warrior's power would never be more than relative. A series of Spaniards, Frenchmen, Mexicans, Anglo-Texans, and Americans understood, if at all, only with difficulty the restrictions upon individual authority among the Comanches and their neighbors. Jean Louis Berlandier was one of those who did understand, writing in 1834, "So ingrained is the love of liberty among the American natives that their chiefs, though recognized as leaders, have strictly limited powers." A chief among the Nuhmuhnuh commanded through force of personal presence and prestige. He had no legal power to compel others.[11] Coercive power, rarely exercised, was the result of consensus in council. So while various forms of influence and authority existed among the People, no Comanche chieftain alone, no matter how renowned, was ever able to exercise more than relative legal, coercive power.

Curiously despite the fact that power among the Comanches rested ultimately upon the supernatural, the People have been called the "Skeptics of the Plains." A contemporary anthropologist, Daniel J. Gelo, has recently demonstrated the falsity of this charge and has shown how a stereotyped and derogatory impression of Comanche religion evolved from the writings of such frontier observers as David G. Burnet (whose "field observations were filtered through a puritan worldview") to the early American ethnologist James Mooney, who stigmatized the Nuhmuhnuh as skeptics. The stereotype has persisted to the present; principally because Comanche elders consistently "downplayed" religion in response to anthropologists' questions (answering, for instance, "We are hunters and warriors . . . ," etc.), and because Comanches in general avoided and still avoid ostentatious religious display. In Gelo's words, the old men's replies indicated "moral courage, intended to impress upon the listener that the speaker is not paralyzed by his regard for the supernatural . . ." Furthermore today's Comanches, when questioned about their rejection of "showy demonstrations of belief," frequently remark that this trait distinguishes them from the Kiowas, with whom it appears they have had a "love-hate" relationship dating back at least to the start of reservation days.[12]

While the Comanches were by no means the "Skeptics of the Plains," their religion did differ significantly from the religions of most other Plains tribes, including the faiths and practices of the Kiowas and Cheyennes. Robert G. Lowie, for instance, argues persuasively that most other Plains Indians were originally southeastern or "western" Woodland peoples, who brought their traditions with them when they moved out upon the Great Plains. These traditions included the glorification of war and the warrior, as well as the sought vision obtained by means of isolation, fasting and self-torture. The Comanches, on the other hand, migrated as Shoshones eastward from the Great Basin, possibly even from California, bringing with them traditions differing from those of the Woodland Indians. Consequently some aspects of their religion are more characteristic of the basin than of the plains.[13] Notably they refused the more masochistic attitudes and rites of Plains culture.

East of the Rockies, noted Ruth Benedict, the vision was typically induced by hunger and thirst, by purgatives and self-laceration. But to the west, although the tradition of the quest also existed, the vision was widely considered to be "unsought, involuntary, a thing of predisposition."[14] The Comanches retained their belief in the fortuitous dream and the spontaneous vision, while incorporating the custom of the vision quest that was characteristic of other Plains tribes. For the quest they adopted the elements of isolation, hunger, and thirst, but rejected the aspect of self-laceration, such as the Cheyenne practice of cutting and peeling off strips of skin.

They also refused to chop off fingers, like the Cheyennes or Mandans, as offerings to the sun or to the Great Spirit.[15]

While the Comanches seem to have held the Sun Dance occasionally from at least 1860 on, they also adapted this ceremony to their own religious attitudes, which rejected the element of self-torture found in its observance by other Plains tribes. The Comanche version, in contrast for example to that of the Kiowas, involved no tearing of the dancers' flesh by cords through their pectoral or dorsal muscles. Comanche dancers were permitted to chew slippery elm bark and to sip fluid extracted from strips of the bark. Even more practical (and humane), if any dancer appeared to be failing, so that there was a question as to whether or not he might last through the ceremony, his father was permitted to arrange for his release.[16] So the Comanches were "pragmatic" about religion, which remained a highly personal affair for each; yet the very assumption of a pragmatic stance toward the supernatural was in itself evidently a form of tribally endorsed ritual.[17]

The warrior ethos of the Comanches included a paramount spiritual dimension while lacking what people of European descent might call moral directives. But what about the Comanches' white adversaries? Many Anglo-Texan pioneers were necessarily warriors too. Convinced of their rectitude, they shared Judeo-Christian values and ideals. Many were devout Christians. What, then, was their attitude toward those peoples whom they classed as "savages?" Attitudes of course varied from person to person, but the following account is probably not unrepresentative of the prevailing point of view toward all Indians on the Texas frontier in the nineteenth century.

In 1823 a Kentuckian named Dewees settled, with a few others, some distance up the Colorado River of Texas. Dewees, a gunsmith and blacksmith, had been raised by a Baptist minister. He was a youngish man of some education and sensibilities. For example after the vengeance killing of some Karankawa Indians, he decided to take a scalp, but he reported to his lady friend in Louisville that the skin of the dead man's head was so thick "and the sight so ghastly, that the very thought of it almost makes the blood curdle in my veins." In another letter, written to the same lady in December, Dewees described another encounter with Texas Indians.

That fall a war party of 180 Tawakonies and Wacos visited his settlement. They assured the alarmed settlers they intended them no harm, that they were seeking their enemies, the Tonkawas. But while waiting for reports from their scouts, they demanded meat. From their camp by the settlement, they compelled one Williams to slaughter a milk cow (a rarity on the frontier) for their use. Uneasy, Dewees and his companions decided to conclude a treaty with the warriors, telling the chiefs they were sending for their "big captain." Of the nine male settlers, the most impressive was a Colonel James B. Ross, a big, good-looking man who had had some experience with Indians. While Ross's wife and daughters were at the house of a neighbor, a mile away, they used his cabin for a council room, where they agreed upon a treaty with the Wichitan leaders.

But Dewees, Ross, Williams, and the other six men had no faith that such a pact would really protect their settlement. Immediately afterward they began trying to contrive a way to kill the people with whom they had just arranged a treaty, "lest on their leaving they should attempt to commit depredations." On reflection, though, they decided they were too greatly outnumbered, and that any attack on the Indians would expose their women and children to reprisals. That evening, when the Wichitan warriors were dancing before a fire, Dewees and the others found "the temptation to cut off their retreat to their wigwams, where they had left their arms, and then fire upon them, was almost too strong to be resisted." Again, though, fearing to leave the women and children unprotected, they reluctantly rejected the idea.

The war party remained camped next to the settlement for three days and nights. On the fourth morning its scouts returned and reported having seen no signs of the Tonkawas. With that the Wichitan chiefs and warriors departed. Dewees concluded his letter to his distant friend by telling her, "We then, all of us, returned to our respective homes feeling very thankful, that the Indians had gone, without committing any depredations, though mortified, that we had been unable to destroy them." [18]

EIGHTEEN

El Tuerto Takes an American Brother, 1823

After independence in 1821, and before becoming a republic in 1824, Mexico was briefly a constitutional monarchy, with neither constitution nor monarch, and with a former royalist officer, Agustín de Iturbide, heading its provisional government. In the spring of 1822 Iturbide's troops pronounced him emperor. But most provinces refused to recognize their new would-be ruler and went on about their business, ignoring Mexico City. Virtually ostracized by the nation, Emperor Agustín I abdicated the following year. By early 1824 delegates from around the country had fashioned the relatively liberal Federal Constitution of the United States of Mexico, a document that, in turn, led to the First Federal Republic.[1]

Meanwhile Comanche-Mexican relations continued on their bumpy road much as they had during the final two decades of Spanish rule, especially in Texas, which was now stuck to Coahuila to form the state of Coahuila y Tejas. Just before losing Mexico, Spanish authorities pardoned a young Spaniard living in American Natchitoches on the condition that he represent the government in negotiations with the Comanches and other Texas tribes. That young man, José Francisco Ruíz, was a native Texan, formerly a lieutenant in the royal army.[2] In 1812 he had joined the Magee-Gutiérrez force of republican adventurers and, upon the expedition's defeat, had been compelled to flee. In the intervening years, he had gained considerable influence with the Comanches, Wichitans, Lipans, and other native peoples.

Mexican officials, after celebrating *la independencia* that spring, confirmed the arrangement with Ruíz, who from then on, until the Anglo-Texan revolt in the fall of 1835, often served as Indian agent to the Comanches. Fatefully for Comanches and mexicanos, at about the same time, Governor Antonio Martínez of Texas (acting prematurely, as it turned out) confirmed Stephen F. Austin's claim to his deceased father's grant east of the Colorado River, where the young empresario soon began establishing the nucleus of an Anglo-American colony.

During the same months the *ayuntamiento*, or town council, at San Antonio commissioned one of its members to work at achieving a peace with the People. This commissioner rode through the Tawakoni villages on the Brazos River to a Comanche encampment. There he met with Pisinape, Paruaquibitse, and several other chiefs. Pisinape was, of course, the alleged troublemaker "Decayed Shoe." In 1810 Chief Cordero had accused him of breaking the treaty with Spain by raiding in Texas and Coahuila and returning with horses that he and his followers reportedly sold to American traders. Paruaquibitse was probably the same as the "Parrow-a-Kifty," or "Little Bear," known in 1819 to David G. Burnet, first (acting) president of the Texas Republic. Burnet called him "brave, enterprising, and intelligent." Little Bear was famed for his "taciturnity and sedateness" and because he reputedly "never laughed, except in battle." Jean Louis Berlandier, who knew Little Bear in 1828 (calling him "Barbakista") observed that this "most famous and important chief," evidently a wealthy man, supported eleven wives.

As a result of talks with the Mexican commissioner, Pisinape visited Béxar in the summer of 1822 in order to sign a truce, so that other leaders of his tribe might journey to Mexico City for negotiations with officials there. That fall a Comanche party set out from San Antonio for the Mexican capital. Accompanying them were José Francisco Ruíz and an escort of soldiers. Several chiefs formed the delegation, including one Guonique and the important Paruaquibitse, or Little Bear. Mexican authorities received them ceremoniously, loading them with gifts. As with visits in later years by chiefs to Washington, these headmen wondered at the size of the buildings and at the throngs of people on the streets.[3]

Early in 1823 the chiefs signed yet another treaty for their followers, vowing everlasting friendship and peace and pledging to control their young warriors. The treaty also established regulations for trade between the two nations. One curious portion of the agreement permitted the Comanches to retain their captives, while the government promised to create trading posts for the tribe's convenience in Texas. In return the Comanches were to maintain a sort of ambassador in San Antonio and, interestingly, were required to send off to boarding schools in Mexico City twelve young men every four years to be educated as Mexicans.

In spite of the treaty, some raiding persisted in Texas, particularly in its northeastern part. There, in the vicinity of the Red River, Comanches periodically stole horses from the new Anglo colonists (squatters, that is), in order to sell them to American traders on the other side of the international boundary. Not that this particular frontier had much significance for either Comanches or Americans. In 1820 for example, the Arkansas Territorial Legislature had created Miller county, brazenly including within its limits Spanish land lying south of the Red.[4] Even earlier thousands of American frontiersmen had forded or ferried the Sabine River, farther south, into Spanish Texas, and it is estimated that between 1821 and 1836 some thirty to thirty-five thousand American squatters crossed those two rivers to settle upon Mexican soil.[5] (In 1821, aside from Native Americans, there were some twenty-five hundred legal residents of Texas.) It would have been surprising if the Comanches had not taken advantage of the proximity of their new neighbors to engage in occasional trading and horse-stealing expeditions.

Fulfilling a condition of the 1823 treaty, José Francisco Ruíz the following year distributed two thousand pesos worth of gifts to the Comanches. Yet the presents bought only a brief interval of calm. The promised trading posts failed to appear, and by 1825, according to Mexican records, hostilities had begun anew. Two years later, after a defeat, chiefs of bands around San Antonio rode into that town, met with Mexican authorities, and agreed upon a truce. The next year Paruaquibitse returned to Béxar and informed officials that he had spent the previous months in sounding out the divisional chiefs and other leaders of his people, and that they all desired peace. Once again for a time, the Comanches substituted a modest trade for marauding.

During this interlude of peace, several Comanche chiefs demonstrated the conscientious behavior of which they were capable, by returning stolen horses to Mexican authorities. Little Bear, for instance, took it upon himself to restore a bunch of horses earlier seized by the Tawakonies, evidently not endearing himself to these sometime allies by his action. In 1831 another Comanche leader, Isazona, brought to Béxar sixteen head previously run off from Goliad. That August yet another Comanche chief, Yncoroy, delivered to Matamoros an additional forty-six head that had been stolen on various occasions.

But shortly afterward, in autumn, a disaster occurred that contained at least two ironies. Paruaquibitse, perhaps the most important friendly Texas Comanche, chose unwisely to camp with a few of his people among the Tawakonies, in an attempt to induce them to make peace with the mexicanos. At the same time, a Mexican force under Captain Manuel LaFuente discovered and attacked their encampment spread along Cowhouse Creek. Upon the dawn assault, Comanches rushed from their lodges, shouting that they were friends and not to shoot. Unfortunately, before LaFuente could control his men, Mexican soldiers and militiamen had killed, besides five Tawakoni warriors, both Little Bear and his son.[6]

The Comanches did not immediately respond with hostilities, presumably because they realized the slayings had been accidental. In fact early in

1832 Chief Isazona sent a message informing Mexican authorities that the People held no bad feelings against them because of Paruaquibitse's death. But the situation continued to worsen as, later in the year, displaced Shawnees from the United States attacked Yncoroy's rancheria, killing a large number of Comanches, including friendly Chief Isazona himself.

Relations between Comanches and Mexicans continued to sour until, by 1833, officials in San Antonio decided to encourage the Shawnees in their hostilities against the Nuhmuhnuh. Not much was done for two years, but in 1835 they placed an Anglo-Texan, Peter Elias Bean, in charge of executing this plan. Bean was busily trying to persuade the Shawnees and Cherokees to raid the Comanches when, in May, General Martín Perfecto de Cos ordered a halt to that policy and a return to the traditional one of offering presents to the so-called "wild tribes." In August, with raids and skirmishes already occurring on the Texas frontier, three hundred Comanches paused at Béxar on their way south to Matamoros, where they were to conclude a treaty with General Cos.[7] Yet by fall the general and his compatriots had an even more critical problem to consider: at the town of Gonzales, on October 2, 1835, Anglo-Texan and Mexican forces fought the first battle of the Texas Revolution.

Thus it was that Mexican soldiers accidently killed Little Bear in 1832. But to glance backward, what had happened meanwhile to Cordero and Pisinape? What had become of Pisinape, alias El Tuerto? What had become of Chief Decayed Shoe?

Pisinape, it appears, had formed a new relationship, found a new "brother."

Between the ages of twenty-five and thirty, when a Comanche man had acquired at least a few horses and gained some reputation as a warrior, he would probably marry. His first wife was likely to be around sixteen years old. Should he have, say, a successful father who was headman of the band, he and his wife (later wives) and children would probably become members of that *nemenahkahne*, or extended family.[8] The band itself would consist of one or more extended families, all within that headman's sphere of influence. It would form, in turn, part of the collection of bands making up the division, a political unit under the direction of a divisional chief, such as Cordero of the Kotsotekas, who would serve also as headman of his own nemenahkahne and band.

Within the extended family, the warrior would have a variety of relationships, including, probably, a cordial one with his parents and a coarse, lusty, joking one with his brother-in-law. With his mother-in-law he could have a respectful but even mildly humorous relationship, since there was no mother-in-law taboo among the People. If he had a sister, the relationship could vary from affectionate to downright hostile. Comanche children, as the ethnologist Thomas Gladwin points out, were under the authority of the oldest sibling at home. When that child was a girl, it sometimes happened that she disciplined her brothers with a whip and "often delighted in teasing them in various more or less nasty ways," including calling them "slave."[9] But the closest family relationship was that between a man and his brothers. There was supposed to be no jealousy among them. An older brother would often leave his wife with a younger one when he departed with a war party. He would assume his brother would sleep with her and would expect reciprocal generosity when that brother married. Yet there was one relationship between men which could be even closer than that between actual brothers.

Comanche men had among them a special category of "friend." This custom of "an institutionalized friendship" was shared with other Plains tribes.[10] The ethnologist Ralph Linton has observed that through the practice a man gained a "brother" or "friend" who was even closer to him than a real brother.[11] The relationship might begin in childhood or later, when two youths courted young women together. Often it began in the stress of battle, when one man or youth might save the life of the other. The two were like "best friends" among later Americans, but closer, since these friendships were tested frequently in warfare. If a man were to ride off and leave his friend lying wounded on a battlefield, he was disgraced among his people. There was, consciously at least, no homosexual element to this relationship. The Comanches scorned homosexuality, and (in contrast to the Cheyennes and other Plains tribes) there was no place for the *berdache*, or homosexual male in a woman's role, in their society.[12] "Friends" assumed the roles of actual brothers. If Comanches made terrible, vengeful enemies, they could also make remarkable friends.

Thomas James believed this band of Comanches now to be friendly toward him.[13] This recent fix had not been as precarious as that of two years ago, in 1821, with Big Star's Yamparicas, but it had been perilous. He was almost positive some of this band had murdered McKnight. If he hadn't succeeded just now, in council, in persuading the chief and the others to smoke with him, he would have had little hope of returning to his temporary fort on the North Canadian. He was sure of that. As it was, he probably now had a good chance of leading the Indians there for trade.

By the tint of the sky outside the tepee, he knew it must be around sunset. He was congratulating himself on having handled the situation as he had, when a shadow flitted across the doorway. Potter ducked in with a grim expression: he held out a gun barrel.

"The One-Eyed Chief's here. He threw this down and said to take it to you."

James regarded the gun barrel. He had heard the One-Eyed Chief was in camp. He had no more dangerous an enemy. "That's all he said?"

"That's all." Potter stared out the door. "He's out there now. On his horse. What shall I say to him?"

James rose and went outside to where the One-Eyed Chief sat his pony. He extended his hand to him. The chief grasped it, all the while gazing penetratingly into his eyes. Meeting the look calmly, the American invited him in Spanish to dismount and enter his lodge. Within the tepee, James seated his guest on a pile of hides. El Tuerto sat silently, with a grave expression. Seating himself, the trader lighted and smoked a pipe with him. Afterward, still in silence, he hung a silver gorget around the man's neck, slipped a silver armband above each elbow, and another upon each wrist. One-Eye continued to sit as if in a trance, submitting in silence. James placed two plugs of tobacco, a knife, and a string of long, colored beads in his lap, while the war chief sat abstractedly. Once again James lighted the pipe. The two men smoked in silence until it had burned out. The Comanche then rose and silently departed. Outside, his pony kicked up dust as it started off at a lope.

James mused, the burnt-out pipe still in his hands, the gun barrel lying at his feet. The last time, in 1821, the One-Eyed Chief had been waiting to kill him up on the Arkansas River. On the third day of his party's enforced stay at the Yamparica encampment, the One-Eyed Chief had ridden in at the head of a hundred warriors, all of them painted black and bearing lances and bows or guns. Luckily Big Star had saved his life by returning the sword the One-Eyed Chief had demanded, and which he himself had then sent to El Tuerto. That was the last time James had seen the One-Eyed Chief, until now.

The following day the entire camp packed up and started its horses and travoises moving toward the fort. Although the One-Eyed Chief said nothing to James, the Taovayas chief, Alsarea, questioned him sharply about the Osages, appearing to suspect that James was delivering them into their enemies' hands. Late that evening the band crossed the North Canadian and set up camp on its bank. A guard of warriors led James to the lodge of the head chief, where he was to spend the night. He was inspecting his goods when the One-Eyed Chief rode up. To the American's astonishment, the Comanche addressed him (it was the first time he had ever spoken to him) in fluent Spanish, inviting him in a cordial manner to accompany him to his lodge.

James suspected treachery. At that moment the old chief called the trader to him. When he learned of the invitation, he advised declining it, because the war chief was "a bad man." On the trader's return to the lodge, El Tuerto repeated his request.

"No," said James, busying himself with his goods.

The warrior walked away, seeming impatient and irritated. Abruptly he turned, focusing his single, black eye upon the American. He walked back to James and suddenly was pleading with him to accompany him. James noticed that while the Comanche was unarmed, he himself was wearing in his belt two pistols, a knife, and a tomahawk. Besides, he and his companions were a mere four Americans in a camp containing hundreds of warriors, at whose mercy they were, in any case.

"I'll come over in the morning," James suggested.

"No, no," exclaimed the war chief. "Come now. Oh, come with me *now*."

James gave in at last. He was walking beside the chief's horse, when a pack of the camp's dogs came at him with such noisy aggression that One-Eye was obliged to spring from his pony to drive them off. After that James rode behind the chief as he galloped to his lodge.

The chief tossed his reins to a wife. In the lodge James was received with smiles by another, evidently the war chief's favorite. He chose a seat opposite the chief, who sat on his buffalo-robe bed, with his weapons dangling from a lodge pole above him. James watched closely as El Tuerto lighted a pipe. Passing it back and forth, the Comanche and the American smoked until the favorite wife brought in buffalo meat.

"I'm sorry it's so poor," she said. "We're out of marrow to cook with, and the buffalo are poor. But it's the best we have right now, and you are welcome to it."

Thomas James thought his hostess charming.

After the meal the two men again smoked in silence. At last the One-Eyed Chief tapped the ashes into his palm. Slowly he raised his head, fixing James with his black, single eye.

"Do you know me?"

"Yes."

"Where did you first see me?"

"On the Cimarron River."

"The second time?"

"At the village on the Canadian."

"Did you know I wanted to kill you?"

"I knew."

"I did. If it hadn't been for Big Star, head chief of the Yamparicas, I would have killed you and your men. I knew you'd been trading with the Osages. You were using their horses, their saddles, their ropes, their skins."

James acknowledged this with a nod.

"The Osages had stolen about two hundred of our horses. My brother and I went out with a war party to get them back and punish the thieves. We caught up with them and fought a battle. They killed my brother. My brother was a great warrior, a hunter, a good man. I loved my brother."

The war chief went on eulogizing his dead brother while the tears slid down his face; until, finally, he could no longer speak and gave way to violent weeping.

James's eyes strayed to the weapons hanging above the chief.

But El Tuerto recovered his composure. He went on to tell of a war party to avenge his brother. During that expedition he had trailed and overtaken James and his men on the Cimarron. He fell silent. Placing the ashes from his hand on the earth, he covered them with a handful of dirt taken from the firepit. Three times he patted the mound. Twice more he covered the ashes, patting again, moaning and once more weeping violently as he did so.

Again James glanced uneasily at the weapons.

When the war chief raised his face, his expression had changed, had become almost rapt. "There. I've buried my brother, but I've found another. I'll take you for my brother." Rising, the One-Eyed Chief came and threw his arms around James, repeating, "my brother, my brother." Around James's neck, he hung an amulet, explaining that it had belonged to his brother. It possessed the power to ward off danger from all enemies. His brother had left it behind the time they had fought the Osages, which was the reason he had been killed. After that, One-Eye spoke more quietly. He wanted to know whether the old civil chief had tried to dissuade James from coming to his lodge.

"He did."

"He's an old fool. He hasn't made up his mind whether to kill you or not. He wants me to be your enemy, so if he decides to kill you, he can count on my help. When he dreams a good dream, he's friendly to you. When he dreams a bad one, he's gloomy and wants me to join in killing you."

James digested this news.

"He's an old fool. He and his men think they'll get back all of the horses they sold you. That's the reason they sold you so many of their best ones. But you're safe now, you and your things. They won't harm you, or take back any of the horses. I may not have many men, but every Comanche in the nation fears me. They'll treat you well. I'll describe you to all our people, so that whenever you travel among us, you'll be safe. I'll tell them you're my brother."

Brother? Who *was* Thomas James's new *hermano*, El Tuerto, alias the One-Eyed Chief? He was, in all likelihood, Pisinape, or Decayed Shoe, the same who as a young man had taken part, with others, in Don Juan Bautista de Anza's 1786 treaty. In 1823, he was probably in his late, vigorous fifties. Speaking, according to James, "fluent Spanish," he was at once a veteran warrior and a man who might be called a "Hispanicized" Comanche. James noted that his body bore the scars of five wounds, "some of them large and dangerous." An arrow had blinded his left eye, a lance had penetrated his side. He had been baptized "in the Spanish country" and had absorbed some notion of Christianity, telling James, "I believe, like you, in the Great Spirit. If I do well, I'll go to a good place and be happy. If I do bad, I'll go to the bad place and be miserable." Yet when Pisinape boasted that everyone in the tribe was afraid of him, that boast probably contained an element of truth. As opposed to an *erda paraivo*, "a 'good' or 'peaceful' chief," El Tuerto was almost certainly known as a *"woha paraivo*, a 'mean' or 'dangerous' chief."[14] His intervention for James now made all the difference in the results of the American's trading expedition to the Comanches.

On departing, Thomas James asked the chief to accompany him to his lodge, because of the camp dogs.

"Take my horse."

"How will I get him back to you?"

"You won't. You'll keep him, my brother. Keep him, in remembrance of me."

The following day on the way to the fort, there was sudden excitement. Warriors appeared to be preparing for battle. Alsarea, the Taovayas chief, loped up to James and his "brother."

"Osages, Osages, a whole heap of them," he exclaimed. "Are you going to stay with us, or go over to them?"

"I'll stay."

"Will you fight with us?"

"I will," said James.

The One-Eyed Chief, riding beside him, laughed. "It's only wild horses."

At the fort, on the Beaver Fork of the North Canadian, the Comanche band spread their lodges over nearby fields. Each day James traded with a throng of the People for horses, mules, beaver skins, and buffalo hides. Most of the time his "brother" sat beside him, advising him. The horses and mules the American sent to a pasture, where his growing herd was guarded by three of his men. But on the third day four well-armed warriors appeared at the pasture, where they intimidated the guards (perhaps some of the men who had earlier bragged of how they would "make a razor strop

of an Indian's skin") and rode off with four of the best horses of the caballada. James reported the theft to his "brother." The war chief mounted his
horse and rode away with his whip in his hand. A couple of hours later he
returned with two of the ponies. That afternoon he led back a third. In the
evening, when he brought back the fourth, his face was contorted with
fury, and his whip was bloody.[15]

After that no more horses were taken.

Some days later a scouting party brought word that the entire Osage
nation was camped only a day's journey from the fort. The chiefs held a
council. The next day they sent their women and children up the river and
then departed toward the Cimarron to attack the Osages.

Before their departure all of the chiefs came to the fort together to say
goodby to James. They spoke of their friendship for him. They wanted
more American traders among them. The Mexicans could give them nothing they really needed in exchange for their horses except for ammunition,
and that they refused to sell to Indians. They wanted to be friends with
Americans. Yet, they protested bitterly, the Americans sold firearms and
ammunition to their enemies, the Osages, who used them to make war on
Comanches. That was wrong.

They asked him to return and visit them in the fall.

"You go up the Red River," explained the One-Eyed Chief. "You'll find
three big mounds near the headwaters. When you get to these mounds,
you'll see smoke from the grass we'll burn every day, so you can find us.
You can travel with only two companions, and you'll be safe. I'm going to
speak of you to all the Comanches. I'll tell them you're my brother. No-
body will harm you. You can travel safely throughout all our country. No
one will dare steal from you or injure you."

One by one the chiefs embraced James in farewell. The One-Eyed Chief
threw his arms around his neck and began weeping violently. Last of all
came Alsarea, the Taovayas. He seated himself with a grave expression.
Several times he struck himself upon the chest, saying his heart was
troubled:

"When you arrived, you had twenty-three men. Now you have only
twenty-two. One is dead. You say he was a very good man?"

"Yes. He was."

"You don't know how he was killed?"

"No. Maybe I'll know someday."

"There are many bad Comanches," Alsarea said. "Many bad Quapaws,
too—and Arapahoes, and Taovayases, and Pawnees. All these nations hunt
in this country. They might have killed your friend. Or he might have
wounded a buffalo and been killed by him, or been bitten by a rattlesnake.

But he is dead, and you don't know how. Here is my war-horse, Checoba. Take him. No Comanche pony will catch him. He'll outrun any enemy or any danger." With that, the Taovayas went a short distance and returned with a black horse which James believed to have been "worthy and fit to have borne a Richard Coeur de Lion or a Saladin into their greatest battles."

In this manner Thomas James parted from his friends.

Whether smoke rose, day after day, from grassfires near the headwaters of the Red River that fall, or even during the succeeding falls, James never knew. He never returned to the southern plains. The trader, with his flair for survival, was unlucky in his business ventures. On the way back to the settlements, his gift horse, Checoba, was bitten by a rattler and permanently lamed. The remaining horse herd died, either from being covered and devoured by flies or from disease. James worked the next twenty-odd years to pay off his debts. Yet after having lost McKnight, perhaps at the hands of Alsarea and the One-Eyed Chief, he had gained for a short while true friendship, found a "brother," an experience not given to everyone and one not available in the marketplace. Though based upon war, as it was, such was brotherhood among the Comanches.[16]

NINETEEN

Comanches on the Santa Fe Trail, 1821–1829

$\mathbf{A}$nd what about Chief Cordero—in 1821 a tall man of around seventy with "bright and piercing eyes," "high, noble forehead and Roman nose," and with the demeanor of a "real commander and a hero?" What had become of him? Thomas James, in his 1823 return trip to the plains, reported that the Comanches had told him Chief Cordero had taken the letter that James had written him, describing the 1821 rescue of the trader and his party, to Natchitoches, where he had presented it to his friend the U.S. Indian agent, Colonel Jamieson. According to the Yamparicas, the colonel had given him "three horses, loaded with presents." The "sagacious, right-hearted patriot" and "brave warrior" had then "returned to his country a rich man" and shortly afterward had become ill and had died.

But wait—there is a discrepancy here. Cordero turns up in New Mexican records in 1826.[1] In that year Santa Fe officials, along with their counterparts from Chihuahua, held a meeting with two important Comanche chiefs on the Rio Gallinas, a stream rising in the mountains northwest of present Las Vegas and flowing southeast through that site, eventually to join the Pecos on the plains. One of the chiefs was Paruaquita (Bear-scat, alias Tawny Bear) of the Yamparicas. The other was Cordero of the Kotsotekas. The assembled Mexican and Comanche leaders negotiated a treaty of trade and peace between the two groups. The treaty stipulated by its terms that the Comanche headmen also represented the Yupe and Tenewa divisions, as well as the Kiowas. Once again the officials promised annual gifts, to be distributed at Santa Fe and San Antonio. Consequently trade was expected to flourish.

As part of the agreement, Chief Cordero, escorted by four troopers and two interpreters, was to ride to Béxar and report the results of the council to the comandante general de oriente. To reward Tawny Bear and Cordero for their cooperation, Mexico pledged to recognize the two chiefs as generals of the republic; so that perhaps the old diplomat was able to add, next to the regimentals of an American colonel, doubtless packed away in a parfleche, the dress uniform of a Mexican general. The following year New

Mexico records refer to Tawny Bear and Cordero as having participated in the celebration of that treaty in Chihuahua City. There were indeed in those decades rewards for being a principal Comanche leader, even if one was, by some standards, an old man.

In 1828 New Mexico authorities dispatched Juan Cristóbal Tenorio, official interpreter, along with a party of comancheros, to confer with the Comanches. Tenorio returned accompanied by a Chief Panchoconuque, who tried to persuade Governor Manuel Armijo to name him leader of the Kotsotekas, claiming that the chief who presently held the position was no longer competent. But New Mexico officials preferred to temporize.

Near the end of August, Comandante Principal Juan José Arocha, along with José Francisco Ruíz of Béxar and others, assembled on the plains with approximately six hundred Kotsotekas. Tenorio read aloud, translating as he went, the treaty of two years before. When the interpreter had finished, Comandante Arocha demanded to know whether the chiefs intended to adhere to the terms of the document. Unanimously all agreed to abide by its terms and, indeed, to ratify them anew. But only after the Kotsotekas themselves had chosen a "general" to lead them did Arocha present to Chief Toro Echicero a medal and cane as symbols of his authority as new divisional leader.[2] These events suggest that by 1828 Chief Cordero had become either physically or mentally incapacitated or had died. So the old warrior passed into history. Yet one clause of the 1826 treaty to which he was a party continues to intrigue. The document stipulated that the Comanche nation "would take care not to interfere with the caravans that came to New Mexico from the United States of the north . . ."[3]

And that nation had taken care not to interfere since the commercial opening of the Santa Fe Trail in 1821. And so it continued to do until 1828, not until that time violating the clause; and then, it would seem, only with good reason.

With the permission of the War Department, Harper and Brothers in 1859 published a guidebook by Captain Randolph B. Marcy, U.S. Army. When Marcy wrote *The Prairie Traveler: A Hand-Book for Overland Expeditions*, he had accumulated years of experience among various Indian tribes and had crossed and explored the southern plains. In his handbook he offered a number of comments about young warriors, of whatever Plains tribe, with a warning. Young men, he wrote, were not accepted into councils until they had proved themselves as warriors. Apparently unaware of the importance of the coup, he asserted that the man who had collected the greatest number of scalps was the most honored of his people. All ambitious young men knew the path leading to success in their culture. It was not surprising that they would be more tempted to take shortcuts along this path than older men who had already earned reputations. He advised travelers to keep a sharp eye on young braves when they met them on the plains.

Captain Marcy cautioned even more emphatically concerning encounters with unsuccessful war parties. As an example he cited the southern Plains Indians' long raids into Mexico for horses, mules, and captives. If the raiders had failed in their objectives, or (worse) if they had lost one or more of their men in battle, they often became reckless. Then they would not hesitate to attack a small party, even one of people with whom they were at peace, providing they believed their act would not become known. To them it was such a disgrace to return to their band empty-handed and with no scalps or other trophies to compensate for the loss of a comrade, that they were likely to show "but little mercy to defenseless travelers" who were unlucky enough to meet them at such a time.[4]

Marcy was of course right. In 1820 for example, Captain John R. Bell of the Stephen Long scientific expedition had encountered such a party of disgruntled "Ietan or Camanch" on the Arkansas River. During the previous night these would-be raiders had been attacked by Otos, who had killed and wounded several and taken most of their belongings and horses. Only through exercising good sense and firmness had Bell and his group of ten avoided a dangerous clash with the humiliated war party.

With all this taken into account, it is surprising that the first seven years of commercial travel over the Santa Fe Trail had been peaceful. William Becknell opened the route to commerce in 1821, taking the long way by Raton Pass and Taos. Neither on the way out nor during his return trip to Franklin, Missouri, did Becknell and his four companions meet with hostile Indians. The following year Becknell pioneered the Cimarron cutoff, a diagonal line running between the Arkansas and Cimarron rivers. This time he traveled with wagons rather than with a packtrain. Before succeeding, Becknell and his fellow traders nearly died of thirst, yet they met with no problems from Comanches or their allies. But the tolerant attitude of the southern Plains Indians toward *los americanos* changed in 1828.

In the same year that the Mexican Comisión de Límites, or Boundary Commission, visited Texas, the two Santa Fe caravans enjoyed, as usual, uneventful journeys from Franklin to New Mexico's capital city. But on the return trip that August, members of the first caravan made two momentous errors. The first cost two men their lives. The second changed for a time the peaceful character of the Santa Fe Trail.

When the first wagon train reached what came to be known afterward as McNees Crossing (through a headwater of the North Canadian River, near today's Clayton, New Mexico), the leading riders discovered two of the party lying bleeding by the stream.[5] Two young men, McNees and Monroe, had ridden ahead, dismounted at the creek, and had carelessly stretched out in the shade to nap. McNees had never awakened. Some unknown Indian or Indians had shot both men with their own guns and had fled. The infuriated traders placed McNees's body, along with Monroe, who was dying, in a wagon and drove them nearly forty miles to the Cimarron River. There Monroe expired.

The Missourians buried both men by the river. The funeral service was just ending when, fatefully, some half-dozen Indians rode up on the other side of the Cimarron. These unidentified Indians were almost certainly Comanches or Kiowas, friendly warriors who surely knew nothing of the murders, or they would have remained miles from the wagon train. A few of the traders wished to parley with the braves, but the majority were so enraged they wanted nothing but revenge, and had no qualms about how they got it. By this time the warriors on the far bank had noticed the belligerent attitudes assumed by many of the traders. One of them spun his pony to flee. A trader fired, bringing down the horse. Instantly other Americans opened fire, killing the man on the ground as well as all but one of the remainder. That one warrior galloped off to tell his people the terrible news of this unprovoked attack.

The traders' rash act had consequences.

Unidentified Indians struck the first caravan shortly afterward near the Arkansas River, running off almost 1,000 head of horses and mules. But it was the second, smaller group of thirty traders who bore the brunt of the Comanches' wrath that year. In September the Missourians began their return journey from Santa Fe with four wagons, 150 head of horses and mules, and a quantity of Mexican silver. Near Upper Cimarron Spring, they were startled to come upon a large Comanche camp lying across the trail.

The chief came out to meet them with a smile. Inviting them to pass the night in his ranchería, he promised them his young men would guard their horses. The traders, after a brief consultation, grimly and silently whipped their mule teams forward. With every firearm drawn and at the ready, they followed the trail between tepees through the center of camp. The wagons and riders passed through safely. But suddenly warriors seized the reins of the three men riding rear guard, simultaneously firing at them. Two of the Americans yanked the reins free, spurred their horses, and dashed from the camp. The third, John Means, the caravan's elected captain, fell dead from his horse and was scalped on the spot.

From that moment the traders' trip became an ordeal that grew worse day by day. After several unsuccessful attempts, the Comanches managed to run off their entire herd of horses and mules, leaving them afoot some three hundred miles from Santa Fe and five hundred miles from Missouri. When the Comanches finally left, the Americans abandoned their wagon-fort and, each carrying what he could, began trudging directly northward toward the Arkansas. After walking with only brief halts for four days and nights, they reached the river. There they cached their heavy silver coins on Chouteau's Island (this island, no longer in existence, was about six miles southwest of modern Lakin, Kansas), then striking out eastward along the river for the settlements.[6] A group of five animated skeletons succeeded in staggering into Independence together. The search party which returned for the others found them scattered, separately, at distances as far as a hundred miles from Missouri. One man, blind from starvation, was discovered lying on his back, with a stick in his hand for beating away impatient coyotes or wolves.

Comanche and Kiowa revenge was not yet complete.

In the settled United States, the deaths of McNees, Monroe, and Means were widely reported in newspapers, especially those near the frontier. Their reports blamed the Comanches, and the news created a stir. Beyond excitement over the loss of life, there was concern over the Santa Fe trade, which was of great economic importance to Missouri. Governor John Miller of that state applied for military assistance and, some five years before the establishment of Bent's Fort, suggested a garrison on the Arkansas. The U.S. Congress denied his request. Finally a group of wealthy merchants approached the newly elected Andrew Jackson, who was always sympathetic to the problems of the frontier. As there was at that time no cavalry in the U.S. Army, Jackson authorized an infantry escort for the 1829 caravan. It was ordered to proceed as far as the Mexican boundary on the Arkansas River.

On July 9, 1829, Major Bennet Riley arrived, with companies A, B, F, and H of the Sixth Infantry, at the Upper Crossing of the Arkansas River, which lay two or three miles below Chouteau's Island. Riley's specially selected battalion had been providing an escort for a train of some thirty-six wagons and seventy traders since June 11. Except for the theft of six horses during the night of June 23, the trip had so far been peaceful. The following day the wagon train crossed the river and international frontier, completing the crossing by four in the afternoon.

The next morning Major Riley himself crossed to confer with Charles Bent, the elected captain of the caravan. Bent, speaking for the merchants, promised him they would meet him on the same spot no later than October 10. Riley, in turn, gave Bent and other leading traders advice about security from Indian attacks, along with a letter for the *Jefe Politico* of New Mexico. Meanwhile two survivors of the previous year's ordeal had led a squad of soldiers to the island, where they had found the cache of coins, exposed by water but intact. Leaving it in Major Riley's care, the traders whipped up their mule teams, and the wagons creaked forward, slowly moving out southward for Santa Fe. Part of the caravan, a single yoke of oxen, plodded at a distance behind a freight wagon. Bent had borrowed a pair of the animals from Riley as an experiment, to see whether they could perform as well as mules on the plains.

That evening around 6:30, as the officers and men of the battalion were relaxing, nine horsemen, soon recognized as traders, appeared on the south side of the river. They were approaching at a gallop. Fording the river, they rode immediately to Major Riley, bringing news that the wagon train had been attacked by some five hundred horse Indians, probably Kiowas. The assailants had killed one man, Sam Lamme, of the advance guard, and would have killed more if the traders had not begun firing their small cannon at them. As it was, the Kiowas, in full view of the caravan, had stripped the dead man naked and hacked off his head. Now if the major didn't come help them, the rest of them expected also to be killed and scalped.

Major Bennet Riley reflected for a moment: a rescue would, of course, mean entering Mexican territory. If the Mexicans protested, it could cause an uproar in Washington and might mean the end of his career. But Riley nodded and told the messengers that the battalion would begin preparing to depart immediately.

The infantrymen trudged into the traders' camp around midnight, after marching about six miles through hills of sand. But that day and those immediately following were anticlimactic. At dawn some traders reported sighting large numbers of Indians. None of the military, though, could discern any either that day or for days to come. The battalion escorted the caravan out of the sand hills, where they had been ambushed, to the relative safety of the open plains. By July 16 the four companies, with all of their oxen and wagons and gear, had once again marched to the Arkansas. They camped at a spot opposite Chouteau's Island. Ten days later Major Riley moved the escort to the American side of the river, where there was an ample supply of firewood and good grass.

On July 31 the enlistments of four soldiers expired. Despite warnings from Major Riley, the four men were determined to walk back to the settlements. They had proceeded eighteen miles down the Arkansas, when a party of mounted Indians crossed the river to them. The Americans made the peace sign, and the two groups parleyed. The Indians invited the ex-soldiers, who were armed with muskets, to accompany them to their camp, even offering them horses to ride. The Americans declined, beginning to move away. The warriors seemed willing to let them go. Suddenly one of the four, named Gordon, impulsively decided to go back, shake hands, and share his tobacco with them. As Gordon stood near the horsemen, who were surely Comanches or Kiowas, one of them shoved his gun at the man and pulled the trigger. The ex-soldier crumpled, sprawling by the hoofs of the ponies. One of the remaining three men aimed, fired his musket, and saw a warrior fall from his horse. The three then retreated, keeping the circling braves at bay until a detail of hunters from camp providentially appeared. The Indians rode off, leaving the Americans to return together to the battalion in a downpour. Once there, the survivors presumably lost no time in reenlisting.

Three days later during early afternoon, the men of the encampment were startled by the sudden popping of gunfire a half-mile upstream, where a guard was assigned to the cattle herd. Quickly assembling their troops, the officers saw masses of warriors riding toward the river from the hills on either side. Major Riley, standing by his tent, realized the attackers' plan was to cut off and stampede the oxen, a tactic that, if successful, would cripple the battalion. Immediately he ordered both the rifle company and the camp guard, which was under Lieutenant Philip St. George Cooke, to advance and assist the five men of the cattle guard.

Lieutenant Cooke knew the rifle company had been drilling with un-loaded guns. They were now marching toward the galloping, painted, whooping warriors in a defenseless state. Cooke ordered his men forward on the double toward the left flank. But he soon learned that the three or four hundred Comanches and Kiowas did not choose to close with them. As soon as the horsemen rode to nearly within range, they would split, like an expert drill team, and ride off in opposite directions. Meanwhile the rifle company had managed to reach and rescue the men of the cattle guard, one of whom was carried by his comrades, mortally wounded. Before them the terrified cattle and mules were scattering, running mostly toward camp.

Major Riley ordered companies F and H to advance northward on the double to attack the greatest concentration of the horse Indians, so as to keep them at a distance from the camp. Simultaneously he ordered a Lieutenant Searight to open up with the fieldpiece.

Cooke, having caught his breath, saw that the Comanches and Kiowas, on either side of the river, were riding in a wide circle around camp, mostly out of small-arms range. Occasionally the companies that remained among the tents would fire at them with platoon volleys. In mingled frustration and admiration, the lieutenant marveled at the enemy's horsemanship, watching Comanche and Kiowa warriors pass at some distance from him, by the camp's rear, where they were closer to the troops and exposed to their fire. All the riders hung extended along the right sides of their ponies, supported by their left heel and arm, "this last," in Cooke's words, "with a bull's-hide shield attached, passed around the horse's neck, from beneath which they repidly discharged their arrows—the shield covering arm, horse's neck, the [brave's] head, and . . . right arm below!" Furthermore he noticed that "excited as they were, they seemed the best of horsemen; and rushed up and down places which few persons in cool blood would think of attempting . . ."[7]

Receiving new orders Lieutenant Cooke marched his men to the fore-front of the camp, which was temporarily undefended. In his position he heard the six-pounder go off. The shot hissed above him and struck about a mile away, amid a cluster of enemy horsemen, creating confusion among them. Searight then fired grapeshot at another group racing their ponies along the base of the sand hills south of the river. A single rider appeared to be hit.

At this time Major Riley spied another group of horsemen driving cattle down a slough between the river bank and Chouteau's Island, somewhat downstream from the camp. He at once ordered company F to leave the front of the camp and to intercept them. Simultaneously he ordered company A to march farther northward, with the intent of possibly trapping the enemy against some timber there. All this time the Comanches and Kiowas on the other, south flank were still attempting to drive off or stam-pede the cattle, while the rifle company, handicapped like the rest of the infantrymen by being afoot, vainly tried to stop them. Ironically, though, the waving and whooping of the horse Indians drove the panicked beasts directly toward the arriving company F, whose soldiers rounded up and defended them, opening fire upon their would-be herders. Observing the musket fire to be ineffective against the warriors' shields, Lieutenant Sea-right swung around his fieldpiece and began slamming shot in ricochet upstream toward this branch of the enemy.

Riley now dispatched company A to a wooded point of the river below camp. He ordered the officer in charge to clean it out and, in conjunction with company F, which was again available, to fire upon the horsemen massed on the south bank. Soon, with all of the horse Indians occupied, the cattle guard managed to corral the oxen, defeating the obvious purpose of the attack.

Their plan frustrated, the Comanches and Kiowas retired out of range. Lieutenant Cooke watched them as they loped for a time around the camp at a distance, whooping and shaking their bows, lances, and guns. Gradually, though, they rode upstream, crossing in little groups, only to reappear later, poised on hilltops against the sky, where they fired their guns into the air once more and dropped out of sight, southward into Comanchería.

After enduring harassment by Indians (undoubtedly Comanches and Kiowas) on the way to Santa Fe, and another misadventure on the return trip, the Missouri caravan rejoined the Sixth Infantry Battalion late, on October 12. Fortunately a Colonel Viscarra and his command of Mexican soldiers had escorted them on that return journey. Anyone examining the freight wagons, when they stood safely on the American shore of the Arkansas, would have seen nailed on the side of at least one of them the entire, drying skin of a Gros Ventre Indian, one of a party who had attacked Viscarra and who had been killed, scalped, and skinned by the traders. But the mexicanos, traders, and American soldiers did not commingle for long. Major Riley, impatient at the delay, soon marched his troops for the settlements. He escorted the caravan as far as the environs of Independence, proceeding from there to Cantonment Leavenworth (present Fort Leavenworth, Kansas), where he and his battalion arrived on November 7.

In his report to General Henry Leavenworth and the War Department, Riley wrote of his forty-five minute battle with the Comanches and Kiowas on August 3. In that engagement the enemy had killed only one man, Private Arrison, of the cattle guard. But they had succeeded in driving off ten government horses and mules, nine officers' horses, and some fifty head of oxen. The major could not judge accurately of enemy casualties, since the horse Indians had removed their wounded and dead. But the Mexican soldiers had reported learning from comancheros that the Comanches and Kiowas had lost eight warriors in the battle, most of them from artillery fire.

Major Riley's report aroused lively interest within the United States Congress, bolstering the Missouri delegation's demand for better protection of Santa Fe traders. But what must have most impressed the representatives and senators was the major's description of his frustration at watching mounted Indians ride away with his cattle and horses, while he and his infantrymen could only stand and watch, helpless spectators. Ultimately the report led to action. Three years later, in 1832, Congress passed a bill authorizing a regiment of dragoons. This was a beginning; first dragoons, cavalry some twenty years later. From then on when battle became necessary against horse Indians, successful American and Texan combatants would be mounted, like generations of Spanish presidials before them. Finally, as a further effect, Riley's report must have brought home to the U.S. government and its military the increasing need for a treaty with those Indians who controlled the southern plains.

Out of the summer the Missouri merchants learned a valuable economic fact: Bent's borrowed yoke of oxen had done well. In the future oxen, far cheaper than mules and edible, would draw most of their heavy freight wagons across the plains. Some few among the traders, like the Bents, probably also realized the events of 1828–29 suggested that Comanches and their allies could not be murdered with impunity. To the majority, though, Indians were Indians; and as Josiah Gregg later observed, there were always occasional whites "disposed to kill, even in cold blood, every Indian that fell into their power, merely because some of the tribe had committed some outrages either against themselves or their friends."

In some instances murders were not even that personal. During a truce with the Comanches in 1837, for example, a Captain Eastland of the Texas Rangers led his company northward from Coleman's Fort, near Austin, up the Colorado River on a hunting and exploring trip. When he turned back, some twenty men refused to follow him. This unruly group pressed on until reaching a cluster of mounds called "the stone houses," where a large gathering of Indians, possibly Caddoans, was camped nearby.

Several Delawares from the encampment soon joined the rangers. While the two groups were conversing, a "wild Irishman," Felix McClusky, spied another Indian warrior approaching alone. At once he spurred his horse and charged the figure. The Delawares yelled after him, saying the man was from a tribe friendly to the Texans. As McClusky bore down on the solitary brave, the man signaled he was friendly. The Irishman, in spite of this, shot him dead, dismounted, scalped him, and searched the body for valuables. On his return, the Delawares warned him that the victim's comrades would surely seek revenge. They departed immediately. The other rangers began to reproach the Irishman.

"For this much tobacco," spat McClusky, displaying a plug taken from the dead man, "I'd kill any Injun."

From the resulting battle, known afterward as "the Stone House Fight," five rangers escaped alive. One of these was Felix McClusky.[8]

On the frontier, even though life was cheap, killing a man, either red or white, was almost certain to create a causally connected series of events resulting in more deaths, in a sequence that might continue indefinitely. Whether the traders who buried McNees and Monroe learned this is doubtful. The Comanches had always known it. But they did learn one new lesson in their first battle with the U.S. Army; it was to beware of "wagons" shooting at them.[9] The loss of eight warriors was an unacceptably high price for a cleverly planned skirmish that could have stranded the soldiers on the plains without draft animals at little cost to the People or their Kiowa allies. This loss made such an impression that they ceased harassing the Santa Fe Trail for a time and in fact did not renew this kind of mass assault until their attacks of the 1850s and 1860s. In the near term, in 1834–37 as it turned out, they had nothing, really, against a treaty with the americanos.

TWENTY

Perspectives from Tejas, 1819–1834

In 1813 when General Joaquín de Arredondo crushed a force of American filibusters and creole revolutionaries at the battle of the Medina River, the survivors fled. Those captured were executed. Many took refuge in American Louisiana, but a few escaped instead into the southern plains and requested asylum among the Comanches, who had been their allies. Among those bold individuals was José Francisco Ruíz.[1] Born in Béxar, Ruíz was a *criollo*, or creole; that is, a descendent of original Spanish settlers. He was educated in Spain, returning to direct his father's haciendas on the Nueces River. He lived, however, in the Texas capital. In 1803 he became San Antonio's first public schoolmaster, teaching in his own home by the Military Plaza. Doubtless inspired by the American and French revolutions, he joined Augustus Magee's republican army in 1811. After the battle of the Medina, he fled at the age of thirty-three to the Comanches and took refuge among them and their allies for the following eight years, moving finally to American Louisiana.

In 1821 José Francisco returned from Natchitoches to his native province, where he represented the interests of Mexico in negotiations with the Lipan Apaches and the Comanches. Eventually he entered the Mexican Army. He was back living in the Texas capital, a lieutenant colonel, in 1828, when he became acquainted with another remarkable man, a young French botanist named Jean Louis Berlandier. Berlandier and Ruíz were to become friends, and the Mexican officer would provide the scientist with much valuable information concerning his former hosts, the Comanche Indians. In the fall of 1829, they would even join a party of Comanches on a hunt for bear and buffalo northwest of San Antonio. In the meantime, though, a few Americans were beginning to enter Texas, legally or illegally. Some of them, too, encountered, formed opinions of, and wrote about *los comanches*.

One of the first of these Americans was David Gouveneur Burnet from Cincinnati, later first interim president of the Texas Republic. But in 1817 he was a sickly young man living in Natchitoches and was about to enter an establishment that traded with the Indians. He changed plans when his doctor told him he was on the verge of tuberculosis, at that time a frequently fatal disease. The physician recommended he try living for a while on the prairies, in the open air. That fall he took the advice. Counting on the friendly attitude of the Comanches toward Louisiana Americans, with whom they had now been trading for nearly a decade, he traveled westward until reaching the plains country at the headwaters of the Colorado River. By the time he arrived there, he was so weak he could scarcely pull himself onto his horse. But after living on the plains "with, or in the vicinity of the Comanches" for much of 1818 and part of 1819, he completely recovered his health and strength. From Texas he returned to Cincinnati, studying and practicing law. In 1824 the *Cincinnati Literary Gazette* printed the first of a series of Burnet's letters describing the Comanches.[2] Although written in a youthfully supercilious and pompous style, the letters demonstrate close observation of the Nuhmuhnuh and contain thoughtful insights concerning them.

His first insight was prophetic. He acknowledged that the People had been and still were friendly toward Americans, but he foresaw a future marked by border warfare, predicting this on the basis of the tribe's love of rapine. On the other hand, Burnet was impressed by the amount of accord existing within the tribe, among divisions and bands as well as between individuals. "Notwithstanding the extreme laxity of their whole economy of government," he wrote, "and their entire exemption from legal restraint, they live together with a degree of harmony that would do credit to the most refined and best organized societies." These "rude and simple children of nature" considered themselves to be, as a people, the greatest in number and most powerful in the world. Yet Burnet (like Berlandier after him) made a conservative estimate of tribal military strength, setting it at only from two thousand to twenty-five hundred warriors, whereas the Mexican government estimated it at around eight thousand fighting men.[3] Although he conceded the Comanches' superb horsemanship, Burnet pronounced their men unfit for "serious and protracted warfare," no doubt contrasting their guerrilla raids to campaigns fought by European armies.

David Burnet either underestimated the fighting capacity of the Comanches or affected to out of bravado. Like most Americans and Europeans, except for certain frontiersmen, he failed to understand the rationale of plains warfare and scorned the martial ability of those braves who, within a couple of decades, would begin bloodying Anglo-Texas, and whose "fantastical and ridiculous" costumes would become symbolic of the nightmare Comanche warriors were creating on that frontier.

In spite of his derisive tone, Burnet did see the Comanches as a threat to the Arkansas Territory. He recommended that its officials take seriously a potential enemy who moved through the wilderness with extreme caution during the day in order to strike its prey at midnight. As an example he described a long-distance raid from Texas into Mexico. Each warrior would set out, he wrote, with two horses, one ordinary pony to ride during the journey and a war-horse, to be kept fresh until needed. The trip would be planned so that the warriors would arrive in the enemy's vicinity at the time of a full moon. There they would establish a secret camp, leaving supplies and the ordinary ponies in charge of a few men and, perhaps, women, wives whose duty it was to take care of chores (and, according to Berlandier, tend to the sexual needs of their husbands, as well as those of their husbands' relatives and friends). The war party would then slip out by moonlight to seek its objectives—principally horses but, whenever possible, scalps and captives as well. (Berlandier estimated that around 1830 there were some five hundred Mexican captives among the Comanches).

The braves would ride their war-ponies bareback, dressed only in breechclouts. Besides his shield, each man would bear a lance and bow and arrows, although a few carried light shotguns. In this way they usually could outmaneuver and outrun the heavily equipped Spanish cavalry. If the party should succeed in surprising a hacienda with a large herd of horses and mules, they would seize the herd and set off at a gallop, forcing the animals night and day until they had crossed the Río Grande, where they felt relatively safe from pursuit. In the desperate rush, many of the horses drowned crossing rivers or fell out of the herd, exhausted, and were abandoned to die or go wild. Burnet estimated that the Comanches, at that time, were stealing some ten thousand head of horses annually out of the interior provinces of Mexico. Of this number he judged that about half died or were abandoned as useless on the way to Comanchería.

And if the hacienda were well defended? Burnet believed that the speed of the braves' ponies, and their riders' knowledge of Mexican geography enabled them usually to surprise the "indolent and inert Spaniards" and to elude pursuit. The effect of the surprise, combined with the inadequate defenses of the provinces, served to inspire the warriors with an "artificial fearlessness" that endowed them, to their "ignorant and spiritless enemies," with all the horrors of the basilisk. Yet, wrote Burnet, all one really had to do was oppose Comanche warriors "with decision and energy," and they would "crouch like the Spaniel, or fly like the 'stricken fawn.'"

This last was not one of Burnet's brightest insights. Might these words have haunted him during the years when each mile's advance of the Anglo-Texas frontier was costing seventeen white lives?[4]

In contrast he had some interesting observations concerning Comanche women. About a decade later, Jean Louis Berlandier was to write of them that, "like anything weak and enslaved," they were "extremely cruel." Burnet went further, holding the women responsible for "the largest portion of the nation's barbarity." He went on to state flatly that they were "infinitely more cruel and ferocious than the men." Certainly if a sense of injustice (probably safely unconscious), as well as long-endured overwork and frustration, make for anger and cruelty, most of the women of the tribe had plenty of motivation to even accounts with the world in the form of a helpless enemy, especially when that enemy was a man. They took a "peculiar delight," wrote Burnet, "in torturing the adult male prisoners."

By custom, at least among the division with which Burnet was familiar, prisoners were delivered over to the women during the first three days of their arrival at the camp. But the amount of torment inflicted upon them varied greatly, according to the degree of success or failure of the war party that had captured them. If the warriors had been successful and had suffered no casualties, the captives' punishment might be light, consisting mostly of whippings. But if the war party had, for instance, lost one or more braves, the torture inflicted upon the captive tended to be extreme, often ending in his death.

For the three days of his ordeal the captive would spend most of his terrible hours on his back, with each hand and foot bound to a stake driven into the earth. Throughout the day the women would take turns, with sharp points, say, and hot coals, in tormenting him, not neglecting his genitals. In the evening the victim would be untied. Forced to bear a stick with the scalps of dead friends or family members, he would be led to the center of a scalp dance and made to join the dancers, while they threatened him, or actually struck him, with clubs, whips, knives, lances, and flaming sticks. When he finally staggered and fell, exhausted, he would again be staked out to wait for the next day's torture, and that of the next.

Interestingly Burnet pointed out that warriors occasionally intervened "to repress excessive barbarities." (One wonders what torments the men might have found excessive!) In any case, if the victim survived his three-day ordeal, he was not punished further. He became, in fact, almost a member of the tribe, as a slave of his captor's family. If prisoners were boys or girls, the Comanches generally treated them in a kindly fashion, according to Burnet, and raised them in a manner not very different from the way in which they raised their own children.

In 1828 General don Manuel Mier y Terán led the expedition of the Comisión de Límites from Mexico City into Texas. The purpose of the expedition was to ascertain the precise boundary between the new nation of Mexico and the United States in the area of the Red and Sabine rivers. Besides this mission it had a mandate to record and bring back scientific information of various kinds concerning the entire region. Jean Louis Berlandier, a Frenchman in his early twenties, was employed to record botanical and zoological data.

Berlandier kept journals of the expedition and later wrote extensively concerning observations made during his journey. Some years afterward he married a Mexican woman and settled in Matamoros, where he practiced medicine until his death by drowning, while fording a river on horseback, in 1851. The American naturalist who purchased the Berlandier collection discovered among his papers a handwritten manuscript of over three hundred pages describing the various Indian tribes of Texas.[5] Although the scientist had not completed the manuscript until around 1834, most of its information was based upon his experiences in Texas during 1828 and 1829. While there Berlandier had become especially interested in the Comanche people, whom he sometimes saw trading their painted buffalo hides, bear fat, smoked and dried meat, and furs in Béxar, in exchange for such items as brown sugar, corn, blackberries, ammunition, and swordblades. Aside from the young scientist's personal observation, the Frenchman's source for most of the details about the People was Colonel José Francisco Ruíz. Young as he was during the Terán expedition, Berlandier was already a trained observer. He seems also to have been interested in everything he encountered. Furthermore he was a Frenchman, and nineteenth-century French candor concerning sexuality, as contrasted to Anglo-Saxon reticence, is reflected in his observations about the native peoples of Texas. He noted for example that the Wacos and Tawakonies always offered women to visitors.[6] The Arapahoes, or "Chariticas" ("Dog-Eaters" to the Comanches, who ate none of the canine family, and who considered the wolf a brother), had a similar custom, but became offended and turned upon anyone who rejected a woman who had been offered.[7] Arapaho men demanded only a bit of vermilion in return.

Colonel Ruíz, Berlandier related, once nearly became embroiled in an altercation with this people for not having immediately accepted such an offer. Quickly reconsidering, Ruíz agreed to the arrangement in order to avoid a dangerous quarrel. As for the native men in general, wrote Berlandier, they rarely practiced sodomy. On the other hand, he contended, bestiality was not unusual, especially among the Tawakonies, who satisfied "all their indecent passions with all their animals, domestic or wild," and, as he mentioned in another context, "living or dead." The Comanches were a "very voluptuous people," whose men were "the most sensual of all the natives." But he observed, in apparent contradiction, that the Comanches were prudes in comparison to the Wichitan peoples, whose women would secretly offer themselves to visitors, if their husbands had not already done so. While unmarried women were dissolute, widows were much more so. Mutual masturbation, he noted, did not occur between individuals of the same sex, but did take place between those of the opposite sex, "as a matter of no consequence."

Still the reader of the manuscript cannot help wondering whether the scientist (or more likely, Ruíz) did not exaggerate. Lieutenant Wheelock, for example, of the 1834 Dragoon Expedition, found the Wichitan Tao-vayas women "infinitely respectable."

In his journal Berlandier recorded hearing that young Comanche males preferred marrying women older than they were, since mature women were thought to work harder. Old men, on the other hand, preferred young girls, who, in their opinion, were more able to appreciate them. He also entrusted to his journal the method by which an older Comanche husband prepared a child wife for future sexual relations. The warrior pur-chased the little girl for a horse or a mule when she was seven or eight years old. The child continued to reside with her parents for the time being. When she was nine or ten, her husband began coming to her father's lodge to sleep with her, without attempting to initiate intercourse. For a long time, on each occasion first greasing his fingers, he masturbated her, using first one finger then two, "in order to dilate the uterus." When at last his two fingers entered her easily, he considered the child ready to take up her wifely duties and brought her home with him to his lodge.[8]

Obviously all brides were not children, although many girls married men considerably older than they. A later French scientist, Leon de Cessac, provides a description of more usual sexual relations among the People. De Cessac visited California in the 1870s and while there interviewed a trapper who had dwelt as a captive with the Comanches for thirteen years. By this man's account, the Comanches believed pressure on a woman's abdomen or the act of holding her thighs apart would either hinder pro-creation or harm any resulting embryo. "Consequently," wrote de Cessac, "their conjugal relations invariably take place *de mare equino* (in the man-ner of the horse)." He added that the tribe considered it the only natural way, since the animals used no other.[9]

On numerous occasions Jean Louis Berlandier gives credit to Colonel Ruíz for his information. Sometimes he refers to the criollo to illustrate a point. For instance in writing of plains warfare, which he understood only a little better than David Burnet, Berlandier tells of a series of events that Ruíz witnessed in 1824, apparently when he was Mexico's commissioner to the Comanches. At that time he attended a great gathering of the

Nuhmuhnuh and their allies. The meeting took place in northern Comanchería, a little below the Arkansas River. The commissioner counted twenty-three hundred tepees belonging to twenty-five hundred warriors in a huge camp stretching along a winding stream. The purpose of this convocation was to be a campaign against a common enemy, the Osage nation.

On a certain day the Plains warriors, with scouts in advance, departed for the enemy villages. Berlandier described elsewhere the impressive appearance of the Comanche horsemen, whose ponies were painted with red, black, and white stripes, and whose own bodies were painted as well. Their shields were surrounded by red and white feathers fluttering along the rims. He also described a "bonnet of feathers" worn by some, with a tail of feathers streaming behind when their ponies galloped. Other warriors wore the long black tuft that grew between the buffalo's horns, while still others wore the whole scalp, with horns attached. Together in an armed mass, the allied force rode out to surprise and destroy the enemy.

Unfortunately the Osages were expecting them. A party of Osage warriors ambushed the approximately fifty scouts riding in advance of the main force. They killed two Comanches and fled. The main body of Comanches and their allies pursued them at a gallop. But suddenly the whole army was blocked by a river, probably a tributary of the Arkansas. Drawn up on the opposite bank was an array of Osages, with fourteen white men among them, almost surely Americans, who, according to the story, carried little flags. Hardly hesitating, the Comanche force turned their ponies and retreated, without being pursued, to their own camp. They had not killed a single enemy, but that was the end of the campaign.

Berlandier found this comic, writing "this campaign, which, by all appearances, was to decide the destinies of two mighty peoples, ended as usual with the death of two or three individuals . . ." [10] Yet the young scientist had failed to understand a culture different from his own. The People's entire concept of warfare was different from that of Europeans and Americans, the reason many of the latter considered Plains warfare to be cowardly and the warriors to be cowards. Even the usually wise physician and merchant Josiah Gregg believed the Comanches not to deserve "the title of brave Indians."

In summing up the characteristics of the Comanches, Berlandier was far from complimentary toward the People. He found them generally "savage and cruel," a view conforming to their later reputation. More surprisingly, though, he declared that once defeated they were "craven cowards."

In this instance Berlandier was mostly wrong. With respect to the charge of cruelty (and the Comanches could be pitiless) it is interesting to compare observations about the Nuhmuhnuh with some concerning other southern Plains tribes, starting with comments by Berlandier himself. Regarding the treatment of prisoners, the scientist asserted that the Comanches, Arapahoes, and southern Cheyennes were "not very cruel." Conversely he found the Lipan Apaches, the Wacos, the Tawakonies, and the Taovayases to be "ferocious and inhuman."[11] Elsewhere he singled out the Apaches for special mention on this subject, writing that "the Lipans are a fine group of men, skilled at warfare, excellent horsemen. . . . But their cruelty is so hideous," he added, "as would never be accepted as historic fact."

Something over a half-century earlier, in 1772, another Frenchman, Athanase de Mézières, had noted that the Comanches practiced "clemency toward their captives . . . , regarding with great disgust the feasts of human flesh" relished by their Wichitan allies. Six years later, while the Nuhmuhnuh were still enemies of Spain, he advised the viceroy that the Comanches were "surpassed by none in numbers, in modesty of dress, in hospitality to their guests, in humanity to their captives, or in bravery, which," he wrote, was "so general that even in the women the most virile sort of valor has been observed." But he warned that they were egregious thieves.[12]

From all the evidence, it appears that the Comanches, though capable of great cruelty, were relatively more humane than many of their Native American friends and enemies south of the Arkansas River. As for their courage, few observers (even including the Texas Rangers) disputed that they were generally brave. In 1812 for example, the prominent New Mexican Pedro Bautista Pino asserted gratefully that only fear of the "brave and honest Comanches" kept the "obnoxious and cruel" Apaches in check, thus helping to preserve his province from the Athapascans' depredations. But perhaps the most accurate and succinct statement concerning both the Comanches' mode of warfare and their courage was that of José Francisco Ruíz, in about 1828: "The Comanches fight," he wrote, "using the technique of constant harassment of the enemy. They engage in a direct confrontation when either owing to the terrain or to superior numbers, they are assured of victory and a swift escape. In the event they are caught, they fight heroically until they die."[13]

But in those direct confrontations, how exactly did Comanche horsemen fight? From the perspective of U.S. troopers, they presented a startling and unorthodox spectacle. Here is how Captain Robert Carter described a battle with Quanah Parker's Quahada Comanches in 1871, when they battled troops of the 4th Cavalry. "Their rapid swing out," he wrote, "or rush into a V-shape formation, and then fanning out to the front from these two wings into an irregular line of swirling warriors, all rapidly moving in right and left hand circles, no two Indians coming together, and their quick extensions, while advancing, to the right or left, and as rapidly concentrating or assembling on the center, but without any close bunching, and their falling back in the same manner, sometimes in a fan-shaped or wing formation, all was most puzzling to all of our Civil War veterans who had never witnessed such tactical maneuvers, or such a flexible line of skirmishers; all without any audible commands, but with much screeching and loud yelling."[14] The Comanches, that is to say, fought on their own terms, whenever they could—and always in their own style.

And Comanche courage?

✝

Three years later, during the 1874 Red River Campaign, according to Carter, a Lieutenant Peter M. Boehm was leading a detachment of scouts at some distance from General Ranald Mackenzie's 4th Cavalry. Besides the lieutenant the group consisted of a Sergeant Charlton, a trooper named McCabe, and two Tonkawas. Abruptly the detail came upon four Comanches sitting on the grass, holding the reins of their horses. The warriors leapt for their ponies. Three of them managed to mount, while the fourth somehow lost his reins, permitting his pony to flee. Lieutenant Boehm shot the horse from under one of the braves, who immediately engaged him in combat, until the officer finally killed him. The two remaining mounted warriors fled, with McCabe and the Tonkawas in pursuit. Meanwhile Sergeant Charlton directed himself toward the warrior whose distant pony was becoming a puff of dust.

This Comanche, who was broad-shouldered and well over six feet tall, was taking deliberate aim with his bow at the lieutenant. Sergeant Charlton shot him before he could release the arrow. In response the warrior discharged a series of arrows at Charlton, whose horse had been plunging and throwing its head each time the American tried to aim his carbine. During the sergeant's struggle with his horse, an arrow drove through his thigh, pinning him to the saddle. The warrior, having used all his arrows, now began firing his rifle, with one shot striking the sergeant's left hand and tearing away parts of two fingers. In spite of this, Charlton finally managed to aim and pull off a round that "shattered the Indian's hips and lower spine." But the Comanche laughed, "tossed his black mane from over his eyes and kept on firing," continuing to do so until Charlton shot him through the head.

Later the sergeant examined the body of his dead foe. He discovered it bore nine bullet holes, "any one of which should have killed an ordinary man."[15] The tall warrior would have been considered an exceptionally brave person in any culture. But in his fight to the death, he personified a Comanche ideal. Not every man, or woman, could live up to it. The ideal, though, was that of a kind of courage able to inspire and motivate the entire People.

✛✛

Even so there were deep cultural differences between those who had inherited the European tradition of war and those whose first thought had necessarily always been that of survival. The Comanche attitude was based on a rationale that was perfectly logical to the People. Berlandier grasped an important point when he wrote that in the view of the Nuhmuhnuh, a single Comanche life was "worth a hundred of the enemy, or more." Europeans and Americans complained that Plains warriors would not "stand and fight." But the horse Indians, even though their populations had increased on the plains, could not and would not tolerate the kinds of losses considered acceptable in battles between European armies. Each warrior was also a hunter. A number of women, old men, and children depended on him for food, perhaps for their very survival during hard times, since other men might feed them out of generosity but were not required to do so. As a result the death of every young warrior was a source of intense grief within his band.

Yet paradoxically, war was the motivating force of Comanche culture and represented the basis of most of its values.[16] The People, then, had to wage war in such a way that they suffered the fewest possible casualties. Like other Plains tribes, they counted upon stealth, the effect of surprise, and the creation of terror to gain a psychological advantage over their enemies. Herman Lehmann pointed out that while Apaches attacked in silence, Comanches whooped and made as much noise as possible. The silent attack was no doubt unnerving. But the Texas Ranger John Salmon Ford wrote of the Comanche war whoop that it possessed "no romance," piercing "even a stout heart with an indescribable sensation."

Like other Plains Indians, the Comanches were reluctant to attack well-armed enemies unless they greatly outnumbered them. Even then they usually would not attack if there were a high risk of casualties. Plains warfare depended upon a strategy of stalking and surprising enemies, throwing them into a panic, with the numbers and odds overwhelmingly in favor of the aggressor. Heavy losses reflected badly upon a war chief. Even a few men killed and wounded might affect his reputation and call into doubt the strength of his medicine. Every war chief kept this in mind throughout each expedition he led.

The United States bought Florida from Spain in 1819. As part of the purchase agreement, America renounced its claim to Texas and that part of New Mexico lying east of the Río Grande. Although the act outraged many western Americans, it removed the excuse for more would-be fili- busters to attempt separating Texas from New Spain with a view of attach- ing it to the United States. But the incursions of the filibusters, as well as the effects of the Mexican revolution of 1810, had already devastated the province. For instance after the battle of the Medina River in 1813, Gen- eral Arredondo had executed, or forced into flight, some thousand Spanish Texans, about a third of the population. In only a few towns, such as Béxar, were there any significant numbers of inhabitants remaining. Even in these, surrounded as they were by abandoned fields, there was a shortage of food. The successful Mexican revolution eight years later further weak- ened Texas, as well as Mexico itself. This protracted turmoil encouraged the Comanches and their allies, despite treaties with Spain and (later) Mex- ico, to intensify their raiding into Texas and southward across the Río Grande.

In the fall of 1821, Stephen Austin, with the blessing of the Mexican government, established his colony on the coastal plains between the Colo- rado and Brazos rivers. After a difficult beginning, the *anglosajones* pros- pered on their rich farmlands. More soon came, with Mexican permission, to join them. The colony was distant from the Comanche raiding range. Austin, in any event, had taken care to maintain good relations with the People. In the meantime, though, another kind of American, the squatter, was immigrating into eastern Texas.

Lieutenant José María Sánchez, draftsman of the Comisión de Límites, noted in 1828 that the norteamericanos had virtually appropriated eastern Texas. They were continually arriving in unoccupied country, he observed. Once there they would settle on whatever land pleased them and build their cabins upon it, without authorization from any Mexican official. Sán- chez was even suspicious of Austin and his colonists farther south. General Mier y Terán, commander of the expedition, and Stephen Austin had es- tablished a friendly relationship during their brief acquaintance. In spite of the mutual respect existing between these two men, Lieutenant Sánchez predicted that the Austin colony would someday produce a spark igniting the conflagration that would deprive Mexico of Texas.

At least the Anglo-Texan farmers, squatters and legal immigrants alike, were able at that time to work their lands in comparative safety. Lieutenant Sánchez observed that, in contrast, the residents of San Antonio dared not venture out of the city to cultivate their fields. Even during periods of peace, the Comanches and their allies harassed the city so frequently that farming at any distance from it was unsafe. Then when officials accused the Nuhmuhnuh and other norteños of violating the peace, they would blame enemy tribes and vehemently protest their innocence.

In 1833 or 1834 Charles and William Bent, along with Ceran St. Vrain, constructed a little picket trading post on the Arkansas River: it was the start of the great adobe edifice, patterned after the Spanish presidio, which became known as "Bent's Fort." The same year, 1834, that Jean Louis Berlandier was completing his manuscript concerning the Texas Indians, Colonel Henry Dodge and his dragoons were peacefully visiting the Comanches at their great encampment near the Wichita Mountains in present Oklahoma. Also in 1834, near present Groesbeck, Texas, a fundamentalist Baptist preacher named John Parker was, along with thirty-three family members and relatives, chopping and sawing and pounding together a stockade on the upper Navasota River, where the whole clan had settled and was beginning to farm. This was a fateful act, both for the Parkers and for the Nuhmuhnuh.

So far Comanches had not attacked the Anglo-Texan settlers, except for the 1826 raid on Gonzales. But now, in the 1830s, the anglosajones, legal or illegal residents, were beginning increasingly to explore northwestward up the Texas rivers and to settle beyond the safe coastal plains in wooded country verging on the Comanche raiding range. So far Elder John Parker had experienced no trouble with Indians, but he was not taking chances; he was building a stockade, a structure that soon became known as Parker's Fort. His clan was safer there than they would have been on the outskirts of San Antonio. Yet in the location he had chosen, sooner or later the People were bound to visit him.

Drawing upon his experiences in 1818 and 1819, David G. Burnet had written, in effect, that when Comanches met with determined opposition, they would "crouch like the Spaniel or fly like the 'stricken fawn.'" Jean Louis Berlandier, doubtless relying on accounts by José Francisco Ruíz, had flatly stated that "native warfare is never very deadly." Often this must have been the case; Ruíz had had plenty of opportunities to observe the Nuhmuhnuh and their allies. Yet when that warfare was motivated by a craving for vengeance, the facts could be otherwise.

Later, much later, in the 1870s, a small band of Comanches (one of the few not already confined to the tribe's Indian Territory reservation) was on its way slowly southward toward the Río Grande. This band of the People was not worried about pursuit. Its men had left all recently encountered enemies either dead or afoot. Presently the band was camped, waiting for

word from the civil chief to pack up and continue the journey. Montechena, a brave, was examining his arrows, one by one, for straightness,
when a commotion at the edge of camp caught his attention. He rose and
went to look. Three warriors, standing by lathered, blowing ponies, were
telling their story. Six of them had been surrounded and attacked by about
thirty well-armed Tonkawas. During the battle these three had escaped to
bring word of the assault. The camp was thrown into a tumult as men ran
to catch their horses. Within minutes some hundred warriors had mounted
their ponies and were riding fast toward the site of the battle. While riding,
Montechena thought about the Tonkawas: many of them were working as
scouts for the white soldiers. It would be a good thing if he and his companions could kill these before they caused the People more trouble.

The war party rode hard for three hours before seeing smoke and, soon,
the enemy's camp. As they approached, the war chief whooped. The warriors joined in—a single drawn out yell. The startled Tonkawas leapt on
their horses and fled, one or two of them falling before the shots and arrows of the charging Comanches. Riding through the abandoned camp,
Montechena heard exclamations of rage and loped, with others, to a group
clustered at the campfire, which gave off the smell of cooking meat. There,
roasting, was a human leg, the leg of a Comanche.

The war chief cried out for vengeance, a cry taken up by the entire party.
Instantly all the warriors were riding at a gallop in the direction of the
enemy's flight. They found the Tonkawas gathered in a ravine, a good
defensive position. The Comanches charged, riders swerving at times as
horses were knocked down at long range, hurling men to the ground before other horsemen. But the charge continued. Montechena, riding in the
front row, was suddenly terrified at facing the concentrated gunfire blazing
from the ravine. But the horses behind him were pressing his horse forward, and he could only bend low over his pony's neck and gallop on. As
the mass of horsemen approached the enemy, Montechena clearly saw individual Tonkawas firing at him, the flash and smoke of their rifles.
Abruptly he became enraged, catching the group spirit of vengeance, and
whipped his pony onward.

Near the ravine the Comanches drew up. A lone Tonkawa rode up out
of the gully in a challenge to single combat. A Comanche responded by
riding straight for him. The Tonkawa fired. The Ietan brave fell, fatally
wounded. Another charged. The Tonkawa shot him, too, from his horse,
killing him. At this, a momentary truce occurred, as if by common consent
of both sides. Men loaded their guns, looked to their arrows and lances.
Then a third Comanche raced out, firing and hitting the enemy warrior.
As the Tonkawa toppled from his horse, an exultant cry rose from the

Comanches, a shout of anger from the horsemen in the ravine. The massed Comanches charged. After the crackling of gunfire from both sides, the attackers reached the ravine and engaged the enemy hand-to-hand. The Tonkawas fought valiantly, but they were outnumbered by more than three to one. Before long, the last of them lay bleeding into the earth. Among the Comanches, eight men lay dying, while some forty more were seriously wounded.

Montechena, knife in his hand, busied himself on the battlefield with other men of his party. Many of the dying Tonkawas were gasping for water. He and his companions paid no attention to their appeals, scalping them, severing their arms and legs, cutting out their tongues. The Tonkawas had built a fire in the ravine. Now Montechena and other Comanches joined in throwing the limbs and bodies of the enemy upon the blazing wood. Some Tonkawas were still capable of showing pain, or of trying to writhe out of the coals and flames, or even of crying out for mercy. But Montechena and his comrades continued to pile the dead and dying together, throwing on more wood and dancing around the fire, watching exultantly as grease and blood ran from the heap, and as skin swelled and popped in little flares.

Later, when Montechena and the other warriors rode in among the lodges, the wounded and dead on ponies behind them, they were met by the women of the band, weeping, moaning, pulling their hair, cutting gashes on their faces, bodies, arms and legs, lacerations that would take months to heal. Soon there would be a funeral dance. But the People had had their revenge.[17]

In 1901 Herman Lehmann Montechena was declared to be a Comanche Indian by an Act of Congress and was presented with a headright of one hundred and sixty acres in Oklahoma, in accordance with the wishes of the Comanche Tribal Business Council. But no act of Congress was needed to make Lehmann a Comanche. Although the pigment of his skin remained white, he had long before become psychically a Comanche warrior. From the time of his return to his family in Loyal Valley, Texas, at the age of nineteen in 1878, until his death in 1932, Lehmann/Montechena remained inwardly a Comanche, unable ever really to adjust to the kind of life lived by his family and their friends. His own friends, such as Yellow Wolf and Quanah Parker, remained upon the reservation, where he visited them frequently, as long as he was able to. But (had he ever seen it) Herman Lehmann might have taken issue with the opinion of José Francisco Ruíz and Jean Louis Berlandier that "native warfare" was "never very deadly."

Mexican Presidial Soldier
(Lino Sánchez y Tapia, Courtesy, The Thomas Gilcrease Institute of American History and Art, Tulsa, Oklahoma)

Omercawbey, or "Walking Face," a Comanche Warrior

Theodore Babb, a Former Comanche Captive

Herman Lehmann with Captain J. B. Gillett of the Texas Rangers
(Courtesy, The Lehmann Family, Boerne, Texas)

Clinton Smith with Old Comanche Friends
(Courtesy, The Arthur H. Clarke Company)

Sam Houston
(Courtesy, Colorado Historical Society)

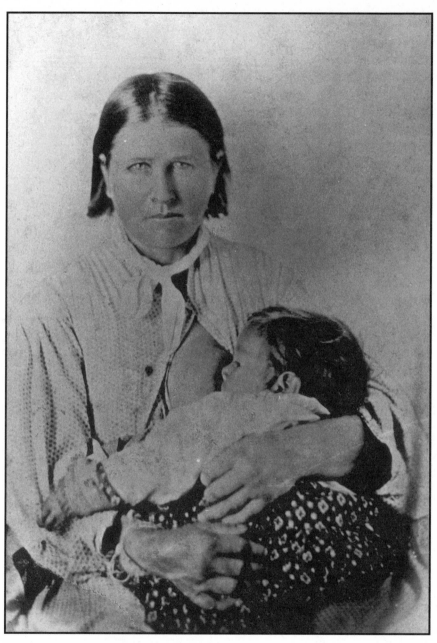

Cynthia Ann Parker, a Former Comanche Captive
(Courtesy, Eugene C. Barker Texas History Center, University of Texas, Austin)

Quanah Parker with Two of His Seven Wives
(Courtesy, Panhandle-Plains Historical Museum, Canyon, Texas)

TWENTY-ONE

Peace, North—War, South, 1834–1835

T he United States Congress in 1830, under the approving eye of the Jackson administration, passed the Indian Removal Act in response to extreme pressure from the states, and citizens, of Georgia, Alabama, and Mississippi. The bill set in motion one of the more disgraceful episodes in American history, providing, as it did, for the eviction of the Five Civilized Tribes (Choctaws, Chickasaws, Creeks, Cherokees, and Seminoles) from their farms and ancestral lands, and for their removal to country west of the Mississippi. (Other tribes, less committed to agriculture, such as the Kickapoos and Shawnees, had already moved west of their own accord.) To the mostly acculturated and horticultural or pastoral Indians of the South, the Removal Act, and its enforcement by federal authorities, was a tragedy. But their compulsory emigration also had bitter ramifications for the Comanches and other Indians of the southern plains.

The forced migrations, while resolving none of the old conflicts in the region, quickly created new ones between the immigrant Indians and indigenous peoples. The principal point of dispute was, for Comanches and Kiowas, the inviolability of their traditional hunting grounds. This concern was reinforced by the gradual start of a discernible decline in the number of buffalo on the plains, enormous though the herds still were. The causes were partly climatic, a change in the precipitation cycle, but as the Texan historian R. N. Richardson points out, "the period between 1830 and 1860 witnessed such destruction" by border Indians and whites among the bison that "hunters of various tribes began to find it exceedingly difficult to kill a sufficient number to sustain their families."[1] By 1841, observes Richardson, the U.S. commissioner of Indian affairs reported that 87,615 eastern Indians had been forcibly transplanted to the West, and more were still to come.[2] The Comanches realized early that encroachments by immigrant Indian hunting parties ultimately threatened their way of life, and they struck back with raids upon the border Indians' farms and cabins, constantly increasing the animosity between the two groups.

Meanwhile the old, traditional hostilities continued.

In 1833 a young Osage chief, Clermont, led 300 of his warriors onto the plains from the general area of Fort Gibson, in present Oklahoma. His purpose was to make war on his enemies, the Comanches, or Kiowas, or the Wichitan peoples. As the great war party proceeded westward, its scouts informed the leaders of passing a Kiowa war party headed in the opposite direction. No doubt using his scouts to trace the enemy's route to its origin, Clermont led his small army to a temporarily defenseless Kiowa encampment lying in the vicinity of today's Fort Sill. Falling upon the camp around dawn, the Osages slaughtered some 150 women, children, and old men. Before departing, the Osages performed a ritual intended to placate certain spirits. This rite consisted of beheading the enemy dead and placing their heads in rows of Kiowa brass buckets in the midst of the ravaged camp. Included with the booty and trophies that the victorious war party carried off with them were horses, scalps, one of the sacred Kiowa Tai-me medicine bundles, and two children, sister and brother.[3]

Curiously, this massacre was the immediate cause of the 1834 dragoon expedition led by Colonel Henry Dodge and accompanied by George Catlin. During each of the preceding two years, mounted expeditions had ridden forth from Fort Gibson for the purpose of finding and making friends with the Comanches and their allies. Each of these had failed. After the massacre American officials on the Arkansas frontier knew that the Kiowas, and probably their allies, would be certain to retaliate against the Osages. This would, in turn, threaten members of tribes (such as Choctaws, Creeks, Cherokees, Shawnees, and Delawares) resettled in present Oklahoma on lands certain to be crossed by war parties moving either east or west. The U.S. government had an obligation to protect these immigrant tribes.

In the latter part of 1832, President Andrew Jackson dispatched his protégé and friend, Sam Houston, to Béxar.[4] Houston, an adopted Cherokee, was a natural choice for the mission. The object of his trip was to meet with Comanche leaders in order to invite them to Fort Gibson (near modern Muskogee, Oklahoma), where they might be persuaded to sign a treaty with the United States. Houston, whose Cherokee name was "The Raven," arrived in San Antonio early in 1833 and succeeded in meeting with Comanches there. They were friendly, he reported, with no objections to signing a treaty with the U.S. government. At his urging they pledged to visit Fort Gibson, a vow they later disregarded. That spring Houston met again with Comanches and recalled to them their promise, yet once more they failed to comply, quite possibly because of the understandable disapproval of Mexican authorities.

In the fall of 1833, one of the U.S. Indian commissioners, Governor

Monfort Stokes of North Carolina, proposed in a letter to the secretary of war that the government purchase from the Osages several of their Kiowa and Wichita captives. An escort of dragoons could return them to their people, who might then be persuaded of American good intentions and consent to attend a treaty council at Fort Gibson. The secretary approved this plan, which became the basis for the dragoon expedition of the following year.

The dragoons had arrived at the "Great Camanchee Village" on July 16, 1834. While camped nearby men and horses alike continued to fall ill from what Catlin called a "slow and distressing bilious fever."[5] On the 18th the expedition departed, following a Skidi Pawnee guide whom Lieutenant Wheelock says they "found." After marching only ten miles, they reached a good stream by a woods. Here Dodge established a sick camp, leaving behind Catlin, along with thirty-six men and three officers.

The following morning Joe Chadwick, Catlin's friend, accompanied Dodge, taking with him the artist's sketchpad and notebooks.[6] After three days of difficult travel, the dragoons arrived at the Taovayas village. It lay on a bank of the Red River's north fork, below jumbled pink granite hills about six hundred feet high (near the mouth of today's Elk Creek and at the entrance to what is now called "Devil's Canyon"). The nearly two hundred conical huts were of grass thatched over poles. Chadwick thought from a distance they resembled beehives. He and the other Americans were surprised to ride by extensive fields of maize, pumpkins, melons, beans, and squash. Lieutenant Wheelock, official journalist of the expedition, found the Taovayas men less "fine looking" than the Comanches, but the women were prettier than Comanche women. In fact some of the girls were very pretty, and went naked except for a garment of deerskin or red cloth worn around the hips. Another member of the expedition was even more enthusiastic, writing later in a newspaper article: "The women are beauties; yes, real first rate copper beauties."

The regiment camped in a defensive square about a mile from the village. On the following day, July 22, Colonel Dodge, with most of his officers, met in the second chief's lodge for council, the head chief being absent. The second chief, Wetarasharo, was old, his age being estimated variously at seventy and ninety. Dodge began by telling the Taovayases what he had told their allies, the Comanches; that he came in peace, representing the United States, for the purpose of establishing friendly relations with them. These would, of course, include trade.

"Do the Spaniards from Santa Fe trade with you?"

The chief replied that, yes, some had visited recently.

"Americans will give you better and cheaper goods than the Spaniards do."

Wetarasharo said he was pleased. He and his chiefs had friendly feelings toward the Americans.

Preliminaries concluded, the colonel broached the subject of a Judge Martin's recent murder while he was hunting on the Washita. The Comanches had informed him, he said, that the Taovayases were responsible for it. They had also told him the judge's little son was presently a Taovayas captive. Before friendly relations could exist between his people and theirs, he explained, they must deliver the boy to him.

The chiefs denied the Comanches' account. With assurance they told Dodge and his officers that their people had had no connection with the murder. And they had no idea of what might have become of the boy. The colonel, skeptical, insisted, continuing to press his demand, while the Taovayases steadfastly denied any knowledge of the affair. Finally the colonel sent for an English-speaking black man whom he had learned was living in the village. This person was soon conducted into the council lodge. Under questioning he told the gathering that, yes, such a boy had indeed been brought among them and was still a prisoner of the tribe. Amid a general stir, the colonel informed Wetarasharo that the council could proceed no further until he produced the boy. The chiefs lapsed into a stubborn silence. Gloom settled over the meeting. As the silence lengthened, the tension grew.

Dodge spoke at last of how, before beginning his trip, he had purchased from their enemies, the Osages, a Kiowa girl, as well as two girls from their own tribe. He had done this to demonstrate the Americans' goodwill toward them. But he would not return the girls before the Martin boy was freed; and furthermore he wanted an American ranger (that is, mounted militiaman) named Abbey, whom they had captured the previous summer. Taking this opportunity to repay their Comanche friends, the chiefs solemnly assured the colonel that while, admittedly, they had seized the man, a party of Comanches had taken him into the Mexican provinces and executed him. As for the boy . . . The chiefs fell into urgent consultation among themselves. Finally they sent out a messenger. Soon the boy was brought in, naked, like the tribal nine-year-olds, from the cornfield where he had been hidden. His entrance created excitement around the council circle. The boy, who was intelligent, looked wonderingly about:

"What! Are there white men here?"

"What's your name, son?" asked Colonel Dodge.

"My name is Matthew Wright Martin."

Taking the boy into his arms, the colonel ordered that the Taovayas girls be brought into the council. Minutes later, amid gathering excitement, they were conducted into the lodge. Kah-kee-tsee, The Thighs, and She-de-a, Wild Sage (attractive girls Catlin had earlier painted) were recognized instantly by their male relatives, who received them with joy. Plainly moved, the old chief rose to his feet. Going to Colonel Dodge, he embraced him, his left cheek pressed against the colonel's, holding him for several minutes in complete silence, "whilst tears were flowing from his eyes. He then embraced each officer in turn," continued Chadwick, "in the same silent and affectionate manner; which form took half an hour or more . . ."

The following day a great number of Comanches arrived, led by Tabbaquena (Sun Eagle, whom Gregg met five years later), second chief of the division.[7] Catlin had depicted him earlier, in paint and by pen, finding him the "largest and fattest Indian" he had ever seen, with an "African face" and a beard two or three inches long. Tabbaquena immediately inquired for Colonel Dodge. Riding to the commander's tent on a fine horse, he dismounted and embraced the colonel, calling him his "great white brother." The two leaders moved into Dodge's tent to confer.

The colonel began by explaining again that the Great American Captain had sent him to bring peace to the various tribes, peace with the Americans and with each other. He told how he had already offered friendship to the Comanches, and how he had trusted them by leaving his sick near their encampment.

"I spent a night in the camp with your sick men," said Tabbaquena. "They treated us well."

Dodge said he was glad to have seen an American flag flying over the main Comanche camp. While it might have come to them from the Pawnees of the Platte River, it was really from their great father, the president.

"I want to be at peace with you Americans," the chief said. "There are many bands of Comanches. I'll visit all of them this year and tell them what you have said to me. They'll all be glad to make peace with you. I'm an old man now, but since I was a boy, I never did kill one of your people."

Dodge nodded.

"You ask who killed the ranger. I can tell you, because I remember when this white man was taken. The Texas Comanches took this white man and brought him over the Red River and killed him there."

The colonel reflected, then changed the subject. "I want some of you to come back with me, so you can see our country and we can make a strong peace between you and other red men, as well as between our peoples. The Panismahas met the Osages, the Delawares, and the Cherokees on our lands, and made peace there. They were enemies before. Now they're friends and don't hate each other any more. We want you to come and make peace with us in the same way."

"You have a girl," said Tabbaquena, "who was taken from our friends, the Kiowas. Now, I have a Spanish girl who was taken from her friends. I'll give you the Spanish girl for the Kiowa girl."

"I want your friendship," Dodge said. "And the Kiowas' friendship. I want you to go back with me, and some of the Kiowas, too. I don't intend to sell the girl to them. I intend to *give* her to her relatives and friends, without asking any price. I'm going to *give* the girl to her tribe. Then they'll understand we're their friends."

"If I go with you," said Tabbaquena thoughtfully. "I'll be afraid to come back through the timber."

"I pledge myself that you'll be escorted safely back."

"No, I can't go myself. My brother will go with you."

Sudden dust and commotion outside caught both men's attention. A group of Kiowas had galloped up, skidding to a halt almost in the doorway of the colonel's tent. Women and children standing there scattered in fright. The Kiowa warriors, just arriving at the great gathering, were enraged: in the Taovayas village they had seen the Osage guides.

At Fort Gibson George Catlin had painted a group portrait of three of some dozen Osage guides and hunters who were to accompany the expedition. The three young men, close friends, are shown with shaved heads, except for a ridge of hair standing up in the center like a horse's roached mane, with twin braids hanging behind. Their heads, decorated with a plume or two, were slightly flattened in the back from having been strapped against cradle boards during infancy. The three were portrayed wearing their summer garb, breechclout, leggings, and moccasins of dressed skins, with garters worn just above the knee. Each held a lance or a bow and arrows. Catlin wrote that the tribe might "justly be said to be the tallest race of men in North America, either of red or white skins; there being very few indeed of the men . . . who are less than six feet . . . and very many of them six and a half, and others seven feet." One of the tribe's three principal chiefs, The Black Dog (the other two being The White Hair and Clermont), stood about seven feet high and weighed from two hundred and fifty to three hundred pounds. (The Osages, however, and perhaps without irony, called themselves informally the "Little Ones.")

Yet the Osages were noted for their speed on foot and for their endurance. In one instance a young Osage warrior, delivering a message, walked and jogged nearly eighty miles in less than ten hours. It was not unusual, reported The *Arkansas Advocate*, for Osage men and women to make the round trip on foot from their village to Chouteau's Trading Post—a distance of about seventy miles—in a single day.[8] The southern Comanches, at least, called the Osages "Los Ligeros," or the Swift Ones, and paid them the compliment, when fighting them, of docking their horses' tails, a sign ordinarily reserved to denote mourning.

Juan Antonio Padilla mentioned this custom in 1819, writing in a report that the Comanches, "to free themselves from the Huasas [Osages] . . . , who are said to be exceedingly swift in a race, . . . use the device of cutting off their horses' tails."[9] At about the same time, the Texas pioneer W. B. Dewees wrote of encountering Osages during a buffalo hunt. "But," he observed, "our company being large we did not fear them. They are only to be dreaded when they catch two or three men alone, as they are so swift of foot as to be able to run down almost any horse and catch him and its rider."[10] Berlandier, writing around 1828, also mentioned this practice.[11] But another member of the Comisión de Límites, Lieutenant José María Sánchez, explained it more graphically than the botanist, writing that the Osages' quickness was marvelous, "for it is a proven fact that when in battle, the Comanches flee, they pursue them on foot, overtake them, and with one leap spear them from the back, or catching the horse by the tail, they throw it down and then put their adversary to death." [12]

Yet . . . is this possible? Yes, possible. Jesse Owens, the American Olympian, could outsprint a thoroughbred in a hundred-yard dash. Of course the race was rigged by firing the starting pistol near the horse's ear.[13] But even with a fair start, the runner might well have outdistanced the animal for the first twenty-five or fifty yards. The Comanche ponies, barely fourteen hands high, and rarely weighing more than eight hundred pounds, were not thoroughbreds or quarter horses. A sprinter could probably have outrun them in a dash, especially if the ponies were starting from a halt or an abrupt turn. Then the trick would have been to fling the pony sideways when two or more of its feet were off the ground. (A galloping horse has, intermittently, all four feet in the air.) Jerked off balance, and made more top-heavy by its rider's weight, the pony would probably have gone down. This would only have to have happened a very few times to have made an unforgettable impression on the Comanches.

The historian Grant Foreman quotes from an 1837 letter by a Major Armstrong, Indian agent, who asserted that "the Osages are held in great terror by the Comanches."[14] This was probably a gross exaggeration, if not slander, especially since the Comanches and Osages had at that time been on friendly terms for three years, thanks partly to Dodge's efforts. Still the

Comanches never underestimated the prowess of the Osages. According to Berlandier the two tribes had been at war since 1752. In 1828, when he knew the Comanches, the two tribes hated each other so intensely that during their campaigns neither side took prisoners. This hatred for the Osages was shared with equal fervor by the Wichitan peoples and the Kiowas. In fact on that July day in 1834 when some thirty Kiowas, with the recent massacre fresh in their minds, nearly rode into Dodge's tent, their anger was so great, wrote a Sergeant Evans, that "it could scarcely be kept in respectful bounds" toward the Americans.

The colonel, doubtless with Tabbaquena's help, managed to placate the Kiowas, explaining through the interpreter that the girl from their tribe, fortuitously present, was to be returned to them without ransom. While most of the warriors remained in their saddles, a relative of the girl dismounted and embraced her, weeping with joy at the prospect.

On July 24 the chiefs attending the great council met at 10:00 A.M. at a designated spot in woods about two hundred yards from the dragoon camp. Of the Americans only Colonel Dodge and his staff attended, while the remainder of the regiment remained under arms. At the same time some two thousand warriors rode continually around the council. After calumets had passed, the colonel, with Tabbaquena seated on his right, addressed the gathering:

"Kiowa chiefs," he declared. "Here is your daughter and relative, given without asking a thing in return. Take her as proof of American friendship. Our great captain, the president, bought this girl from the Osages. He has sent me to restore her to the arms of those who love her. This is only one of the acts of kindness he will show you. You and the Indians who accompanied us have been at war a long time. It is the president's wish you now make peace. As a friend of you all, he will send traders among you who will bring blankets, guns, and other things you need. The buffalo are becoming scarce. There are fewer every year. But the president will give you cattle to replace them, and you will be able to plant corn and work the soil, as the Cherokees and other Indians do. Now—I want you to think over my invitation to return with me. I promise you will receive presents, and you will be escorted safely back through the timber country."

"You are leaving tomorrow?" asked one of the chiefs.

"I want to leave as soon as possible. We have far to go."

The Kiowa head chief, Titchetochecha (known to whites as Dohasan) agreed to go, as well as a Waco chief.[15]

Wetarasharo, the old Taovayas, urged the others to believe the colonel's words, because, "he is a good man."

"White men and brothers," declared Dohasan. "This day is the most interesting period of our existence. The Great Spirit has made a light shine all around us, so we can see each other. The Great Spirit has sent these white men and brothers to see us. Kiowas, take them by the hand and treat them well. They are your friends. They have brought home your lost relative. When you meet a white man, take him to your lodge. Give him buffalo meat and corn. Then he will always be your friend."

The expedition departed on July 25, moving first toward the sick camp. Riding along the second day, Lieutenant Wheelock managed somehow to converse with one of the Taovayas chieftains. He learned from him that the Wichitan peoples did not much like the Comanches, although the two tribes had long maintained friendly relations. The trouble was, apparently, that these allies habitually cheated them, then rode away. Their newer friends, the Kiowas, they found "more honest and gentle."[16] (On the other hand, Lawrie Tatum, Quaker Indian agent for the Comanches and Kiowas, 1869–73, considered the Kiowas to be "the worst tribe . . . in Indian Territory.") Wheelock himself, though, was rather favorably disposed toward the Nuhmuhnuh, writing in his official journal that "The Camanche is a fine looking Indian, in general naked . . ." The "appearance of a Camanche fully equipped on horseback, with his lance and quiver and shield by his side, is beautifully classic."[17]

On the twenty-seventh the dragoons reached the sick camp, where they found two lieutenants ill and Catlin worse. But the major event of the day was the departure of Tabbaquena and the Comanche delegation, because of "the sickness of the squaw." This seems to have left only that "gallant little fellow," Jesús Sánchez, as representative for the Comanches. Since Tabbaquena had earlier told Colonel Dodge he would send his brother, it is interesting to speculate as to whether "the little Spaniard" might not have been "brother" to the chief. Catlin described Sánchez as "one of the leading warriors of the tribe," certainly worthy to be the chief's "brother." Because he was a former captive (not half-Comanche as Catlin thought), he still spoke some Spanish and was able to communicate with the americanos. Although this is conjecture, it would seem possible that as a leading warrior, the "brother" of the second chief, would have been a logical choice for delegate to the great council at Fort Gibson.

Sánchez was also a bold man, as he had demonstrated upon first meeting Colonel Dodge and the dragoons. But the huge majority of the Comanches, starting with Tabbaquena, appeared to look upon the colonel's invitation with cautious suspicion. Certainly they did fear leaving their own buffalo plains to pass through the Cross Timbers. There, as on the long-grass prairie, with its occasional groves, and in the forest, they would be vulnerable to the Woodland Indians. Did they fear treachery? Possibly. And, after all, the americanos had returned no captive Comanches. Although the People were now disposed to be friendly to the Americans, and the chiefs were pleased with the guns and pistols Dodge had given them, apparently no Comanche but Jesús Sánchez was willing to accompany the Kiowas.

On August 16 the expedition reached Fort Gibson, where George Catlin transferred from a litter to a bed. Yet he had accomplished his personal mission, bringing back the notebooks and sketches and portraits which are a part of his contribution to American art and history. Colonel Dodge had almost accomplished his, though at the terrible price of some 150 dead and dying dragoons. As Catlin began recovering, Dodge continued to carry out his instructions. He dispatched an officer to return Matthew Martin to his mother, returned the unfortunate black man to his master, and sent runners to the Cherokees, Creeks, Choctaws, Delawares, Senecas, and Osages, calling them to meet in a great council with the Plains delegates who had returned with him.

The council of about 150 members began in the fort's crude theater on September 2 and continued, off and on, for three days.[18] Americans present included Colonel Dodge, Major Armstrong, and Governor Stokes. Chiefs or other leading men represented all of the tribes Dodge had convened. The colonel opened the meeting by explaining its purpose, declaring that after long years of war, it was now time for the chiefs of the various tribes to bury the tomahawk and, together, smoke the pipe of peace. This would be in accordance with the wishes of their Great Father, the president, who would then extend his protection to all of their people, as well as providing other benefits. To begin with the colonel wanted them to come forward and shake hands.

Interpreters conveyed his words, endlessly, it seemed, into the various languages represented. But Dodge's address created an atmosphere that was sufficiently friendly so that all of the chiefs of the immigrant tribes went in turn to Wetarasharo and the Waco chief, shook their hands, and promised to be friends. They next turned to Dohasan, who hugged them, one by one. But when Dodge requested the Osage chief to advance, he appeared reluctant to do so. When he did come forward, Chief Dohasan sat down. An awkward interval followed before the Kiowa would agree to shake hands with his enemy. But finally Dohasan rose, advanced, and embraced Clermont.

On the second day Colonel Dodge repeated the handshaking ritual among the Osage, Taovayas, and Kiowa chiefs. Young Chief Clermont (the Third) had complained to him of detecting a coolness in the manner of the

Kiowas toward him. Accordingly he and Dohasan embraced again. This time, by Lieutenant Wheelock's account, the Kiowa chief was enthusiastic and warm, while the Osage was cold and withdrawn. In spite of this tension, Dodge succeeded before long in establishing a mood of relative harmony and concord among the delegates. One chief after another was soon orating, expressing his friendship for his former Plains enemies, while the Plains leaders, not to be outdone, responded similarly.

On the final day, September 4th, the Cherokees and Senecas presented the Plains chiefs with white beads and tobacco, both symbolic of peace. Momentarily the envoys from the immigrant tribes raised the question as to whether or not they should recognize Jesús Sánchez, that mexicano (or even nuevomexicano) as the official Comanche representative. After brief discussion they did so. Continuing the ceremony the Seneca chief gave the bold little warrior gifts of beads and tobacco for Tabbaquena and the People.

Afterward in the cordial atmosphere established during the course of the council, the delegates smoked and passed the pipe. More speeches followed prior to adjournment. Even Chief Clermont seems finally to have fallen into the prevailing mood.

"The Great Spirit has brought us together today," he declared, "to smoke as friends. He watches us. This tobacco comes from the white man's hand. Its smoke mixes his friendship with ours, your red brothers. There are no clouds today. The whole earth is clear. The sky over us is clear. When the Plains people and Osages next meet—remember, we meet as friends." [19]

Once more Clermont and Dohasan embraced, this time with warmth on both sides.

In 1835 at Camp Holmes on the Canadian River west of the Cross Timbers, the Nuhmuhnuh ratified their first treaty with the United States. It was at a time when both sides were less cynical about such pacts than they were to become. By the treaty's terms, the immigrant tribes were to have hunting rights in Comanchería to the Mexican boundary. Americans were to have safe passage through the same region and were to remain unmolested on the Santa Fe Trail. Two years later at Fort Gibson, the Kiowas, Kiowa-Apaches, and the Tawakonies agreed to a similar treaty.

For the Comanches the treaty with the Americans held, more or less, to 1845 and beyond. The treaty with the immigrant Indians was shaky from the beginning, since the eastern tribes found the buffalo to be irresistible game, while the Comanches resented each intrusive hunting party. The quantity of encroaching Indian hunters, as time passed, rekindled their wrath against the intruders. But to the Nuhmuhnuh the important treaty was that with the Osages, an agreement they owed to the Kiowas and perhaps to Jesús Sánchez. After eighty-two years of warfare between Comanches and Osages, the 1834 agreement at Fort Gibson established peace between them. The two peoples became trading partners, Comanches bartering stolen Mexican horses and mules for white man's goods that the Osages obtained at frontier trading posts. It was a good arrangement for both tribes. The treaty was never broken.[20]

Meanwhile in the same year in which Comanches, Taovayases, and Wacos approved a treaty with Americans at Camp Holmes, a volunteer force of eighteen Texans, under a Major Coleman, attacked a Tawakoni village on the Navasota River. Presumably this action was in retaliation for Tawakoni raids upon, or thefts of horses from, local settlers, since the Texans had by this time encroached into Wichitan territory. The volunteers had planned a dawn attack, creeping near the village, but barking dogs revealed their presence. The Tawakonies responded in force, ultimately driving Coleman and his men, with one dead and three badly wounded, to Parker's Fort, where they were secure.

Shortly afterward, General Edward Burleson and Colonel John H. Moore raised a large force of men in order to attack the village again. This time they found it deserted, the corn still growing in its fields. For more than a hundred miles they trailed the fugitives, finally surprising a small camp of Tawakonies. Opening fire at once, they killed three of them, capturing five or six others. The main body of the tribe was camped ahead. Forewarned, probably by the gunfire, they fled in such haste that they actually cut their horses' stake ropes, not taking the few seconds to untie them.

Because the Texans and their horses were nearly exhausted from the long pursuit, they turned back, bringing their prisoners with them. One of these, a woman, had with her a lively three-year-old daughter. The little girl was bright and pretty, and the men paid much friendly attention to her. But one morning, after camping for the night on the Brazos River, they discovered to their horror that the child's mother had killed her with a knife. Afterward she had attempted to kill herself. By this time the command had to depart. General Burleson called for a volunteer to end her agony. One Oliver Buckman stepped forward. Somehow moving the Tawakoni woman to the river bank, he drew a large "hack knife" he had made himself. While she stared straight into his eyes, he severed her head from her body with a single stroke. The head and body rolled into the river.

In concluding his account of this raid, the Texas pioneer John Holland Jenkins related how a Colonel Neill had "adopted a singular, if not barbarous, method of sending destruction upon the Indians." Injecting one of the captive braves with smallpox virus, he "then released him to carry the infection into his tribe!" Jenkins went on to reflect that, unfortunately, "nothing was ever heard as to the success or failure of this project."[21]

As it happened, though, the raids and perhaps the "project" seem to have produced results the following year.

TWENTY-TWO

Lone Star . . . and Captive Anglo Women, 1836

In 1835 Mexico's President Antonio López de Santa Anna dissolved his Congress. The following spring a new, conservative Congress began to rewrite the liberal constitution of 1824, ushering in a profound change from federalism to centralism; that is, appropriating power from the individual states and transferring it to Mexico City. The nation's northern frontier provinces revolted in varying degrees, but nowhere to the same extent as in Texas. Texas was of course a special case, owing to the enormous quantity of immigration, legal and illegal, from the United States. A trickle of settlers before and during the early 1820s had become a deluge by the middle 1830s. It is estimated that between 1821 and 1836 approximately thirty to thirty-five thousand Americans crossed the Red and Sabine rivers to build their dogtrot cabins in Mexican Texas.[1] These new immigrants outnumbered the Texan mexicanos by something like ten to one.

On March 2, 1836, Anglo-Texans, assembling at Washington-on-the-Brazos, declared themselves independent from Mexico. Among that body were two Hispanic Texans, one of whom was José Francisco Ruíz. In succeeding weeks Santa Anna invaded Texas, the Alamo fell, and settlers fled in confusion, a panic ever afterward known as the "runaway scrape." But on April 21, Sam Houston and his army defeated General Santa Anna's troops at San Jacinto and succeeded in capturing the president as well. The settlers returned to their homes, even to such out-of-the-way places as Parker's Fort, and went on building new lives. Texans had to continue to fight for it, but they had won their independence.

On the morning of May 19, 1836, a war party of Comanches and Kiowas, along with some Caddoans and Wichitans, drew up their ponies in woodland by the upper Navasota River, some forty miles east of modern Waco. From a distance of about three hundred yards, they scrutinized the two-year-old stockade fort that lay within the traditional hunting grounds of the Wacos and Tawakonies. Had some Tawakonies brought their friends here for a purpose? Or was this, as had been suggested, merely a mixed and random group of raiders? Given the Texan attacks on the Tawakonies the previous year, the first hypothesis seems the more likely. The desire for vengeance, when combined with that for plunder, was a powerful motivator.

The braves sat their ponies, studying the fort. Its stockade, with loopholes, enclosed nearly an acre, with two-story blockhouses guarding diagonal corners. Parker's Fort appeared highly defensible. Yet as the war chief probably knew, most of the men of the little colony of thirty-four people were absent, working in neighboring fields. One of the braves waved a white flag from his lance.

Within the fort twenty-seven year old Rachel Plummer watched the mounted Indians anxiously, holding the hand of her eighteen-month-old son, James Pratt.[2] Her two uncles, Benjamin and Silas, stood nearby, along with several other settlers and her grandparents. She noticed one of the settlers, Mr. Dwight, beginning to shepherd his wife and child and mother-in-law, Mrs. Frost, out of the stockade.

"Good lord, Dwight," cried Silas, turning. "You are not a-going to run?"

"No. I'm going to take the women and children to the woods."

Silas was watching the some two hundred warriors again. "Stand and fight like a man. And if we have to die, we'll sell our lives as dear as we can."

Dwight promised to return. Her uncle Benjamin walked out to greet the Indians, two of whom had come to the fort to declare they were friendly and wished to make a peace treaty with the tejanos. Benjamin walked the two hundred yards to where the main body of horsemen was now standing with the white flag. The warriors remained mounted while communicating with him by signs. Soon he was walking back. To the settlers in the stockade he reported his belief that the Indians planned to fight. He warned the men to look to their arms. Besides the old couple, only Rachel's two uncles and Samuel Frost, with his son, Robert, remained. Silas tried to persuade his brother not to return to the party of warriors but to stay and help defend the fort. But Benjamin stubbornly walked back toward the waiting Comanches. As Rachel watched Benjamin parley, Silas ran back to his house for his shot pouch. Returning a minute later, he asked whether the Indians had commenced killing his brother. She replied that they were gathering around him.

"I know they'll kill him," said Silas, examining his rifle. "But I'll be good for one, anyhow."

Rachel swept up her son and fled out the small back gate that opened toward her father's farm. As she came into the field, she saw horsemen plunging their lances into her Uncle Benjamin. She ran as fast as she could, but a group of mounted warriors headed her off. Several flung themselves from their ponies, chasing her on foot. A large brave snatched up a hoe and knocked her down. Another tore James Pratt from her arms. Still another seized her long hair and began dragging her. She heard a confusion of war whoops, screams, shots. As she managed to twist and scramble to her feet, she heard her Uncle Silas shout a triumphant, "Huzza!"

At the main body of warriors, two Comanche women greeted her with whips. As she stood weeping, blood running from her scalp wound, one of them lashed her several times, her ritual welcome as a captive.

After an interval of screaming from the stockade—silence. In the distance Rachel could see warriors plundering the house; the air around it was snowy with feathers ripped from bed ticks. Little figures brought out and dropped her father's books and medicines. Before she could watch further, warriors seized and threw her on a horse, tying her securely there. Next she heard shouts. Men were coming from the fields with rifles. The raiders at the fort leapt upon their ponies, whipping them away. Suddenly the entire war party departed, as if in a stampede, heading northward toward the Trinity River.

They rode all day and continued for hours in the dark, forcing the ponies. Exhausted, bruised, her scalp wound aching, sick with fear and anxiety about her child, she was relieved finally to stop. She judged it to be about midnight. Men built fires and led off horses. She noted there were fewer in the party now. Two braves removed her from the blowing, sweat-drenched pony. Tightly they bound her wrists behind her with thongs, then bound her ankles, carrying and dumping her face-down on the ground near a fire and other bound forms. She was at first unable to make out who the other captives were. The rough handling had started her scalp bleeding profusely again. Trying to turn her head, she wondered whether they would let her choke, or drown, in her own blood.

By the time the gash in her head had begun to clot, the victorious warriors were dancing, waving fresh scalps as they shuffled and leapt around the fire. A figure from the dark tossed on fresh wood. In the sudden blaze and flying sparks she recognized the gray hair of her grandfather whipping from a hand. She also made out the other captives—three children and Elizabeth Kellogg, a widow about her age. The children were Cynthia Ann and John Parker, nine and six, and her own little John Pratt. Thank God! As the dance gathered momentum, the dancers grew more and more frenzied. In passing they kicked and stamped on her and the others, finally beating the captives with bows.

By the end of the scalp dance, Rachel was dazed and numb, so that she hardly felt any pain from the last blows, only the impact. She hardly felt the warriors untying her wrists and ankles. Yet she still could be shocked, and was, when she saw other braves yanking clothing from Elizabeth Kellogg—saw them hold her white and struggling and naked by the fire, within the circle of dim figures. One began tormenting her with a burning stick. Rachel now tried to fight when they pulled off her own clothes. Naked, she heard herself cry out time after time, and twist away from the stabs of red coals. When one of the men holding her flung her down on her face and mounted her, she hardly knew what was happening. Detached from her body, she felt a paralysis as warrior after warrior copulated with her. Once, for an instant, she turned her face toward the fire and saw Elizabeth palely visible under another humping brave. Although James Pratt slept as if dead, the other two children watched, with great eyes.[3]

The previous month, on April 4, near the southern tip of what would soon be the Republic of Texas, a group of dissatisfied and frightened colonists had fled from their settlement in ox-drawn wagons. Mostly Americans with some Germans and English, this group was among the last to desert the colony of a British empresario named Beales. The aptly named Villa de Dolores had risen on land between the Río Grande and Nueces River by Las Moras Creek. Dr. Beales could hardly have known that his site lay nearly across one of two well-worn Comanche war trails leading from the southern plains through the Río Grande into Chihuahua. But when nervous colonists learned of recent murders and scalping of shepherds and farmers in the vicinity, when they discovered unshod pony tracks near their settlement, when the Mexican officer assigned to protect them hastily departed with most of his men, they decided to abandon the village and travel to Matamoros, where they might book return passage to New York and London. In addition they feared Santa Anna, who, with his army, was waging ruthless war against the rebellious Anglo-Texans fighting for independence. Two days earlier, on the road to San Patricio, they had heard the guns of Mexican soldiers hunting game on their way north to quash the revolt. The two women in the party, with an infant and two small children in charge, were especially fearful and apprehensive.

About one in the afternoon, the group reached a lake, where they planned to camp. The men released the oxen to feed. Some started a fire and began cooking a deer, while others fished or cleaned their guns. Sarah Ann Horn, a young Englishwoman, held the three-month-old baby of the other woman, a Mrs. Harris.[4] Mrs. Harris, who was in poor health, was a short distance away, gathering wild fruit. Nearby Sarah's husband was seated on the ground with their two sons, John, about five, and Joseph, not yet four. Recently some Americans had killed an alligator at the lake. Horn had collected some of the animal's teeth and was drilling holes through them with a gimlet, so that he could amuse the children by stringing them around their necks. Sarah Ann finished washing the baby. As she stepped up on the front part of the wagon to find a clean dress for it, she saw forty or fifty "strange-looking," nearly naked men riding mules toward the camp. Alarmed, she ran to Horn, the infant in her arms. She told him what she had seen. Looking up from his task, which the two boys watched, engrossed, he smiled:

"I doubt that there's any danger. Why don't you dress the baby?"

Did the dream then flit through her mind, the dream that had haunted her for three nights in New York?

She was responsible for two beautiful babies not her own. Neither of her sisters would help her care for them. She laid one of them down on a crib in a corner. Regarding it, she thought it was the most beautiful creature she had ever seen. She took up the other, nursing it from her right breast. While doing so, she returned to the crib to gaze at the other. She was shocked to find its beauty gone—the baby lay naked and filthy, looking as if it had died some time ago. As she stared, the other child continued to suckle her right breast, while milk poured so freely from her left as to chill her entire body.

The war party came in view while Horn was speaking. Something made Sarah start and stare at one of the men standing next to her. An arrow was jutting from his chest. With both hands he pulled it out. As blood spurted, he pitched forward onto the earth and died. Men began falling on all sides. Sarah leapt to her husband, who was on his feet, grasping a boy by either hand. The warriors were off their mules and running. While some tore Sarah and her sons from Horn, another smashed the back of his head with a double-barrelled gun. Horn crumpled to the earth upon his face. Sarah watched him draw up his arms, raise his head once. With a deep sigh, he collapsed, lifeless.

The strange-looking men shoved Sarah and the children to the wagon. They were joined by Mrs. Harris, whom the Comanches had discovered hiding nearby in the bushes. Sarah passed her the baby girl, trying to console the grieving, terrified boys. At once warriors tore the shaking children from her. With knives they showed the boys how they would kill them if they approached their mother. Other braves climbed into the wagon and threw everything out of it, while members of the party ransacked through the goods, choosing those they wished to take. When this was done, the raiders mounted their mules again, placing the women behind two of them, while others took the boys. The war party rode off, leaving the dead men lying naked and scalped next to the empty wagons and flickering fire.

The Comanche camp was concealed in a dense thicket only about two miles from the lake. At a quarter of a mile from the camp, a crowd of warriors greeted the party, dancing and whooping in celebration. As the captives entered the encampment, they were nauseated by the stench of the putrid horsemeat that lay about. When the women had dismounted, they were made to sit on the ground under guard. Members of the war party took their bonnets, handkerchiefs, combs, and rings, while others stripped the boys, leaving the baby naked, as she had been. The men began eating, but they offered no food or water to the captives. Before lying down to sleep, they bound the two women with thongs around the wrists and ankles, throwing a blanket over them. Throughout the night Sarah Ann lay listening to her boys call for her and their dead father, asking for water, while mosquitoes buzzed and stung. The baby slept almost until dawn, when she began crying from hunger and cold. After the braves had unbound Sarah Ann, she asked them in Spanish for flour with which to prepare the infant some food, since its mother was unable to nurse it. The warriors smiled:

"Yes, it will have something to eat."

A powerful brave came up to her and took the crying child. Gripping her by the arms, he hurled the baby as far as he could into the sky, letting her plummet and smash on the earth.

As the war party traveled, Rachel Plummer was fed nothing for five days and given little water. Once James Pratt was brought to her, abused and bloody. The eighteen-month-old child cried out and extended his arms. But as soon as the braves saw she had weaned the child, they took him away. On reaching the plains, the party split into two sections. James Pratt was borne away with the other group. Hers crossed the Red River. The remainder of that spring they traveled. Even after they joined the band to which the party belonged, they continued to move northwestward, crossing the headwaters of the Arkansas and pushing farther into what is now Colorado. That July and part of August the band camped in what Rachel called the "Snow Mountains," or Rockies, where she suffered from cold much of the time.

Pregnant when captured, she gave birth to a child during her travels. When the infant reached the age of six or seven weeks, it became inconvenient to her mistresses. Several warriors entered the lodge where she lived. Taking the baby from her, one of them hurled it to the ground. When he had repeated this once or twice, he handed it back to her. Under her frantic efforts, the infant showed signs of life. The braves again wrested the infant from her, carrying it outside. One of them mounted his pony and dragged the baby back and forth through cactus, until it was a torn and bloody corpse. This they gave back to her, permitting her to dig a hole and bury it.

The band continued to journey until they were northwest of the Río Grande's headwaters. Rachel grieved for her dead baby, as well as for James Pratt, wherever the child might be. On one occasion the People camped near a cave. Rachel entered with a Comanche woman. When the woman turned back and called to her, she kept going in a cavern illuminated by the large candles she had made from buffalo tallow. During her time in the cave, she had a vision of an angel, who comforted her. She was surprised, on returning to the daylight, to learn she had been gone two days and a night. Although she continued to suffer under a mean old woman and a cruel young mistress, she emerged from her experience strengthened, writing later that "The impressions made upon my mind in this cave, have since served as a healing balm to my wounded soul."

Sarah Ann Horn traveled with part of the original war party, still over a hundred men, until mid-June, when they reached the village of her master, the brave who had first seized her. During this time they rode their mules at first south, then north, from twenty or thirty miles above Matamoros to somewhere well within the southern plains, a journey of at least six hundred miles. Naked or nearly so, herself, Sarah Ann found that her greatest anguish came from the sight of her naked, sun-blistered, peeling sons. On one occasion Joseph, seated behind a Comanche boy, slipped from a mule while it was struggling to climb a bank out of a stream. She turned in time to see her son, still not quite four, desperately trying to thrash his way out of the water. A warrior, furious at the child, swung around and jabbed at him with his lance, striking him beneath an eye. The child slipped back into white water, but—fighting for his life—he managed to thrash and flounder forward, until he stood at the bank with blood flowing over his naked body. At that, Sarah Ann lost control and shrilly scolded the man. In return the brave forced the boy to walk over rough terrain the remainder of the day, driving a lame mule.

When the war party stopped that evening, the warrior, still sitting on his mule, beckoned Sarah Ann to him. Approaching, she saw he gripped his whip in one hand, his knife in the other. By this time she had suffered so severely, both physically and emotionally, she no longer feared dying and scarcely feared further pain. When the brave swung his quirt against her skin, each stroke seemed to her, she recalled later, "of no more weight than a feather." Afterward he seized her by the hair. With his knife he sawed it from her head. She watched while he tied it within his own long braid.

On another occasion, two days later, the party crossed a stream so deep the mules had to swim, battling the current. On a hilltop beyond it, they halted. Sarah Ann watched a number of warriors take her sons back to the stream. About an hour later she saw them returning, supporting the children by their hands. Each time the men let go of them, the boys fell and lay still. When the group arrived at the camp, she saw that the children's starved bodies were grotesquely bloated. Joseph, in particular, looked dreadful, with his face already discolored and swollen from his wound. Both lay unconscious for a time, with water running from their mouths, noses, and ears. She concluded that the men had been amusing themselves by throwing the boys into the stream, each time pulling them out just before they drowned. Had they been punishing her further? Or had this been a brutal "swimming lesson?" Or had they, perhaps, been "making men" out of the boys? In any event, this time she said nothing.

A little before the Comanches reached their lodges, the three portions of the war party rejoined. Sarah Ann found Mrs. Harris a pitiful remnant of her previous self, but the two women were happy to see each other alive. For several days the entire party of from three to four hundred warriors rode together. Then one day when Sarah Ann had been placed within the vanguard, she happened to look back and discover that the party was breaking into little groups, which were drifting off in different directions. Included, together or apart, in one or more of these groups of dwindling horsemen bound for the horizon, were Joseph and John.

Soon her party arrived at the village of her master. Her mistress turned out to be as pitiless as the men had been. The Comanche woman spoke broken Spanish, but when Sarah was unable to understand her, she would become enraged and hurl the nearest object at the captive's head. By this time, though, Sarah Ann had toughened to hardwood; she would grab the object and fling it back at the other woman. Later she remembered she had "fared much better for it."

Sarah Ann's mistress put her to work at once dressing buffalo hides. She had difficulty learning that process, but she soon became accomplished at the chore. In her master's family, which filled three lodges, there were five sons and no daughters. It became Sarah Ann's task not only to dress buffalo skins but to make them into clothing and moccasins. She also had to slice and dry buffalo meat, pound it for use, and cook for the entire family. Her master's mother, an aged widow, was the single kind person among those around her. She spent as much of her time as possible with this old woman, who, "by her acts of kindness and soothing manner," did a great deal to make her life bearable. In this way Sarah Ann Horn, the genteel English-woman, became Sarah Ann, the Comanche slave.

As the months wore on, Rachel Plummer grew increasingly restive under the tyranny of her two mistresses. One day she rebelled, fighting back against the younger woman. After a fierce struggle, she forced the Comanche to the ground, subduing her. She expected to be killed, or at least harshly punished. To her astonishment, the Nuhmuhnuh treated her with new respect. She could by now speak some Comanche and understood when a chief told her, "You are brave to fight—good to a fallen enemy. You are directed by the Great Spirit." He explained to her that Indians rarely spared a fallen foe.

Soon afterward she revolted against the oppression of the old woman. In the ensuing battle the two women snapped a lodge pole. The tepee collapsed upon them. But under the buffalo hide, Rachel wrestled down her tormenter. The old woman angrily went to the chiefs and complained about the captive. The chiefs held a council in which they tried Rachel. They ended by sentencing her to replace the lodge pole, and dropped the matter. But she found that from then on her status was higher, and her life under her mistresses became more tolerable.

In March 1837 several Plains tribes gathered for a council of war. Rachel spent as much time as she dared near the council lodge, eavesdropping. Among all of the oratory, she heard the purpose of the meeting: the tribes proposed to make war on the advancing Texas frontier. They would first conquer and occupy Texas, then vanquish Mexico, then the United States. The white men, they said, had "driven the Indian bands from east to west and now they would work this plan to drive the whites out of the country."

Although much of the talk probably consisted of threats and rhetoric, its basis was serious. Two years after concluding a treaty with the United States, the Comanches were awakening to what had happened to the eastern tribes and to what was happening throughout North America. They continued to be generally friendly toward Americans, although there were emerging problems. During the previous month, for instance, American frontier officials had received reports that the important Comanche chief Isacony, whom Catlin had met three years before, had ripped up his copy of the 1835 Camp Holmes Treaty, supposedly because he had not understood that it permitted immigrant Indians to hunt in his part of Comanchería.[5] Yet one can speculate that Isacony, or Returning Wolf, had known the terms of the treaty from the beginning, but that the continued, and probably augmenting, intrusion of hunters into his region was making him increasingly uneasy and angry.

During the previous winter, a Choctaw hunting party had informed a trader of their tribe, Israel Folsom, that (according to a band of Kichais encountered on the plains) "all the different tribes of Indians in the West were uniting with a view to declare war against the United States." Furthermore American officials learned that the Comanches had sent word to the Osages to avoid Comanchería that spring, since they intended to destroy the U.S. post, Camp Mason, along with its garrison.[6] Alarmed, frontier officials commissioned Colonel Auguste Pierre Chouteau to seek out Isacony, as well as important chiefs of other tribes, and attempt to placate them. Chouteau, who was apparently liked by all Indians, succeeded in achieving the treaty of 1837 with the Kiowas, Kiowa-Apaches, and Tawakonies. He also evidently pacified the Comanches to some extent, since that May they brought in three Anglo women to Camp Holmes, and traders were later able to buy the release of others.[7] In any event the rumored attacks never occurred.

The southern Plains tribes, even the divisions and bands within them, were probably too independent and individualistic, too reliant on visions and dreams, to take concerted action for long. It is likely that after the great council, much of the cooperative energy dissipated. Yet these Indian nations, whichever they were, had reached a consensus. From the southern plains the Comanches, with their allies, would carry out at least a part of the council's plan: they would wage guerrilla warfare against the new, encroaching Republic of Texas.

Three months later, on June 19, New Mexican comancheros, acting for an American trader, bought Rachel Plummer and delivered her to Santa Fe. About the same time, other comancheros ransomed Mrs. Harris. They also tried to purchase Sarah Ann, but her master refused to sell her. By late September, though, when she was twenty-eight, he had changed his mind and sold her at San Miguel del Vado for a horse, four bridles, two blankets, two looking glasses, some tobacco, and some powder and shot. She soon learned, through inquiries by other New Mexican traders, that her son John had been ordered to hold a horse all night outside a lodge. His Comanche family had found him sitting there, frozen to death, in the morning. Joseph, after all his trials, had been adopted into the tribe as well. His new mother was a former Mexican captive married to a Comanche brave. The couple would not part with him at any price.

All three women returned with Missouri merchants to the United States by the Santa Fe Trail. They were received back into a society whose puritanical sexual attitudes made them appear to be tainted creatures, even if through no fault of their own. (Possibly the poor women were literally tainted, since many warriors returning from Mexico had contracted syphilis). Suffering as well from continued anguish over the loss of their children, in addition to the emotional and physical pain they had endured, all three women died within a year of their release. More than anything, though, they were destroyed by thoughts of their dead or captive children. At the end of her narrative account of her ordeal, Rachel Plummer cried out:

> But oh! Dreadful reflection, where is [*sic*] my little children? One of them is no more—I buried its bloody body in those vast regions of prairies—but I hope its soul is now in Heaven. My body is covered with scars which I am bound to carry to my grave; my constitution is broke—but above all and every trouble which haunts my distracted mind is WHERE IS MY POOR LITTLE JAMES PRATT?

How did male Texans react to the bondage and abuse of their women? In 1849, during a truce, Ranger Captain Rip Ford was in a huge encampment of the People, where he saw from nearby a woman with golden-brown hair and blue eyes. She was on horseback. Her attractive face was scarred with long slashes on her cheeks. Jim Shaw, the Delaware, told him these were probably signs of grief for the loss of a husband. Shaw also warned him not to speak to her, "as it might cost him his life." To Ford the woman's face was "the personification of despair." Always after that when the captain led a charge against the Comanches, "the woman with auburn hair, slashed cheeks, and countenance of extreme sorrow appeared to lead him. She was before his mind's eye, and he struck for her and for vengeance."[8]

After remaining a captive among the Nuhmuhnuh for six years, James Pratt Plummer was ransomed in 1842. From Fort Gibson he was sent home to Texas, where, in the care of his grandfather, he grew to manhood, becoming a respected member of the frontier community in Anderson county.

Many years later, in the 1870s, another Texan boy captive, Clinton Smith, entered the lodge of his foster father before an imminent battle.

"Potaw," he said, placing his arms around the chief's neck. "I'm begging you not to send me out this time. I've got a big boil on the back of my neck, and I can hardly ride. It hurts so much I can't sleep at night."

Tosacowadi thoughtfully puffed on his pipe, then drew it from his lips. "Boxickeloc, you can have your wish. You can stay here with Monia."

Monia was the chief's twelve-year-old son.

Tosacowadi turned Smith across his lap and examined the boil. Calling one of his wives, he told her to make a poultice of prickly pear. As soon as the woman placed the poultice on his neck, Smith felt relief. That day he remained in camp, while his chief and the other warriors rode out to fight the Otos.[9]

The Comanches, of course, habitually killed and scalped adult male enemies. Sometimes they tortured them. Yet among the People, with their warrior culture, young male captives, because they were male, almost always did better, in the long run, than women or girls.

TWENTY-THREE

A Ranger Resides with Comanches, 1837–1838

Lt was a strange sight: two Comanche chiefs, a half-dozen braves, and a lone white man riding along together. The white man was not bound. He was armed. Even more curious, this was in Texas in early summer of 1837, and this particular tejano was a ranger. When the horsemen reached a small Penateka camp on Brushy Creek, about twenty-five miles from Austin, its inhabitants, some hundred warriors and their families, thronged out of their lodges to stare. The party drew up on their ponies before the tepee of the head chief, old, bald Muguara, or Spirit Talker, who was also the principal medicine man of the southern Comanches.[1] As the ranger swung off his horse, the old chief stepped forward and embraced him. Conducting the Texan into his lodge, Muguara offered him every mark of hospitality of which he was capable. For the following three months, Noah Smithwick lived with Chief Muguara and his band as their guest.[2]

Earlier that spring a delegation of Mexicans had visited all of the frontier tribes. In the words of P. L. Chouteau, brother of Auguste Pierre and American agent for the Osages, they made "the most seductive offers" to the various chiefs, in an attempt to persuade them to make war upon the Texans, promising to supply them with arms, ammunition, and so forth. More important they succeeded in convincing many leading men of what was, in fact, the truth—that the tejanos intended to seize all of their lands and drive them from the region. As a result the Comanches and their allies increased depredations against the settlements.

The Texas Congress declared war against them, but President Houston also dispatched a Major A. Le Grand, of the Texan Army, that same spring to arrange a treaty with one of the principal, and most hostile, Comanche chiefs, Isacony, or Returning Wolf. The major finally found the chief camped on the Washita River in present Oklahoma. Isacony, however, informed him that as long as he saw the Texas frontier advancing, he would continue to believe what the Mexicans had told him. Consequently he would remain an enemy of the Anglo-Texans. Le Grand returned to the capital at Houston without a treaty.

Still, about this time, the chiefs of the *orientales*, or Penatekas, whose hunting range bordered the Texan frontier, decided a treaty would be to their advantage, especially if they could persuade the Texans to agree to a dividing line that neither side would cross. As a result two of them had appeared one day early that summer at Coleman's Fort, on Walnut Creek, six miles below Austin. As they approached they waved a white flag. The fort, a group of log cabins within a stockade, housed a company of rangers commanded by Captain Michael Andrews. Since Noah Smithwick spoke more fluent Spanish than the other men, he rode forth with several companions to learn what the Comanches wanted. Chiefs Quinaseico and Puestia told him the Penatekas desired a treaty with the whites.[3] To implement this they wished to have a commissioner accompany them back to their camp, so that he might discuss terms in council with the chiefs. Smithwick conducted the party of eight into the fort, where the two chiefs explained their proposal to Captain Andrews.

The captain soon discovered that the Anglo-Texan settlers, tired of living under a state of siege, were delighted at the prospect of peace and willing to accept a treaty with the Nuhmuhnuh under nearly any circumstances. The single problem was that no one was eager to take on the position of commissioner, because the Comanches, and all Indians, were considered to be so treacherous. But this difficulty was partially resolved when the chiefs themselves chose Smithwick to fill the post, while giving their word that no harm would come to him. Smithwick, believing there was "a degree of honor even among Indians touching those who voluntarily became their guests," valiantly agreed to undertake the job. After saying farewell to his friends, many of whom never expected to see him again, he rode out of the fort that day in June, a lone white Texan among eight Comanches.

Since "Smithwick" was a difficult word for the People to pronounce, one of Chief Muguara's first courtesies toward his guest was to provide him with a new name. To do so he called a council. The assembled headmen decided to call the ranger by the name of a dead chief. Muguara then announced to the entire camp, in a stentorian voice, that from this time forward the name of their white brother would be "Jauqua," pronounced as a Spanish word. All of the individuals of the band repeated it, the men loudly and jokingly, the women shyly, nearly under their breaths, and the children, as Smithwick later recalled, with a look and sound reminding him of "the little bark or squeak of the prairie dog as he disappears into his burrow at the approach of an enemy."

As "Jauqua" began his life among the People, he at once took an interest in the six captives in camp. Of these, two were women, one white and one mexicana. Of the remainder, two boys were Mexican and two white. All of the boys had forgotten their lives before their captivity. Only the Mexican woman, who had been seized as an adult, wished to go home, and she wept when she told Smithwick her story. The white woman had been captured (possibly by Tawakonies or Wacos, then traded) when she was so young that she, too, remembered nothing of her former life and was apparently contented with her Ietan husband and her children by him.

Smithwick recognized one of the Anglo boys, a youth of about eighteen, now a Comanche warrior. Twice the Texans had recaptured him. Each time the youth had remained with the rangers for a few days, appearing happily at ease, then had disappeared, along with several of the company's best horses. For the other white child, "a bright little fellow, five or six years old," the ranger tried trading a fine horse. But the woman who had adopted him clutched the little boy affectionately to her:

"No, he's mine—my own child."

Clearly this was a lie. Yet, observing her obvious love for the boy, Smithwick did not persist. This child was, he noted, "petted by the whole tribe."

The Texas Ranger was not only brave, he was intelligent and observant. At the beginning he noticed his hosts were careful not to reveal military information, such as the total number of Kotsoteka oriental, or Penateka, warriors. Also, strangely, he was not allowed to examine the dolls of the little girls. But virtually all else lay before him to record without interference. Old Chief Muguara even showed him the contents of his medicine pouch, which included a yellow substance with the supposed power of deflecting arrows or bullets from a body upon which it had been rubbed. He studied the Nuhmuhnuh's Shoshone dialect, asking questions and making notes. He recorded the Comanche diet, in this instance consisting entirely of meat except for such delicacies as "the curdled milk taken from the stomachs of suckling fawns and buffalo calves," which his own stomach "absolutely declined to do honor to." Another Comanche favorite that his stomach rejected was entrails, which the women merely dragged over grass to clean before broiling. On the other hand, he found Muguara quickly acquired a liking for the coffee he offered him in an effort to be sociable.

Strolling among the lodges, Smithwick took an interest in the most mundane activities, even pausing again and again to watch women working and ornamenting hides. First a woman would stake the hide to the earth, hair side down. With a bone scraper, she would remove every fragment of flesh. She would then spread lime on the clean surface to absorb its grease, afterward rubbing in the animal's brains and working the skin until it became soft. These stages required days of labor.

When the hide was soft and supple, the woman would paint a symbolic design upon it, using paint made from colored chalks and brushes fashioned from tufts of hair. A favorite image was that of the sun. With the hide still stretched on the earth, the woman would bend patiently over it, beginning her design in the middle. From this center she would paint "a multitude of different colored rays . . . radiating out in finely drawn lines, the places made by the divergence again and again filled in." Some of these designs, he thought, showed remarkable skill. In the end the painted robe would be hung over shoulders (almost surely male), with the hair side underneath, and the design displayed.

Smithwick also speculated about the People's religion, opining that they held a belief like that of sun worship. But since they were reticent about their beliefs, he could only judge from his own observations. When the men killed game, for example, he noted they immediately made a fire and roasted meat. Before taking a bite, the chief present would cut off a piece and bury it. Then all could eat. He also noticed that these Comanches would never touch a dead animal's heart. They would cut all the flesh from the skeleton, leaving the heart intact inside it.

The ranger was also intrigued by the Ietan custom of greeting each new day with a song, as the first man to awake in the morning would do. But the practice seemed to him more like the spontaneous outpouring of the birds than a religious ritual, especially since the song was wordless, merely "Ah, ha, ha," repeated several times, ending with a yell. From dawn to dark, Smithwick of course spent most of his time with the warriors of the band. At the beginning he had noted that among them there were none who had been maimed or lamed in battle, although all of them were proud of their battle scars, particularly those made by bullets. These they had tattooed lines around, in order to make them more conspicuous.[4] While the men were not hunting, they amused themselves by lounging around telling tall stories of war and the chase. (The ranger surmised that the first variety was for his benefit). They also raced their horses and sometimes raced on foot. Smithwick could beat most of them in a fifty yard dash, but the warriors preferred at least a quarter of a mile. Knowing they would beat him at the longer distances, he refused to race over his limit, keeping his dignity secure.

The men (the ranger called them "bucks") were also passionate gamblers. Smithwick would spend hours watching them play a game in the summer sun, with sweat rolling from their faces. This game was played on the smooth side of a buffalo robe, which had been divided into several parts by chalk lines. As instruments the warriors employed special short sticks, snapping them against a flat stone in the middle of the robe. The sticks, released, would rebound and land in various divisions of the robe. Each player would gain points according to the position of his sticks and the divisions in which they fell. The Texan later recalled that while the players would wager their last deerskin on the game, he had never witnessed a quarrel resulting from its outcome.

On other occasions Smithwick would ride out with a party of hunters. Rarely, he remembered, did he see any of them kill an animal in wanton sport, in the manner of white hunters. The exceptions were the times he saw them bait old bulls. After they had killed a sufficient number of bison for meat, the warriors would sometimes single out an old bull and would play with it somewhat in the spirit of a Spanish or Mexican bullfight. Though less dangerous than the bullfight, this sport also had its risks.

The hunters would begin by shooting arrows into the animal's hump. When it became infuriated and charged one of them, another would gallop beside it and jerk an arrow from its hump. At the fresh pain the bull would turn and attack its new tormentor. It was then that a well-trained horse was essential. Smithwick recorded seeing old bulls whirl so quickly that it was "all the Indian's pony could do to get out of the way." But then another warrior would race in and snatch an arrow, and the bull would turn on him. The hunters would keep this up until the animal was exhausted, when they would dispatch it and retrieve their arrows.

Another sport also practiced on horseback was the roping of deer, mustangs, buffalo calves, and wild turkeys. In the first instance, the hunter would conceal himself and his pony and wait patiently near a waterhole. When deer finally came and drank, they would, in Smithwick's word, "become stupid and any good mustang could run upon them with ease." A similar technique was employed in capturing mustangs. Since the wild horses frequently grazed ten or twelve miles from water, they would, when thirsty, run to a stream, then, sweating and tired, drink their fill. The Comanche roper, mounted on his fresh pony, could easily catch up with and toss his loop over a waterlogged mustang. In pursuing buffalo calves, the Comanches would start a herd running, pressing them so hard and closely that the calves would fall behind and could be roped by the warriors.

The Nuhmuhnuh used a variation of this method in taking wild turkeys, probably for their feathers alone, since fish and fowl were taboo as food. When a flock of turkeys ventured onto the plains, seeking grasshoppers, a horseman would follow them at a distance until the birds were a mile or more from a woods or other cover. Then he would race at them, causing them to fly. Whipping his pony, he would ride underneath the flock, forcing them to remain in the air until they became exhausted. When they fluttered to the ground, he would rush among them and rope as many as he wished.

Smithwick visited Muguara's ranchería in summer, of course. Winter camps also enjoyed various forms of recreation. For the men, restricted as they were by snow and weather, these were more nearly limited to the storytelling and gambling which the ranger describes. But for children and women, there were possibilities unavailable in summer, when their band or division was frequently on the move. In 1821 for instance, Jacob Fowler, a surveyor, led a trading expedition deep into the plains. Fowler kept a journal and, though an educated man, used a uniquely personal style of spelling and punctuation. In his entry for November 23, he describes the children of a huge camp of Plains Indians (Comanches, Kiowas, Kiowa-Apaches, Arapahoes, and Cheyennes) playing on the Arkansas River in what is now Pueblo County, Colorado:

> . . . a Snow fell about one foot deep and the Weather is now Cold the River frosen up the Ice a great thickness and the Indean Children that is able to walk and up to tall boys are out on the Ice by day light and all as naked as the Came to the World Heare the are at all kinds of Sport Which Their Setuation Will admit and all tho the frost is very seveer the apper quite Warm and a lively as I Heave Ever seen Children In mid Summer I am shure that We Have Seen more than one thousand of these Children on the Ice at one time and Some that Ware too young to Walk Ware taken by the larger ones and Soot on a pece of skin on the Ice and In this Setuation kick its [legs] Round and Hollow and laff at those Round it at play . . . [5]

Colonel Richard I. Dodge, writing of a later period, the 1850s and 1860s, but generalizing about Plains tribes, observed that even old women enjoyed winter. During these months they were relieved of endlessly pitching and taking down lodges, of continually packing and unpacking the horses. In winter their chores were reduced to fetching wood and water, cooking, overseeing the horses, and occasionally dressing a few skins. But for young men and women, whether married or not, this was, by Dodge's account, a time for dancing and feasting, for visiting and for fun of every kind. Above all, he noted, it was "the season for love-making," probably including in the term both flirting and courtship.

Evenings were, of course, the time of greatest excitement in camp. By day the men gambled or slept, the women worked or relaxed, as they wished. But as soon as darkness fell, everyone was ready for any amusement offered. Only a few beats on a drum brought people out of their tepees to join in a gambling game, such as the Plains version of "button, button, who's got the button?," in which both men and women played, or a dance, either of which could continue nearly until dawn. Generalizing further,

Dodge declared his belief that these Native Americans were "habitually and universally the happiest people" he had ever seen.[6]

But what about the horses in winter, the Comanches' immense herds? In June of 1852 Captain Randolph B. Marcy, exploring to the headwaters of the Red River, was moving through the present Texas panhandle some eleven miles west of today's Mobeetie, when he and his men encountered a "beautiful stream of good spring water, flowing . . . through a valley about a mile wide, covered with excellent grass." This creek passed through many old winter camps. The earth for several miles along it was littered with cottonwood sticks whose bark had been gnawed away by horses. Marcy observed that the Plains tribes habitually fed "their favorite horses" cottonwood bark during the winter. In this instance there was also "fine mezquite and grama grass," which the captain believed would carry a herd through most of a winter. When the grass gave out, there remained the cottonwood bark, surely a reason why Comanches or Kiowas had probably wintered along that stream year after year.[7]

Colonel Dodge, writing years after Marcy, confirms the captain's observation about the Plains pony's winter sustenance, noting that "exposed to the terrible cold and piercing winds of the Plains . . . he would undoubtedly starve, but that the squaws cut down acres and acres of young cottonwood for him to browse upon. At this season, with coat long, shabby and rough, matted with bark and burrs, hips extended in the air, belly puffed out with sticks and bark swallowed in the vain attempt to appease the hunger that consumes him, forlorn, downcast and miserable, he looks an uncouth monster rather than a horse." But each spring, with the new grass, according to Dodge, a metamorphosis occurs. Then the Plains pony, whether Comanche, Kiowa, or Cheyenne, "sheds the rough coat, scours the protuberant belly, and with rounded, supple form, head erect, ears and eyes full of bright intelligence, he is again ready to bear his master in fight and foray, to be trusted even to death."[8]

The People resumed their nomadic life every spring, following the buffalo. By the time summer came round, their best ponies, both buffalo horses and war horses, were ready for raiding into Coahuila, Chihuahua, or Nuevo Leon, for penetrating the Texas frontier, or even for grazing under the eyes of boys and captives outside the peaceful encampment of a chief like old Muguara; that is, his ordinarily peaceful encampment.

From time to time warriors from another tribe would visit, men with whom Muguara's *orientales* "swapped lies." Smithwick observed that sometimes his Comanche companions and the strangers communicated entirely and expertly by signs, evidently not understanding each others' languages. On one occasion, though, the visitors were Wacos wearing war paint. The ranger, always conscious of the possibility of treachery, began fearing he truly might never see his comrades again.

He knew the Comanches and Wacos warred against each other sporadically. In fact one little boy in camp was a Waco who had been adopted by old Chief Quinaseico. Noting that all the chief's other children were adults, he had once asked him whether the child were his.

"Yes," said the old man, embracing the little boy. "Mine, now."

Quinaseico explained that some years before, while the Comanches and Wacos had been at war, he and his braves had surprised an enemy encampment and killed everybody except for this one child.

"After the battle," the chief said, "I went into a lodge and found him, about two years old, sitting beside his dead mother, crying. My heart felt sorry for him. So I took him up in my arms and brought him home on my pony. My wife took him to her bosom, and fed him, and now he's mine."

But at this time the Comanches and Wacos were again allies. These particular Wacos had gone on a horse-stealing raid to the settlements. During a skirmish the Texans had killed several of their warriors. Now, having heard of a white man in Muguara's camp, they came to demand Jauqua as a sacrifice.

From the occasional words of Spanish that Smithwick caught, he suspected the meeting between the two bands concerned him in some ominous way. By using a Mexican boy as an interpreter, he soon learned the nature of his predicament. At once he knew his life was in extreme danger. He determined to fight to the death if the Comanches should decide to surrender him, rather than face torture by the Wacos.

But old Muguara, he later recalled, stood up for him "like a man and a brother." The Comanche chief drew his tall figure erect, towering above the Waco chief.

"*No*," he roared. "*This man is our friend.* You'll have to step over my dead body to reach him! Hurt him at all, and not one of you will get away alive!"

Penateka warriors gathered behind Muguara, clutching lances and bows as the confrontation continued. For a time it seemed to Smithwick that the situation would erupt in a bloody battle. But the Comanches outnumbered the Wacos, who finally gave way and rode off muttering threats of vengeance against all whites.

So much, in this instance at least, for the "treachery" of the Comanches!

Both the ranger and the Comanche chief feared that the Wacos, unable to obtain Jauqua by force, might attempt to seize or kill him by stealth. Muguara warned him to remain close to his Penateka companions while out hunting. When the ranger visited the settlements, as he did several times during his stay with the band, the old chief sent a sizable bodyguard with him. On other occasions Smithwick conducted parties of Comanches into the settlement of Bastrop, where the townspeople, enjoying the period of peace, made them presents.

Once Mother Muguara ("mother" because the chief and his head wife called the ranger "*hijo,*" or "son") accompanied the party. Jauqua escorted her into Palmer and Kinney's general store, so that she might trade her buffalo robes and buckskins for calico and tobacco. The Texan was busy helping her do this when two young ladies, friends of his, entered. Glad to see them, he went over to them and chatted briefly, then returned to the Comanche woman, who was critically examining the white girls.

"Jauqua," she asked in Spanish. "Are both of these your wives?"

"No," laughed the ranger.

"Then," she demanded. "Which one of them is?"

"Neither," insisted Smithwick.

"Och," cried the old woman, shaking her finger in his face. "You lie."

Smithwick burst out laughing.

On another occasion the ranger had come to Bastrop with the old chief himself. Muguara differed from the great majority of the People, as he did in his baldness, by occasionally drinking whiskey. Jean Louis Berlandier had written some three years before that the Comanches refrained entirely from alcohol, calling it *agua tonta,* or "stupid water." Later, in 1846, Ferdinand von Roemer observed some Comanches watching a drunken Delaware stagger down a street in San Antonio. "I shall never forget," he wrote, "the disgust registered on their faces." But generalizations have exceptions. On this occasion, just as the Comanche party was about to leave Bastrop, Muguara turned to the Texan, surely with a twinkle in his eye:

"Jauqua," said he. "Hadn't we better get a bottle of fool's water? We might meet hostile Indians on the road, and it would make us brave."

Dramatic and entertaining moments aside, Smithwick was living with the People for a purpose. During those summer months he had many long and serious talks with the Comanche chiefs, who ultimately succeeded in making the ranger see their point of view. The country was theirs, they told him, because they had inherited it. The Great Spirit, they said, had placed the buffalo, their cattle, on the land for their use. Now the white men would run into a herd of bison and shoot them down in a wanton slaughter that they considered sport, often not even taking the hides.

"We've pitched our lodges in this timber and swung our babies from these branches as long as anyone can remember," Muguara told him. "When the game leaves, we pull down our lodges and move on, leaving nothing behind to scare it. In a little while it comes back. But the whites come and cut down trees and build cabins and fences. The buffalo get scared and go away and never come back. The Indians are left to starve—or, if we follow the game, we trespass on the hunting grounds of other tribes, and then there's war."

"What if you had land, and a way to cultivate it, like white men?"

"No," insisted Muguara. "The Indians were not made to work. If they build houses and try to copy white men, they will all die."

The ranger listened thoughtfully.

"If the white men would just draw a line showing what land they claim, and then keep on their side of it, the red men wouldn't bother them."⁹

Smithwick must have sighed. He knew that the immigrant eastern Indians (such as the Delawares and Cherokees) had told the Comanches of how they had lost their homes and hunting grounds to the whites. He knew also that they had warned the Plains tribes that the same was about to happen to them. This was one of several reasons the Penatekas were becoming increasingly uneasy and wished an agreement with the tejanos that would secure their hunting grounds for their own permanent use.

Finally Jauqua, the Texas Ranger Indian commissioner, persuaded five of the principal Penateka chiefs to accompany him to the republic's capital in Houston. (Of these, two were probably Muguara and Quinaseico; another may have been Potsanaquahip, or Buffalo Hump, a war chief whom Texas would hear much from later). The commissioner found an interested listener in the president. Sam Houston sympathized with the native races, the ranger wrote later, as he himself "had also learned to do." But when Smithwick had explained the Comanches' wish for a precise line to be drawn between the settlements and themselves, Houston sadly shook his head.

"If I could build a wall from the Red River to the Río Grande," he said. "So high that no Indian could scale it, the white people would go crazy trying to devise a means to get beyond it."

At least President Houston listened receptively to the Comanches' concerns. Ultimately he would attempt to satisfy their demand for a boundary, as events will demonstrate. But the question of admitting any Indians' right to land they had occupied for generations had been, in effect, settled as early as the first days of the Texas revolution. The great majority of Anglo-Texans, as well as most of their leadership, were willing to yield absolutely nothing in the way of land rights to Indians. "It is a matter of great importance to secure the entire neutrality at least of the Indian tribes . . . ," wrote David Gouveneur Burnet, first Texas president, to M. B. Menard in March of 1836. "But I must enjoin it upon you to avoid with great caution entering into any Specific treaty relating to boundaries, that may compromit the interests of actual settlers . . ."[10]

The following year the Texas Congress reacted to Comanche peace-feelers by authorizing the president to appoint a commission to improve relations between the People and the "Republick," yet the members insisted that "no fee simple right of soil be acknowledged."[11] Then in 1838, the year that Muguara's delegation met with President Houston, a body of 150 warriors entered San Antonio to ask that a group of Texans accompany them back to their camp in order to discuss a peace treaty with their chiefs. A number of tejanos complied, including Mosely Baker, a member of the Texas Congress. The chiefs received them in a cordial manner, but the citizens were dismayed to learn in council that as a condition of any treaty, the Penetekas insisted upon a boundary to their territory that would allot some of the choicest land in Texas to comanchería. The Comanches wanted all of the country lying north of the Guadalupe Mountains, a vast region equal to approximately a quarter of the republic. On the other hand, they warned that they would kill any surveyors who entered their country.

That same spring two Penateka chiefs, Isawacony and Isananica (Turtle Wolf and Howling Wolf) visited Béxar to seek out the commander of the Texas Army, Albert Sidney Johnston. To him they repeated their demands for the proposed boundary. But Johnston refused to discuss the subject with them, and the chiefs no doubt rode away frustrated and angry.[12] An indication of the Penateka's mood during the same spring is that a party of them, on leaving the town of Houston where they had just concluded a treaty, killed two Texans while still within sight of the city. Near Gonzales they abducted a fourteen-year-old girl. A little later, near San Antonio, they slew six more men.[13] Whether or not this was Muguara's party, or more likely some portion of it, the Comanches were clearly frustrated by their inability to obtain any substantial commitment from the Texans; and just as clearly were in an ugly and murderous frame of mind.

In the end Houston and Noah Smithwick and the five chiefs "fixed up a treaty." The ranger wrote that he failed to recall its terms. But this was of no importance, because neither side ever observed them. Peace continued for a time, he remembered, "and gave the settlers a chance to quarrel among themselves," while some of the bolder ones moved closer to the Comanche hunting grounds. One of the treaty's provisions decreed that a trading post be established on Brushy Creek, at the site of an abandoned blockhouse. But the Texas Republic did not see fit to carry through this commitment. When the Penatekas came with their hides to trade and found no post, they went to call on Jauqua in the settlements. Since Smithwick was unable to offer a convincing excuse for the omission, they accused him of lying to them, and he lost all influence with them. The whites, on the other hand, accused him of favoring and shielding the Indians.

After his three-month stay in Muguara's peaceable community, Smithwick had come to see the justice of the People's claims against the Texans. But he remained ambivalent toward his former hosts. On the one hand, looking back years later, he wrote, "I really felt mean and almost ashamed of belonging to the superior race when listening to the recital of the wrongs the redmen had suffered at the hands of my people." Yet "when they made hostile incursions into the settlements I joined in the pursuit and hunted them as mercilessly as any one." Not only that but he confessed he had "treacherously turned to account" certain signs the Nuhmuhnuh had shown him, such as how to distinguish Indian friends from enemies. In the end, though, he valued his "vivid recollections of the kindness and friendship" shown him "by the Comanches, especially the old chiefs," during that summer of 1837.

By early 1838 the Texas Republic was beginning to thrive. The number of inhabitants had substantially increased, owing to an influx of immigrants arriving the previous year. Farmers were beginning to realize a profit. For example, according to the early Texas historian Henderson K. Yoakum, cotton alone was "estimated at fifty thousand bales, and worth at the selling prices of two millions of dollars." Galveston was flourishing. With ships arriving every day, it was beginning to resemble an Atlantic port. Land had increased in value, and early that year land offices had begun opening in the frontier communities. Locators and surveyors were riding out beyond the settlements, eager to claim the best lands.

The Penatekas watched this flurry of activity. They knew what surveyors meant. When Smithwick had been staying with them the previous year, they had run off the horses of a survey party on Brushy Creek, blaming the deed on another tribe. Now they became convinced that the Mexicans had been telling them the truth all along when they had predicted that the Anglo-Texans would try to seize their land and drive them away.

That August 10, two hundred Comanche warriors attacked Colonel Henry Karnes, Texas Army commander of the southern region, along with a company of twenty-one men. Although the Comanches succeeded in wounding the colonel, Karnes and his men defeated them and drove them off with no further Texan casualties. Next, on October 20, another war party struck a group of surveyors working within five miles of San Antonio, killing two of them. Thirteen residents of the town rode out to reconnoiter. Some hundred Comanches attacked them three miles from the place of the previous assault. The tejanos bravely charged, and the warriors faded backward, only to close in behind the party, killing eight and wounding all the others, but one. And so it continued. "The irrepressible conflict," declared Smithwick, "recommenced with redoubled vigor." In Yoakum's words, "the whole frontier was lighted up with the flames of a savage war."

TWENTY-FOUR

Diplomacy North and South, 1840

I n 1840 two events occurred that had great significance for the future of the Comanches. The first of these took place that spring in San Antonio. It hardened the People's attitude toward Anglo-Texans from that time forth. The second occurred in the summer on the Arkansas River. The first event, which came to be called "the Council House Fight," involved the southern Comanches, or Penatekas, while the second involved mostly the northern Comanches, the Kiowas, and Kiowa-Apaches. Yet both affairs affected all of the People and their allies, no matter where they roamed or hunted on the southern plains. The first event focused tribal hatred on an enemy whom, from then on, they would neither forgive nor trust, as long as they were a free people. The second gained them new allies, with warriors fierce as they were, tribes who were destined to fight along with them, finally, back to back, until no one among them would any longer have the heart to fight.

But that was a long way off.

About three miles east of Bent's Fort, there was a site where fields stretched north and south on either side of the Arkansas River. That summer of 1840, probably in June, the banks on both sides were lined with tepees. Behind them the fields were specked with hundreds and hundreds of additional lodges, with smoke drifting above them. The air resounded with a confusion of shouts, the neighing of horses, the barking of dogs. This was the place that came to be known as the Treaty Ground, because here the Comanches, Kiowas, and Kiowa-Apaches, who were camped on the south bank, made a permanent peace with the Cheyennes and Arapahoes, who were camped on the north bank.

After all of the ceremonies had taken place, and friendship between the tribes had been firmly established, one of the Cheyenne chiefs urged his Comanche counterpart to ride up to the fort with him, saying there were good people there, Americans, not Texans, and he and his followers ought to trade there, like the Cheyennes. The two rode side by side to the fort, where the sentry at the gate admitted them through the opening below the belfry, with its pair of captive bald eagles. When the Comanche peace chief, Old Wolf, met William Bent, the boss of the fort soon offered to buy from him the old man's son-in-law, James Hobbs, along with another young captive named John Batiste (probably Jean Baptiste). Old Wolf replied that he would part with John for very little. His son-in-law was another matter. He would not sell him, unless the young warrior wanted to leave the band. But he did send for the two captives.

Later that day three riders approached the fort. Apparently Plains Indians, they led an extra horse behind them. When they had been admitted, Bent realized he saw before him the two young men who had been captured from the west-bound caravan of his brother, Charles, some four or five years before. Today they were dressed in buckskins and breechclouts and resembled Comanches. But there was a difference between them. One of the young men looked around him with a cowed air, while the other moved as confidently as any Plains warrior.[1] Bent guessed that was Old Wolf's son-in-law. Walking behind him was a pretty young Comanche woman, carrying on her back a child of about three. She had been crying, and often her gaze rested apprehensively on Hobbs, who seemed filled with joy and with eyes for nothing but the fort and the white men gathering around the group, welcoming him.

That night the traders celebrated, and the whisky passed around. The Cheyenne chief and Old Wolf were included in the celebration. But about midnight a messenger appeared and told the revelers that some thousand warriors were waiting outside the walls, demanding their chiefs. Suspecting treachery, they wanted to know why the Cheyenne and Comanche head men had not returned to their camps. Old Wolf led Hobbs and his daughter out upon the wall with him, making a speech to the assembled braves—he and the Cheyenne chief were being entertained by good men who were friends of the Cheyennes and Comanches, he said, and presents would be distributed to everybody in the morning.

The next morning William Bent succeeded in ransoming James Hobbs from a reluctant Old Wolf for six yards of red flannel, an ounce of beads, and a pound of tobacco. Standing by his wife and child, Hobbs must have felt a pang of regret mingled with his elation. Joyful as he was, memories of his captivity, his years as one of the People, must have flitted behind his eyes.

Of course none of it would have happened if he and John, with his pack mule, had not run off after that buffalo cow he had wounded with his pistol. . . . After all, though, he had been hired as a hunter, even if he was only sixteen at the time. His pride had been hurt by the laughter of the men. He had got the cow, all right, but by the time they had finished butchering her and loading the meat on the mule, it was nearly dark, and they had lost track of where they were in relation to Charles Bent's caravan or the Arkansas River. After spending the night out, they had come upon Comanche hunters the next day. Nine braves had caught up with them in a little ravine.

He would remember all of his life that first conversation—in English, as it happened:

"How do you do?" a muscular war chief asked him.

He nodded, swallowing. "How do you do?"

"Texas?" queried the chief politely.

"Nope, we're friendly. Going to set up a trading post for the Comanches and other nations."

"Friendly, uh? Better come with us for a while, though. Got any tobacco?"

Back at the Comanche encampment, the warriors, who behaved in an affable manner, presented the boys to Old Wolf, a big, tall old man with braided hair hanging to his waist. James, hoping to please the old chief, offered him brandy, first swigging, himself. After staring suspiciously at the bottle for a time, Old Wolf seized it and drank off the contents like lemonade. Because of the effects of the brandy, the council called to decide the boys' fate was postponed.

Eventually a twelve-year-old captive Texan named Harry Brown informed them of the chiefs' decision. As long as they were really not Texans, he translated, and if they would behave and make no attempts to run away, the People would not kill them. In fact the band would allow them to live with them. The braves for whom Harry was translating pointed to some dried scalps. Three Mexican captives, they told him, whose job it had been to guard the horses, had run away. They had caught up with the three and brought back only their scalps. Watching as the boys listened, the men looked at them with deadly serious expressions. James and Jean Baptiste, who had no knowledge of the surrounding country, decided not to try escaping.

John took the chiefs' command so seriously he never left camp. But James had a restless and daring nature. About three months after the youths' capture, a war chief began raising a war party to go fight the Pawnees. Some of this group asked the boys to accompany them and help in the attack. While John declined, Hobbs accepted. Later, when the force departed, a brave returned his Hawkins rifle. During the ride out, he noticed the war party was retracing the route his captors had used, even passing by the spot where he had been seized. To his chagrin Hobbs reflected that if he had not been captured, he might have been on the way to becoming a rich trapper or trader by this time.

At the Arkansas River, just below the area known as The Caches, the Comanches surprised some two hundred Pawnees camped in a thicket of wild plums. The startled Pawnees fled, escaping by running, flinging themselves into the stream and frantically swimming. Angry and determined to prove his worth to the warriors, Hobbs aimed at a Pawnee in the middle of the river. When he squeezed the trigger, the swimmer shouted and sank. Immediately several Comanches leapt from their horses, ran to the river, entered the water and retrieved the body, which they scalped on the bank. This was the only scalp taken.

On the war party's return to the ranchería, Chief Old Wolf himself helped Hobbs from his pony, greeting him with a hug:

"You have a big heart," he told him through an interpreter. "John, he has a little heart—he wouldn't go and fight."

After a scalp dance and celebration, Hobbs's status among the People improved. Old Wolf offered him his daughter, Spotted Fawn, and he married into the tribe, becoming a Comanche. Two months later he accompanied another war party south to Monclova, Mexico. This war party returned with nine Mexican captives and some fourteen hundred horses and mules. Although James did nothing special to distinguish himself during this campaign, he found his position among the band even more secure simply from having successfully taken part in it. The seasons continued to flow by, and year followed year. His son was born. On the whole his life among the People was satisfying. But Hobbs never got over his restlessness, his desire for freedom. So one day when a trader named Kit rode into camp and James was called upon to interpret, he managed to give Carson a message for the Bents: he and John, lost from Charles's caravan in '35, were captives in this camp. After that one thing had followed another—until here he was, standing before William Bent, once more a free man.

But before that there had to have been the treaty, because the Cheyennes and Comanches had been at war. In 1835 William Bent had ridden south and traded with some two thousand Comanches on the Red River. But the Nuhmuhnuh would not have peacefully visited the fort on the Arkansas, because the Cheyennes were friends of the Bents and traded at the fort. In fact only a couple of years before, a party of Comanches had galloped into the horse herd grazing outside the fort, killed the herder, and run off about fifty head. But even before that, some Cheyenne Bow String soldiers had set out to raid the Comanche and Kiowa horse herds, and the Comanches and Kiowas had killed all forty-two of them. So the next year, in 1838, the

Cheyennes had attacked a Comanche-Kiowa encampment near the Cimarron River. One party had encountered and killed thirty-one Kiowa men and women hunting buffalo on the plains. The main force of Cheyennes had surprised the camp, after pausing to kill a dozen women out digging roots. But then the Comanches and Kiowas had mounted a successful defense, finally forcing the attackers to withdraw, after killing an important Cheyenne chief named Gray Thunder.

For another two years, sporadic horse raiding and fighting continued, partly because the Cheyennes needed horses. But it happened that one of the Arapahoes, who were friends of the Cheyennes, married a Kiowa-Apache woman. One day during the winter of 1839, a delegation of Kiowa-Apaches visited an Arapaho camp and informed the chiefs that the Kiowas and Comanches wanted peace with them and their allies. The Cheyennes and Arapahoes held councils, and it turned out that the mood for peace was general. So at a given time during the following summer, the five tribes or parts of each camped below Bent's Fort on the Arkansas River.

After the chiefs had smoked, the peoples gathered on either side of the river gave each other presents.[2] The first day the Arapahoes and Cheyennes waded the stream and sat in rows facing the Comanches and their allies, men first, then women and children. The Comanches, Kiowas, and Kiowa-Apaches signaled their boys and Mexican captives to bring the horses down from the hills. As soon as the ponies arrived, in herd after herd, they began giving them to their former enemies—even to children among them. The Cheyennes must have been amazed, knowing that among the northern tribes (the Blackfoot, for instance) a poor family might have to borrow a horse whenever their band moved camp. The Ietans and their allies gave ordinary men and women from 4 to 6 apiece, but they reserved the most and best for the chiefs. All the Comanche and Kiowa and Apache chiefs gave great numbers of ponies to their counterparts and others, in a display of their generosity and power. The Kiowa chief, Sa-Tank, was supposed to have given away the most of all—250 head of horses, more or less. In fact the Comanches and their allies gave away so many ponies that the Cheyennes and Arapahoes lacked sufficient ropes to lead them with, and had to herd them in bunches across the river.

The next day the Cheyennes and Arapahoes, of course, had to outdo themselves to equal the generosity of their southern plains neighbors. High Backed Wolf, the Cheyenne chief, had asked his guests to bring their ponies, in order to carry back their gifts. The Comanches and others rode across the river and seated themselves in rows within a bare circle at the center of the Cheyenne camp, with the chiefs in front. The Cheyenne women appeared with the banquet in kettles, and everyone feasted on exotic food from the fort—corn meal, rice, dried apples, and molasses. Afterward High Backed Wolf called for the presents, first warning his guests not to be alarmed when they heard shooting; it was Cheyenne custom to fire a gun in the air before giving it away. For a time the camp sounded like an American settlement Fourth of July celebration. Finally the Cheyennes piled gift after gift before their new friends—blankets, brass kettles, calico, beads, and guns.

"We have made peace," proclaimed High Backed Wolf, at last, to the guest chiefs. "We have made presents to each other. Tomorrow we can start trading with each other. Your people can come here and trade, and my people will go trade in your camp."

Now, in an attempt to comfort his wife, Hobbs bought her an assortment of beads and a red dress. But the gifts failed to reconcile her to the loss of her husband. Continuing to weep, she begged her father to allow her to go with James. But Old Wolf said he preferred to have her remain with him and that her husband could visit her as often as he cared to, which Hobbs promised to do.

The old chief slept at the fort every night but one during the nine days the tribes devoted to trading with each other and with the Bents, and every one of those nights his warriors assembled outside the walls and insisted that he appear in order to reassure them he was safe. On the ninth morning, Chief Old Wolf complimented William Bent on his trade goods and whisky and promised to return in a few months with plenty of horses and mules from Mexico. For his part Bent agreed to give the Comanches the going rate for all they could supply and, like most American traders, exhibited no fussy concern regarding the source of the animals.

When it came time to part with his wife, Hobbs, by his own account, seems to have remained unmoved, no doubt having plans that did not include her. Spotted Fawn presented him with a good bay horse he liked. Picking up their three-year-old son, she gave James a last tearful hug and, with a little shriek, turned away and departed. Old Wolf, who had greatly enjoyed his meals and entertainment at the fort, gave Hobbs two mules and Jean Baptist a pony when he said goodby to them. Then he, too, was gone out the gate.

From the east wall Hobbs must have watched the old chief, with his daughter and the child, ride away down the river, with a group of warriors following them. Anyhow he was free! He couldn't help thinking, though, of the two Brown girls, both married to war chiefs, sons of Old Wolf, and their younger brothers, Henry and Jim. These four, the only survivors of their San Antonio family, were still captives. He had told William about them. Bent had made efforts to ransom them, but Old Wolf had adamantly refused to consider it. Maybe, speculated James, they would have to stay with the Comanches for the rest of their lives.

James Hobbs picked up his frontiersman's life where he had left it some five years before. Only once or twice over the years did he return to the People to visit his wife and son. During one of these visits, or at Bent's Fort, he learned that he had been only partly right about the Browns. Around three months after he had left, the peace chief's oldest son was killed in Mexico. Old Wolf sold the widow to Bent, and the girl finally made her way back to Béxar. At the same time, or later, Bent also ransomed her younger sister, Matilda. But the chief refused to permit her son, his grandson, to accompany her. Matilda, a free woman, moped around the fort for a few days, then—remarking she was no longer fit to live among civilized folk—she returned to the Nuhmuhnuh. As for her two brothers, neither cared ever to leave the Comanches.

During that same year, 1840, a Colonel Len Williams and a trader named Sloat, with a Delaware guide, traveled into Comanchería with mules to trade. On the Canadian River they found a band of Pahayuco, an important Tenewa chief with whom they were on good terms, despite the mutual animosity existing between Texans and Comanches.[3] While engaged in trading, the Texans discovered Cynthia Ann Parker in camp. The girl, who had been seized during the raid on Parker's Fort, was now thirteen or fourteen. At the white men's request, Chief Pahayuco persuaded the child's adoptive family to allow them to talk to her, which they did. But the girl remained silent. There was no question of ransoming her. Her foster father would not consider it.

Cynthia Ann later became almost a legend in Texas history, but she was only one of many Anglo-Texan captives. Around that time Texas officials estimated there were approximately two hundred such prisoners scattered among the Comanche divisions.[4] The republic was determined to retrieve its own by any means possible.

Earlier, that January, a party of Comanches had ridden into Béxar under a white flag. Their chiefs had parleyed with Colonel H. W. Karnes, then left town in a blast of dust. Karnes sent a message to Albert Sidney Johnston, secretary of war under Mirabeau Buonaparte Lamar, president of the Texas Republic since 1838. He reported that the Comanches, responding to Texan peace feelers, had asserted that they, too, wished peace. As confirmation of this desire, they offered to bring in their Texan captives. Actually the southern Comanches, or Penatekas, wanted another cessation of hostilities, at least for a time, because too many of their young war chiefs and warriors had been dying in retaliatory attacks by the Rangers, a small, mounted force formed in 1835 to defend the Texas frontier. The Rangers, armed with six-shot revolvers by 1840, were composed of adventurous young men who fought and scalped like Indians and who rarely took prisoners. They were formidable fighters, whom the people called "Those-Who-Always-Follow-Our-Trails."

President Lamar, unlike his predecessor, Sam Houston, did not, in 1840, desire the annexation of Texas by the United States. On the contrary he possessed (or was possessed by) a vision of a great, self-sufficient republic reaching from Louisiana to the Río Grande, a vast region including more than half of Nuevo México. There was one inconvenience. Hunting and camping in the path of this expansion were the southern Plains tribes. Again in contrast to Houston, Lamar had no patience with or sympathy for Indians. In dealing with them, his administration was directed to be stern: the Comanches and others were to move out of the way of settlers and to leave them alone. Furthermore there would be no more gifts to the chiefs and their followers. Yet, on the other hand, the Texans did badly want their abducted women and children back. The Lamar administration wanted peace—on its own terms.

The Penatekas who spoke with Karnes promised to return by a certain time with their most important chiefs, who would discuss the proposed treaty with the headmen of the tejanos. Meanwhile Johnston, secretary of war, dispatched Lieutenant Colonel William S. Fisher to march with three companies of the First Infantry Regiment to San Antonio. He ordered Fisher, in case the Comanches appeared without captives, to seize and hold hostage most of the delegation, sending word to the People that their chiefs and the others would be detained until they surrendered the Texan prisoners. Since everyone knew the Comanche delegation had been ordered to bring with them all of their Texas captives, there was surely a mood of expectation in San Antonio as the date of the meeting approached.

On March 19 twelve Comanche chiefs rode into Béxar, accompanied by fifty-three warriors, women, and children. The presence of their women and children was, of course, a sign that they expected, as in all councils, nothing but discussion and bargaining.[5] Faces painted, they wore their most colorful finery. They drew up their ponies by the courthouse, a single-story stone building always known afterward as the "Council House." Their policy, agreed upon in advance, was going to be that of offering one captive at a time for ransom, then driving a hard bargain for each. In keeping with this decision, they brought with them only a little Mexican boy, along with a sixteen-year-old white girl, Matilda Lockhart.

Owing to their ignorance of Anglo-Texan culture and of whites in general, the Penateka chiefs could not have known what a blunder they were committing in delivering up the Lockhart girl. If they had possessed some understanding of white customs, values, and attitudes, they would have realized that bringing in the girl, as she was, was a crazy act of provocation. Matilda Lockhart, it turned out, had not only been raped by the men, as was customary with female captives, but had been horribly abused by the Comanche women, some of whom may have been avenging husbands or sons killed by Texans.

Mrs. Samuel Maverick was one of the women who helped bathe and dress Matilda. The child, she later recorded, was covered with bruises and sores from beatings and burns. Worst of all, the Ietan women had burnt off the fleshy part of her nose, leaving holes for her nostrils and a scab at the end of the bone. Like an adulterous woman of the People, Matilda would be disfigured for life. She told her shocked listeners of how the women would wake her to herd the ponies by holding a flaming coal to what remained of her nose. When she screamed they would shout and laugh. Matilda did not want to be seen by anybody; she felt degraded, she said, and would never be able to hold up her head again.[6]

If the Ietans made a deadly error through their ignorance of white culture, the Texas authorities committed an equally disastrous blunder out of ignorance of the People. To have expected important chiefs meekly to surrender their arms, even when trapped and outnumbered, was to show a complete lack of understanding of the "Hatey" ("haughty," Fowler's word) Comanches. From the outset each side was insulated in arrogant ignorance of the other.

The difference between them, though, was that the Texas government had determined not to abide by the traditional rules of the council. Its officers and soldiers had the dozen chiefs more or less at their mercy. Furthermore the Texans were already infuriated by the mistreatment of the Lockhart girl. They were doubtless concealing their anger with difficulty.

Chief Muguara was to be spokesman for the Penatekas. The old, bald chieftain waited impassively, seated cross-legged, while the other Comanches sat in a row beside him on the hard dirt floor. The commissioners, along with a few other military officers and city officials, sat stiffly in chairs on a platform facing the chiefs. Near the door lounged Captain Tom Howard, whose company of rangers remained on duty outside in the court house yard. The commissioners opened the session by demanding to know why no more prisoners had been brought in. The civil chief gravely explained that many were held by bands other than his. Still he did believe that, in time, all of them could be purchased. It would, of course, cost a lot. Their captors wanted a great deal of ammunition, blankets, vermilion, and other trade items for them. Muguara paused, then queried, "How do you like that answer?"

The Texan response was not what the chiefs expected. Colonel Fisher ordered a squad of soldiers into the courtroom. One man remained near Captain Howard, to guard the door, while others placed themselves at intervals along the walls. Beginning to be uneasy, the chiefs gripped their bows and muskets, looking around them. Colonel Cooke ordered the interpreter to inform Muguara that he, Spirit Talker, and the other chiefs would be detained until every white captive had been surrendered. Meanwhile the soldiers present were to be their guards. The interpreter, a former Comanche prisoner, blanched and shook his head at the message. He warned, in effect, that hell would break loose if he were to deliver it. But the commissioners insisted. The interpreter turned to the chiefs, who were watching him intently. The room became still. Flies buzzed. Through open windows came the quiet laughter of bystanders outside, who were tossing coins for Comanche boys to shoot arrows at. The interpreter translated the ultimatum, then quickly left the room.

After an instant of stunned silence, Muguara and the other chiefs leapt to their feet, war-whooped, and began shooting arrows. Scrambling commissioners yelled for the soldiers to fire. Muguara reached the door, where he stabbed Captain Howard in the side with his knife. Almost simultaneously the tall old chief collapsed from a shot fired point-blank by the soldier standing there. Other soldiers were firing, striking both Indians and whites. An off-duty ranger, Captain "Old Paint" Caldwell, caught a bullet in the leg but managed to wrest a musket from one chief, kill him with the charge, then club another Comanche to death with the weapon. Somehow during a pandemonium of shouts and war-cries, reverberating shots and drifting gunsmoke, several of the chiefs succeeded in fighting their way to and out the door.

Outside the curious crowd of Anglo and Mexican Texans realized too late what the noise in the courthouse signified. But the Comanches of both sexes and all ages understood immediately the import of the war whoops and shots. They reacted by beginning to loose arrows into the crowd, killing at least one spectator, a visiting judge. (Colonel McLeod, the Texas adjutant general, reported later that in the ensuing fight the Comanche arrows, "when they struck, were driven to the feather.") The shouts of the chiefs who managed to burst out of the courthouse roused their followers and families to further anger—and terror. They began to flee in panic. An officer ordered the infantry drawn up outside the building to fire. The soldiers responded by shooting into the crowd, wounding and killing both fleeing Comanches and Texans.

During the melee, soldiers, rangers, and armed citizens found it difficult to distinguish warriors from women and children, who fought as fiercely as the men, so that in the confusion they killed three women and two children. The Texans also killed all of the chiefs and warriors, hunting down those who had temporarily escaped. Afterward soldiers herded the surviving women and children, many of them wounded, into the stone *calabozo*, or jail, adjoining the court house.

The immediate cost of the fracas to the Republic of Texas was seven citizens dead, including a judge, sheriff, and an army lieutenant. Ten more were wounded. The long-term cost was, of course, incalculable. In return they had slain thirty-three Comanches, including at least part of the Penateka top leadership. They had in addition seized and jailed the surviving thirty-two women and children.

The following day the authorities arranged a truce with the demoralized survivors. A chief's widow was mounted upon a horse, given supplies, and ordered to return to the Penatekas with a message: the People were to bring in all fifteen of the Anglo captives reported by the Lockhart girl, as well as the few Mexicans. The woman promised to return in five days, although the Texans allowed her through the end of the month. But they warned her that if she were not back by then, with a reply from her tribe, they would execute all of the hostages.

The woman never returned, and the Texans executed none of the hostages, who all were exchanged or escaped to rejoin their people over a period of time. But on March 28, Chief Isananica (Howling Wolf) arrived at the beginning of town with some three hundred warriors.[7] He and a single brave rode into San Antonio, circled the city square, and rode up and down Commerce Street. Painted for battle and naked, except for breechclout, he yelled out insults, challenging the townspeople to come out and fight. In front of Black's Saloon, he drew up his pony and whooped out his challenge. Some of the customers, crowding to the door, told him in Spanish that the soldiers were quartered at Mission San José; he should go there if he wished a fight.

Howling Wolf led his warriors to the mission. Colonel Fisher, as it happened, was sick in bed. The second in command, Captain Redd, explained through an interpreter that he was under orders to observe a twelve-day truce, for the purpose of exchanging prisoners. If the chief and his braves would wait for three days, until the truce ended, he would be glad to accommodate them with a fight. But the Comanches, probably suspecting another trap, refused to wait. Shouting more taunts at the mission walls, Chief Isananica turned his pony and departed, followed by his warriors.

Meanwhile Captain Redd had packed a number of his furious soldiers into the San José church, in order to prevent them from firing upon the Comanches. Another officer, Wells, disapproving of this, called him a coward. Redd challenged Wells, the two dueled, shot each other, and died, adding two more lives to the short-term Texan death toll resulting from the Council House Fight. But there were still more lives to be added, as the people of Béxar soon learned. In early April Chief Piava of the Comanches negotiated the trade of three Texan captives for several of the hostages. The Texans were a five-year-old girl with the family name of Putnam, a Mexican boy, and another boy, Booker Webster, whose mother had previously escaped on horseback with her three-year-old. Booker and the Putnam child had been adopted into the tribe by families who had since been persuaded to relinquish them.

Their adoption had saved their lives. Booker Webster told of how the Penatekas had received the news of the devastating losses sustained in San Antonio. The woman had wailed and howled and moaned. Tearing off their clothes, they had put on leather rags. They had slashed their faces, arms, legs, and breasts. Some had cut off their hair and all had painted their faces black. Some of the braves may have slashed their arms and legs like the women. But the men were mostly occupied for several days in killing the horses of the dead chiefs, a custom that had been disappearing but that must have seemed called for at this time as a means of expressing their profound shock, grief, and sense of outrage.

Finally the warriors turned over the remaining thirteen Texan captives to their women. Vengeful women staked out the naked children and young women, singly, by fires. Slowly, night and day, they sliced and burned them, in the end roasting them until there was no longer any response to knife or flame, and all that remained were charred corpses with open mouths and staring eyes.

These acts of vengeance brought the Texan short-term death toll to twenty-two, eleven fewer fatalities than those of the Comanches at Béxar. But the Council House Fight was to continue having consequences over the next thirty-five years. Although the Texans had reduced the leadership of the Penatekas, there were at least four other divisions of the People. When these others learned about the Texan treachery at the Council House in San Antonio, they reacted with a rage equal to that of their southern branch. The Nuhmuhnuh knew that they themselves were sometimes treacherous, but the violation of a council represented an almost unthinkable degree of perfidy. The council was sacred not only to the People but to all Native Americans, even to the Lipans, who, eighteen years before, after the outbreak of renewed war with the Ietans, had slit the throats of all Comanche men who had married into their tribe during the interval of peace. Jean Louis Berlandier described one "native" of an unspecified tribe who developed a nosebleed during a council. Even though "he was choking from the severe hemorrhage, he was not allowed to leave," for that would have violated the sacred character of the meeting.

No, the only parallels in tribal experience had been the seizure and jailing of El Sordo and his little group in 1811; or, especially, the earlier treachery of New Mexico's Governor Manuel Portillo Urrisola in 1761, when he had seized several chiefs at a Taos trade fair, then (by his account) had slaughtered four hundred of their warriors attempting to rescue them. When Governor Vélez had resumed office in 1762, he had succeeded in reestablishing peace with the tribe. No such thing would happen this time. There was one Texan who might have been able to forge a durable peace with the Comanches, but he was the antithesis of Lamar and his administration. Besides, Sam Houston was, at this juncture, without power. So from the spring of 1840 forward, there could be little trust and no lasting peace between the Nuhmuhnuh and the settlers of the Texas frontier. This time the entire People and their allies went to war, in their own fashion, and for as long as they were able to fight, against los tejanos.

TWENTY-FIVE

Sam Houston's Peace Policy, 1841–1845

F or the remainder of the spring and most of the summer of 1840, the northwestern frontier of Texas remained quiet. When people gathered, in the smallest settlement or in Austin or San Antonio, they wondered aloud to each other what had become of the Comanches. Then, on August 5, townsfolk of Gonzales, below and east of Béxar, discovered a wide trail of unshod pony tracks and reported it to the nearest company of rangers. The local captain, Ben McCulloch, immediately sent out riders to alert the district.

Chief Potsanaquahip, or Buffalo Hump, led the vengeance party of at least four hundred horsemen.[1] This man was one of the surviving major Penateka chiefs, and was (or earlier had been) according to the Texas pioneer John Holland Jenkins, "a magnificent specimen of savage manhood." In 1847 Frederick von Roemer, the German geologist, met with Buffalo Hump and two other principal chiefs. Von Roemer found the Penateka leader to be "the genuine, unadulterated picture of a North American Indian." In contrast to many in his tribe at that time, the war chief disdained all articles of European dress. Naked from the waist up, he wore a buffalo hide wrapped around his hips, copper bracelets on his arms, and a string of beads around his neck. As Buffalo Hump sat in council with German settlers, von Roemer noted his grave and dignified expression, which seems to have been at once earnest and so impassive as to appear apathetic. In this meeting, or during the visit of several days, the chief "drew special attention to himself" because he had formerly "distinguished himself for daring and bravery in many engagements with the Texans."[2]

In 1840 the war chief's followers were mostly Penatekas, along with some Kiowas and a scattering of angry volunteers from other Comanche divisions.[3] On August 6, Buffalo Hump seized the town of Victoria, killing some fifteen residents; all, that is, who were not "forted up" in a stone house. When he departed he and his braves drove with them almost two thousand head of horses. Two days later the vengeance party reached Linnville, a hamlet on Lavaca Bay and a port for shipping goods inland to

San Antonio. Most of its citizens fled in boats, while the Comanches spent the day sacking and burning the village, killing, as they did so, five more tejanos.

After that, having, he believed, begun to even scores, Buffalo Hump headed north. This was a mistake. Slowed by a caballada of from two to three thousand horses and a train of mules heavily loaded with plunder, the war chief chose to retrace his route, more or less, instead of making for vacant country to the west. On August 12, at Plum Creek, a stream feeding the San Marcos River, a force of Texans (regular army, local militia, and companies of rangers) hit the Comanche caravan on its flank, stampeding the horses and mules. In the following running battle, the Texans, with their Tonkawa scouts, killed some eighty warriors, with the loss to themselves of only a single man. Buffalo Hump and his remaining braves abandoned their loot to flee northward into Comanchería.

It was a notable Texan victory. President Lamar, however, was not yet satisfied. That September his secretary of war, Albert Sidney Johnston, dispatched Colonel John H. Moore, with a command of about ninety rangers and twelve Lipan scouts.[4] Moore's orders were simple: to ride northwestward until he found Comanches, then to destroy them. The colonel led his rangers far up the Colorado River, deep into the plains, where the Lipans discovered a small Ietan encampment near present Colorado City. Moore succeeded in taking the band entirely by surprise. Jean Louis Berlandier had earlier remarked, to his astonishment, that the Comanches posted no sentinels at night, even when at war and in enemy country. (Apparently such lack of precaution was not unusual among Plains tribes; the ethnologist John C. Ewers noted that the Blackfoot usually posted no guards at night). During the hours of darkness, Moore stationed riflemen by the river to cut down those who attempted to flee. At dawn on October 12, mounted Texans charged the sleeping camp. Since, as Governor Mendinueta had once written, shot and shell have no respect for age or sex, Moore and his rangers and Lipans slaughtered some 130 men, women, and children. Many died in the river, which supposedly ran red with blood. Still the Texans did take 34 women and children prisoners. These included one fourteen-year-old boy who tried to fend off the attackers with a mesquite branch. A ranger was about to kill him, when a Judge Eastland knocked up the man's gun, declaring the boy should be spared because of his courage.

The colonel and his rangers left the wounded Comanches in a tepee under the care of several of their women. Destroying the remainder of the camp, they departed with the prisoners and a herd of five hundred ponies. In Austin Moore's report must have satisfied even Mirabeau Lamar; Texans, this time, had taught the Comanches a lesson.

The people did not forget. But the Penatekas, who had lost much of their leadership as well as a great number of warriors (up to three hundred of them), migrated northward beyond the Red River to a safer part of Comanchería.[5] The ensuing interval of quiet convinced frontier Texans that Lamar's Indian policy was the correct one, and for a time it did appear to be a success. During 1841, for example, the frontier remained mostly quiet. The Comanches continued to raid deep into Mexico, but they avoided the Texas settlements.

Yet Lamar was ensnaring himself, at the same time, in difficulties that would cause his reputation to plunge at the end of his term, when the cost of Indian affairs alone would amount to the (then) extraordinary sum of $2,552,319.[6] (The expenditure for Indian Affairs during Houston's second term, 1842–45, would reach only $94,092). Although Lamar's bellicose policies had succeeded in pacifying the frontier, opening vast tracts of land for settlement, and had helped win recognition for the republic from France and England, his military campaigns had created debts the nation could not pay. By the end of his administration, the Texas dollar was worth twenty cents. Lamar's filibustering expedition to Santa Fe during the summer of 1841, ending with the capture by New Mexicans of the entire force, was his final blunder, and it assured the defeat of his chosen successor, David G. Burnet, in the election that fall, along with the victory of Sam Houston.

Lamar had served as vice-president under Houston from 1836 through most of 1838. Mirabeau Buonaparte, as has often been noted, probably hated his rival as much as he hated Indians. For one thing Houston could accurately be labeled an "Indian lover," an expression of opprobrium on the frontier. Especially in the Republic of Texas, where nine-tenths of the Anglo population came from the South, Sam Houston was an anomaly. Perhaps only the man who had decisively defeated Santa Anna's Mexican army at San Jacinto in 1836 could have shown sympathy for "red niggers," as Texans called Native Americans, and still have remained immensely popular with all but his enemies, such as Lamar, Burnet, and their supporters.[7]

Even after the Council House Fight, Houston (like Vélez and de Anza before him) might conceivably have concluded a meaningful treaty with the Comanches.[8] Certainly the monumental leader had the presence. Referred to by the Lamar faction as a "bloated mass of iniquity," he was a womanizer and drinker, a man of strong passions who had once caned a member of the U.S. Congress for making derogatory remarks about him. Yet Sam Houston was also a man of extraordinary courage who in battle had, as a young man, won the respect of Andrew Jackson. Politico and opportunist, with a talent for the dramatic, Houston possessed a cool, clear intelligence and a command of the language which, with his other attributes, made him a powerful orator. He was in addition capable of an understanding and a compassion that permitted him to look upon American Indians as fellow human beings with profound cultural differences from whites.

In spite of these qualities, Houston seems not to have quite understood the warrior ethos of the southern Plains tribes. This is surprising, because "The Raven" was, among other things, a warrior himself. But the American Indians he knew and loved, and with whom he had spent significant parts of his boyhood and manhood, were the Cherokees, an acculturated people markedly different from Comanches, Kiowas, Kiowa-Apaches, or Wichitans. Apparently drawing upon his experience with the Cherokees, Houston seems to have believed that the People and their allies raided almost entirely from economic motives.[9] He was right of course, in thinking that Indians desired access to the white man's trade goods, items they had come to need or want, such as guns and ammunition, bright bolts of cloth, beads and vermilion, sugar and coffee. He may even have been aware that some southern bands, owing to a reduction of the buffalo herds, were at times "half-starved" by now, as a correspondent of the *Telegraph and Texas Register* had noted in 1838, and relied on trade as one source of their sustenance.[10]

But still Houston failed to take fully into account the Comanches' territorial anxiety, as well as their nonmaterial needs. He seems not to have realized that the values of the nomadic tribes rested upon the display of courage and the appeasement of anger, hatred, and wounded pride through vengeance and war honors. Plunder, scalps, horses, and captives were symbols of a man's success, as well as of his religious "power"; but it was that "power" and its success itself that counted most, those actual deeds that he could legitimately boast about to his people, and that at this time may have taken on an additional luster if vaguely construed as having been performed in defense of the Comanche homeland.

Mirabeau Lamar knew, in part, how to achieve peace on the frontier. But his was only a partial solution to the problems presented by guerrilla warfare. He was right in assuming that, apart from his Council House blunder, Texans could impress the Nuhmuhnuh by repeatedly defeating them in battle. The Comanches were impressed by these adversaries. They respected ranger captains like Jack Hays, Shapley P. Ross, and Rip Ford. But Lamar's policy of patrols and punitive expeditions had been tried by Mendinueta before him. They could bring about only temporary intervals of calm. The People were persistent in war.

With the wisdom of hindsight, one can speculate that Sam Houston, if he had better understood Comanche culture, might have followed Lamar's military successes not only by offering peace and trading posts, but also by proposing an alliance against the Mexicans, with whom both the Texans and Comanches were, in effect, already at war. Mexico had never reconciled herself to the loss of Texas in 1836; for her leaders, war with the Republic had never ended. In 1842, for instance, the Mexican army twice invaded Texas, twice captured San Antonio, only to withdraw quickly southward after each campaign. The Mexicans had also attempted to set the Comanches, Cherokees, and other tribes against the Texans. If Sam Houston personally, in command of a strong military force, had managed to gather together and confer with all the major Comanche chiefs, if he had offered to arm and supply them and their warriors in a guerrilla war against Mexico, he might have achieved a genuine peace on the Texas frontier, perhaps from early 1842 through the end of the Mexican War in 1848. After that, of course, and even earlier, that frontier became the responsibility of the United States. Such an alliance, even if temporary, might have left a residue of tolerance for a time between Texans and Comanches. It might have reduced the agony of the frontier.

Yet it is all too easy to second-guess past events. Other considerations suggest that such a course probably would have been impossible, even for Sam Houston. For one thing the republic was poor, too impoverished to send out an impressive force led by its president. At the time of Houston's inauguration in December 1841, its indebtedness amounted to more than an estimated twelve million dollars in gold; while, by that time, its paper currency was bringing as little as three cents to the dollar. For another thing, in contrast to New Mexico's static eighteenth-century eastern border, the Texas frontier continued aggressively to advance. Finally the racial attitudes held by a majority of Texans would probably have precluded an alliance like the one de Anza fashioned with the proud Comanches.

Houston abided by his belief in the Comanches' economic motive for raiding settlers. Of course there was much truth in this conviction. The power of economics, like that of territoriality, should never be underestimated. The Nuhmuhnuh and other southern Plains tribes did want trading posts located near them. Beginning in 1842 the Texas government established several posts manned by licensed traders. The Comanches regularly used Torrey's Trading House on the upper Brazos, another at the site of the old presidio on the San Sabá, and a third at Comanche Peak, near the present town of Granbury. These posts proved to be profitable for the traders and provided the People with almost any trade item they might wish. Furthermore their presence may have helped to keep war parties en route to or from Mexico at a distance from the settlements.

Yet despite these efforts by the Texas Republic, the Comanches, still

outraged, had determined upon revenge. Houston probably underestimated the force of this cultural imperative. Generally the Comanches and
their allies refused to forgive or even to treat with an enemy until scores
had been evened. Still there were among the People and their allies some
fascinating individual exceptions to the rule. Sometimes their anomalous
behavior grew out of Plains, and Native American, admiration for courage, when that admiration was curiously combined with the concept of
brotherhood.

The practice of two warriors becoming "brothers" was by no means
restricted to the Comanches. John C. Ewers writes of such a custom
among the Blackfoot, for example, calling the two men "partners." These
relationships could sometimes be paradoxical, overcoming even the claims
of vengeance. In 1855, for instance, Ranger Captain Shapley P. Ross became agent for the Indian agency on the Brazos River. He was chosen
because of his fairness and courage by the Wacos, Tawakonies and other
Indians themselves. Shortly after Ross's appointment, Jim Shaw, the Delaware interpreter, told him a Tawakoni wished to speak with him privately.
Ross went into his office and seated himself, doubtless busying himself with
papers while waiting. When he next raised his head, a large warrior stood
before him.

"Get up," said the Tawakoni.

Startled, Ross got to his feet.

"You killed my brother."

Ross suddenly remembered he was unarmed.

"He was my only brother," the warrior continued. "He was the bravest
man around here."

Ross waited.

"Now I want you to be my brother. If you'll agree, I'll do everything
you say."

Ross nodded, or somehow signified assent.

The Tawakoni displayed a long mesquite thorn. He pinched the skin
and muscle over his heart, pierced the gathered flesh, leaving the thorn
within it, then cut out the bloody spine with his knife. Holding it up, he
appealed to the Great Spirit to witness he was taking the captain as his
"brother."

"To the credit of the red man," wrote Rip Ford, who related this anecdote, the Tawakoni "complied faithfully with his promise."[11]

Ford himself, about four years earlier, had acquired a Comanche
"brother," although by no particular wish of his own. A warrior named
Pinohiachman (Saddle Blanket) was, by his ironic account, "famishing for
another brother upon which to lavish his pent-up affections." Apparently

Ford agreed to the arrangement, writing that Saddle Blanket "conferred that distinguished honor on the ranger captain, and they became a modern edition of Jonathan and David . . ." Later Warren Lyons, one of his rangers and a former captive raised as a Comanche, warned him that the relationship might have its inconveniences, since "brothers" were obligated never to fight each other, and were required to assist one another during moments of danger. Yet no problems ever arose, and the captain later gave Pinohiachman due credit, recalling that when he was again in the field, in 1858 and 1859, "chasing Indians, Mr. Saddle Blanket remained true to his pledge." [12] If brotherhood and forgiveness are to be counted as attributes of the Christian, certain of the Comanches and their allies would seem to have been better Christians in those respects than some of their Anglo adversaries!

Rip Ford's experience occurred around a decade after the Council House Fight. An individual warrior's admiration for the courage and repute of an enemy war captain had, in both instances, his and Ross's, overcome the cultural demand for vengeance. An equally interesting exception, this time without the "brother" concept, was that of the Comanche chief, Sanaco, whom Ford had encountered during a truce in 1849. (He called him "Shanaco"). The chief's father had died in the Council House Fight. Sanaco told Captain Ford that he had once believed he could never bring himself to make peace with the Texans. Yet having done all he could to avenge his father's death, he had at last "buried the hatchet," which presumably means he had forgiven the tejanos, at least for that particular catastrophe. Finally there is an instance of a principal Comanche peace chief setting aside the tribal imperative for revenge (and this in the face of unanimous opposition from his peers) in order to argue the case for clemency and diplomacy.

President Houston soon succeeded in concluding a preliminary treaty with the Wichitans, but he was long frustrated in his desire to treat with the Comanches. Even when he sent word by Taovayases or Tawakonies, the chiefs of the Nuhmuhnuh refused to attend councils called by Texans. To add to Houston's difficulties, the envoys were unable to locate the Penatekas within the republic.

At last, in 1843, a small Texan delegation, led by the commissioner of Indian affairs, Colonel J. C. Eldredge, and guided by polyglot Delawares and a Waco chief, traveled far north beyond the Red and found a large Penateka encampment along the Canadian River. Besides Eldredge the Anglo-Texans consisted of Tom Torrey, trader, and Hamilton Bee, a young man along for the adventure. The party was halted, eating fruit, in a grove of wild plum trees, when a Comanche riding a splendid horse, with a little boy seated before him, entered the grove and fearlessly approached them.

The warrior, as it turned out, was blind, and the little boy his guide. After the child had picked all the plums the man wanted, the two of them led the party to the camp of Pahayuco, the major civil chief.

The party entered under a white flag. The chief being absent, his wives welcomed the envoys hospitably, vacating the chief's lodge for them. But the weather was hot, so that the Texans preferred to pitch their own tent, which was open at both ends and breezy. For several days Pahayuco did not appear. In the meantime the tejanos were objects of curiosity to the women of the camp, who would gather to stare at them, while some of the bolder ones would hoist the envoys' sleeves to show their children the white skin.

Meanwhile messengers on swift horses had undoubtedly reached Chief Pahayuco. The peace chief was presented with the urgent problem of what to do about these emissaries from the People's treacherous, mortal enemies, the Texans. As a first step, he convened a meeting of the principal men in his division.

When Pahayuco finally arrived, on August 10, he behaved in a neutral manner toward the commissioner and his two Anglo companions, neither smoking nor eating with them. The following morning at sunrise, a great council of some hundred chiefs and warriors gathered together in a huge tepee, seating themselves in a diminishing circle around the old civil chief. All day the envoys waited in their own tent, while the Delawares and the Waco represented them, urging the Comanche leaders to attend a council with President Houston. At least that was what Eldredge, Torrey, and Bee believed was happening, so that it was a shock when one of their Delaware hunters entered and informed them, with an impassive expression, that the Comanches had decided to kill them.

Eldredge sent for the Delaware interpreters. They returned with Acequash, the Waco (whom Bee called "Old Squash"). Chief Acequash came in with tears dripping from his cheeks. Jim Shaw, a Delaware chief, told the Texans that all the Comanches with a right to speak had spoken, except for one. They had, without exception, called for the envoys' death. Shaw, Acequash, and the others had made every possible appeal in their effort to save them. They had at last declared they would die with them, since they had promised Houston to return them safely. There was only one hope, Shaw said, before returning to the council: Pahayuco had not yet spoken.

Eldredge, Torrey, and Bee, who was only twenty-two, considered their situation. Their horses were at a distance, grazing with the Comanche ponies. There was no escape. They did still possess the pistols in their belts. They resolved, finally, to kill as many warriors as they could and, rather than to be tortured, each to save a last bullet for himself. As they waited, the hours dragged on. From noon until four o'clock there was silence in the council, while the old chief deliberated. Abruptly they heard running footsteps. Jumping to their feet, they drew their pistols. Chief Acequash rushed into the tent and embraced Colonel Eldredge. A moment later the Delawares ran in and told them they were saved: Pahayuco had spoken in their favor and had persuaded a sufficient number of the most important men to share his opinion, so that "when the vote was taken," they were saved.

Young Hamilton Bee (later General Bee in both the Texan and Confederate armies) recorded that moment in his journal: "Prostrate upon the earth were the red and white men—creatures of a common brotherhood, typified and made evident that day in that tent in the wilderness. Not a word was spoken—each bowed to the earth; brothers in danger, brothers by that holy electric spark which caused each in that moment, in his own way, to thank the God of his fathers for this great deliverance."[13]

The man responsible for saving them, Chief Pahayuco, was noncommittal about the prospects for a future treaty, but perhaps mollified by their returning two captive Comanche children, he eventually agreed to meet with Houston the following year.

On October 7, 1844, Sam Houston did finally meet with the Comanches, as well as with the chiefs of several other tribes, including the Tawakonies and Wacos. The meeting took place at the falls of the Brazos River, near the settlement of Bucksnort (later, Marlin). Although the president of the Texas Republic usually dressed casually (in shoes, for example, without laces); he was probably wearing for the occasion a scarlet silk robe given him by the Sultan of Turkey. Flanked by officers and dignitaries, he opened the great council by smoking and passing the calumet. Then Houston addressed the gathered chiefs and warriors through interpreters:

> To the Chiefs of the Comanche, and to all the Chiefs;—We the Chiefs of the white people are very glad to see you. You are welcome to our presence. We are glad that you are here. We have been very far apart, and the path that led from your villages to us has been a long and bloody one . . . we have now met to take away the blood from the path of the Comanche and the white people.
>
> Six years ago, I made a peace with the Comanche: that peace was kept until a bad chief took my place. That Chief made war on the Comanche and murdered them at San Antonio: he made war, too, on the Cherokee, and drove them from the country. Now this has to be mended, war can do us no good . . .

On the second day of the council, Houston read the proposed treaty and presented blue robes to the two major Comanche chiefs who were present—Mopechucope, or Old Owl (whom von Roemer later portrayed as "a small old man" marked only by "his diplomatic crafty face"), and Potsanaquahip.[14] On the following day the president asked for reactions to the treaty from council members, starting with the Comanches.

"I like the treaty well enough," said Buffalo Hump. "All but one thing, the line is too far off, too far up the country."

Here the war chief touched upon the issue that had haunted relations between Texans and Comanches since the beginning of the republic. At last Houston had offered a dividing line between the hunting grounds of the People and the whites. His treaty forbade individuals of either race to cross that line without permission from the president or from an Indian agent. Potsanaquahip now objected that the boundary line was drawn too far north and west of the Texan settlements. The proposed boundary ran from the upper Cross Timbers and Red River to Comanche Peak, slanting southward to the old presidio on the San Sabá, and stretching from there in a southwesterly direction to the Río Grande. Buffalo Hump rejected it on the basis that his people needed to follow the bison, even when the herds drifted toward the settlements, as they had done that very year. In his discussion with Houston, which at times approached an argument, the war chief made some startling statements, such as "I want to live by the white people." But when the president proposed moving a trading post deeper into Comanchería, Buffalo Hump again objected.

> I want the Trading House to remain where it is; and I want my friends, these other Indians, to settle on the line and raise corn and I can often come down among them. I am like the bird flying through the air. I can travel and am always traveling and can easily come down here. I want the Trading House to remain where it is and I will come to it.[15]

Sam Houston wanted one dividing line and the war chief wanted another. In the end the president, frustrated, ordered the boundary proposal stricken from the treaty. No doubt within a few years the Nuhmuhnuh would have been happy to have had the line as it had been offered. But such a boundary would have been, in any event, a fiction; neither the president of the Republic of Texas nor any Comanche chief, given the bad blood between the two peoples, could have enforced an agreement of that sort. The astonishing thing was that Houston had made the offer, considering the attitudes of his constituents toward land and, further, toward Indians, who many among them thought no better than "varmints," to be shot like coyotes, the Plains people's "medicine wolf," on sight.

TWENTY-SIX

Burial of a Nation, Birth of a State, 1845–1846

The senate of the Republic of Texas ratified the Comanche treaty in early 1845. President Anson Jones, Houston's chosen successor, signed it shortly afterward. The following February of 1846, just as Texas was about to join the Union officially, Jones's superintendent of Indian affairs, T. G. Western, was optimistic about relations between the people of Texas and the Indian tribes residing or roaming within its perimeter. "It must be a source of congratulation," he wrote in his final report, "that during the past year as well as at the close of our separate national existence, we have been and are at peace with *all* men both *red* and *white*."[1]

Presidents Houston and Jones gave the republic a longish truce of four years. But even at that, Western's report was a bit too rosy to accord entirely with facts on the frontier. Starting in early 1843, raiding parties of up to a dozen Comanches had begun trickling, during the seasons of good grass, down wooded canyons toward the Texas settlements. Using extreme caution these war parties would have been difficult even for rangers to apprehend. As it was the raiders, often on moonlit nights, would surprise and assault isolated homes, where they would murder or abduct settlers, seize their horses, lance other livestock, and then ride hard for a hundred miles with their captives and stolen horses, until they were virtually secure from pursuit.

Paradoxically that same year the townspeople of Béxar held a precursor of the modern rodeo, pitting Texas Rangers against Mexican caballeros and Comanche braves. The contestants performed such feats as plucking a glove from the ground at a gallop, shooting bullets or arrows into a target from a dead run, and breaking wild horses. The judges, who were presumably Anglos, awarded first prize to a ranger named McMullen, second to a Comanche warrior named Long Quiet, third to a Colonel Kinney, and fourth to a ranchero, Señor don Rafael. Those in charge closed the performance by distributing presents to the Comanches, with whom, it would seem, they were momentarily on good terms.[2]

Yet the following January of 1844, the Texas Congress authorized Captain Jack Hays once again to recruit a company of rangers for the defense of the frontier. Many of the repeated Comanche and Kiowa forays were offshoots of the great annual raids into Mexico. Motivated by a desire for plunder, as well as by their blood feud with the Texans, warriors from any of the tribal divisions might form a war party. Sam Houston, though, at the start of his second term, had removed the capital from Lamar's frontier town of Austin to Houston, that port city named for him. There, at a distance from the settlements, reports of occasional Indian depredations seemed of minor importance and, more or less, to lie in the nature of things. During Houston's second term, coastal planters considered Indian relations to be good. In their view the peace policy had wrought an immeasurable improvement in the affairs of the republic since the time of Lamar's expensive Indian wars. They had. But the folk residing in the expansionist western counties and on the frontier, who were closer to the sporadic raiding, had an altogether different attitude toward Indian relations and Native Americans of any tribe. Like Joseph Conrad's European, Kurtz, in his *Heart of Darkness*, they may be imagined crying out to each other, while building their cabins closer and closer to Comanchería, "Exterminate all the brutes!"[3]

The same was true, of course, of most American settlers on their various frontiers.

Meanwhile, though, what of New Mexico? In New Mexico the historic relationship between nuevomexicanos and Comanches had not altered significantly. In 1821, the year that Chief Cordero and the Spanish officers rescued Thomas James and his party, another American trader, Jacob Fowler, and his associates, tried to ransom a "Spanish Prisnor" from "Ietans " up on the Arkansas River near present Pueblo, Colorado. This unfortunate person had lived near San Antonio, with which, remarked the trader, "the Indeans are at war—tho at Peece With new maxeco and the Spanish in Habetance there." The 1820s continued for the most part peacefully, with the '30s and '40s not much different. The most serious interruption of this general harmony seems to have occurred, according to Mexican documents, in September of 1827, when "several hundred Comanches" were reportedly raiding between Abiquiù and Taos. But the following month another, smaller, group of the People came for trade with New Mexicans to a site known as "Punto de Salinas."[4]

While New Mexican officials, both Spanish and, after 1821, Mexican, tried diligently (though unsuccessfully) to persuade Comanche leaders to cease their raiding in Texas and beyond the Río Grande, the populace was generally more interested in their own long-standing friendship with these Plains nomads, as well as in their long-established mutual relationship as trading partners. In 1835, for instance, when authorities in Santa Fe proposed a campaign against the Comanches, a commission of Taos citizens protested to the governor, saying in effect that they would by no means make war upon the Comanches, who had maintained a loyal friendship over the years and had thereby contributed to a genuine peace in the territory.[5]

Six years later, in 1841, George Wilkins Kendall, the American journalist with the Texan Santa Fe expedition, found further evidence of the tranquil relations existing between nuevomexicanos and Comanches. During the expedition's ill-conceived and ill-fated journey, whose object was in effect to "liberate" New Mexico from Mexico, the Comanches' Kiowa allies had massacred one of its details, a lieutenant and four soldiers out in search of water. Finally, with the main command lost and virtually out of food, Kendall and a small group of officers and men hurried ahead to try finding help in the New Mexican settlements. After some days, at about where the plains meet the western mountains, this half-starved group suddenly encountered a remarkable sight—an enormous flock of sheep.

There were seventeen thousand of them, tended by a small group of *pastores.* The Texans at once purchased twenty fat ewes, and that night feasted. The next day Kendall had a chance to look around. He must have contrasted the landscape and the men and animals inhabiting it with his recent ordeals. Here, at the edge of the Sangre de Cristo range, at the western limit of the southern plains, he rested his eyes upon a pastoral scene. Under the care of only a few shepherds with crooks in their hands and under the gaze of many big, gentle dogs, which were constantly patrolling its outer perimeter, an enormous flock stretched away, bleating and grazing, on the brown-yellow plain. Whenever a sheep would begin to stray, one of the watchful dogs would "walk gently up, take him carefully by the ear, and lead him back to the fold." Here at the edge of Comanchería was a biblical scene of peace.[6]

Four years later, after narrowly missing the fate of the Texan lieutenant and his men ("Here my heart whispered to me that he might be an American, and I did not shoot"), Lieutenant James W. Abert, Topographical Engineers, and his companions arrived safely at Fort Gibson. Several days later, on October 24, 1845, they departed one shining morning, after a night of rain, for the settlements and the United States. The road was good. But it contained, as they progressed, and unknown to them, unhappy auguries for the future of the People and their friends. "The way from

Fort Gibson," Abert later reported, "was literally lined with the wagons of emigrants to Texas, and from this time until we arrived at St. Louis we continued daily to see hundreds of them."

The long, ferocious war between Comanches and Texans has been called a racial war. From the point of view of the majority of Texans it surely was. But from the Comanches' viewpoint, it was not. The Nuhmuhnuh had many faults. They were vengeful, sometimes treacherous, sometimes extremely cruel. As the "People" they had a high opinion of themselves. But they were not racists.[7] Toward white Americans they had a mostly friendly attitude through 1845, and even beyond. They adopted some Anglo-Texan children, as well as mexicanos, into the tribe. Once children were adopted, the People usually treated them well. White girls, such as Matilda Brown and Cynthia Ann Parker, could become Comanches. Captive Mexicans, like Jesús Sánchez, and captive Anglos, like Herman Lehmann and Clinton Smith, could *become* Comanches. These psychic transformations point up the fraudulence, and tragedy, of establishing a person's or a people's identity on the basis of skin color or race.

Spain, it is true, had a long history of racial attitudes based upon "whiteness of skin," "purity of blood," and even place of birth, since native-born Spaniards discriminated against criollos such as José Francisco Ruíz by unofficially denying them the highest positions in the Spanish bureaucracy.[8] Yet certain eighteenth-century Spaniards (Tomás Vélez Cachupín, Juan Bautista de Anza, Jacobo Ugarte y Loyola, Fernando de la Concha) came closer to dealing successfully with the Comanches, on grounds of mutual understanding and respect, than did any Texan official during the period of the republic. The Texas historian Rupert Norval Richardson has observed that "by 1786 the Spaniards knew more about the Comanches than the Anglo-Americans succeeded in learning before 1850."[9] If Richardson included Anglo-Texans among the Anglo-Americans, as he surely must have, his statement was decidedly correct.

In the summer of 1843, when Colonel Eldredge, Tom Torrey, and Hamilton Bee learned their lives were to be spared, they still had one matter to attend to before departing from the great Comanche encampment on the Canadian River.[10] President Houston had ordered Eldredge, as a demonstration of good will, to return two Comanche children captured in 1840 by Colonel John H. Moore on the upper Colorado. Bill, named after a Colonel Hockly, who had adopted and helped raise him, was now fourteen, while the girl, Maria, was eleven. The white couple who had cared for Maria had obviously been kind foster parents. On parting with them, the little girl wept and begged to remain.[11] Maria had forgotten the Shoshone dialect of her people and spoke only English. She feared the "wild Indians" as much as any white child living on the frontier. But Eldredge had his orders and brought her with him.

For the long trip he placed her on a gentle Indian pony rigged with a miniature side saddle, so that she rode along with the others like a proper lady. When the group reached the first Indians, an encampment of Wacos and Delawares on Tehuacana Creek, above present Waco, the Wichitans and their friends were greatly amused by the sight of this shy, timid Comanche child riding in a manner so different from that of her people.

At the camp Bill Hockly, who had forgotten neither his language nor the Nuhmuhnuh, traded his Anglo-Texan clothes for buckskins. Immediately he became a Comanche again. During the long search into the plains, he proved more sharp-sighted in perceiving bison, in distinguishing a distant buffalo from a horse, or in telling a riderless pony from one carrying a man, than any of the adult Delaware guides or hunters. Maria, on the other hand, remained inwardly a white child. Every time scouts believed the expedition was nearing a Comanche camp, she would withdraw into herself, becoming silent and fearful. The remainder of the time, when the scouts would, as usual, report their failure to find evidence of the People, the envoys would hear her cheerful chatter as they rode along or would watch her playing around the fire in the evenings.

At Pahayuco's great encampment, Maria tried to be as inconspicuous as possible. Her appearance, though, riding on a sidesaddle, created a sensation throughout the ranchería. She was, as it turned out, the daughter of an important chief, who had received his mortal wound at the battle of Plum Creek the same year Moore had captured her. Her true name, it appeared, was Nosacooiash, but she was unable to respond to the friendly greetings many of the People gave her, and remained as close to her Texan friends as she was able. Bill, in perverse adolescent fashion, did the same, having decided he would not speak Comanche to anyone.

Bill's manner changed abruptly when he was presented to the old peace chief. Pahayuco addressed the boy sternly, upon which the adolescent replied in his native tongue. After that Colonel Hockly's namesake returned to his own people, only rejoining the envoys a final time, during the formal ceremony restoring Maria and him to the Nuhmuhnuh.

The night before the concluding council, the three Anglo-Texans tried to imagine an appropriate way of dressing the little girl. Her ordinary clothes were by now ragged and threadbare. From somewhere, perhaps from among Torrey's trade goods and presents, they found a dress that would suffice. The skirt was right, but the sleeves were too long for the child. One of the men cut them off at the elbows. Afterward the fit was satisfactory, a fact that had absolutely no interest for Maria in her state of acute anxiety.

The following morning the three men dressed the little girl in her new red dress. Placing strings of brass beads around her neck, they slipped brass bracelets on her arms, tied a red ribbon around her braided hair, and crowned her with a wreath of wildflowers. One of the three, as a finishing touch, painted her unhappy face with vermilion.

Later that morning the council met, probably in Eldredge's tent. The colonel stood holding the hands of the two children. Speaking through a Delaware, he began with a reference to President Houston:

"As a sign of his desire for peace with the Comanche nation, the Great White Father returns to you these children, captured in war . . ." Eldredge began transferring the children's hands to the outstretched hand of Pahayuco. At that instant Maria tore away, beginning to scream and jumping behind the colonel.

"Please, for God's sake," she cried. "Don't leave me with these people!" Falling on her knees, she continued to shriek, hugging his legs.

Except for the child's sobbing, an icy silence fell upon the council. Pahayuco and his chiefs regarded the girl with expressionless faces, as the three Texans tried without success to comfort her.

"This is the daughter of our long-lamented dead chief," said Pahayuco at last. "She is of our blood. Her grandmother is here to accept her. But she has forgotten her own people. She does not wish to return to us. If the Great White Chief merely sent her so we could see she was fat and well cared for, then thank him for me, and she may go back."

Young Hamilton Bee, moved, murmured to Eldredge that this was possibly a way of keeping the child. The colonel, also agitated, still felt compelled to follow out Houston's orders.

"I was told to return the child to you," he said. "I now have done that. She's yours. But you see she's no longer a Comanche. She has learned the language of another people—and I beg you to give her back to me, and let me take her to my home and care for her the rest of my life."

"No," replied Pahayuco. "If she's mine, I'll keep her." The old chief seized the child, roughly swinging her up behind him into the arms of her grandmother, who carried her off, screaming. Later, when Eldredge, Torrey, and Bee rode out of camp with their escort of Delawares and Acequash, they could still hear distant wails from the disconsolate little girl they were leaving behind.[12]

Nearly a quarter-century later, in about 1867, another parting took place, at the camp of Chief Horseback, a powerful Nokoni Comanche leader. An equally important leader of another band, Chief Esserhaby, who was at that time friendly to the Americans, had just spent five weeks at the ranchería persuading Horseback and his brother, Pernerney, to release Theodore Adolphus Babb. Finally Horseback had agreed to allow the boy to chose his own future, confident he would wish to remain with the People. But Babb surprised his captors by opting to return to his father, who waited for him, with the sister from whom he had been separated, at Fort Arbuckle, on the Washita River. Esserhaby, knowing he would be repaid by Babb's father, presented Horseback with several good horses, bridles, blankets, saddles, and other goods in exchange for the boy. After that Babb, still only fifteen, was free to depart with the chief and his entourage of warriors and wives.

But Theodore found parting was not easy. After having lived with the Nuhmuhnuh for only two years, he had formed strong attachments. His departure, he wrote later, seemed to hang a black cloud over the camp. A few friends wept openly, especially the Comanche woman and her son whose family he had joined, and whom he called, respectively, "mother" and "brother." His foster mother was a sister of Horseback, Pernerney, and Tuchispooder. As Babb came to realize later, their intimate companionship had formed "bonds of affection almost as sacred as family ties." "Their kindnesses to me," he wrote, "had been lavish and unvarying, and my friendship and attachment in return were deep and sincere, and I could scarcely restrain my emotions when time came for the final good-bye."[13]

In the end Theodore Adolphus had come to love the people whose warriors he had watched murder his mother. As for Maria, or Nosacooiash, General Bee received a friendly message from her years later and sent her some presents. She had become a principal interpreter for the People and frequently sat in council with Comanche chiefs and white officials. But General Hamilton Bee was certain he would never forget that "bright but desolate child and her prayers and tears when she was forced to be left with her strange people . . ."[14]

The Comanche band of which Clinton Smith was a member was for a long time increasingly on the run from American soldiers. Way up on the Yellowstone River, or so Clinton believed, they engaged in a battle with the Americans. In this battle Chief Tosacowadi was fatally wounded, dying shortly afterward.

"I always claimed Tosacowadi as my father," Smith said later. "And his three squaws as my mothers. Now my father was dead, and I had three squaw mothers left. They buried my best friend on a high point of a mountain, upon a scaffold, wrapping his body in a red blanket, and placed his bow and quiver by his side, and left him there in that solitude. With a heavy heart and bowed head I followed the wailing squaws back to camp, until my grief became too great to silently bear when I, too, joined in the wailing."

Later some members of the band, now led by Chief Black Bear, told Smith that white children were being taken by the tribe into Fort Sill and exchanged, presumably for goods or for Comanche women captives. They wanted him to go, telling him his father was there, waiting for him.

"No, no," cried Clinton, refusing to go. "My father was killed on the Yellowstone River." [15]

In February of 1845 the United States Congress passed a bill admitting Texas into the Union as a state coequal with all others; or maybe a little more so. The bill permitted the state of Texas to retain all of its public lands. This meant that the federal government owned no land in Texas and, consequently, could reserve none for the Comanches or the Wichita peoples or for any other tribe of American Indians. That October the citizens of the Texas Republic voted to accept the annexation treaty, as well as their new state constitution. The United States Congress at once accepted the latter document. In December President Polk, who had been elected as an expansionist candidate, signed the act joining Texas to the Union, even though it meant certain war with Mexico.

The following February at the capital in Austin, a crowd of representatives, officials, and spectators watched as President Anson Jones read the valedictory, concluding with the words: "The Republic of Texas is no more." Artillery boomed while the Lone Star flag fluttered down, to be replaced by the rising Stars and Stripes. If there was a sense of loss ("the funeral of a nation," wrote Rip Ford) there was also jubilation, "joy for the present, and radiant hope for the future." Throughout the new state, people celebrated, especially in the western counties. Now the U.S. Army would defend the frontier; settlers and their families would be safe, at last, from the "murder raids" of the Comanches and their allies.

None of the elated settlers could have foreseen that the Comanche war with Texas would continue for another thirty years. Nor could anyone have imagined that among those years (the time of the Civil War, for instance) there would be some even worse than those they had seen. For their children, perhaps, or their grandchildren, the real terror lay ahead.

On the other hand, a New York editor had that previous December written the phrase that would, within thirty years, foreclose the People's future and destroy their way of life. John L. O'Sullivan, expressing the expansionist mood of the times, wrote in the *Morning News* the sentiments of most Americans, when he recognized "our manifest destiny to overspread and possess the whole continent which Providence has given us for the development of the great experiment of liberty . . ." [16] The Comanches, who still considered themselves the most powerful nation on earth, were mercifully ignorant of that slogan, which summed up the ambitions of the Americans with its combination of Christian piety and brutal acquisitiveness. Yet it was, though suspended, the People's death sentence.

Epilogue

In the spring of 1846, United States Commissioners met with Comanche chiefs Pahayuko, Mopechucope, Santa Anna, and Saviah. The American envoys negotiated a treaty, succeeding that of 1835, with the People. But the U. S. government failed to follow through with promised gifts. By fall the Torreys sent word from their Brazos River trading post that the Comanches were accusing President Polk of lying to them, contrasting their new "great father" to their "good friend" Sam Houston. "We want to see our friend, Sam Houston," they reportedly told the traders. "*He* never told us lies."[1]

So began a new era, very much like the old.

All this, of course, is "history," even "ancient history." Yet sometimes facts, the basis of histories, combine to form a story with the strength of legend, because that story has been told again and again. One such story, like those of Thomas James, owes part of its power to the few seeds it contains of reconciliation. Not many of course. But within the bitterness of history a few floating seeds.

There was a child once named Cynthia Ann. When she was nine, in 1836, a war party of Comanches, Kiowas, and Wichitans abducted her from Parker's Fort, along with Rachel Plummer and others. When Cynthia Ann was thirteen, and living with Chief Pahayuco's band, white traders tried to ransom her, but her Comanche father would not hear of it. Permitted to speak to her, the traders noted that, although she maintained a stubborn silence, her lip trembled. Four or five years later, U. S. government representatives tried to ransom her. She was now about seventeen and had become Naudah, or "She-Carries-Herself-with-Dignity-and-Grace." Her husband, Peta Nocona, or "He-Who-Travels-Alone-and-Returns," was the head chief of the Nokoni Comanches. Whenever the officials attempted to approach her, she would run and hide. They left the Comanche camp without her. Some years later, in 1851, white hunters spoke to her in a ranchería on the upper Canadian. Didn't she want to return to her family? Pointing at two tiny boys playing by her feet, she shook her head.

Nine years after that encounter, a mixed force of volunteers, Texas Rangers, and U.S. troops fell upon a Comanche supply camp on the Pease River. The cowman Charles Goodnight, then a young scout for the party, tried to comfort Naudah, one of some three survivors of the massacre, only to discover that his captive was blue-eyed and white. Back at the settlements, her uncle identified her when she leapt to her feet at the words, "Cynthia Ann." But Naudah, even though accompanied by her infant daughter, Prairie Flower, was bitterly unhappy as the virtual prisoner of her Parker relatives. She grieved at her absence from the People and from her other two children. During the Civil War years, she once implored a former Comanche captive, Coho Smith, to help her steal some horses and to guide her back to the Nuhmuhnuh. Switching back and forth between Comanche and Spanish, she begged for help, because, in her words, "Mi corazon esta llorando todo el tiempo por mis dos hijos!" ("My heart's continually crying for my two sons!")[2] But in 1864, shortly after the death of her daughter from a childhood disease, Naudah died at the age of thirty-seven, evidently of grief.[3]

The elder of the two little boys playing at Cynthia Ann's feet in 1851 had been Quanah, a word meaning approximately "Sweet Smell." Later, on the reservation, he took "Parker" as a last name. In 1867 Quanah was present at the great council in what is now Kansas with the U. S. commissioners for the Medicine Lodge Treaty; the chiefs of the Quahada division, to which he belonged, did not sign. The next year, along with eight other warriors, he followed a Kiowa chief on a raid into Chihuahua. But by 1871 Quanah was leading his own men, as a Quahada war chief. Captain Robert Carter, in his reminiscences, described Parker charging into a skirmish with the 4th Cavalry in order to kill a white trooper whose horse was lagging. Quanah held his pistol balanced in his hand, pointing skyward, as he galloped in, mounted on a black race horse. Black war paint "gave his features a satanic look." His eagle-feather warbonnet sailed out behind him, reaching over the black's tail, sometimes nearly brushing the ground. Closing on the isolated trooper, the war chief shot him dead; then, not pausing to scalp his victim, spun his horse and raced away, followed by his warriors.[4] On another occasion besieged buffalo hunters at the June 1874 Battle of Adobe Walls observed Quanah gallop through heavy fire to lean and swoop up a wounded Comanche named Howea. Hanging from his horse by an arm and a foot while supporting the injured man, Parker succeeded in reaching cover, although he himself was later wounded.

Adobe Walls was an abandoned Bent trading post on the Canadian River in the present Texas panhandle.[5] The attack by Comanches, Kiowas, and southern Cheyennes upon buffalo hunters established there began, in effect, what came to be called the "Red River War." During that campaign Ranald Mackenzie's 4th Cavalry struck the remaining nonreservation Comanches and their allies a decisive blow. On September 28, 1874, the brevet general's Tonkawa trackers led him to Palo Duro Canyon, also in the

Texas panhandle, south of today's Amarillo.⁶ Concealed below the plain, within the canyon's red walls, were the lodges of a great encampment of Comanches, Kiowas, and southern Cheyennes. The troopers descended a steep trail into the valley and attacked. Plains warriors, at first disorganized, rallied and fought a delaying action, while their women and children escaped up the canyon walls. The men followed, disappearing after their families.

In this engagement Mackenzie and his troopers killed only four braves. But they captured virtually all of the belongings, supplies, and horses of the Plains Indians. Among the supplies Mackenzie found ammunition and crates of new carbines that New Mexico comancheros had sold to the Nuhmuhnuh and their allies.⁷ To this extent, at least, de Anza's pact with the Comanches, prepared for by Vélez Cachupín and the Marqués de Rubí and ordered by Teodoro de Croix and Jacobo Ugarte, had held for nearly ninety years.

Mackenzie burned the tepees, buffalo robes, blankets, flour, sugar, jerked buffalo meat, and other possessions and supplies. The following day, after giving his Tonkawa scouts several hundred ponies, the pick of nearly two thousand head, he ordered the remainder shot. General Mackenzie, himself a grim warrior, remembered with chagrin the time when Comanches had stampeded and retrieved a captured herd from him; on this occasion it would not happen. That winter those Comanches and Kiowas and Cheyennes who had escaped from Palo Duro had few options except to straggle across the plains to Fort Sill and surrender, which many of them did.

As for Quanah and the Quahadas, Ranald Mackenzie never caught up with them. But Quanah and the other Quahada leaders were intelligent men. During the Red River Campaign, they had escaped the fate of those camped at Palo Duro; they still had their lodges and supplies and ponies. But they recognized that their situation was becoming untenable. With the mass slaughter of bison by professional white hunters, the herds that had sustained the People were vanishing. The soldiers had discovered most of the Quahada hiding places and were by now familiar with the southern plains, even with the remote Llano Estacado. The last free, integral division of Comanches was tired of running, and was probably hungry. The chiefs knew it would be only a matter of time before the soldiers hunted them down. That battle, when it came, might end in the massacre of all the Quahadas, including the women and children.

In April of 1875, Ranald Mackenzie dispatched the Fort Sill interpreter, a Dr. Jacob Sturm, along with three Comanches, to seek out the Quahadas. On May 1 Sturm and his guides rode into Quanah's camp, which lay along a creek near the present town of Gail, in west Texas. The Quahadas greeted Mackenzie's messenger amicably and, after meeting in council with him, agreed to return together to the Comanche-Kiowa reservation, where they promised to lay down their arms without any conditions. On June 2, 1875, Quanah and the other chiefs surrendered to the U.S. Army troops, giving up their arms, as well as their ponies, which would not be suitable for dragging plows. Soldiers escorted them into Fort Sill as prisoners. This moment marked, in effect, the end of Comanchería and of the People's free, nomadic life on the plains.

By around 1881 the buffalo, too, were gone from the southern plains, along with much of that land's multitude of wild animals. A new people had moved in who shot or poisoned nearly every creature that was not domesticated and capable of being raised or sold for a profit, concentrating especially upon the predators, who might compete with them; foxes, coyotes, bobcats, hawks, and eagles were decimated, cougars and bears mostly eliminated. Professional wolfers and ranch hands set out traps and strychnine for wolves. Some four or five decades after the buffalo, the *lobos*, too, departed, with the Texas gray wolf now thought to be extinct and the Buffalo wolf virtually so. This slaughter, along with barbed wire, the windmill, and stock tank, constituted a value in which the new people had almost as much faith as the Bible. They called it Progress.[8]

Quanah Parker, a born leader and politician, was in his twenties when he surrendered. In the reservation years that followed, he not only became the principal chief of his people, but also the friend of Charles Goodnight, Burk Burnett, Daniel W. Waggoner, C. T. Herring, and other Texas cattle barons. In 1884 Quanah, with a delegation of Comanche and Kiowa chiefs, traveled to Washington to lobby for a legal leasing system with Texas ranchers, an arrangement that, when authorized, proved profitable to the two tribes, since it was impossible to keep Texas cattle from Indian land in any event.

As a recompense for Quanah's help, Burk Burnett built him a two-story, twelve-room mansion, where the Comanche chief lived with his wives from about 1885 until his death in 1911. By 1901 at the latest, he was employing a white couple as housekeepers. While Parker never learned to read, he spoke satisfactory (if broken) English and subscribed to several newspapers, which he had read to him daily. Active in politics, Quanah entertained over the years many notable guests, including the British Ambassador Lord Brice; the Apache Chief Geronimo; Generals Hugh Scott, Nelson Miles, and Frank Baldwin; the Kiowa Chiefs Lone Wolf, Big Tree, and Big Bow; the Commissioner of Indian Affairs Robert G. Valentine; the Comanche Chiefs Wild Horse, Isa-tai, and Powhay; as well as, of course, the Texas cattle barons. But the high point in his social life presumably came in 1905, when he entertained President Theodore Roosevelt as his dinner guest. After that the president's picture hung in the dining room behind Quanah's chair at the head of the table. In this way the man who is considered by many to have been the last great Comanche war chief embraced a curiously American fate—he became a celebrity.[9]

But the fact that Quanah Parker was the son of a celebrated Texan captive undoubtedly helped him in his relations with whites. His story, agreeable as it may be, with its thread of reconciliation and success, was in no way typical of the experience of the great majority of Comanche chiefs and their followers. For these people, stunned and bewildered by the change in their lives, the "white man's road" led into an alkali waste. The trauma of defeat by the uniformed agents of an alien, inexplicable culture was devastating to them. An early and more typical example of a perceptive Comanche leader's fate was the experience of Chief Santana (not to be confused with the Kiowa, Satanta) around 1846.

According to Richard I. Dodge, Santana was one of the most prestigious and influential Comanche chiefs at the time of Texas annexation. Because he and his warriors were preying relentlessly upon the Texas frontier, representatives of the U. S. government sought him out and met with him in council. These officials presented him with gifts and persuaded him to visit the "Great White Father" in Washington. The trip was a shock to Santana. As Dodge pointed out, the distances traveled through country populated by whites, the teeming cities, the quantities of arms and troops, all of this constituted a terrible revelation to the Comanche chief. What he saw convinced him it would be impossible to defeat the whites in warfare.

Santana reported this conclusion, with details of what he had observed, to his fellow chieftains and, through them, to his people. He emphasized the importance of keeping the peace with their powerful neighbor. But the Comanches refused to believe his description of circumstances so different from their own view of the world. The result? His fellow chiefs and their followers came to regard him with suspicion, believing the whites had corrupted him and that he had fabricated a packet of tall tales in order to help the tejanos achieve their purposes. The People believed he had betrayed them. Rapidly his power declined. By Colonel Dodge's account, he was soon "deserted by all except two faithful wives." He died, in Dodge's words, "heart-broken," shortly afterward.[10]

Some twenty years later, Ten Bears, head chief of the Yamparicas, also visited Washington. At the council for the 1867 Medicine Lodge Treaty, he spoke in his oration of that visit:

> When I was in Washington the Great Father told me all the Comanche land was ours, and that no one should stop us from living on it. So, why do you

ask us to leave the rivers, and the sun, and the wind, and live in houses? Do not ask us to give up the buffalo for the sheep. . . .

If the Texans had kept out of my country, there might have been peace. But that which you now say we must live in is too small. The Texans have taken away the places where the grass grew the thickest and the timber was best. Had we kept that, we might have done the things you ask. But it is too late. The whites have the country which we loved, and we wish only to wander on the plains until we die.[11]

Ten Bears, too, knew the power of the whites. Like Santana before him, he had urged peace upon his people. But the Yamparicas had doubted him, neither able nor wishing to believe in what he said he had seen. When he lay dying in 1872, tended by Thomas Battey, the Quaker schoolteacher, he expressed among his last words the wish that his people cease their raiding in Texas. But of his people, only his son was present to hear his words.[12]

In the first year of the Red River War, 1874, an incident occurred on the Comanche-Kiowa reservation that illuminates the plight of the two chiefs. Separated in time by more than twenty years, they faced the same dilemma. They had both seen with their own eyes a vision they could not adequately communicate and whose ramifications were terrible to them. The incident took place among Kiowa chiefs and warriors, yet it illuminates equally circumstances among the Comanches, with whom the Kiowas were to share an identical fate.

That March Thomas Battey decided to instruct some of his charges by means of the "Alphabetical Object Teacher." The gadget was a stereoscope. The Quaker, in relating this anecdote, also remarked upon several characteristics of his pupils. First they believed pictures could not lie. Second, they were highly skeptical concerning all accounts of the United States east of the plains. Their disbelief included, especially, reports of the size of the towns and cities as well as those of the great spaces inhabited by the Americans. In addition they believed that white men had somehow bewitched the chiefs who had traveled east.[13]

As a result, when Battey exhibited images of buildings, towns, rural scenes, and soldiers, they were stunned. All of this became even more convincing when Battey showed some mountain landscapes from Colorado, country with which they were familiar and which they recognized. Slowly they realized that what they had previously taken for gross exaggerations or lies had been, instead, barely half the truth. In particular the Quaker noticed one middle-aged war chief, a prominent skeptic. Unable sufficiently to express his surprise, he "beat upon his mouth in utter astonishment."

"What do you think now?" demanded the well-traveled Chief Sun Boy in Kiowa. "You think they're all lies now? You still think all chiefs who've been to Washington are fools?"

Again and again the war chief peered into the stereoscope, "his hand over his mouth, dumb with amazement."

Soon he called in his warriors and showed them the pictures, haranguing them the while. Battey recorded that he understood only a portion of what the chief was saying, but that he made out such expressions as these:

"Look—see what a mighty, powerful people they are! We're fools! We don't know anything! We're just like wolves running wild on the plains!"

Along with buildings, towns, garrisons, locomotives, and probably steamboats, the chief had seen an apocalyptic vision, under whose weight his own reality began to buckle and collapse. The vision was of a sort of power, even of a sort of medicine, and of a sort of future he could scarcely imagine. Its import was: adapt or die. In crying out to his warriors, the Kiowa, under the impact of his revelation, exclaimed not only for his own people but for their long-time allies, the Comanches, crying—

"We don't know anything! We're just like wolves running wild on the plains!" [14]

But there was still worse—worse before and worse afterward. A few years earlier Colonel Richard I. Dodge had been "on a scout," when he had encountered a Plains Indian encampment that appeared recently to have been abandoned. [15] Broken weapons, scraps of destroyed lodges, dead horses, and signs of blood were scattered about. After closely examining the site, Dodge decided that all of this indicated the death of an important man. He soon found a track where a heavy body had been dragged over the earth. Following the path he discovered a mound of dry leaves, which he scooped aside. To his amazement there lay the body of a leading Comanche war chief, perhaps one not altogether unlike James's "brother"— "a man greatly loved and feared by his tribe."

Mourners had painted the chief's face. They had dressed him, after dragging him unceremoniously to the spot (doubtless because of the manner of his death) in a uniform coat and a hat with a feather. His gun lay beside him. In a blue and stiffened hand he clutched a box of matches. Only months later did the colonel learn that the man had died of delirium tremens. What vision, worse even than that of the Kiowas, had this chief beheld before his death?

Or after the horrors, might he, on the other hand, have hallucinated while dying a scene at once as mysterious and terrible and beautiful as the one witnessed by Lewis Garrard in 1846 along the Arkansas River, in the silent plains above Comanchería? It was on a late fall afternoon, nearing that dusk the French call *entre chien et loup*, when he sighted a band of buffalo running across the Santa Fe Trail and "two hundred or more large wolves, who, with outstretched necks and uplifted sharp heads, were in sure, noiseless, though swift pursuit. It was a magnificent sight to watch them dashing along—the poor buffalo straining their utmost to elude the sharp fangs of their persecutors—the wolves gaining at every stride. On they went, now out of sight, now in the river, where the buffalo had the advantage; a cool swim invigorated the pursuers, who, loping with dripping hair, howled, as they pressed on . . ." [16]

One night many years afterward, but not so many years ago, a Comanche woman in present Oklahoma heard footsteps padding back and forth outside her front door. Upon opening it she saw a large wolf pacing on her porch. She said to him, "Tell me some good news, brother." [17]

The Comanche people have waited a long time. May that good news come soon . . .

Notes

PREFACE

1. That is, from the moment of annexation, conflict between Comanches and Americans became inevitable. See, for example, Mooney, *Calendar History*, 170.

2. Foreman, *Advancing the Frontier*, 241, 278–79.

3. Richardson (*The Comanche Barrier*, 172) observes that between 1830 and 1860, encroachments by outside hunters upon the southern plains caused such destruction among the buffalo herds that the nomadic tribes living there "began to find it exceedingly difficult to kill a sufficient number [of bison] to sustain their families." Although the Comanches tended to blame white and border Indian hunters, a variety of factors were responsible for the decline in bison population. Flores ("Bison Ecology," 483), for example, notes that "drought, Indian market hunting, and cow selection [for the best robes] must stand as the critical elements—albeit augmented by minor factors such as white disturbance, new bovine diseases, and increasing grazing competition from horses—that brought on the bison crisis of the midcentury Southern Plains."

4. For example, "the notion that Indian peoples are best understood in relation to ourselves has informed Euro-American thinking from the very beginning" (Foster, "'Being Comanche,'" 1988, 8). For a discussion of this subject, see ibid., 1–56 ("Euro-American Images of Indians") or see Foster, "'Being Comanche,'" 1991, 3–5.

5. Kavanagh, "Comanche Politics," 6.

6. See Foster, "'Being Comanche,'" 119–20, or his *Being Comanche*, 1991, 54–57.

7. For example see Thurman, "A New Interpretation," 578–79. Fehrenbach (*Comanches*, 51) thinks that Comanche "survivors of the twentieth century no longer understood exactly what their forefathers had truly believed. They no longer believed it themselves. Most had become at least nominal Christians, and their belief in most, if not all, magic was shattered." Linton ("The Comanche," 47) declares that "many features of [the Comanches'] original culture were . . . forgotten, and . . . they tended to accept constant changes in their ways of living," even after contact with Anglo-Americans.

8. Bancroft, *Native Races* 1:506. Foster (*Being Comanche*, 1991, 32–33) believes it to be "entirely possible that Comanches were active on the Plains for some centuries before European contact." See also Flores, "Bison Ecology," 468.

9. Shimkin ("Words of Acculturation," 198), for instance, believes the migration occurred after 1600. "Nuhmuhnuh" was, and is, the Comanche people's name for themselves as a group. According to the ethnologist Daniel Gelo, the word is pronounced accenting the first syllable (personal communication). Fehrenbach uses "Nermernuh," while Foster prefers "Numina," and Thurman, "Nemena." To this writer's ear, "Nuhmuhnuh" sounds closer to the spoken word. The first Americans to encounter Comanches called them "Hietans" or "Ietans," terms which will be used occasionally in the present work.

10. Parkman, *La Salle*, 1001.

11. Horgan, *Great River*, 68.

12. *Times Atlas*, 149.

13. See Forbes, *Apache, Navaho, and Spaniard*, xxii.

14. See Flores, *Journal of an Indian Trader*. Philip Nolan, incidentally, may have been a spy for the traitorous James Wilkinson, commanding general of the U. S. Army (as of 1800). See Jackson, *Thomas Jefferson & the Stony Mountains*, *100–101*.

15. Dodge, *Plains of the Great West*, 3.

16. Please note that Marcy's report in *Senate Document No. 54* and his *Adventure on Red River*, both referred to repeatedly in the present work, are virtually identical, except that the Senate Document includes a good deal of scientific data about his itinerary.

17. Fehrenbach, *Comanches*, 499.

PROLOGUE

1. There is disagreement among scholars as to when the Comanches, or their forebears, moved onto the plains. Flores ("Bison Ecology," 468), for instance, writes that "perhaps as early as 1500 the proto-Comanches were hunting bison and using dog power to haul their mountain-adapted four-pole tipis east of the Laramie Mountains."

2. Kavanagh, "Comanche Politics," 60; Ewers, *The Horse*, 9.

3. Trenholm and Carley, *The Shoshonis*, 19. Shimkin ("Words of Acculturation," 198) believes the migration started earlier, writing that "Beginning about 1600, the Comanche-Shoshone peoples . . . migrated rapidly onto the High Plains, reaching central Saskatchewan in the north . . . and the Arkansas River in the south by around 1730. Yet in the light of information from the Ulibarrí and Valverde expeditions (1706 and 1719, respectively), the 1730 date would appear to be late. John (*Storms*, 256), for example, holds that "the Comanches carried their triumphant sweep of the northern plains to the upper reaches of the Red River in the early 1720's . . ."

4. Wallace and Hoebel, *The Comanches*, 12.

5. Details are drawn from Winship, *The Coronado Expedition*, and from Hammond and Rey, *Don Juan de Oñate*.

6. De Benavides, *Revised Memorial of 1634*, 81.

7. For accounts of early Spanish-Apache relations, see Kessell, *Kiva, Cross, and Crown*, as well as Moorhead, *The Apache Frontier*.

8. Cordero, Antonio. "Cordero's Description of the Apache," 350, trans. and ed. Daniel S. Matson and Albert H. Schroeder.

9. Gunnerson, *Jicarilla Apaches*, 258. Hyde (*Indians of the High Plains*, 63–92) refers to archaeological evidence for Padouca-Apache settlements reaching as far north as present Nebraska and South Dakota.

10. There is some question concerning the quantity of horses possessed by Plains tribes in the early eighteenth century. The Comanches seem to have had at least a modest sufficiency of them by 1700. According to Ponca tradition (Wallace and Hoebel, *Comanches*, 39), "the Comanches taught the Poncas how to ride . . . Soon afterward they left the country and the Poncas knew not where they went." This must have been

in the late seventeenth century, when the Poncas lived in the Black Hills or at the mouth of the Niobrara River in present Nebraska. In 1700 a Father Gabriel Marest noted that the Poncas, among other tribes, possessed Spanish horses (cited by Ewers, *The Horse*, 4). In southern Ute tradition there is a suggestion that the Utes acquired horses from Spaniards "probably around 1640" (cited by Ewers, ibid., 3). At the time of the Spaniards' return to New Mexico in 1693, the "Utes had reorganized their lives around horses and were purveying the animals to other Indians farther north. Most receptive to the equestrian life were the Comanches. The turn of the century marked an epoch of change . . . When Comanches came in increasing numbers to join forces with them the Utes commanded an unprecedented potential for raiding and for war" (John, *Storms*, 231). Conversely, though, it must be mentioned that in 1726 Brigadier Pedro de Rivera wrote of the Comanches that "they halt at any camp site and set up their campaign tents, which are transported by large dogs which they raise for this purpose" (Kessell, *Kiva, Cross, and Crown*, 371). Still, Catlin (*Letters and Notes*, 2:62) depicted dogs harnessed to Comanche travoises in 1834, when the band (or division) he visited possessed "at least three thousand" head of horses and mules.

    11. The Comanches possessed so many horses that one modern scholar (Canty, "New World Pastoralism," 6) considers them to have been "a formative example of New World pastoralism . . . " Canty contends (ibid., 91) that "Comanche ownership of horses with a ratio of six animals per person made this tribe very wealthy. It had at least three times as many horses as any other group . . . They were the pastoral repository of animals which passed to other tribes . . ." Thurman observes ("Comanche," 55) that "the horse rich Comanches were one of the few Plains tribes to use pack horses and pack saddles (made of rawhide pads)."

    12. Population estimates for the Comanches vary greatly. There were probably never many more than twenty thousand of them on the plains, and even that figure may be inflated; see Wallace and Hoebel, *Comanches*, 31–32. Richardson (*Comanche Barrier*, 1991, 4) observes, however, that they had been greatly reduced by the mid-nineteenth century, when there were probably no more remaining than eight or ten thousand. Thurman ("Comanche," 67) estimates an even lower figure, stating that "there are no compelling reasons . . . to believe that the Comanches ever numbered more than 6 to 8,000." On the other hand, Flores ("Bison Ecology," 479, and n.36) comments that "six of the seven population figures for the Comanches estimated between 1786 and 1854 fall into a narrow range between 19,200 and 21,600." He notes that while anthropologists estimate lower figures, he has a "historian's bias in favor of documentary evidence," and that "Plains observers computed village sizes relatively easily by counting the number of tents."

    13. Dodge, *Our Wild Indians*, 426–27.

    14. Canty (citing George E. Hyde's *Life of George Bent*, Univ. of Oklahoma Press, 1968) observes that the Cheyennes used a slip noose (a loop tied open along a willow hoop frame, or a loop tied to a pole) until after the midnineteenth century, when they mastered the lariat. She ("New World Pastoralism," 93) notes that the Comanches "excelled in the used of the lasso from the early nineteenth century." It seems possible, however, that the Comanches, having to manage large *caballadas*, may have learned the art of the lariat earlier.

    15. Smith, *The Boy Captives*, 57.

16. Dodge, *Our Wild Indians*, 427.

17. This practice evidently spread to other Plains tribes. Nye (*Plains Indian Raiders*, 83) writes of raids along the Smoky Hill Road in Kansas during the summer of 1867, without specifying the Indians, who were probably Cheyennes, or Cheyenne Dog Soldiers: "If one of the raiders was shot from his horse, two Indians would ride up at full speed and lift him from the ground without dismounting, and often without stopping. This was a difficult and spectacular stunt which they had practiced since childhood, and it made the tallying of Indian casualties practically impossible."

18. Bollaert, *William Bollaert's Texas*, 361.

19. There appears to be no available translation for "Sanaco." Generally, the present work has preferred translations of Comanche names by the ethnohistorian, Thomas W. Kavanagh. When Kavanagh offers none (and apparently certain words have been lost from the Comanche language), the traditional translation has been used, when one exists. In the event that no translation is available, the historical rendering of the Indian name has been used, e.g., "Sanaco." The author has translated the Spanish names of Comanche chieftains.

20. Marcy, *Senate Document No. 54*, 96–97.

Chapter 1

1. The epigraphs quoted from New Mexico folksongs (on part I title page), along with their translations, are provided courtesy of Enrique R. Lamadrid. For the source of events described in this chapter, see Thomas, *Plains Indians*, especially his translation of Vélez's report to Viceroy Revilla Gigedo, 68–76.

2. John (*Storms*, 321) gives a somewhat different account of these events, writing that Vélez trapped the Comanches "in a box canyon and drove them back toward a deep pond at the head of the canyon . . . ," etc.

3. See the report by Lobato to Vélez in Thomas, *Plains Indians*, 114–17.

Chapter 2

1. New Mexico was both kingdom and province. "The Spanish used the word *kingdom* in the early days to describe any extensive area ruled over by a governor who was in turn subordinate to the viceroy. Towards the end of Spanish colonial rule, the word *province* was substituted for *kingdom* in official documents and maps" (Burke, "*This Miserable Kingdom*," i).

2. Accounts of the Valverde and Ulibarrí expeditions are based, respectively, upon the governor's and the sergeant major's diaries, trans. and ed. by Thomas, in *After Coronado*.

3. Rayado Creek, which does not appear on most maps, can be found in *Roads of New Mexico*, 35. Evidently the Mountain Branch of the Santa Fe Trail later crossed the creek near the community of Rayado, located in Colfax County at the southeastern tip of today's Philmont Scout Ranch.

4. Those who doubt that the Comanches possessed a moderate number of horses early in the eighteenth century might consider this passage from Valverde's diary: "After they marched some two leagues, the track of the enemy was recognized, which left

a clear trail wherever it went, both on account of the great number of people and the multitude of horses, as well as the tent poles they carried dragging along behind" (Thomas, *After Coronado*, 127). While it appears that many individuals were walking, many others were evidently riding "the multitude of horses," some of which were dragging travoises. Surely the Comanche and Ute warriors, at least, were mounted, if there were horses available to drag the baggage.

5. See Conrad, "Reluctant Imperialist," 93–105.

6. Parkman (*A Half-Century of Conflict*, 570) writes: "In 1703, twenty Canadians tried to find their way from the Illinois to New Mexico . . ." While "Canadian" was not a nationality at the time, Parkman evidently uses the term to indicate place of origin, a practice the present work will follow when convenient. Another French, or Canadian, explorer coming from the Illinois was Lieutenant Claude-Charles Du Tisné. It has been generally believed that de Tisné visited Wichita villages in the Arkansas Valley, "on the bank of a small stream twelve leagues west of the Arkansas" (John, The Taovayas Indians," *Chronicles of Oklahoma*, 275–76. But M. M. Wedel ("Claude-Charles Dutisné," 147–73) argues persuasively that the villages were actually on the Verdigris near today's Neodesha, Kansas. At one of these villages, incidentally, de Tisné found 300 head of horses.

7. Details from the Villasur campaign are taken from the portion of Villasur's diary trans. and ed. by Thomas, in *After Coronado*.

8. Accounts of both de Bourgmont's and the Mallet brothers' expeditions are drawn from Margry, *Mémoires et documents* 6.

9. Traditionally the Padoucas were thought to have been Comanches. The prevailing view today among historians and ethnologists is that the people whom de Bourgmont sought out and met were Plains Apaches. Some modern scholars still hold to the former opinion. See, for example, John, *Storms*, 219–20, and Shimkin, "Words of Acculturation," 200. (Compare his view with that of Forbes, *Apache, Navaho and Spaniard*, xxii; and especially with that of Gunnerson, *Jicarilla Apaches*, 223–24.) Incidentally, the detail in Margry of carrying de Bourgmont on a buffalo hide may support Forbes and Gunnerson. Kessell (*Kiva, Cross, and Crown*, 194–95), drawing on Spanish documents, describes a similar scene in 1660. The bearers honoring one Diego Romero were Plains Apaches, whose custom this may have been. This writer knows of no comparable incident described in records relating to Comanches. Hyde investigates (*Indians of the High Plains*, 86) the Padouca question thoroughly and concludes that "the Bourgmont evidence explodes the legend that the Padoucas were Comanches. In Kansas, as elsewhere, the Padoucas were Apaches."

10. See Fehrenbach, *Comanches*, 190.

11. Americans, particularly during the Jefferson years, thought of all Comanches as "Hietans" or "Ietans" (Dan Flores, ms. review, 1/20/92, in possession of University of New Mexico Press), which is how "Ietan" will be employed in this work, i.e., as an occasional synonym for "Comanche," unless otherwise specified. The term, however, also has a narrower meaning. Elizabeth A. H. John considers the Ietans to have been Kotsoteka Comanches, while the historian, Odie B. Faulk, thinks they were Yamparicas. The ethnohistorian, Thomas W. Kavanagh, believes, like Faulk, that the "Ietans," in the narrower sense of the word, were Yamparica Comanches. See Kavanagh, "Comanche Politics," 187, n.102.

12. The New Mexico historian E. A. Mares tells the author that *genízaro* derives

from *janissary.* In the Ottoman Empire, war captives and young Christians were pressed into service, converted to Islam, and strictly disciplined into an elite corps. New Mexico Spaniards settled ransomed Indians, genízaros, along their eastern frontier to form a buffer against incursions by plains raiders.

13. Kessell (*Kiva, Cross, and Crown,* 378–80) suggests that Governor Vélez exaggerated casualty figures in order to discredit his predecessor, Governor Codallos, and to boost his own reputation. Certain events around 1749, and before then, are difficult to date since historians disagree. John, for instance, writes (*Storms,* 313) that "sometime before 1735, a breach occurred between the Comanches and their erstwhile allies, the Utes." But Bancroft (*History of Arizona and New Mexico,* 249) has New Mexico Governor Codallos in 1747, "with over 500 allies," overtaking "the Comanches with some Yuta allies beyond Abiquiù" and defeating them, after which "four Yuta captives were shot." Clearly the two tribes were still allied in 1747, if Bancroft is correct. Kessell (*Kiva, Cross, and Crown,* 383) believes that the Ute-Comanche breach occurred "late in the 1740s." Hyde declares (*Indians of the High Plains,* 106–7) that the Comanches began attacking their former allies in 1749, the same year that, in his view, the People became allied with the Wichitas and began trading with their new friends for French muskets. In any event it would seem likely that these two important events, which may have been related, took place around the middle of the eighteenth century.

Chapter 3

1. Lehmann, *Nine Years with the Indians.*

2. Close-knit, that is, as a single cultural community, though not necessarily unified politically. See Foster, *Being Comanche,* 1991, 58–59.

3. Gladwin, "Comanche Kin Behavior," 78–82.

4. Berlandier, "Casa del Oso y Cibolo," 178.

5. Neighbors, "The Na-ü-ni," 133–34.

6. Unless specifically identified otherwise, all material drawn from Berlandier may be found in his *Indians of Texas.*

7. Domenech, *Journal d'un Missionaire,* 137–39.

8. Uniquely among this writer's sources, Thurman ("Comanche," 53) observes that "Comanches were very concerned with personal cleanliness . . . Adults bathed every morning, to the point of breaking ice on streams, and washed before eating."

9. Cited by Neeley, *Quanah Parker,* 571; see also Haley, *Charles Goodnight,* 57.

10. See Hoebel, *Law-Ways,* 54.

11. As cited by Foreman, *Advancing the Frontier,* 192.

12. "The prairie Indians do not put their prisoners to death by prolonged tortures, but invariably compel the females to submit to their lewd embraces" (Marcy, *Adventure on Red River,* 169). Robert S. Neighbors ("The Na-ü-ni," 132) noted a year later, in 1853, that when women were captured by the Comanches, "their chastity [was] uniformly not respected." "To the Plains tribes all females were chattels, and despite a great deal of studied delicacy on the subject, there was never to be a known case of white women captives who were not subjected to abuse and rape. . . . Until the last half of the nineteenth century, Comanche warriors proudly asserted such exploits" (Fehrenbach, *Comanches,* 287).

13. Emphasis added; Linton, "The Comanche," 61. Newcomb (*Indians of Texas*, 180) notes, further, that "in a very literal sense Comanche culture came into being through military prowess, blossomed through raiding . . . , and nearly every aspect of life became intertwined in one way or another with the art of war."

14. Writing of Plains Indians in general, Dodge (*Our Wild Indians*, 213–14) observes that "it is regarded as effeminate in a man to show any special affection for his wife in public. A very notable exception . . . is Powder Face, a prominent chief of the Arrapahoes, a desperate and dangerous man, covered with scars and celebrated for the . . . scalps he has taken . . . His [only] wife is a woman of average good looks, and of some thirty years of age. They have been married for about fifteen years and have no children. . . . He will sit for hours before his lodge door combing her hair, painting her face, petting and fondling her; *conduct which would disgrace a less determined or well-known warrior*" (emphasis added). This chief owed his name to having suffered gunpowder burns on his face when he was younger. For his photograph with his wife, by Soule, see Nye, *Plains Indian Raiders*, 347.

15. "From infancy a Plains Indian boy had it dinned into his ears that bravery was the path to distinction, that old age was an evil, while it was a fine thing to die in battle. . . . Thus, every lad was conditioned to emulate the example of eminent warriors" (Lowie, *Indians of the Plains*, 106).

16. Emphasis added; cited by Moorhead, *Apache Frontier*, 160–61.

17. Linton, *Study of Man*, 121; see also Linton, "The Comanche," 55.

18. Most contemporary ethnologists seem to have discarded the notion that there was a "typical" Plains tribe. Thurman ("Comanche," 49) however, does assert that in the period of about 1850–74, "the Comanches were a typical Plains tribe . . ."

19. John ("Kiowa History," 387) writes that "it was in the first half of 1806 that the Kiowas and Comanches celebrated the enduring peace between those two markedly different nations."

20. See Gelo, "Comanche Belief and Ritual," 116–17.

21. The Kiowa tribal medicine was the equivalent of "the medicine arrows of the Cheyenne, the sacred pipe and the wheel of the Arapaho, . . . the Okipa drums of the Mandan, and the buffalo calf pipe of the Dakota" (Wissler, *Indians of the Plains*, 110). For the distinction between the individual medicine bag and the group bundle, see Holder, *The Hoe and the Horse*, 41–42.

22. Gelo, "Comanche Belief and Ritual," 75.

23. "Comanche culture . . . was comparatively poor in content and full of all sorts of minor maladjustments which were due in large part to their recent arrival in the southern Plains and their extensive borrowings from the various groups with whom they were in contact" (Linton, *Study of Man*, 364). Hoebel (*Law-Ways*, 17) also writes of the Comanches as "a tribe with a simple culture."

24. Dodge, *Plains of the Great West*, xxvii. Wallace and Hoebel state that Farnham called the Comanches the "Spartans of the Plains"; this writer could find only "Arabs of the Plains" in that reference.

25. Gelo, "Comanche Belief and Ritual," 32.

26. Dodge, *Our Wild Indians*, 136–38.

27. "Bravo!" is an interjection in Spanish. But "Bueno!" would have served as well.

28. Smith, *The Boy Captives*, 95–97.

CHAPTER 4

1. For the circumstances and treatment of such genízara slaves as Manuela in colonial New Mexico, see Gutiérrez, *When Jesus Came*, 179–90.

2. For the principal sources of this chapter, see Thomas, *Plains Indians*, especially documents under the following headings: "The Frontier Policy of Don Thomas Vélez Cachupín," 61–81; "Governor Vélez and the French intrusion of 1752," 82–110; and "Governor Vélez Establishes Peace with the Comanches, Utes, and Apaches," 111–56. See also Kessell, *Kiva, Cross, and Crown*, 378–85.

3. Zebulon Montgomery Pike (*Journals* 2:58), on the other hand, in 1807 called the New Mexicans "the bravest and most hardy subjects in New Spain . . ."

4. In May of 1837 an incident occurred that illustrates the contrast between the attitudes of one Spaniard and one Texan toward the Comanches. Chiefs meeting in San Antonio with Albert Sidney Johnston, commander of the Texan army, "demanded" that a guard be placed over their horses. "Johnston told them that they must recollect that they were dealing with Americans [*sic*, Texans] who would not tolerate their insolence—they must therefore take care of their own horses" (as cited from Mirabeau Buonaparte Lamar's notes by Kavanagh, "Comanche Politics," 195, n.159).

5. See Hackett, *Historical Documents*, 486–87. Section 55, from which the quote above is taken, consists of forty-four lines. In lines six through eight, Fray Pedro Serrano declares that during the trade fairs the fleet is in. "The fleet being, in this case, some two hundred . . . tents of barbarous heathen Indians, Comanches as well as other nations . . ." On line thirty-five begins the quoted passage that provides the basis for the account dramatized in this chapter. In the interim Father Serrano mentions no Utes or Apaches, only Christian Indians, who form part of the audience. It seems plausible to believe that Comanche traders were those "heathen Indians" he refers to.

6. Cited by Bancroft, *History*, 257–58, n.7.

7. The Franciscans went so far as to charge that "the governor's reports of Indian campaigns had often no foundation in fact" (Bancroft, *History*, 256). The campaign described above, in chapter 1 was, of course, independently verified by the Kiowa woman who had been a Comanche captive. John L. Kessell (*Kiva, Cross, and Crown*, 383) takes a somewhat more critical view of Vélez than does this writer; yet in the end, he concedes that "despite the nasty things the friar partisans of ex-governor Codallos said about Vélez, he, like Vargas before him and Anza after him, seemed to grasp intuitively the key to peace with the raiders: an active personal diplomacy backed by proven prowess in battle and a supply of gifts or trading opportunities." For the seventeenth-century background to the bitter feuding between clergy and civil government in New Mexico, see Scholes, "Church and State."

8. Trenholm and Carley (*The Shoshonis*, 27) note that the Plains Shoshones ate "yamps, or wild carrots." Might this be the same plant?

CHAPTER 5

1. Dodge (*Our Wild Indians*, 31) called the Comanches "the most cunning, the most mischievously artful, of all the United States Indians . . ." A modern anthropolo-

gist (Gelo, "Comanche Belief and Ritual," 113–14) notes a parallel between the Comanche warrior and "Coyote as trickster." He goes on to observe that "ethnographic accounts emphasize the Comanches' resourcefulness, opportunism, and predatory lifestyle, and so tacitly draw the analogy between Comanche and Coyote."

2. Scholars disagree as to whether or not Cuerno Verde died on this occasion. Thomas (*Plains Indians*, 167, n.68) believes he did not. John (*Storms*, 469), on the other hand, believes that the original chieftain died at Ojo Caliente and that his son recovered his headdress and replaced him. A careful reading of Thomas's translation renders her opinion the more persuasive of the two. According to Pino ("Exposicion," 131), Cuerno Verde's Comanche name was "Tabivo Naritgante," supposed to translate as "handsome and brave."

3. Thomas, *Plains Indians*, 184. (Mendinueta to Bucareli, Santa Fe, August 19, 1775).

4. Thomas, *Teodoro de Croix*, 111; John, *Storms*, 583.

5. See Thomas, *Teodoro de Croix*, as well as *Plains Indians*, "Policy of Croix for the Eastern Frontier of New Mexico, 1777–1778," 190–211.

Chapter 6

1. Babb, *Bosom of the Comanches*, 28–34.
2. See Thomas, *Plains Indians*, 167, John, *Storms*, 585.
3. Thurman ("Comanche," 59) declares, somewhat ambiguously, that "captive children were often adopted, but young children were usually tortured to death." This writer is skeptical of the second clause. Berlandier (*Indians of Texas*, 83), for instance, writes that "small boys are better treated [than adult male captives] because they grow up with such good tutors that they become so active and so evil the garrison people fear the prisoners more than the natives." Burnet (*Letters*, 130) observes that when the Comanches "capture boys and girls . . . they usually treat them with much lenity and kindness, and retain them in a kind of filial servitude, very little inferior to the condition of native children." Furthermore Flores ("Bison Ecology," 471) points out that "widespread adoption of captured children and polygyny . . . were designed to keep Comanche numbers high and growing." In n.19 on the same page, he cites nineteenth-century Indian Agent Thomas Fitzpatrick as insisting that Comanche raids were for children, "to keep up the numbers of the tribe."
4. Jenkins, *Recollections*, 226–31.
5. Sánchez, "Trip to Texas in 1828," 263. It is perhaps also worth noting the following observation by Sánchez: "When [the Comanches] find young Mexicans, they take them captives, raise them, and permit them to live with the same freedom as Indians themselves enjoy."

Chapter 7

1. For de Anza's account of this campaign, see Thomas, *Forgotten Frontiers*, 122–39.

2. This deed alone would seem to demonstrate that the Comanches were already a politically advanced people!

3. See in Thomas, *Forgotten Frontiers*, 294–321; 325–27.

4. Marcy, Senate Document No. 54., 100–101.

5. As cited by Moorhead, *Apache Frontier*, 157.

Chapter 8

1. John, "Nurturing the Peace," 346.

2. For a general description of the comancheros and their commerce, see "The Comanchero Trade, 1786–1860," in Kenner, *New Mexican-Plains Indian Relations*, 78–97.

3. See Brown, "Los Comanches."

4. "Men could, and often would, beat their wives on any pretext they chose . . ." (Gladwin, "Comanche Kin Behavior," 85).

5. Gelo, "Comanche Belief and Ritual," 30. For Francesca's story, see Corwin, *Comanche and Kiowa Captives*, 7–13.

6. As cited by Moorhead, *Apache Frontier*, 157. Sixty-six years, later Marcy (*Senate Document No. 54*, 102) referred to the Comanche woman as "a beast of burden and a slave to the will of her brutal master," while at the same time seeming "contented with her lot . . ." Dr. John Sibley ("A Report from Natchitoches," 78) wrote in 1807 that "the Women seem in the Most Abject & degraded State of Servility . . ." Roe (*The Indian and the Horse*, 323–24) would seem to have misinterpreted Marcy in concluding that "among the Comanche the impact of the horse had evidently favored the 'emancipation of women,'" partly at least because women rode astride and often expertly. Citing Richardson (*The Comanche Barrier*, 1933, 216), Roe also refers to Comanche chief Santa Anna's widow, who was wealthy and "one of the best hunters in the tribe." Probably this woman was one of some few exceptions. Flores, for example, notes (*Caprock Canyonlands*, 90) that Comanche women lost status when the tribe became horse nomads. He believes that (*Journal of an Indian Trader*, 133, n.40) "as bison hunters, the Comanches had a culture forged upon a sexual division of labor that—whether interpreted in anthropological or modern feminist terms— rarely allowed women to escape the role of subordinate and inferior."

7. Berlandier calls this chief "Barbakista." Kavanagh ("Comanche Politics," 183, n. 65) gives the name as "Paruaquibitse," or "Little Bear."

8. Ford was nicknamed "Rip" because of his habit of writing R.I.P. by the names of the dead in his casualty reports.

9. Marcy (*Senate Document No. 54*, 102) noted that Comanche boys were "nurtured with care and treated with great kindness by their mothers, while the girls [were] frequently beaten and abused unmercifully."

10. Conversely, according to Gladwin ("Comanche Kin Behavior," 85), "An illegitimate child was a great shame to all members of the family, and especially to the girl's brother . . ." Wallace and Hoebel (*Comanches*, 142) report that Comanche women practiced abortion by beating their bellies with stones. Flores (manuscript review, 12/22/91, in possession of University of New Mexico Press) observes that "Comanche

women also used birthspacing and stoneseed, an herbal birth control that researchers have found to interfere with conception." Among the Cheyennes, in contrast, abortion was considered homicide. In their attitude toward sexuality, the Comanches represented an antithesis to the Cheyennes, for whom chastity was an ideal. Elsewhere Hoebel (*The Cheyennes*, 95) writes that every Cheyenne girl, after her first period, received a chastity belt from her mother. Until she married she wore it constantly, continuing to wear it when her husband was absent hunting or at war. She even wore it whenever she left her lodge to fetch wood or water.

11. John, "Wichita Village," 428.

12. Hoebel, *Law-Ways*, 73.

13. Neighbors, "Comanches of Texas," 132. Hoebel (*The Cheyennes*, 38) notes that among the Cheyenne ruling Council of Forty-four, the chiefs were supposed to be imperturbable. Should a wife of one of these men run off with another man, he might remark casually to his warrior friends, "A dog has pissed on my tepee." The matter would end there.

14. Von Roemer, *Roemer's Texas*, 271.

15. Berlandier, *Indians of Texas*, 117. Neighbors ("Comanches of Texas," 133), writing in 1853, or a little before, stated that the Comanches formerly killed the favorite wife, "but this custom has been done away with, from intercourse with the more civilized Indians." Berlandier (*Indians of Texas*, 117) was also shocked by the practice of burying alive a nursing infant with its dead mother, unless the child had already cut its baby teeth, because the Comanches believed that "no one should be forced to shoulder the burden of so little an existence." Usually Comanche children were not weaned until the age of four or even five, when they could chew buffalo meat.

16. Nye (*Plains Indian Raiders*, 276) writes, opposite a Soule photo of a Cheyenne woman: "Though the wife or daughter of a Plains Indian worked hard, she was by no means the downtrodden slave that she is sometimes described as being. In the Cheyenne tribe especially and also in the other southwestern Plains tribes, the women occupied a coequal status with the men. In their own sphere of responsibility, which was the care of the lodge and the upbringing of the children, they had the final word; but they were consulted on other matters, too, including tribal affairs."

17. Carter, *On the Border*, 286.

CHAPTER 9

1. Loomis and Nasatir's *Pedro Vial and the Roads to Santa Fe* provided the information and documents that are the principal sources for this chapter.

2. Kavanagh ("Comanche Politics," 180, n.22) notes that "Zoquiné is probably / soquina/ 'hazy' or 'smoky.'"

3. See John, "Kiowa History," 386–87 and n.18.

CHAPTER 10

1. Loomis and Nasatir, *Pedro Vial*, 437.

2. Don Facundo Melgares was the last Spanish governor of New Mexico

(1818–22). Zebulon Montgomery Pike, who was earlier in Melgares's custody as a prisoner, thought highly of him. See Loomis and Nasatir, *Pedro Vial*, 237, n.5.

3. Emphasis added. As cited by Flores, *Jefferson and Southwestern Exploration*, 322.

4. Flores (*Jefferson*, 26–27) notes that "in order to overcome the handicap of unfamiliarity the United States would have in the inevitable boundary dispute with Spain, Jefferson sought to provide the American diplomats with correct geographical information through extensive scientific exploration of the West. He also points out that American exploration of the Southwest brought the United States and Spain to the verge of war.

5. In contrast to the view expressed in Loomis and Nasatir's *Pedro Vial*, 178 (that the Pike expedition was a partial cause of Melgares's march), Flores (manuscript review, 12/22/91, in possession of University of New Mexico Press) holds that "since Melgares left Santa Fe before Pike even was ordered west, Melgares could not have been in pursuit of Pike—despite Pike's self-serving claim."

6. Barker, *Life of Stephen F. Austin*, 41.

7. See Kavanagh, "Comanche Politics," 50.

8. Ibid., 94–95. Dr. Sibley, who in 1804 already had a budget of three thousand dollars for presents to Indian tribes in the region, was implementing Jeffersonian, and American, policy to disaffect Spain's Indian allies, especially the Wichitan peoples and the Comanches. See also John, "Nurturing the Peace," 353; and Flores, *Journal of an Indian Trader*, 18–20.

9. Pike, *Journals*, 260–62. Elizabeth John ("Nurturing the Peace," 358) comments that "while Sibley had no interpreter of Comanche, he understood their leader to prefer the American over the Spanish flag and grandly presented him one." However, in the quoted passage, Sibley does refer to an interpreter. See also Sibley, "Report from Natchitoches in 1807," 54; and Flores, *Journal*, 24–26.

10. Kavanagh, "Comanche Politics," 295, n.10.

11. Sibley, "Report," 49.

.CHAPTER 11

1. As early as 1833, when Sam Houston, as envoy of President Jackson, met with Comanches in Béxar, the People knew the difference between americanos and tejanos. But after the United States-Comanche treaty in 1835, the Comanches grew increasingly resentful of displaced eastern Indians encroaching upon lands they had traditionally considered their own. They bitterly resented these Indians hunting in Comanchería. Part of their anger was directed, quite rightly, at the government that had placed the immigrant Indians next to them. Still as a matter of national policy, the U.S. Army succeeded in maintaining good relations with the tribe. Consequently from the mid 1830s on, the Comanches made a clear distinction between the (mostly alright) americanos north of the Red River and the (mostly bad) tejanos south of that international boundary. See, for example, Fehrenbach, *Comanches*, 374–75.

2. See Loomis and Nasatir, *Pedro Vial*, 462–509.

3. Thurman ("Comanche," 62) states that "in 1758 [the Comanches] attacked the Lipan Apaches . . . at the San Saba mission . . ." There were no Apaches at the mission

when the Comanches and their allies attacked. See Fehrenbach, *Comanches*, 201–4, and John, *Storms*, 297–98.

4. The ruins of the presidio, somewhat stabilized, may still be seen at Menard, Texas, near the community golf course.

5. See Thomas James, *Three Years among the Indians*, 100–128.

6. For information on Glass, see Flores, *Journal*, 26–27.

7. For Glass's diary account of his expedition see John, "Wichita Village"; or Flores, *Journal*.

8. See Gregg, *Commerce of the Prairies*, 1967, 171–205.

9. Catlin painted his portrait in 1834, mistakenly naming him "The Mountain of Rocks." At that time Dragoon Sergeant Hugh Evans wrote in his journal ("Journal," 195) that "the old chief come riding on a verry fine horse he was a verry large man corpulent and muscular in appearance . . ."

10. See Abert, *Country of the Comanche Indians*, 35–40.

11. Abert and his men were, of course, not a civilian survey party, which the Comanches would have recognized by 1845, but military cartographers.

12. Flores (manuscript review, 12/22/91, in the possession of University of New Mexico Press) observes that "the 'rose and blue striped agates' mean they were at a sacred place, the Alibates flint quarry, now a national monument in the Canadian Breaks of the Texas Panhandle."

13. "Isa" means "Wolf." The meaning of the remainder of the chief's name is unknown.

14. Hatcher was a mountain man as well as a plainsman. Garrard, who knew him in 1846, wrote of him (*Wah-to-Yah*, 153) as "an unerring shot" with "an inexhaustible fund of anecdote and humor." According to young Lewis, "he was the *beau idéal* of a Rocky Mountain man."

CHAPTER 12

1. Kavanagh, "Comanche Politics," 78; also see Barker, *Life of Stephen F. Austin*, 48–49.

2. See DeShields, *Border Wars*, 74.

3. Again, "Isa" means "Wolf." The meaning of the rest of the name is unknown.

4. See Yoakum, *History of Texas*, 282–90.

5. Flores (manuscript review, 12/22/91, in possession of University of New Mexico Press) notes that "Comanches certainly were materialistic when it comes to horses and arms, and this is what the cessation of trade meant—fewer arms." Still, curiously, the Comanches, as "light cavalry," seem eventually to have preferred the bow to the musket or rifle, until the advent of Colt revolvers and of Henry and Winchester repeating rifles. See Fehrenbach, *Comanches*, 298, 498. For an example of the speed and accuracy with which a Comanche could discharge arrows, see Gregg, *Commerce of the Prairies*, 1967, 200–201.

6. A family would hold a Give-Away Dance, for example, to celebrate the first coup of a son. This action also demonstrated to everyone the family's confidence in their supernatural "power"; see Wallace and Hoebel, *Comanches*, 131. Foster, for one,

postulates an apparent economic determinism to explain Comanche behavior, writing ("'Being Comanche,'" 71) that the historic Comanches "were consistently guided by economic considerations" in their relations with Euro-Americans. While such considerations had to be important, and may have been neglected in past studies (see De-Mallie, xii), they alone surely cannot represent the complex of Comanche motives for this people's actions vis-à-vis Spaniards, Frenchmen, Mexicans, Anglo-Texans, and Americans. An overriding emphasis on economics not only denies the dynamics of friendship and hatred, as well as territoriality and the Plains warrior ethos, but it reduces these proud predators with "a high sense of honor" (Mooney, "Comanche") to a community of calculating traffickers in stolen livestock. This writer must concur with Smith (*Nation Comes of Age*, xv), when he writes that "with careful reservation for the Divine," he "can discover no 'forces,' economic or astral, other than the individual and collective wills of human beings, that guide or direct human history."

7. Richardson, *The Comanche Barrier*, 1933, 76.

8. Wilbarger, *Indian Depredations in Texas*, 5–7.

9. See DeShields, *Border Wars*, 119.

10. Much of Fort Gibson was reconstructed during the 1930s. The Fort Gibson Military Park may be visited today.

11. Catlin may be wrong here. Fourteen feet for a lance seems extreme. Most Comanche lances were apparently six to eight feet long. Curiously Fehrenbach (*Comanches*, 298) refers to the "supple, sixteen-foot Plains lance." Yet von Roemer (*Roemer's Texas*, 106) mentions "a thin [Comanche] lance eight feet long." A lance of from fourteen to sixteen feet would seem quite unwieldy when carried on a Plains pony of only fourteen hands. Furthermore Gregg (*Commerce*, 1933, 433) comments that "the Comanches employ usually short-handled javelins or lances, declaring, like the Spartan mother, that cowards only need long-handled weapons."

12. See Catlin, *Letters and Notes*, 55–62.

CHAPTER 13

1. Flores (manuscript review, 12/22/91, in the possession of University of New Mexico Press) observes that "Los Adaes was 16 miles west of Natchitoches, which was on both banks of the Red. The dividing line [between French Louisiana and New Spain] was the 'Gran Montane,' a wooded ridge about 150 ft. high."

2. "By mid [eighteenth] century, Apaches and Spaniards joined battle along a new front south of New Mexico and Texas, competing for horses and thus for survival" (John, *Storms*, 271–72). And "thus, in just a half century, the Comanches . . . had driven the Apaches from the Plains, all the way from the Arkansas to the Texas coast" (Hyde, *Indians of the High Plains*, 116).

3. See Faulk, "The Comanche Invasion of Texas," 12.

4. See John, *Storms*, 370–74, 434–35.

5. These, the "Naytanes," have been called Yamparicas by one historian, Odie B. Faulk; while another, Elizabeth A. H. John, considers them to have been Kotsotekas. The ethnohistorian Thomas W. Kavanagh ("Comanche Politics," 187, n.102) believes, like Faulk, that the "Naytanes," or "Ietans," were Yamparica Comanches. He points

out, furthermore, that "Naytane" was the Caddoan word for "Snake." A quick, backward, wiggling motion of the finger drawn across the chest denoted "Comanche," in plains sign language. (Note that in this instance "Naytanes," or "Ietans," is used to designate a specific Comanche division, the Yamparicas, and not the entire tribe.)

6. See Bolton, *Athanase de Mézières* 2 : 83–100.

7. For the principal sources of this chapter, see Kavanagh, "Comanche Politics," 60–68; and John, *Storms*, 612–96.

Chapter 14

1. See Babb, *In the Bosom of the Comanches*, 20–42.

2. For two accounts of the events related in this chapter, see Kavanagh, "Comanche Politics," 68–73, 93–96; as well as John, *Storms*, 736–73 and "Nurturing the Peace," 345–56.

3. John ("Nurturing the Peace," 346) observes that, in contrast to Spanish/Comanche relations in New Mexico, "much less stable conditions confronted eastern Comanches on the Texas frontier. There distances were so vast, population so sparse, horses so numerous, and passage of Comanche war parties after Lipan Apaches so frequent as to invite mischief." Kavanagh ("Comanche Politics," 70), in addition, attributes the contrasting relations in New Mexico and Texas to a loss of Comanche leadership in the latter province, noting that "for the last fourteen years of the eighteenth century there does not seem to have been a single Texas Comanche with sufficient prestige, authority, or power to warrant the status "Principal Chief."

4. "Parua" means "Bear." The meaning of the rest of the name is unknown.

5. For some general background to this chapter from the viewpoint of Comandante General Jacobo Ugarte y Loyola, see Moorhead, *Apache Frontier*, 143–69.

6. Josiah Gregg's "belief that trade was the key to the Comanche peace [in New Mexico] unquestionably was correct. In addition, the bonds that had developed between the New Mexicans and Comanches were far warmer and deeper than Gregg realized" (Kenner, *New Mexican-Plains Indian Relations*, 73).

7. The meaning of the Comanche word *encanaguane* has apparently been lost.

8. John, "Nurturing the Peace." 353. "Isazat," by the way, is "Wolf" + something, while "Sargento" is, of course, "Sergeant."

9. Pike, *Expeditions* 2 : 700.

10. See John, "Nurturing the Peace," 354–55.

Chapter 15

1. Clinton Smith, *The Boy Captives*, 74–75.

2. For two (similar) accounts of the El Sordo affair, see Kavanagh, "Comanche Politics," 77–80; and John, "Nurturing the Peace," 360–64.

3. John, "Nurturing the Peace," 359.

4. Schilz and Schilz, *Buffalo Hump*, 5.

5. Padilla, "Report," 55. Padilla also admonishes that "the greatest insult you

can offer a Comanche is to pull his braids," an act probably not attempted often or by many.

6. In May of 1822 Stephen F. Austin wrote General Anastacio Bustamante, captain general of the provincias internas, that the Comanches "had been used by the insurgents as allies in 1812, and after Arredondo's defeat of Toledo's army some of the American soldiers of fortune who were serving with him had settled around Natchitoches. There they connected themselves with unscrupulous traders, and, through their acquaintance with the Comanches and Lipans, established an extensive commerce with them, exchanging store goods for horses and mules, which they sold in the United States" (Barker, *Life of Stephen F. Austin*, 48).

7. Weber, *The Mexican Frontier*, 95. See his chapter 5, 83–105, for a discussion of this problem.

8. See Fehrenbach, *Lone Star*, 120–31.

9. Babb, *In the Bosom of the Comanches*, 42–43.

CHAPTER 16

1. See Thomas James, *Three Years among the Indians*, 128–39.

CHAPTER 17

1. The epigraph (on PART III title page) quoted from the *Telegraph and Texas Register*, is cited by Richardson, *Comanche Barrier*, 1933, 101.

2. Thurman ("Comanche," 58), however, observes that lances and warbonnets "almost all had ritual obligations attached to them." Power may thus depend upon "force of arms" or its threat, or upon other means such as political influence, wealth, prestige, or even beauty. Actually (except for certain possible forms of supernatural power) it means simply the capacity to "get one's way." Hall, a cultural anthropologist, notes (*Anthropology of Everyday Life*, 206) that "power and the symbols of power are the currency of our land," meaning the United States.

3. Berlandier, *Indians of Texas*, 91, 116.

4. Burnet, "Letters," 125.

5. Benedict, "Guardian Spirit," 28.

6. Gladwin ("Personality Structure," 118) notes that "the guardian spirit came to the Cheyenne through suffering."

7. Wallace and Hoebel, *Comanches*, 160–61. For details of the vision quest and for other aspects of Comanche attitudes and practices concerning "medicine," see ibid., 155–84.

8. See Benedict, "Guardian Spirit," 67. Hoebel (*Cheyennes*, 85), however, notes that "The Cheyenne medicine man is . . . more of a priest than he is a shaman. The main road to supernatural power is through acquisition of ritual knowledge learned from one who is already a priest."

9. Linton ("Comanche," 82), in discussing the change from Plateau culture to Comanche culture, observes that "the most powerful and influential figure in the so-

ciety did however change from the medicine man in the old culture to the war chief in the new."

10. Wallace and Hoebel, *Comanches*, 246–50. Yet Gladwin ("Personality Structure," 121) observes that most Comanche bands did not bother to count coup, concentrating instead on killing the enemy and seizing his horses.

11. Kavanagh ("Comanche Politics," 49) believes that headmen did possess the power "to impose physical sanctions."

12. Gelo, "Aboriginal Skeptics," 21. See also Mooney, *Calendar History*, 242. Gelo believes the "skeptic" stereotype can be traced from Mooney back to Burnet's and Neighbor's contributions to Schoolcraft's monumental compendium.

13. Gelo, "Aboriginal Skeptics," 19. He points out, for instance, that the Comanche custom of acquiring "power" from ghosts of forebears as well as from animal tutors is a Shoshonean trait.

14. Benedict, "Guardian Spirit," 26.

15. See for example Catlin's "Letter No. 22," describing self-torture in Mandan religious ceremonies in *Letters and Notes* I:155–84.

16. Linton, "Comanche Sun Dance," 420–28. Modern scholars disagree about the frequency of Comanche Sun Dances. Gelo ("Belief and Ritual," 75), for example, believes that the Comanches "had virtually no Sun Dance . . ."

17. Gelo, "Aboriginal Skeptics," 19.

18. Dewees, *Letters*, 47.

CHAPTER 18

1. For the background to Mexican political struggles and independence, see Weber, *The Mexican Frontier*, 1–31; see also McElhannon, "Imperial Mexico and Texas," 117–50.

2. For information regarding Ruíz, see Berlandier, *Indians of Texas*, 11–12; Ruíz, "Report," 1–3; and Stuck, *José Francisco Ruíz*.

3. Schilz and Schilz, *Buffalo Hump*, 9.

4. Pool, *Historical Atlas of Texas*, 35.

5. Ibid., 44.

6. Schilz and Schilz, *Buffalo Hump*, 12–13.

7. See Kavanagh, "Comanche Politics," 82–87.

8. Ibid., 49.

9. Gladwin, "Comanche Kin Behavior," 82–83. Note that after puberty, and the warpath, boys "could and would occasionally whip their sisters, even after they were married."

10. Ibid., 91.

11. Linton, "Comanche," 57.

12. There was however a role for the rebel and nonconformist in Comanche culture among "The Crazy Dogs." "The Crazy Dogs were contraries. They did everything backwards. Tell them to bring water and they would bring fire . . . Such men were a great nuisance. They urinated like dogs. Going about the camp they could shoot an arrow into anybody's pot of meat, taking whatever piece stuck to the shaft . . . Most

Crazy Dogs started out as wayward youths." On the other hand, most were released from the role after some act of exceptional courage. "By their war records ex–Crazy Dogs were always men of importance in the tribe" (Hoebel, *Law-ways*, 33–34). The Cheyennes also had contraries known as Crazy Dogs, "undoubtedly influenced in part by the Crow Indian Crazy-Dogs-Wishing-to-Die . . ." (Hoebel, *The Cheyennes*, 33).

13. See Thomas James, *Three Years among the Indians*, 213–56.

14. See Kavanagh, "Comanche Politics," 53.

15. Wallace and Hoebel make a distinction between "war chief" and "peace " or "civil" chief. In this view the war chief was young and aggressive, while the peace chief was old and conciliatory. Kavanagh ("Comanche Politics," 54) argues otherwise, writing that "in contrast to . . . kinship relations, political relations with [Comanche] non-kin were based on pragmatic considerations of relative power. The difference between 'peace chief' and 'war chief' is one of role, not of status, and the decision of which role to take when is dependent on a situational evaluation of the power differential."

16. Thomas James was a fighter, a man of intemperate views and violent prejudices. Note for example his attitude toward the governor of New Mexico in 1821: "The doughty Governor, Facundo Melgares, on foot, in his cloak and chapeau de bras, was reviewing this noble army [of "tatterdemalions"]. He was five feet high, nearly as thick as he was long, and as he waddled from one end of the line to the other I thought of Alexander and Hannibal and Caesar, and how their glories would soon be eclipsed by this hero of Santa Fe" (James, *Three Years among the Indians*, 166–67). Zebulon Montgomery Pike, on the other hand, liked and admired Melgares. James exaggerated, particularly with regard to money, it would seem, as well as with respect to the virtues of his friends and the failings of his enemies. Yet he appears to have been, in spite of these traits, an intelligent and courageous man with a talent for leadership. This view is supported by the fact that his neighbors and fellow citizens elected him in 1825 to the Illinois State Legislature and, in addition, elected him general of the Second Brigade, First Division of Illinois Militia. (Ibid., xxiv). See also Loomis and Nasatir, *Pedro Vial*, 258–60.

CHAPTER 19

1. See Kavanagh, "Comanche Politics," 88–91.

2. "Toro," of course, means "Bull." An *hechicero* is "One-who-casts-spells." The chief's name translates roughly as Sorcerer Bull or Medicine Bull.

3. As cited by Kavanagh, "Comanche Politics," 89.

4. Marcy, *The Prairie Traveler*, 205–6.

5. See Young, *The First Military Escort*.

6. See Simmons, *Following the Santa Fe Trail*, 119–20.

7. Cited by Young, *The First Military Escort*, 114–15.

8. Smithwick, *Evolution of a State*, 142–43.

9. Elizabeth John (*Storms*, 591) declares that according to Spanish documents, in the winter of 1779, during the American Revolutionary War, uniformed troops from east of the Mississippi attacked and destroyed two Comanche camps, supposedly having

been asked to do so by the "A" tribe. The Spanish first believed the troops to have been British, later, American. This odd incident raises so many questions that the present writer prefers not to consider it the "first" battle between American soldiers and Comanches.

CHAPTER 20

1. See chapter 18, n.2.
2. See Burnet, "Letters," 115–40.
3. As has been mentioned previously, estimates of Comanche population as well as military strength vary considerably. Flores (manuscript review, 12/22/91, in possession of University of New Mexico Press) believes the Mexican government's figures were more accurate, since Burnet saw only the Texas division. The anthropologist John C. Ewers, citing Rister's *Border Captives*, observes that Paul L. Chouteau, who knew the Comanches in 1836, calculated the number of their warriors to be forty-five hundred. (Berlandier, *Indians of Texas*, 121, n.161).
4. Fehrenbach, *Comanches*, 304; and *Lone Star*, 469.
5. John C. Ewers, the ethnologist who edited the Berlandier manuscript, observes in his introduction that "in the future Berlandier may be remembered as one of the most enlightened and most objective amateur ethnographers of the American West during the frontier period" (Berlandier, *Indians of Texas*, 22).
6. Ibid., 61.
7. "The wolf was regarded as a brother who often warned the Comanches of impending trouble . . ." (Richardson, *Comanche Barrier*, 1991, 14).
8. Berlandier, *Indians of Texas*, 61, n.56.
9. De Cessac, "Ethnographic Information," 40.
10. Berlandier, *Indians of Texas*, 67–73.
11. Ibid., 76.
12. Bolton, *Athanase de Mézières* 1 : 298, 2 : 174.
13. Ruíz, "Report," 9.
14. Carter, *On the Border*, 289–90.
15. Carter, *Old Sergeant's Story*, 93–94.
16. For instance: "War was viewed as a man's pre-eminent occupation . . ." (Thurman, "Comanche," 59).
17. Lehmann, *Nine Years*, 159–63.

CHAPTER 21

1. Richardson, *Comanche Barrier*, 1933, 172.
2. Ibid., 77, n.131.
3. See Nye, *Carbine and Lance*, 5–7.
4. See Kavanagh, "Comanche Politics." 102.
5. Nye (*Carbine and Lance*, 10) says the dragoons suffered from "acute dysentery and malaria."

6. See Catlin, *Letters and Notes* 2:70–72; see also Wheelock, *Journal*, 376–81; and Evans, *Journal*, 192–205.

7. It is unclear which Comanche division Dodge encountered; see Kavanagh, "Comanche Politics," 190–91, n.127.

8. Foreman, *Advancing the Frontier*, 119. For the preceding "Little Ones" reference, see Foley and Rice, *The First Chouteaus*, 32, n.31. Formally the Osages designated themselves the "Children of the Middle Waters." See ibid.

9. Padilla, "Report," 53.

10. Dewees, *Letters*, 16.

11. Berlandier, *Indians of Texas*, 140. It is Berlandier who noted that the Comanches called the Osages "Los Ligeros."

12. Sánchez, "Trip to Texas," 262.

13. Devaney, *Great Olympic Champions*, 85.

14. Foreman, *Advancing the Frontier*, 150.

15. Nye (*Carbine and Lance*, 12) translates "To-hauson" as "Overhanging Butte." Mayhall (*The Kiowas*, 82) translates "Dohasan" as "Top of the Mountain" or "Little Bluff." He has also been called, "Little Mountain."

16. Fowler (*Journal*, 68), too, had preferred the Kiowas, writing in 1821, "It is but Justice to Say We find the Kiawa the best Indeans possing [*sic*] more firmness and manly deportment than the arrapoho and less arogance and Hatey Pride than the Ietan . . ."

17. Sergeant Hugh Evans ("Journal," 188) took an opposite view of the Nuhmuhnuh, writing that "Those Commanch Indians are the most homely featured being verry large & corpulent in size not to [so] tall as the Osages but of a heavy square and inelegent perportion . . ."

18. For an account of this council, see Foreman, *Advancing the Frontier*, 131–37; see also Evans, "Journal," 212–14.

19. Cited by Foreman, *Advancing the Frontier*, 136.

20. Mayhall, *The Kiowas*, 82.

21. Jenkins, *Recollections*, 23–26.

CHAPTER 22

1. Pool, *Historical Atlas of Texas*, 44.

2. For the events described in this chapter concerning Rachel Plummer, see Plummer, *The Rachel Plummer Narrative*, 1st and 2d eds.

3. Fehrenbach, *Comanches*, 287.

4. For a description of the events relating to Sarah Ann Horn, see Horn, *A Narrative of the Captivity of Mrs. Horn*.

5. Catlin had painted his portrait in 1834, misnaming him "The Bow and Quiver." Usually he is called "Traveling Wolf," but Kavanagh ("Comanche Politics," 190, n.127) believes that "Returning Wolf" is more accurate.

6. Foreman, *Advancing the Frontier*, 149. Camp Mason, named for Major R. B. Mason, was on a creek near present Purcell, Oklahoma. It seems to have been near, if

not identical with, Camp Holmes. Ibid., 232, n.31; see also Van Zandt, "History of Camp Holmes."

7. Richardson, *Comanche Barrier*, 1933, 85.

8. Ford, *Rip Ford's Texas*, 119–20.

9. Clinton Smith, *The Boy Captives*, 107–8.

CHAPTER 23

1. Muguara may have been the Penateka divisional chief, although here he is camped with what appears to be his own band. Kavanagh ("Comanche Politics," 194, n.156) observes that Fehrenbach gives Muguara's name as "Mook-war-ruh," or "Spirit Talker." The ethnohistorian considers this etymology to be "doubtful," but offers no alternative. Consequently "Spirit Talker" will translate "Muguara" in the present work.

2. For Smithwick's own account of his stay with the Comanches, and related matters, see his *Evolution of a State*, 125–40.

3. Kavanagh ("Comanche Politics," 194, n.155) believes "Quinaseico" probably represents "Quena Sieca," or "Eagle Feathers." He opines that "Puestia" might signify the Spanish *puesta*, from *puesta del sol*, or "sunset."

4. While out of office, Sam Houston is said to have received Count Saligny, minister from the French government to the Republic of Texas, in this manner: The Raven, drunk, stood upon a table wrapped in an Indian blanket, but with his battle-scarred chest bare. "An humble republican soldier who wears his decorations here," he cried in greeting, striking his chest, "salutes Monsieur le Comte, representing the great French nation!" (Day and Ullom, *Autobiography of Sam Houston*, xiv–xv).

5. Fowler, *Journal*, 56–57.

6. Dodge, *Our Wild Indians*, 241–48.

7. Marcy, *Adventure on Red River*, 60–61.

8. Dodge, *Our Wild Indians*, 588.

9. The southern Comanches desire for a boundary again illustrates the limitations inherent in overemphasizing economics as the sole or even principal determinant of Comanche behavior. Foster ("'Being Comanche,'" 71), for example, fails even to mention territoriality as a possible motive for Comanche actions. While he does refer to the availability and quantity of bison, the plains herds pertained by no means strictly to Euro-American/Comanche relations. As early as 1796, for example, Colonel Antonio Cordero ("Description of the Apache," 355) wrote of the Lipans, calling them "most bitter enemies of the Comanches, with whom they have continuous bloody struggles for the proprietorship of the buffalo, which each one wants for itself." W. W. Newcomb, Jr., (*The Indians of Texas*, 180) carries this thesis further: "To gain a foothold on the teeming Buffalo plains the Comanches had to be willing to fight and fight hard, and once they had won their land they had to fight with equal vigor to defend themselves against a varied assortment of white and Indian enemies." See also Hall (*Silent Language*, 51): "The history of man's past is largely an account of his efforts to wrest space from others and to defend space from outsiders. . . . To have a territory is one of

the essential components of life; to lack one is one of the most precarious of all conditions."

10. Winfrey and Day, *Indian Papers of Texas* 1:17.

11. As cited by Kavanagh (from Winfrey and Day), "Comanche Politics," 113.

12. Richardson, *Comanche Barrier*, 1933, 94–95; Kavanagh, "Comanche Politics," 113.

13. Muckleroy, "Indian Policy of the Republic of Texas," 140.

CHAPTER 24

1. For an account of the events involving Hobbs, as well as related occurrences, see Lavender, *Bent's Fort*, 199–203; see also Hobbs, *Wild Life*, 22–50.

2. The Comanche-Cheyenne treaty is described in Grinnell, *Fighting Cheyennes*, 63–69.

3. "Pahayuco" has been translated variously to mean either "Sexual Intercourse," or "He-Has-Relations-with-His-Aunt," or "He-Has-Relations-in-the-Water." Although Pahayuco has traditionally been considered a Penateka, more recent research (Kavanagh, "Comanche Politics," 194–95, n.157) suggests he might have been a Tenewa (or "middle") Comanche.

4. As early as 1808, Sibley wrote of the Comanches that "many of them both men and women are nearly as fair as Europeans with long straight sandy or light Hair with blue eyes and freckles. I have seen many women so fair that if they were taken into the United States and dressed like American women and kept a short time out of the sun no one would ever suspect they had a drop of Indian blood in them. Yet the Chief asserts they are pure Hietans. They [*sic*] are many shades whiter than their Neighbours the Spaniards" (Flores, *Journal*, 81, and n.39). As Flores observes, surely some of these fair-skinned individuals had been captured from Spanish settlements as young children or were the result of Comanche marriages with captive women. He also believes that Sibley was exaggerating. Yet it is difficult to think of a motive for such exaggeration.

5. For an account of the Council House Fight and related events, see Mayhall, *Indian Wars of Texas*, 19–30; and Fehrenbach, *Comanches*, 322–33. See also the report of the Texas adjutant general, Colonel Hugh McLeod, to President Lamar, in Muckleroy's "Indian Policy of the Republic of Texas," 142–43.

6. Wilbarger (*Indian Depredations*, 4) states that as a result of the abuse Matilda Lockhart suffered as a captive, on her return to her family she died, "after lingering some two or three years."

7. Usually this chief's name is given as "Isamanica" and translated as "Hears-the-Wolf" or even as "Echo of the Wolf's Howl." Kavanagh ("Comanche Politics," 195, n.158) believes the name to be "Isananica," or "Howling Wolf."

CHAPTER 25

1. Two modern historians (Schilz and Schilz, *Buffalo Hump*, 51, n.2) give the chief's name as "Po-cha-na-quar-hip," translating this as "Erection that won't go down." Kavanagh ("Comanche Politics," 194, n.157). , however, in a more likely ver-

sion, translates "Potsana" as "young male buffalo," leaving the meaning of the final syllables unknown.

2. Von Roemer, *Roemer's Texas*, 269.

3. For accounts of the Comanche raids on Victoria and Linnville and of the battle of Plum Creek, see Jenkins, *Recollections*, 60–68; Webb, *Texas Rangers*, 57–62; Richardson, *Comanche Barrier*, 113–14; and Fehrenbach, *Comanches*, 334–46.

4. See Jenkins *Recollections*, 171–74; Richardson (*Comanche Barrier*, 114–15; Fehrenbach, *Comanches*, 347–48.

5. "During the Comanche wars of 1840 at least three hundred warriors of that nation were killed" (Muckleroy, "Indian Policy," 242).

6. The historian W. Eugene Hollon (*Southwest*, 128) comments that "at the end of the inept and extravagant Lamar administration the public debt was the equivalent of seven million United States dollars, while Texas scrip was worth only fifteen cents per dollar."

7. "To the frontier white, all Indians were vermin. Searching for the most damning epithet to dehumanize the race, Texans called them 'red niggers' " (Fehrenbach, *Lone Star*, 452).

8. For details of the contrasting Indian policies of Lamar and Houston, see Muckleroy, "Indian Policy."

9. In his 1836 inaugural, address Houston declared: "Treaties of peace and amity and the maintenance of good faith with the Indians, present themselves to my mind as the most rational ground on which to obtain their friendship. Abstain on our part from aggression, establish commerce with the different tribes, supply their useful and necessary wants, maintain even-handed justice with them and natural reason will teach them the utility of our friendship" (Muckleroy, "Indian Policy," 8). Two years later Houston referred specifically to the Comanches: "The Comanches have lately come in desiring peace. They are powerful, and if peace is made with them, they will find it to their interest and security to obtain from the hostile tribes on their borders, obedience to them and peace to us. The reason is obvious, because should depredations occur, they would be liable to suspicion, which would interrupt their trade and intercourse with the Texans" (Ibid, 10).

10. Cited by Richardson, *Comanche Barrier*, 1933, 101. But elsewhere Richardson (ibid., 88) finds it "significant that all accounts [in the 1830s], including Catlin's sketches, give evidence of the absence of want and hunger, and indicate beyond a doubt that . . . these Indians as yet knew nothing of that poverty which later drove them to desperation." Half-starved Comanches in 1838 were apparently unusual but were an augury of things to come, when for a variety of reasons the bison population on the plains began rapidly to diminish. Flores ("Bison Ecology," 480), observes, for example, that "the Comanches were reported to be eating their horses in great numbers by 1850 . . . Bison were becoming less reliable, and the evolution toward an economy based on raiding and true horse pastoralism was well under way." The increasing scarcity of buffalo, then, even in the 1840s, would seem to have driven the Comanches to a compensatory increased raiding and trading for their very subsistence. Hence the establishment of trading posts certainly was relevant to Comanche needs.

11. Ford, *Rip Ford's Texas*, 452.

12. Ibid., 182–83.

13. Wilbarger, *Indian Depredations*, 42–49.

14. Houston's Indian agent had been unable to find Pahayuco. Documents indicate that he had lost a son in Mexico and was inconsolable. He had gone north, far from familiar surroundings, in an attempt to recover from his grief (Richardson, *Comanche Barrier*, 1933, 121–22, n.214).

15. Winfrey and Day, *Indian Papers of Texas* 2:103–14.

Chapter 26

1. As cited by Muckelroy, "Indian Policy," 199.

2. Wilbarger, *Indian Depredations*, 290–95.

3. Conrad, *Heart of Darkness*, 111.

4. Kavanagh, "Comanche Politics," 90. For an overview of New Mexican-Comanche relations, see also Kenner, *New Mexican-Plains Indian Relations*, 53–77.

5. Kavanagh, "Comanche Politics," 92.

6. Kendall, *Texan Santa Fe Expedition*, 358–59.

7. Gladwin ("Comanche Kin Behavior," 84), however, in writing of marriage, does point out that "a captive (especially a Mexican) made the most dependent, and hence reliable, son-in-law of all, though the lowered prestige of the resultant half-Comanche grandchildren was a deterrent to this practice."

8. E.A. Mares, New Mexico writer and historian, told the author of this custom.

9. Richardson, *Comanche Barrier*, 23.

10. Colonel Eldredge's matter-of-fact official report of these events differs considerably from Hamilton Bee's journal notes, upon which the account in this work is based. For Eldredge's December 1843 report to Houston, see Winfrey and Day, *Indian Papers of Texas* 1:265–75.

11. Most Native American captives were, of course, eager to escape back to their own people. But there were exceptions. Much depended on the child's age when captured. Writing of himself in the third person, Rip Ford related the following anecdote in his memoires (*Rip Ford's Texas*, 237): "Captain Ford had picked up a young boy while returning from the pursuit of the foe . . . He was reputed to be the son of the chief, Iron Jacket. He was four or five years old at the time of capture. It was not long before he expressed a preference for the American mode of living.

"Me go back to Comanches? They got no sugar, no coffee, nothing but buffalo meat and pecans. No Go."

The boy was finally raised by Anglo-Texans.

12. Wilbarger, *Indian Depredations*, 186–90. According to Wilbarger, this narrative of Bill and Maria first appeared in *The American Sketch Book*, ed. Mrs. Bella French Swisher of Austin, who had the story firsthand from General H. P. Bee. See also Corwin, *Comanche and Kiowa Captives*, 21–24.

13. Babb, *In the Bosom of the Comanches*, 58.

14. Wilbarger, *Indian Depredations*, 190; Corwin, *Comanche and Kiowa Captives*, 24.

15. Clinton Smith, *The Boy Captives*, 161–62.

16. As cited by Billington, *Far Western Frontier*, 149; see also Merk, *Manifest Destiny*, 24–60.

Epilogue

1. As cited by Kavanagh, "Comanche Politics," 121.

2. As cited by Neeley, *Quanah Parker*, 60–61.

3. For what is known about Cynthia Ann's life, see Hacker, Cynthia Ann Parker; see also DeShields, *Cynthia Ann Parker;* and Haley, *Charles Goodnight,* 54–59.

4. Neeley, *Quanah Parker*, 11.

5. The post was built by John Hatcher and another man, probably in 1845; see Lecompte, "Bent, St. Vrain & Co.," 283.

6. For a good account of Mackenzie's "Palo Duro Canyon fight," see Fehrenbach, *Comanches,* 541–42.

7. Kenner (*New Mexican-Plains Indian Relations,* 212) observes that after 1846 there was an "informal alliance" between Hispanic New Mexicans and Comanches against "the Anglo intruders who had occupied the Southwest."

8. See Flores, *Caprock Canyonlands,* 56–58.

9. For details of Parker's life, see Neeley, *Quanah Parker.*

10. Dodge, *Our Wild Indians,* 81–83.

11. Richardson, *The Comanche Barrier,* 1933, 303-4.

12. Richardson (*The Comanche Barrier,* 1991, 15) explains that Comanches abandoned a dying person out of "fear of the spirits which possessed the unfortunate one."

13. See Battey, *Life among the Indians,* 257–58.

14. Nye (*Plains Indian Raiders,* 244–45) tells of a Yamparika chief, Howea (Gap in the Woods), who was familiar with Fort Sill in the 1870s. Yet "so great was his ignorance of the outside world," that traveling as a delegate by rail to Washington in 1885, "when the train plunged into a tunnel, he went into convulsions."

15. Dodge, *Our Wild Indians,* 160–61.

16. Garrard, *Wah-to-Yah,* 31–32. *Entre chien et loup* translates as "between dog and wolf."

17. Gelo, "Comanche Belief and Ritual," 138.

Bibliography

Unpublished

Brown, Lorin W. "Los Comanches." (9 pages) From the files of the New Mexico Writer's Project, History Library, Palace of the Governors, Santa Fe, circa 1937.

Canty, Carol Shannon. "New World Pastoralism: A Study of the Comanche Indians." Master's thesis. San Antonio: University of Texas, 1986.

Foster, Morris W. "'Being Comanche': The Organization and Maintenance of an American Indian Community, 1700–1986." Ph.D. diss. New Haven, Conn.: Yale University, 1988.

Gelo, Daniel. "Comanche Belief and Ritual." Ph.D. diss. New Brunswick, N. J.: Rutgers University, 1986.

Kavanagh, Thomas W. "Political Power and Political Organization: Comanche Politics 1786–1875." Ph.D. diss. Albuquerque: University of New Mexico, 1986.

Zimmer, Stephen. "The Kiowa Tribe and Inter-Tribal Relations on the Southern Plains." Master's thesis. Albuquerque: University of New Mexico, 1976.

Published

Primary Sources

Abert, Lieutenant James W. *Through the Country of the Comanche Indians in the Fall of the Year 1845: The Journal of a U.S. Army Expedition Led by Lieutenant James W. Abert of the Topographical Engineers.* Edited by John Galvin. San Francisco: John Howell Books, 1970.

Adams, Eleanor B., ed. and trans. "Bishop Tamarón's Visitation of New Mexico, 1760." *New Mexico Historical Review* 28 (July 1953):192–221.

Babb, Theodore Adolphus. *In the Bosom of the Comanches.* 2d ed. Dallas: Hargreaves Printing Company, 1923.

Battey, Thomas C. *The Life and Adventures of A Quaker among the Indians.* Introduction by Alice Marriott. Western Frontier Library, vol. 36. Norman: University of Oklahoma Press, 1968. (First published Boston, 1876.)

Becknell, William. "Journals of Capt. Becknell." *Missouri Historical Review* 4(1910): 68–84.

Bee, Hamilton. [Journal excerpt and firsthand account.] See Corwin, *Comanche and Kiowa Captives,* 21–24; and Wilbarger, *Indian Depredations,* 40–49, 186–90.

Berlandier, Jean Louis. "*Casa del Oso y Cibolo, en el Noroeste de Tejas.*" 1828. Mexico City: *El Museo Mexicano,* tomo 3, n.d. (Facsimile provided through the courtesy of the Bancroft Library, Berkeley, California.)

———. *The Indians of Texas in 1830.* Edited and introduced by John C. Ewers. Translated by Patricia Reading Leclercq. Washington: Smithsonian Institution Press, 1969.

Bollaert, William. *William Bollaert's Texas.* Edited by W. Eugene Hollon and Ruth Lapham Butler. Norman: University of Oklahoma Press, 1956. Published in Cooperation with the Newberry Library, Chicago.

Bolton, Herbert E., ed. *Spanish Exploration in the Southwest, 1542–1706*. Original Narratives of Early American History series. New York: Barnes and Noble, 1946. (First published New York, 1908.)

Brown, Lorin W. See under "Unpublished."

Burnet, David G. "The Comanches and Other Tribes of Texas; and the Policy To Be Pursued Respecting Them." In *Information Respecting the History, Conditions, and Prospects of the Indian Tribes of the United States*, edited by Henry R. Schoolcraft. 6 vols. Philadelphia: Bureau of Indian Affairs, 1853.

———. "David G. Burnet's Letters Describing the Comanche Indians." Introduction by Ernest Wallace. In *West Texas Historical Association Yearbook* 30(1954):115–40. (First published in *Cincinnati Literary Gazette*, 1824.)

Cabeza De Vaca, Alvar Nuñez. *Adventures in the Unknown Interior of America*. Translated and edited by Cyclone Covey. New York: Crowell-Collier Publishing Company, Collier Books, 1961.

Carter, Capt. R. G. *The Old Sergeant's Story: Winning the West from the Indians and Bad Men in 1870 to 1876*. New York: Frederick H. Hitchcock, 1926.

———. *On the Border with Mackenzie, or Winning West Texas from the Comanches*. Reprint. New York: Antiquarian Press, 1961. (First published 1935.)

Catlin, George. *Letters and Notes on the Manners, Customs, and Conditions of North American Indians*. 2 vols. Reprint. New York: Dover Publications, 1973. (First published London, 1844.)

Cook, John R. *The Border and the Buffalo: An Untold story of the Southwest Plains*. Reprint. Austin: State House Press, 1989. (First published Topeka, Kans., 1907.)

Cordero, Lt. Col. Don Antonio. "Cordero's Description of the Apache—1796." Translated and edited by Daniel S. Matson and Albert H. Schroeder. *New Mexico Historical Review* 32(Oct. 1957):335–56.

Cremony, John C. *Life among the Apaches*. Glorieta, New Mexico: Rio Grande Press, 1970. (First published 1868.)

Day, Donald, and Harry H. Ullom, eds. *The Autobiography of Sam Houston*. Norman: University of Oklahoma Press, 1954.

De Benavides, Alonso. *Fray Alonso de Benavides' Revised Memorial of 1634*. Edited by George P. Hammond, Frederick Webb Hodge, and Agapito Rey. Albuquerque: University of New Mexico Press, 1945.

De Cessac, Leon. "Ethnographic Information on the Comanches Gathered from the Mouth of a Trapper Who Was Their Prisoner for Thirteen Years." In *Two Nineteenth Century Ethnographic Documents*. Berkeley: Archeological Research Facility, Department of Anthropology, University of California, 1973.

De la Concha, Ferdinand. "Advice on Governing New Mexico, 1794, by Ferdinand de la Concha." Translated by Donald Worcester. *New Mexico Historical Review* 24(1949):236–54.

De Lafora, Nicolas. *The Frontiers Of New Spain: Nicolas de Lafora's Description, 1766–1768*. Edited by Lawrence Kinnaird. Berkeley: Quivira Society, 1958.

De Mézières, Athanase. *De Mézières and the Louisiana-Texas Frontier, 1768–1780*. Translated, edited, and annotated by Herbert Eugene Bolton. (2 vols. in 1.) New York: Kraus Reprint Co., 1970. (Originally published Cleveland, 1914.)

Dewees, W. B. *Letters from an Early Settler of Texas.* Waco: Texian Press, 1968.

Dodge, Richard Irving. *Our Wild Indians: Thirty-Three Years of Personal Experience among the Red Men of the Great West . . .* Reprint. Freeport, N. Y.: Books for Libraries Press, 1970. (First published 1882.)

––––––. *The Plains of the Great West: Being a Description of the Plains, Game, Indians, etc. of the Great American Desert.* Reprint. New York: Archer House, 1959. (First published 1877.)

Domenech, Emmanuel Henri Dieudonné. *Journal d'un missionaire au Texas et au Mexique, par l'Abbé E. Domenech, 1846–1852.* Paris: Gaume Frères, 1857.

––––––. *Seven Years' Residence in the Great Deserts of North America.* 2 Vols. London: Longman, Green, Longman and Roberts, 1860. [Translation from the French; translator's name not given.]

Duval, John C. *The Adventures of Big-Foot Wallace, the Texas Ranger and Hunter.* Reprint. Alexandria, Va.: Time-Life Books, 1983. (First published Philadelphia, 1871).

Evans, Hugh. "The Journal of Hugh Evans, Covering the First and Second Campaigns of the United States Dragoon Regiment in 1834 and 1835." Edited by Fred S. Perrine and Grant Foreman. *Chronicles of Oklahoma* 3(1925):175–275.

Farnham, Thomas J. *Travels in the Great Western Prairies.* 2 vols. Vol. 28 of *Early Western Travels, 1784–1897.* Edited by Reuben Gold Thwaites. Cleveland: Arthur H. Clark Co., 1905.

Faulk, Odie B. "A Description of the Comanche Indians in 1786 by the Governor of Texas." Translated and edited by Odie B. Faulk. *West Texas Historical Association Year Book* 37(1961):177–82.

Flores, Dan L., ed. *Jefferson and Southwestern Exploration: The Freeman and Custis Accounts of the Red River Expedition of 1806.* Norman: University of Oklahoma Press, 1984.

––––––, ed. *Journal of an Indian Trader: Anthony Glass and the Texas Trading Frontier, 1790–1810.* College Station: Texas A&M University Press, 1985.

Ford, John Salmon. *Rip Ford's Texas.* Edited with an introduction by Stephen B. Oates. Austin: University of Texas Press, 1963.

Fowler, Jacob. *The Journal of Jacob B. Fowler, . . .* Edited, with notes, by Elliott Coues. Reprint. Minneapolis: Ross & Haines, 1965. (First published 1898.)

Garrard, Lewis H. *Wah-To-Yah and the Taos Trail . . .* Vol. 5 of the Western Frontier Library. Introduction by A. B. Guthrie, Jr. Norman: University of Oklahoma Press, 1955. (First published 1850).

Glisan, Rodney. *Journal of Army Life.* San Francisco: A. L. Bancroft and Company, 1874.

Gregg, Josiah. *Commerce Of The Prairies: The Journal Of A Santa Fe Trader.* Reprint. Dallas: Southwest Press, 1933. (First published 1844).

––––––. *The Commerce of the Prairies.* Edited with an Introduction by Milo Quaife. A Bison Book Reprint of No. 24 in the Lakeside Classics Series (originally published in 1926). Lincoln: University of Nebraska Press, 1967.

Hackett, Charles W., ed. and trans. *Historical Documents Relating to New Mexico, Nueva Vizcaya and Approaches Thereto, to 1773.* 3 vols. Collected by Adolph F. Bandelier. Washington, D. C.: Carnegie Institution, 1923–37.

––––––, ed. *Pichardo's Treatise on the Limits of Louisiana and Texas.* 4 vols. Austin: University of Texas, 1931.

Hammond, George P., and Agapito Rey. *Don Juan De Oñate: Colonizer of New Mexico, 1595–1628.* Albuquerque: University of New Mexico Press, 1953.

Hobbs, James. *Wild Life in the Far West.* Reprint. Alexandria, Va.: Time-Life Books, 1983. (First published Hartford, 1872).

Horn, Sarah Ann. *A Narrative of the Captivity of Mrs. Horn and Her Two Children, with Mrs. Harris, by the Comanche Indians.* Edited by E. House, annotated by Carl Coke Rister. In *Comanche Bondage . . . ,* by Carl Coke Rister. Glendale, Cal.: Arthur H. Clark, 1955. (First published St. Louis, 1839.)

Humfreville, James Lee. *Twenty Years among Our Hostile Indians . . .* 2d ed., rev. and enl. New York: Hunter, 1903.

Irving, Washington. *A Tour on the Prairies.* Edited with an introduction by John Francis McDermott. Vol. 7 of the Western Frontier Library. Norman: University of Oklahoma Press, 1956. (First published London, 1835).

James, Edwin. *Account of an Expedition from Pittsburgh to the Rocky Mountains.* Reprint. Ann Arbor: University of Michigan Microfilms, 1966. (First published Philadelphia, 1823).

James, Thomas. *Three Years Among The Indians And Mexicans.* Reprint. The Lakeside Classics Series. Edited, with an introduction by, Milo Milton Quaife. Chicago: The Lakeside Press, 1953. (First published 1846)

Jenkins, John Holland. *Recollections Of Early Texas.* Edited by John Holms Jenkins, III. Forward by J. Frank Dobie. Austin: University of Texas Press, 1958.

Kendall, George Wilkins. *Narrative Of The Texan Santa Fe Expedition.* Historical Introduction by Milo Milton Quaife. The Lakeside Classics Series. Chicago: The Lakeside Press, 1929 (First published, 1844).

Lehmann, Herman. *A New Look At Nine Years With The Indians, 1870–1879.* Edited and revised by Garland Percy and Kitti Focke. 3d Ed. San Antonio: Lebco Graphics, 1985. (Autobiographical narrative originally told by Lehmann to J. Marvin Hunter; first published 1927.)

Marcy, Randolph B. *Adventure on Red River: Report on the Exploration of the Headwaters of the Red River By Captain Randolph B. Marcy and Captain G. B. McClellan.* Edited and annotated by Grant Foreman. Norman: University of Oklahoma Press, 1937.

————. Capt., Fifth Infantry, assisted by George B. McClellan, Brevet Capt., U.S. Engineers. "Exploration of the Red River of Lousiana in the Year 1852." *Senate Document No. 54,* 32nd Cong., 2nd sess. Washington, D. C., 1853. [Note: the *Senate Document* consists of all the material included in *Adventure on Red River,* as well as additional scientific data.]

————. *The Prairie Traveler: A Hand-Book for Overland Expeditions.* Reprint. Alexandria, Virginia: Time-Life Books, 1981. (First published New York, 1859).

————. *Thirty Years of Army Life on the Border.* Introduction by Edward B. Walbee. Philadelphia: J.B. Lippincott Company, 1963. (First published New York, 1866).

Margry, Pierre, ed. *Mémoires et documents pour servir à l'histoire des origines françaises des pays d'outre mer: découvertes et établissements des français dans l'ouest et dans le sud de l'Amérique septentrionale (1614–1754).* Vol. 6. Paris: Maisonneuve et cie., 1879–88.

Marriott, Alice. *The Ten Grandmothers.* Vol. 26 in the Civilization of the American Indian series. Norman: University of Oklahoma Press, 1945.

Neighbors, Robert S. "The Naüni, or Comanches of Texas." In *Information Respecting the History, Conditions, and Prospects of the Indian Tribes of the United States.* Edited by Henry R. Schoolcraft. 6 vols. Philadelphia: Bureau of Indian Affairs, 1853.

Padilla, Juan Antonio. "Report on the Barbarous Indians of the Province of Texas." Translated by Mattie Austin Hatcher. *Southwestern Historical Quarterly* 23(1919): 47–60.

Parkman, Francis. *The Oregon Trail.* 1849. Edited from his notebooks and introduced by Mason Wade. New York: Heritage Press, 1943.

Pattie, James Ohio. *The Personal Narrative of James O. Pattie of Kentucky.* Edited by Timothy Flint; historical introduction and footnotes by Milo Milton Quaife. Chicago: R. R. Donnelley and Sons, 1930.

Pike, Zebulon Montgomery. *The Expeditions of Zebulon M. Pike.* Edited by Elliott Coues. 3 vols. New York: Francis P. Harper, 1895.

———. *The Journals of Zebulon Montgomery Pike with Letters and Related Documents.* Edited and annotated by Donald Jackson. 2 vols. Norman: University of Oklahoma Press, 1966.

Pino, Pedro Bautista. "Exposicion sucinta y sencilla de la Provincia del Nuevo Mexico . . ." In *Three New Mexico Chronicles,* translated with introduction and notes by H. Bailey Carroll and J. Villasana Haggard. Albuquerque: Quivira Society, 1942. (First published in Cádiz, Spain, 1812.)

Plummer, Rachel. *Narrative of the Capture and Subsequent Sufferings of Mrs. Rachel Plummer . . .* In *The Rachel Plummer Narrative,* 2d ed., rev. 1839, copyright 1926 by Rachel Lofton, Susie Hendrix, and Jane Kennedy, descendents of J. W. Parker. (First published Louisville, 1844, as an appendix to Rachel Plummer's father's *Narrative . . . of James W. Parker . . .*)

———. *Rachel Plummer's Narrative of Twenty-One Months Servitude as a Prisoner among the Commanchee Indians.* In *The Rachel Plummer Narrative.* Reprint. Austin: Jenkins, 1977. (First published Houston, 1838.)

Ruíz, José Francisco. "Report on the Indian Tribes of Texas in 1828." Facsimile and translation edited and with an introduction by John C. Ewers. Translated from the Spanish by Georgette Dorn. No. 5, Western Americana series. New Haven: Yale University Library, 1972.

Russell, Charles M. *Good Medicine: Memories of the Real West.* With introduction by Will Rogers and biographical note by Nancy Russell. Garden City, N. Y.: Garden City Publishing Company, 1929, 1930.

Sánchez, José María. "A Trip To Texas in 1828." Translated by Carlos E. Casteneda. *Southwestern Historical Quarterly* 29(1926):249–88.

Schoolcraft, Henry R., ed. *Information Respecting the History, Conditions, and Prospects of the Indian Tribes of the United States.* 6 vols. Philadelphia: Bureau of Indian Affairs, 1853.

Sibley, Dr. John. "A Report from Natchitoches in 1807." Edited with an introduction by Annie Heloise Abel. New York: Museum of the American Indian, Heye Foundation, 1922.

Simmons, Marc, ed. *Border Comanches: Seven Spanish Colonial Documents, 1785–1819.* Introduction and translation by Marc Simmons. Santa Fe: Stagecoach Press, 1967.

Smith, Ashbel. *Reminiscences of the Texas Republic.* Brasada Reprint series. Austin: Pemberton Press, 1967.

Smith, Clinton Lafayette. *The Boy Captives: Life among the Indians.* Written by J. Marvin Hunter. Bandera, Tex.: Frontier Times, 1927.

Smithwick, Noah. *The Evolution Of A State; Or Recollection Of Old Texas Days.* Compiled by author's daughter, Nanna Smithwick Donaldson. Austin: Gammel Book Company, 1900 (facsimile, Austin: Steck Company, n.d.).

Stanley, Henry M. *My Early Travels and Adventures in America.* Reprint. Lincoln, Nebraska: University of Nebraska Press, Bison Book, 1982. (First published as *My Early Travels in America and Asia.* Vol.1, London, 1895.)

Tatum, Lawrie. *Our Red Brothers And The Peace Of President Ulysses S. Grant.* Lincoln: University of Nebraska Press, 1970.

Thomas, Alfred Barnaby, ed. and trans. *After Coronado: Spanish Exploration Northeast of New Mexico, 1696–1727: Documents from the Archives of Spain, Mexico, and New Mexico.* Vol. 9 of the Civilization of the American Indian series. Norman: University of Oklahoma Press, 1935.

———, ed. and trans. *Forgotten Frontiers: A Study of the Spanish Indian Policy of Don Juan Bautista de Anza, Governor of New Mexico, 1777–1787.* Vol. 1 of the Civilization of the American Indian series. Norman: University of Oklahoma Press, 1932.

———. *The Plains Indians and New Mexico, 1751–1778: A Collection of Documents Illustrative of the History of the Eastern Frontier of New Mexico.* Coronado Cuarto Centennial Publications, 1540–1940. Albuquerque: University of New Mexico Press, 1940.

———, ed. and trans. *Teodoro de Croix and the Northern Frontier of New Spain, 1776–1786: From the Original Documents in the Archives of the Indies, Seville.* Norman: University of Oklahoma Press, 1941.

Thompson, David. *David Thompson's Narrative of His Explorations in Western America, 1784–1812.* Edited by J. B. Tyrrell. Toronto: Champlain Society, 1916.

Von Roemer, Ferdinand. *Roemer's Texas.* Reprint. Waco, Tex.: Texian Press, 1967. (Originally entitled *Texas, with Particular Reference to German Immigration and the Physical Appearance of the Country* . . . Translated from the German by Oswald Mueller, 1935; first published in German in 1849.)

Wheelock, Lieutenant T. B. "Journal Of Colonel Dodge's Expedition from Fort Gibson to the Pawnee Pict Village (1834)." *American State Papers, Military Affairs* 5(1934):373–82.

Wilbarger, J. W. *Indian Depredations in Texas: Reliable Accounts of Battles, Adventures, Forays, Murders, Massacres, etc.* Reprint. Austin: Eakin Press, Statehouse Books, 1985. (First published Austin, 1889.)

Winfrey, Dorman H., and James M. Day, eds. *The Indian Papers of Texas and the Southwest 1825–1916.* 5 Vols. Austin: Pemberton Press, 1966.

Winship, George Parker. *The Coronado Expedition, 1540–1542.* Chicago: Rio Grande Press, 1964. (First published in 1896 as part of the Annual Report of the Bureau of American Ethnology of the Smithsonian Institute, 1892–93.)

Secondary Sources

Adams, Alexander B. *Sunlight and Storm: The Great American Plains.* New York: G. P. Putnam's Sons, 1977.

Bailey, L. R. *Indian Slave Trade in the Southwest.* Los Angeles: Western Lore Press, 1966.

Bancroft, Hubert Howe. *History of Arizona and New Mexico, 1530–1888.* Vol. 17 of the Works of Hubert Howe Bancroft. San Francisco: History Company Publishers, 1889.

———. *Native Races of the Pacific States.* Vol. 1, *Wild Tribes.* New York: D. Appleton and Company, 1875.

Bannon, John Francis. *The Spanish Borderlands Frontier, 1513–1821.* Histories of the American Frontier. New York: Holt, Rinehart and Winston, 1970.

Barker, Eugene C. *The Life of Stephen F. Austin: Founder of Texas, 1793–1836.* Austin: Texas State Historical Association, 1949.

Beck, Warren A., and Ynez D. Haase. *Historical Atlas of New Mexico.* Norman: University of Oklahoma Press, 1969.

Benedict, Ruth. "The Concept of the Guardian Spirit in North America." American Anthropological Association Memoir 24. Menasha, Wis., 1923.

Billington, Ray Allen. *The Far Western Frontier, 1830–1860.* New York: Harper and Row, 1956.

Bloom, Lansing B. "The Governors of New Mexico." *New Mexico Historical Review* 10 (April 1935):152–57.

Bolton, Herbert E. *The Hasinais: Southern Caddoans as Seen by the Earliest Europeans.* Edited with an introduction by Russell M. Magnaghi. Vol. 182 in the Civilization of the American Indian series. Norman: University of Oklahoma Press, 1987.

———. *Texas in the Middle Eighteenth Century: Studies in Spanish Colonial History and Administration.* New York: Russell and Russell, 1962; Austin: University of Texas Press, 1970. (Originally published Berkeley, 1915.)

Brinkerhoff, Sidney B. *Lancers for the King: A Study of the Frontier Military System of Northern New Spain.* Including Sidney B. Brinkerhoff's and Odie B. Faulk's translation of the Royal Regulations of 1772. Phoenix: Arizona Historical Foundation, 1965.

Burke, Rev. James T. *This Miserable Kingdom . . . : The Story of the Spanish Presence in New Mexico and the Southwest from the Beginning until the 18th Century.* Santa Fe: Cristo Rey Church, 1973.

Cash, Joseph H. *The Comanche People.* Indian Tribal series, edited by Joseph H. Cash and Gerald W. Wolf. Phoenix: 1974.

Connell, Evan S. *Son of the Morning Star: Custer and the Little Bighorn.* San Francisco: North Point Press, 1984.

Conrad, Glenn R. "Reluctant Imperialist: France in North America." In *La Salle and his Legacy: Frenchmen and Indians in the Lower Mississippi Valley,* edited by Patricia K. Galloway. Jackson: University Press of Mississippi, 1982.

Conrad, Joseph. *Heart of Darkness* and *The Secret Sharer.* Reprint. New York: New American Library, 1950. (First published 1899.)

Corwin, Hugh D. *Comanche and Kiowa Captives in Oklahoma and Texas.* Guthrie, Oklahoma: privately printed, 1959.

Demallie, Raymond J. "Preface." In *Indians of the Plains,* by Robert Lowie. Lincoln: University of Nebraska Press, 1982.

DeShields, James. T. *Cynthia Ann Parker: The Story of Her Capture at the Massacre of the Inmates of Parker's Fort . . .* St. Louis: The author, 1886.

————. *Border Wars of Texas; Being an Authentic and Popular Account . . .* Revising editor and publisher Mat Bradley. Tioga, Texas: Herald, 1912.

Devaney, John. *Great Olympic Champions.* New York: Putnam, 1967.

Dines, Glen. *Sun, Sand, and Steel: Costumes and Equipment of the Spanish/Mexican Southwest.* New York: G. P. Putnam's Sons, 1972.

Dobie, J. Frank. *The Mustangs.* Boston: Little Brown and Company, 1952. (First published 1934.)

Dozier, Edward P. *The Pueblo Indians Of North America.* New York: Holt, Rinehart, and Winston, 1970.

Egan, Ferol. *Fremont: Explorer for a Restless Nation.* Garden City, N. Y.: Doubleday and Company, 1977.

Eggan, Fred. *The American Indian: Perspectives for Social Change.* Chicago: Aldine Publishing, 1966.

Ewers, John Canfield. *The Blackfeet: Raiders on the Northern Plains.* Vol. 49 of the Civilization of the American Indian series. Norman: University of Oklahoma Press, 1958.

————. *The Horse in Blackfoot Indian Culture, with Comparative Material from Other Western Tribes.* Bureau of American Ethnology Bulletin 159. Washington, D. C.: Smithsonian Institution, 1955.

Faulk, Odie B. "The Comanche Invasion Of Texas, 1743–1836." *Great Plains Journal* 9(1969–70):10–50.

————. *The Leather Jacket Soldier: Spanish Military Equipment and Institutions of the Late 18th Century.* Pasadena, Cal.: Socio-Technical Publications, 1971.

Fehrenbach, T.R. *Comanches: The Destruction of a People.* New York: Alfred A. Knopf, 1974.

————. *Lone Star: A History of Texas and the Texans.* New York: Collier Books, 1968.

Flores, Dan L. *Caprock Canyonlands: Journeys into the Heart of the Southern Plains.* Austin: University of Texas Press, 1990.

————. "Bison Ecology and Bison Diplomacy: The Southern Plains from 1800 to 1850." *Journal of American History* 78(Sept. 1991):465–85.

Foley, William E., and C. David Rice. *The First Chouteaus: River Barons of Early St. Louis.* Urbana: University of Illinois Press, 1983.

Forbes, Jack D. *Apache, Navaho and Spaniard.* Vol. 115 of the Civilization of the American Indian series. Norman: University of Oklahoma Press, 1960.

Foreman, Grant. *Advancing the Frontier, 1830–1860.* Vol. 4 of the Civilization of the American Indian Series. Norman: University of Oklahoma Press, 1933.

————. *Fort Gibson: A Brief History.* Muskogee, Okla.: Press of Hoffman Speed Printing Company, n.d.

————. *Indian Removal: The Emigration of the Five Civilized Tribes of Indians.* Vol. 2 of the Civilization of the American Indian series. Norman: University of Oklahoma Press, 1953.

————. *Indians and Pioneers: The Story of the American Southwest before 1830.* Vol. 14 of the Civilization of the American Indian series. Norman: University of Oklahoma Press, 1936.

Foster, Morris W. *Being Comanche: A Social History of an American Indian Community.* Tucson: University of Arizona Press, 1991.

Friend, Llerena. *Sam Houston: The Great Designer*. Austin: University of Texas Press, 1954.

Galloway, Patricia K., ed. *La Salle and His Legacy: Frenchmen and Indians in the Lower Mississippi Valley*. Jackson: University Press of Mississippi, 1982.

Gard, Wayne. *Rawhide Texas*. Norman: University of Oklahoma Press, 1965.

Gelo, Daniel. "The Comanches as Aboriginal Skeptics." Forthcoming. *American Indian Quarterly* 17(January 1993).

———. "On a New Interpretation of Comanche Social Organization." *Current Anthropology* 28(1987):551–56.

———. Review of Wallace and Hoebel: *The Comanches: Lords of the South Plains*. *Plains Anthropologist* 33(1988):539–41.

Gibson, Charles. *Spain In America*. The New American Nation Series. New York: Harper and Row Publishers, 1966.

Gladwin, Thomas. "Comanche Kin Behavior." *American Anthropologist* 50(1948): 73–94.

———. "Personality Structure in the Plains." *Anthropological Quarterly* 30(1957): 111–24.

Goya, Francisco. *The Disasters of War*. New York: Dover Publications, 1967.

Grinnell, George Bird. *The Fighting Cheyennes*. Vol. 44 of the Civilization of the American Indian series. Norman: University of Oklahoma Press, 1956. (First published 1915.)

———. "Who Were the Padouca?" *American Anthropologist* 22(1920):248–60.

Guderjan, Thomas H., and Carol S. Canty. *The Indian Texans. The Texians and the Texans series*. San Antonio: University of Texas Institute of Texan Cultures at San Antonio, 1989.

Gunnerson, Dolores A. *The Jicarilla Apaches*. DeKalb: Northern Illinois University Press, 1974.

Gutiérrez, Ramon A. *When Jesus Came, the Corn Mothers Went Away: Marriage, Sexuality, and Power in New Mexico, 1500–1846*. Stanford, Cal.: Stanford University Press, 1991.

Hacker, Margaret Schmidt. *Cynthia Ann Parker: The Life and the Legend*. Southwestern Studies No. 92. El Paso: Texas Western Press, University of Texas at El Paso, 1990.

Hail, Barbara A. *Hau, Kóla: The Plains Indian Collection of the Haffenreffer Museum of Anthropology*. Vol. 3 of Studies in Anthropology and Material Culture. Rev. ed. Bristol, R. I.: Haffenreffer Museum of Anthropology, Brown University, 1983.

Haines, Francis. "The Northward Spread of Horses among the Plains Indians." *American Anthropologist* 40(1938):429–37.

———. "Where Did the Plains Indians Get Their Horses?" *American Anthropologist* 40(1938):112–17.

Haley, J. Evetts. *Charles Goodnight, Cowman and Plainsman*. Boston: Houghton Mifflin Company, 1936.

———. Fort Concho and the Texas Frontier. San Angelo, Tex.: San Angelo Standard Times, 1952.

Hall, Edward T. *An Anthropology of Everyday Life: An Autobiography*. New York: Doubleday, 1992.

———. *Beyond Culture*. Reprint. Garden City, N. Y.: Anchor Press/Doubleday, 1976.

————. *The Hidden Dimension.* Reprint. Garden City, N. Y.: Doubleday and Company, 1966.

————. *The Silent Language.* Reprint. Greenwich, Conn.: Fawcett Publications, 1959.

Hoebel, E. Adamson. *The Cheyennes: Indians of the Great Plains.* Case Studies in Cultural Anthropology. New York: Holt, Rinehart and Winston, 1960.

————. "Comanche and Hekandika Shoshone Relationship Systems." *American Anthropologist* 41(1939):440–57.

————. *The Political Organization and Law-ways of the Comanche Indians.* Memoir no. 54. American Anthropological Association, 1940.

Holder, Preston. *The Hoe and the Horse on the Plains: A Study of Cultural Development among North American Indians.* Lincoln: University of Nebraska Press, 1970.

Hollon, W. Eugene. *The Southwest Old and New.* Lincoln: University of Nebraska Press, 1968. (First published 1961.)

Horgan, Paul. *Great River: The Rio Grande in North American History.* Reprint (2 vols in 1). New York: Holt, Rinehart and Winston, 1971. (First published New York 1954.)

Hyde, George E. *Indians of the High Plains: From the Prehistoric Period to the Coming of Europeans.* Vol. 54 of the Civilization of the American Indian series. Norman: University of Oklahoma Press, 1959.

Inman, Henry. *The Old Santa Fe Trail: The Story of a Great Highway.* Minneapolis: Ross and Haines, 1966. (First published 1897.)

Jackson, Donald. *Thomas Jefferson & the Stony Mountains: Exploring the West from Monticello.* Urbana: University of Illinois Press, 1981.

John, Elizabeth A. H. "An Earlier Chapter of Kiowa History." *New Mexico Historical Review* 60(1985):379–97.

————. "Nurturing the Peace: Spanish-Comanche Cooperation in the Early Nineteenth Century." *New Mexico Historical Review* 59(1984):345–69.

————. "Portrait of a Wichita Village, 1808." *Chronicles of Oklahoma* 60(1982):412–87.

————. *Storms Brewed in Other Men's Worlds: The Confrontation of Indians, Spanish, and French in the Southwest, 1540–1795.* College Station: Texas A&M. University Press, 1975.

————. "The Taovayas Indians in Frontier Trade and Diplomacy, 1719–1768." Part I. *Chronicles of Oklahoma* 31 (1952).

————. "The Taovayas Indians in Frontier Trade and Diplomacy, 1769–1779." Part II. *Southwestern Historical Quarterly* 57(1952):181–201

————. "The Taovayas Indians in Frontier Trade and Diplomacy, 1779–1835." Part III. *Panhandle-Plains Historical Review* 46(1953):41–72.

Jones, David E. *Sanapia: Comanche Medicine Woman.* Case Studies in Cultural Anthropology. New York: Holt, Rinehart and Winston, 1972.

Jones, Oakah L., Jr. "Pueblo Indian Auxiliaries in New Mexico, 1763–1821." *New Mexico Historical Review* 37(1962):81–109.

————. *Pueblo Warriors and Spanish Conquest.* Norman: University of Oklahoma Press, 1966.

Kardiner, Abram, ed. *Psychological Frontiers of Society.* New York: Columbia University Press, 1945.

Kenner, Charles L. *A History of New Mexico-Plains Indians Relations.* Norman: University of Oklahoma Press, 1969.

Kessell, John L. *Kiva, Cross, and Crown: The Pecos Indians and New Mexico, 1540–1840.* Washington, D. C.: U.S. Department of the Interior, 1979.

Lamadrid, Enrique R. "Los Comanches: The Celebration of Cultural Otherness in New Mexico Winter Feasts." In the 1992 New Mexico Festival of American Folklife Archive. Washington, D. C.: Smithsonian Center for Folklife and Cultural Studies.

Lamar, Howard Roberts. *The Far Southwest, 1846–1912: A Territorial History.* Reprint. New York: W. W. Norton and Company, 1970. (First published 1966.)

Lavender, David. *Bent's Fort.* Lincoln: University of Nebraska Press, 1972. (First published, 1954).

Leckie, William H. *The Military Conquest of the Southern Plains.* Norman: University of Oklahoma Press, 1963.

Lecompte, Janet. "Bent, St. Vrain and Co. among the Comanche and Kiowa." *Colorado Magazine* 49(1972):273–93.

Linton, Ralph. "The Comanche." In *The Psychological Frontiers of Society,* by Abram Kardiner and Associates (with the collaboration of Ralph Linton, Dora DuBois, and James West). New York: Columbia University Press, 1966.

———. "The Comanche Sun Dance." *American Anthropologist* 37(1935):420–28.

———. *The Study Of Man.* New York: Appleton Century, 1936.

Loomis, Noel M. and Abraham P. Nasatir. *Pedro Vial and the Roads to Santa Fe.* The American Exploration and Travel Series. Norman: University of Oklahoma Press, 1967.

Lowie, Robert H. *Indians of the Plains.* Anthropological Handbook No.1, published for the American Museum of Natural History. New York: McGraw-Hill Book Company, 1954.

Lozano, Ruben Rendon, with new material added by Mary Ann Noonan Guerra. *Viva Tejas: The Story of the Tejanos, the Mexican-born Patriots of the Texas Revolution.* San Antonio: Alamo Press, 1985. (First published 1936.)

Mayhall, Mildred P. *Indian Wars of Texas.* Waco: Texian Press, 1965.

———. *The Kiowas.* Vol. 63 of the Civilization of the American Indian series. Norman: University of Oklahoma Press, 1962.

McElhannon, Joseph Carl. "Imperial Mexico and Texas, 1821–1823." *Southwestern Historical Quarterly* 53(1949):117–50.

McHugh, Tom. *The Time of the Buffalo.* Reprint. Lincoln: University of Nebraska Press, 1979. (First published New York, 1972.)

Merk, Frederick. *Manifest Destiny and Mission in American History.* New York: Vintage Books, 1963

Montejano, David. *Anglos and Mexicans in the Making of Texas, 1836–1986.* Austin: University of Texas Press, 1987.

Mooney, James. *Calendar History of the Kiowa Indians.* 17th Annual Report of the Bureau of American Ethnology, part 1, 1895–96. Washington, D. C.: Government Printing Office, 1898.

———. "Comanche." In *Handbook of American Indians North of Mexico,* Bulletin no. 30 of the Bureau of American Ethnology. Edited by Frederick W. Hodge. Washington, D.C.: U.S. Government Printing Office, 1912. (First published 1907.)

Moorhead, Max L. *The Apache Frontier: Jacobo Ugarte and Spanish-Indian Relations in*

Northern New Spain, 1769–1791. Vol. 90 of the Civilization of the American Indian series. Norman: University of Oklahoma Press, 1968.

Morris, John W., Charles R. Goins, and Edwin C. McReynolds. *Historical Atlas of Oklahoma.* 3d ed. Norman: University of Oklahoma Press, 1986.

Muckleroy, Anna. "The Indian Policy of the Republic of Texas." Parts 1, 2, 3, 4. *Southwestern Historical Quarterly* 25, 26 (April 1922; July 1922; October 1922; January 1923):229–60, 1–29, 128–48, 184–206.

Murdock, George Peter, and Timothy J. O'Leary. *Ethnographic Bibliography of North America.* New Haven: Human Relations Files Press, 1975.

Neeley, Bill. *Quanah Parker and His People.* Slaton, Tex.: Brazos Press, 1986.

Newcomb, W. W. Jr. *The Indians of Texas from Prehistoric To Modern Times.* Austin: University of Texas Press, 1961.

Nye, Colonel W. S. *Carbine and Lance: The Story of Old Fort Sill.* 3d ed. Norman: University of Oklahoma Press, 1969.

———. *Plains Indian Raiders: The Final Phases of Warfare from the Arkansas to the Red River,* with original photographs by William S. Soule. Norman: University of Oklahoma Press, 1968.

Oglesby, Richard Edward. *Manuel Lisa and the Opening of the Missouri Fur Trade.* Norman: University of Oklahoma Press, 1963.

Opler, Marvin K. "The Origins Of Comanche And Ute." *American Anthropologist* 45(1943):155–58.

Parkman, Francis. *A Half-Century of Conflict.* In *France and England in North America.* 2: New York: The Library of America, 1983.

———. *La Salle and the Discovery of the Great West.* In *France and England in North America,* 1: New York: Library of America, 1983.

Pool, William C. *A Historical Atlas of Texas.* Austin: Encino Press, 1975.

Richardson, Rupert Norval. *The Comanche Barrier to South Plains Settlement: A Century and a Half of Savage Resistance to the Advancing White Frontier.* Glendale: Arthur H. Clark, 1933.

———. *The Comanche Barrier to South Plains Settlement.* Edited by Kenneth R. Jacobs. Abilene, Tex.: Hardin-Simmons University, 1991.

Rister, Carl Coke. *Border Captives: The Traffic in Prisoners by Southern Plains Indians, 1835–1875.* Norman: University of Oklahoma Press, 1940.

———. *The Southwestern Frontier—1865-1881* . . . Cleveland: Arthur H. Clark, 1928.

The Roads of New Mexico. Fredericksburg, Tex.: Shearer Publishing, 1990.

Roe, Frank Gilbert. The Indian and the Horse. Vol. 41 of the Civilization of the American Indian series. Norman: University of Oklahoma Press, 1955.

Rollings, Willard H. *The Comanche.* Indians of North America. New York: Chelsea House Publishers, 1989.

Savage, Candace. *Wolves.* Text and Photographic Selection by Candace Savage. San Francisco: Sierra Club Books, 1988.

Schilz, Jodye Lynn Dickson and Thomas F. *Buffalo Hump and the Penateka Comanches.* Southwestern Studies Series No. 88. El Paso: Texas Western Press, University of Texas at El Paso, 1989.

Schilz, Thomas F. *Lipan Apaches in Texas.* Southwestern Studies Series no. 83. El Paso: Texas Western Press, University of Texas at El Paso, 1987.

Scholes, France V. "Church and State in New Mexico." In *New Mexico Past and Present: A Historical Reader.* Edited by Richard N. Ellis. Albuquerque: University of New Mexico Press, 1971.

———. "Civil Government and Society in New Mexico in the Seventeenth Century." *New Mexico Historical Review* 10(April 1935):71–111.

Schroeder, Albert H. *Apache Indians I: A Study of the Apache Indians, Parts 1, 2, 3.* New York: Garland Publishing Inc., 1974.

Secoy, F. R. "The Identity of the 'Paduca.'" *American Anthropologist* 53(1951):525–42.

Shimkin, Demitri B. "Comanche-Shoshone Words of Acculturation, 1786–1848." *Journal of the Steward Anthropological Society* 2(Spring 1980):195–248.

Simmons, Marc. *Following the Santa Fe Trail: A Guide for Modern Travelers.* 2 ed. Santa Fe: Ancient City Press, 1986.

———, ed. *On the Santa Fe Trail.* Introduction by Marc Simmons. Lawrence: University Press of Kansas, 1986.

Smith, Page. *The Nation Comes of Age: A People's History of the Ante-Bellum Years.* Vol. 4 of A People's History of America. New York: McGraw-Hill, 1981.

Smith, Ralph A. "The Comanche Bridge between Oklahoma and Mexico, 1843–1844." *Chronicles Of Oklahoma* 39(1961):54–69.

Stuck, Walter Goodloe. *José Francisco Ruíz, Texas Patriot.* San Antonio: Witte Memorial Museum, 1943.

Swadesh, Frances Leon. *Los Primeros Pobladores: Hispanic Americans of the Ute Frontier.* Notre Dame, Ind.: University of Notre Dame Press, 1974.

———. *Twenty Thousand Years of History: A New Mexico Bibliography.* Santa Fe: Sunstone Press, 1973.

Terrell, John Upton. *The Plains Apache.* New York: Thomas Y. Crowell, 1975.

Thurman, Melburn D. "Comanche." In *Dictionary of Indian Tribes of the Americas* 2:48–67. Newport Beach, Cal.: American Indian Publishers, 1980.

———. "A New Interpretation of Comanche Social Organization." *Current Anthropology* 23(1982):578–79.

———. "Reply to Gelo." *Current Anthropology* 28(1987):552–55.

Thwaites, Reuben Gold. *France in America, 1497–1763.* Reprint. New York: Haskell House, 1969. (First published 1905.)

Times Atlas of World History. Produced and published by The Times in collaboration with Geoffrey Barraclough and Son Ltd. London: Times Newspapers Ltd., 1972.

Trenholm, Virginia Cole. *The Arapahoes, Our People.* Vol. 105 of the Civilization of the American Indian series. Norman: University of Oklahoma Press, 1986. (First published 1970.)

Trenholm, Virginia Cole, and Maurine Carley. *The Shoshonis: Sentinels of the Rockies.* Vol. 74 of the Civilization of the American Indian Series. Norman: University of Oklahoma Press, 1964.

Twitchell, Ralph Emerson. *The Leading Facts of New Mexico History.* 2 vols. Albuquerque: Horn and Wallace, 1963.

VanDerBeets, Richard. *The Indian Captivity Narrative: An American Genre.* Lanham, Md.: University Press of America, 1984.

Van Zandt, Howard F. "The History of Camp Holmes and Chouteau's Trading Post." *Chronicles Of Oklahoma* 13(1935):316–37.

Wallace, Ernest, and E. Adamson Hoebel. *The Comanches: Lords of the South Plains.* Vol. 34 of the Civilization of the American Indian Series. Norman: University of Oklahoma Press, 1952.

Weaver, Bobby D. "Relations Between the Comanche Indians and the Republic of Texas." *Panhandle Plains Historical Review* 53(1980):17–33.

Webb, Walter Prescott. *The Great Plains.* Reprint. New York: Grosset and Dunlap, 1947. (First published 1931.)

———. *The Texas Rangers: A Century of Frontier Defence.* 2d ed. Austin: University of Texas Press, 1989. (First published 1935.)

Weber, David J. "American Westward Expansion and the Breakdown of Relations between Pobladores and Indios Barbaros on Mexico's Far Northern Frontier, 1821–1846." *New Mexico Historical Review* 56(1981):221–38.

———. *The Mexican Frontier, 1821–1846: The American Southwest under Mexico.* Histories of the American Frontier. Albuquerque: University of New Mexico Press, 1982.

Wedel, Mildred Mott. "Claude Charles Dutisné: A Review of his 1719 Journeys." *Great Plains Journal* 12(1973):147–73.

Wedel, Waldo Rudolph. *Prehistoric Man on the Great Plains.* Norman: University of Oklahoma Press, 1961.

Wissler, Clark. *Indians of the United States.* Rev. Ed. Garden City, N. Y.: Doubleday and Company, 1966. (First published 1940.)

———. "The Influence of the Horse in the Development of Plains Culture." *American Anthropologist* 16 (1914):1–25.

———. *North American Indians Of The Plains.* Handbook Series No.1. New York: American Museum of Natural History, 1912.

Worcester, Donald E. *The Apaches: Eagles of the Southwest.* Vol. 149 of the Civilization of the American Indian series. Norman: University of Oklahoma Press, 1979.

———. "The Beginnings of the Apache Menace in the Southwest." *New Mexico Historical Review* 16(1941):1–14.

———. "The Spread of Spanish Horses in the Southwest." *New Mexico Historical Review* 19(1944):225–32; 20(1945):1–13.

Wright, Muriel H. *A Guide to the Indian Tribes of Oklahoma.* Vol. 33 of the Civilization of the American Indian series. Norman: University of Oklahoma Press, 1986. (First published 1951.)

Yoakum, Henderson K. *History of Texas from its First Settlement to 1846.* 2 vols. New York: Redfield, 1856.

Young, Otis E. *The First Military Escort on the Santa Fe Trail, 1829 . . .* American Trails Series, no.7. Glendale, Cal.: Arthur H. Clark, 1952.